STIEGLITZ

1   Alvin Langdon Coburn, *Alfred Stieglitz, Esq.*

STIEGLITZ

A BEGINNING LIGHT

KATHERINE HOFFMAN

YALE UNIVERSITY PRESS

NEW HAVEN AND LONDON

Designed by Gillian Malpass

Printed in Singapore

Library of Congress Cataloging-in-Publication Data

Hoffman, Katherine, 1947–
    A beginning light : the early work of Alfred Stieglitz / Katherine
Hoffman.
      p.   cm.
Includes bibliographical references.
    ISBN 0-300-10239-9 (cl : alk. paper)
   1. Stieglitz, Alfred, 1864–1946.   2. Photographers–United
States–Biography.   I. Title.
   TR140.S7H64 2004
   770′.92–dc22

                                2003019486

A catalogue record for this book is available from
The British Library

To my children,
Kristen, Geoffrey, and Ashley,
and my husband, Graham,
with love

To Stieglitz, the prime objective of art is the affirmation of life, and unless this affirmation is considered in time as well as in contemporary experience, it is without validity.

Alfred Stieglitz was my friend and counselor, noble among men, and the most lucid prophet of our age.

Ansel Adams[3]

Stieglitz, nor any man like him, can enjoy more than notoriety among us. Fame is something somewhere else.

Frank Lloyd Wright[4]

Let me tell you in French that "la pureté et la simplicité que Stieglitz exprime dans son travail est le fruit d'une profonde connaissance de l'Humain."

Henri Cartier-Bresson[5]

[Stieglitz] is the one artist in America today whose work matters. His photographs are in the great tradition. In his prints precisely the right values are expressed. Symbols are used correctly. His photographs are "absolute" in the same sense that Bach's music is absolute music.

Amanda K. Coomaraswamy[6]

People think that I am interested only in art. That is not true . . . Whether it is scrubbing a floor or painting a picture – only the best work of which man is capable will finally satisfy him . . . only work born of a sacred feeling . . . And what interests me is whether a man will fight for the opportunity of doing the best work of which he is capable. It seems to me that people will fight for almost anything except that right. And yet nothing else will fulfill in the end.

Alfred Stieglitz[7]

CONTENTS

In placid houses well pleased we dream
Of many a brave unbodied scheme.
But form to lend, pulsed life creak,
What unlike things must meet and make:
A flame to melt – a wind to freeze;
Sad patience – joyous energies;
Humility – yet pride and scorn;
Instinct and study; love and hate;
Audacity – reverence. These must make,
And fuse with Jacob's mystic heart,
To wrestle with the angel – Art.

Herman Melville, "Art"[1]

The abuse of freedom is undeniably greater than the understanding of what freedom really is.

Alfred Stieglitz, letter to Guido Bruno, 28 December 1916[2]

ACKNOWLEDGMENTS

This book has been a project of many twists and turns. Instead of a long list of names, I should like to acknowledge the institutions with whom I worked and those individuals who were particularly helpful. Institutions included the Beinecke Rare Book and Manuscript Library at Yale University; the Georgia O'Keeffe Foundation in Santa Fe, New Mexico; the Philadelphia Museum of Art; the Metropolitan Museum of Art in New York; the National Gallery of Art in Washington, D.C.; the Museum of Modern Art in New York; the Musée D'Orsay, Paris; the Art Institute of Chicago; the J. Paul Getty Museum, Los Angeles; the Lee Gallery, Winchester, Massachusetts; George Eastman House, Rochester, New York; the New York City Public Library; the Adirondack Museum, Blue Mountain Lake, New York; and the interlibrary loan department at St. Anselm College, Manchester, New Hampshire. Individuals included Peter Bunnell, Robert Sobieszek, Judy Lopez, Sarah Greenough, William Homer, Barbara Hilary, and Waltrud and Ellen Heinemann. The scholarship of William Homer, Peter Bunnell, Richard Whelan, and Sarah Greenough, in particular Sarah Greenough's catalogue for the National Gallery's "Key Set" of Stieglitz's photographs, were helpful foundations for this project. I was most grateful for the kind hospitality of William Homer, who welcomed me into his home one afternoon, and for the many hours Waltrud and Ellen Heinemann spent with me sharing their knowledge of Wilhelm Hasemann's work. St. Anselm College provided me with a summer research grant to develop the initial proposal. Madeleine Greiner diligently typed my manuscript. Gillian Malpass, my editor, is to be thanked for her support of the book.

To my friends and family, thank you for your support as the project waxed and waned – in particular, thank you to the Silverthorne family, who provided me with a place to stay in their busy household on my trips to Washington, and to Liz and Dick Meryman, whose barn provided a special space for my beginning days of organizing and writing.

Above all, thank you to my family for the time I stole from them to work on this book – to my husband, Graham Ward, who patiently accompanied me on various research trips and endured my sometimes frantic working hours; and to my three dear and creative children, Kristen, Geoffrey, and Ashley, for their support of the project and for their understanding of the power of photography. And, finally, an accolade to Alfred Stieglitz himself, whose life and work still stands spirited and strong as we enter the twenty-first century.

About the Illustrations

Owing to circumstances and situations beyond the author's control or understanding, as well as expense, it was impossible to obtain a number of illustrations that were initially intended for this book. Some photographs are described in depth to give the reader a sense of the image. The reader is referred to the National Gallery of Art's comprehensive two-volume Key Set of Stieglitz images, which were given to the museum by Georgia O'Keeffe. Therein are some of the images that are described but not pictured. It is with regret that the author was not able to include all that were intended. It is hoped that those illustrations that are here will serve as representative examples of the "beginning light" of Stieglitz's rich body of work. To those institutions who provided images, a grateful thank you is extended.

All recent photographs of the sites where Stieglitz spent time and/or photographed were taken by the author, with the exception of that of the Realgymnasium in Karlsruhe (private collection).

PROLOGUE

> The arts equally have distinct departments and unless
> photography has its own possibilities of expression, separate
> from those of the other arts, it is merely a process, not an art;
> but granted that it is an art, reliance should be placed
> unreservedly upon these possibilities, that they may be made to
> yield the fullest results.
>
> Alfred Stieglitz, 1901[1]

Many years ago, as a young graduate student in New York City studying art history as well as painting and photography, I was, among other
things, photographing and painting clouds. Indeed, I was obsessed with
clouds – their exterior beauty and changing light patterns and their
intrinsic capacity to evoke different aspects of emotions. Somehow I
wanted to capture the essence of those clouds and their varied levels of
meaning. One of my instructors at New York University suggested I look
at the works of Georgia O'Keeffe and Alfred Stieglitz, in particular
Stieglitz's series of cloud photographs, the *Equivalents* and *Songs of the
Sky*. From those early student days I have been forever hooked. I devoted
my career to art history, writing, among other things, two books on
Georgia O'Keeffe, *An Enduring Spirit: The Art of Georgia O'Keeffe*
(1984) and *Georgia O'Keeffe: A Celebration of Music and Dance*
(1997). And now once again I return to my early inspiration, this time
to the magic of Stieglitz's photographs.

Stieglitz was American, born in Hoboken, New Jersey in 1864. His
early work in both the United States and Europe formed a significant
foundation for his later, more well-known work. During much of his
career, Stieglitz fought tirelessly for the recognition of photography as a
significant fine art, in his own work as a photographer, as a collector, as
a gallery director, and as a writer and speaker about photography. In
the May 1999 issue of *ARTnews*, Stieglitz was listed as one of the
twentieth century's most influential artists.

This book is about the early work of Stieglitz, his first fifty-three years, from 1864 to 1917. Here the story ends with the closing of his 291 gallery, the last issue of *Camera Work*, as Stieglitz's first photographs of Georgia O'Keeffe, and the United States' entry into World War I. Stieglitz's work of these early years may be viewed as both a mirror and a lamp for the times, reflecting others' innovations and also providing innovations and insights, both technical and aesthetical, for photography.

This book is not a straight biography, nor a technical guide to photographic experiments of the last century. Rather it is an attempt to understand the early Stieglitz in the context of his times and to explore more fully his life and work as they were intertwined during those early years, both in the United States and in Europe. As Dore Ashton wrote,

> No matter how banal the thought that the artist is a man of his time, the fact is that the history of art and literature is filled with statements, more or less eloquent, affirming the artist's sense of being shaped by the epoch in which he performs his art. In some cases, he is not so much shaped as prodded. In many statements, there is a distinct impression of the artist being drawn forcibly forward; to be reeled in by a future that cannot be evaded. The "time" of an artist makes itself felt, even if only as tyranny against which the artist reacts.[2]

The interplay between Stieglitz and his times was a complex one that involved social, economic, political, philosophical, technological, and cultural strands which, when woven together with Stieglitz's life and work, created a tapestry that was rich with detail. The result produced innovations in design and artistic technique.

One of the threads that may be seen to run through much of Stieglitz's work is the role of "place". The power of place was significant for Stieglitz at various times. Such places included New York City, Lake George in New York State; Berlin; Katwyk in the Netherlands; Gutach, Germany; Paris; and Chioggia in Italy. To better understand their power for Stieglitz, I travelled to some of the places that were important in his early career. As is seen in some of my own photographs, a number of these places are in some ways unchanged. Stieglitz, in many instances, was able to give the viewer a sense of a particular place and at the same time provide a sense of the universal. The poet William Carlos Williams, an admirer of Stieglitz, voiced this same notion – he felt that the universal can exist in the local and that there can be a "radiant gist" in objects and places.

Another thread that can be seen to wind through Stieglitz's life and work was the influence and inspiration sparked by the presence of various women in his life – from his first wife, Emmeline, to his daughter, Kitty, to Sophie Raab, Marie Boursault, Rebecca Strand, Ellen Koeniger Morton, and, of course, Georgia O'Keeffe, who was to become his second wife in 1924.

A significant strand was the role of music, which both directly and indirectly influenced Stieglitz and his work. From his early days as a student, Stieglitz played the piano and went to hundreds of musical and theatrical performances, particularly in his youth. And many of the artists whose works Stieglitz showed at his 291 gallery demonstrated affinities with music and the performing arts. Indeed, Stieglitz may be seen as a kind of Orpheus figure, enchanting those around him both as musician and poet.

Stieglitz's well-known September 1923 statement, "How I Came to Photograph Clouds," points to the continuing importance of music for him:

Thirty-five or more years ago I spent a few days in Murren (Switzerland), and I was experimenting with ortho plates. Clouds and their relationship to the rest of the world, and clouds for themselves, interested me, and clouds that were most difficult to photograph – nearly impossible. Ever since then clouds have been in my mind most powerfully at times, and I always knew I'd follow up the experiment made over thirty-five years ago. I always watched clouds. Studied them. Had unusual opportunities up here on this hillside. What Frank [Waldo Frank] had said annoyed me: what my brother-in-law said also annoyed me. I was in the midst of my summer's photographing, trying to add to my knowledge, to the work I had done. Always evolving – always going more and more deeply into life – into photography.

My mother was dying. Our estate was going to pieces. The old horse of 37 was being kept alive by the 70-year-old coachman. I, full of the feeling of to-day: all about me disintegration – slow but sure . . .

So I made up my mind I'd answer Mr. Frank and my brother-in-law. I'd finally do something I had in mind for years. I'd make a series of cloud pictures. I told Miss O'Keeffe of my ideas. I wanted to photograph clouds to find out what I had learned in 40 years about photography. Through clouds to put down my philosophy of life – to show that my photographs were not due to subject matter – not to special trees, or faces, or interiors, to special privileges, clouds were there for everyone – no tax as yet on them – free.

2   Alfred Stieglitz, *Music: A Sequence of Ten Cloud Photographs, No. 1,*
1922

. . . I had told Miss O'Keeffe I wanted a series of photographs which
when seen by Ernest Bloch (the great composer) he would exclaim:
Music! Music! Man, what that is music! How did you ever do that?
And he would point to violins, and flutes, and oboes, and brass, full
of enthusiasm, and would say he'd have to write a symphony called
"Clouds." Not like Debussy's but much, much more.

And when finally I had my series of ten photographs printed,
and Bloch saw them – what I said I wanted to happen, happened
verbatim.[3]

Continuing his musical emphasis, Stieglitz wrote to his friend, the
writer Sherwood Anderson, in November 1923: "I've been crazily mad
with work – fun – some great sky stories – or songs. "[4] And in
December of 1923, Stieglitz wrote to the poet Hart Crane, who espoused
a theory of "ultimate harmonies": "I'm most curious to see what the
'clouds' will do to you . . . Several people feel I have photographed God.
May be . . . I know exactly what I have photographed. I know I have
done something that has never been done. Maybe an approach occa-
sionally [found] in music. I also know that there is more of the really
abstract in some 'representation' than in most of the dead representations of the so-called abstract so fashionable now."[5]

Two years later Stieglitz wrote to J. Dudley Johnston, president of the London Royal Photographic Society: "My photographs are ever born of an inner need – an Experience of Spirit . . . It's because of the lack of inner vision amongst those who photograph that there are really but few true photographers. The spirit of my 'early' work is the same spirit of my 'later work.'"[6] In 1924, Stieglitz was awarded the Royal Photographic Society's Progress Medal for his services in founding and fostering pictorial photography in the United States, and particularly for his initiation and publication of *Camera Work*, the most artistic record of photography ever attempted.

Approximately forty years earlier, Stieglitz had bought his first camera and begun to study in Professor Hermann Wilhelm Vogel's classes in photochemistry in Berlin. In those forty years, in particular in his work up to 1917, Stieglitz created work that may be seen as a foundation and set of guideposts that were to lead to the culminating *Equivalents* series and to his famous composite portrait of Georgia O'Keeffe. Without those early years of experimentation, interaction with specific individuals, and exploration of various places, it is doubtful whether Stieglitz could have done what he did in his later years. It is to these early years that I devote my attention.

In trying to understand Stieglitz's early work, it should be remembered that many of the "stories" about Stieglitz are those told by him, with his great gift as a raconteur. In some instances, these narratives come second-hand, recounted years later by the author Dorothy Norman or others such as Doris Bry (O'Keeffe's agent and assistant for a period of years), Sue Davidson Lowe (Stieglitz's niece), or one of the critics, such as Paul Rosenfeld, a "disciple" of Stieglitz. To be "objective" about Stieglitz is sometimes quite difficult. Responses to his work and to his engaging personality were frequently intense, ranging from laudatory to pejorative. He engendered both love and hate, and he could be volatile. As Herbert Seligmann, his gallery assistant for many years wrote:

> He wasn't a saint. He was vain and theatrical; he could be vindictive and cruel. He could go to extremes in his admiration and in his subsequent depreciation of people. He was a romantic. He erupted with the continuing energy of a volcano . . . Wherever he was, Stieglitz created a magnetic center to which flocked musicians, workers, painters, aspiring and seeking human beings in all walks of life. For them he achieved moments of all but blinding awareness and release.[7]

Shortly after Stieglitz's death in 1946, Dorothy Norman wrote that she felt that any writing concerning Stieglitz "is born of deep feeling: that those who are moved to write about him invariably do so from a desire to share a sense of wonder about him, rather than actually to 'explain' his meaning or importance. This, again, is as it should be, for Stieglitz's entire life was dedicated to the sense of wonder – his own, as well as that of others."[8] This book is certainly meant "to explain" but it is also meant to generate that sense of wonder that Norman suggests.

I have written this book in the long, dark shadows of global political unrest. I have asked myself many times how Stieglitz would have responded to acts of terrorism and the events of September 11, 2001, but am somewhat unsure how he would respond to my question. One wonders if Stieglitz would have made a new series of *Equivalents*? Would he have taken photographs from the windows of his gallery at the foot of Fifth Avenue? Apolitical, sometimes anarchistic, an incessant, indefatigable fighter for what he believed in, Stieglitz, I suspect, would have fought for what he felt was the truth and would have responded deeply and compassionately. Since September 11 his words seem to ring with an even stronger resonance: "I can do nothing because another does it; nothing that is not for me to do because of some deep inner need. I clarify for myself alone. I am interested in putting down an image only of what I have seen, not what it means to me. It is only after I have put down an equivalent of what has moved me, that I can even begin to think about its meaning . . . I feel that all experiences in life in any particular form must be an equivalent of any other truly felt experience."[9]

It is that sense of searching for equivalents that our world still needs. The light of Stieglitz's early work, in both the literal and figurative sense, still has much to show us as we enter into the first few years of a new century and a new millennium.

Katherine Hoffman
Peterborough, New Hampshire
September 2003

Part 1

THE NINETEENTH CENTURY

Out of the cradle endlessly rocking,
Out of the mocking bird's throat, the musical shuttle,
Out of the ninth-month midnight,
Over the sterile sands, and the fields beyond, where the child leaving his bed,
wandered
  alone . . .

Walt Whitman, "Out of the Cradle Endlessly Rocking"[1]

Afoot and light-hearted, I take to the open road,
Healthy, free, the world before me,
The long brown path before me leading wherever I choose.

Walt Whitman, "Song of the Open Road"[2]

3   Alfred Stieglitz,
My Father, 1894

4   Alfred Stieglitz.
"*Ma,*" 1914

5   Unknown
photographer, studio
print, *Flora and Alfred
Stieglitz*, c.1868

It was New Year's Day, 1864. The United States was three years into a bloody civil war. On that crisp winter day, in Hoboken, New Jersey, at One Sea View Place, where the island of a growing Manhattan could be seen, Edward and Hedwig Stieglitz celebrated the birth of their oldest son, Alfred. It is perhaps fitting that Janus, the ambivalent Indo-European deity with two faces, should be the mythological figure associated with Stieglitz's birthday. Janus, originally the god of gods, god of beginnings, and benevolent creator, was later also seen as a god of change. He was also god of the Gate, watching entrances and exits and looking into the internal as well as the external world. In the spirit of Janus, Stieglitz was to become a man who initiated and ended a number of things, and would be concerned with internal emotions as well as external facts and details.

The new child, Alfred Stieglitz, was born into a world that was already beginning to experience changes in art and culture that were to become more pronounced and rapid at the turn of the century. Photography had just been born with the announcement in 1839 of the development of the daguerreotype by French inventor Louis Daguerre, deriving its name from the Greek words for light and writing. In the same year Hippolyte Bayard made positive images on paper and Henry Fox Talbot made known his photogenic drawings. Then, in the 1850s, inexpensive photographic portraits became available to all social classes, produced by large-scale photographic operations like that built by French photographer André Adolphe Eugéne Disdéri. (The portraits measured about 4 by 2.5 inches.) In France the possibilities for artistic expression were beginning to be explored by members of the Société Française de Photographie, founded in 1853–4. In Britain, London's Photographic Society was founded at the same time to promote a new scientific art of photography on the international level. In 1859 photographs were admitted for the first time into the official Salon in Paris. But many, including Charles Baudelaire, were not willing to accept photography as an art. Several years later a controversy over copyright issues covering works of art brought the status of photography to the French courts. On 4 July 1862, Independence Day for Americans, the French court declared photography to be an art.

Back in America, as the Civil War was fought, photographer Alexander Gardner in his *Photographic Sketchbook of the War* (1866) chronicled events in distant, removed images that were also seen in various mass periodicals of the time. The well-known images of Matthew Brady and his staff documenting the Civil War were displayed, along with portraits, in Brady's successful gallery of national portraiture in New York City. The lure of photographic expression drew the American William Henry Jackson to the western United States, where he became known for his photographs of the landscape and of Native Americans.

Other cultural milestones around the time of Stieglitz's birth include the publication of Charles Baudelaire's *Fleurs du Mal* and of Gustave Flaubert's *Madame Bovary* in 1857 and of Victor Hugo's *Les Misérables* in 1862; Jules Verne's *Journey to the Center of the Earth* and Fyodor Dostoyevsky's *Notes from Underground* in 1864; the first performance of Richard Wagner's *Tristan and Isolde* in 1865, and the publication of Karl Marx's *Das Kapital* in 1867. From 1864 to 1869 the Russian novelist Count Leo Tolstoy composed his epic novel, *War and Peace*, chronicling Napoleon's invasion of Russia.

In the visual arts, the British artist William Morris co-founded Morris, Marshall, Faulkner and Co. for the hand manufacture of home décor, fostering the Arts and Crafts Movement with its emphasis on fine design and decorative arts such as stained glass, furniture, and wallpaper. These artists looked frequently to forms in nature as their inspiration.

The French graphic artist Honoré Daumier painted *The Third Class Carriage*, establishing further the significance of depicting the lower and working classes, emphasized earlier in paintings such as Gustave Courbet's *The Stone Breakers* (1849) or *The Burial at Ornans* (1849). Daumier's *The Laundress* (1863) brought dignity to a woman burdened with her laundry, holding fast to the hand of a small child as she wearily climbs steps leading towards the viewer. Jean-François Millet's depiction of peasants near Gruchy in rural northern France in the 1850s and 1860s brought forth a quiet heroicism found in the beauty of the everyday life and surroundings of women spinning, men harvesting, a shepherdess calling her sheep, or laborers stopping in the fields to pray as the distant angelus sounds. Stieglitz was later to turn to depictions of the working class in his photographs.

In 1863, the famous Salon des Refusés displayed works of art rejected by the official salon. The secession was sparked by Edouard Manet's controversial painting of 1863, *Dejeuner sur l'herbe*, in which a well-known model, Victorine Meurent, is depicted in the nude, having a picnic with two clothed men. Manet's flattened forms and lack of detail in certain areas of the canvas began the journey to Impressionism and twentieth-century abstraction. His *Olympia*, painted in the same year, depicting a nude prostitute in a pose drawn from Titian's *Venus of Urbino*, also created controversy. The Salon des Refusés marked a giant stride forward in asserting the rights of the individual artist to express him or herself as an individual and not be dominated by the "rules" of the official salon. Such freedom of expression was to be important for Stieglitz.

In American painting, the Hudson River School, with the vast panoramic landscapes of artists such as Albert Bierstadt or Frederick Church, still expressed the American Romantic spirit and America's sense of its Manifest Destiny as new vistas in the West were discovered. This was maintained by the subsequent Luminist generation of painters such as Fitz Hugh Lane, Martin Johnson Heade, or John Frederick Kensett, with their emphasis on stillness and quiet luminosity. George Innes, influenced by the Barbizon School and the Hudson River School, developed softer, atmospheric depictions of nature following his move to an artists' colony in Eagleswood, New Jersey, in 1863. His landscape paintings became harmonies in color, light, and space. Genre paintings, such as those by George Caleb Bingham of the 1840s depicting fur traders, raftsmen on the river, and so on, still had a place in the American psyche, which valued work and the open road.

On 19 November 1863, Abraham Lincoln delivered his famous Gettysburg Address, speaking the forever-famous lines, "this nation under God shall have a new birth of freedom" and that a "government of the people, by the people and for the people shall not perish from this earth." Slaves were also freed through the Emancipation Proclamation of the same year on New Year's Day. That heritage of freedom was to become a part of Stieglitz's psyche.

But when Stieglitz was approximately sixteen months old, the American actor John Wilkes Booth assassinated President Lincoln during a performance of the British play *Our American Cousin* at Ford's Theater in Washington, D.C. The event had a strong enough impact on the Stieglitz family to prompt them to save the *New York Evening Express* from 15 April 1865, reporting Lincoln's murder. (The newspaper is now in the Beinecke Library files.)

Stieglitz's father, although of German Jewish descent, had served in the military during the Civil War. Born in Hannoversch Münden, Germany, in 1833, the young Edward Stieglitz came to the United States following the European economic and political upheavals of 1848. Edward grew up on a farm, and loved nature and art. He also had a business sense and became a partner in a prosperous wool business after serving in the Civil War. In 1862 Edward married Hedwig Werner, originally

from Offenbach, Germany, near Frankfurt. Hedwig had come to
the United States when she was eight; Alfred was born when she was
nineteen. She was devoted to her family and friends and was reported
to be a woman of generous spirit who loved reading.

Edward was a man with flare and a sense of style. Tall, slender, and
well dressed, he carried himself in an aristocratic fashion. He loved
flowers, fishing, and horse racing, and owned his own fine saddle horse.
The Stieglitzs' home at 109 Garden Street, where they moved in August
1864, was filled with guests and activity. Stieglitz was later to look back
on his early days:

> Our house was filled with guests, forever guests, expected and unex-
> pected, from all classes of society, but mainly musicians, artists, and
> literary folk, rather than business people. We had many books and
> pictures . . . our dining room in Hoboken was in the basement (fashion
> had not yet decreed the first floor back as such – not that my parents
> were guided by what others did) and the room was simple. I had my
> hobby horse there and while the men would drink, talk, and smoke,
> I loved to sit on my horse, riding, and listening to the conversation.
> This was when I was four until about seven years old . . . my parents'
> way of life doubtless left a lasting impression on me. They created an
> atmosphere in which a certain kind of freedom could exist. This may
> well account for my seeking a related sense of liberty as I grew up.[3]

There are several stories from Stieglitz's childhood that seem to be harbingers of his later career as a photographer and as a kind of impresario
through his work as a gallery director and editor. When he was two years
old, during the family's six-month trip to Europe, he insisted on carrying around with him a photograph of a handsome young male cousin,
much like a child carries a teddy bear or blanket. He was fascinated and
attached to the seemingly magic object. Another story involved his great
admiration for one of his father's cousins and friend of his mother's, "a
lady in black":

> After her visits, my heart would sink. The lady in black was tall. She
> had dark hair, smoothed down, and white skin. While she was in the
> room, I had a lovely but sad feeling about her. I awaited her appear-
> ance, knowing the days when she was expected. I know of no pain
> any more intense than the one I experienced when she departed. My
> heartache, I realized later, was the same as that in which all love, like
> all art, is rooted. I always have been fascinated by black. I believe this

may be related to my early infatuation with the lady in black. And I always have been in love.[4]

With thick black hair and dark eyes and often dressed in black, Stieglitz was sometimes called "little Hamlet" by his mother and friends. As an adult, he frequently wore a long, flowing black cape.

Alfred was the first child of a rapidly growing family. Within seven-and-a-half years there were six children: Alfred, Flora, the twins Leopold and Julius, Agnes, and Selma. It is easy to see how attention lavished on a first-born child was quickly diluted. Alfred was often jealous of the twins, who were intense creatures and had each other. As Richard Whelan notes in his biography, Stieglitz, not having a twin, from a very early age searched for a soul mate: "In at least partial fulfillment of his wish, he was given to discerning 'reflections' of himself – narcissistic projections – often in rather unlikely people and phenomena. Surely, one factor that drew him to photography was that the medium would allow him to capture and collect those reflections."[5]

Late in 1865, Hedwig's sister Rosa Werner came to live with the family and remained there until her death in 1899. She appears to have been a stabilizing influence on the household and helped much with the children. Later, as a student in Europe, Alfred frequently remembered her in his letters sent home. In June of 1871, just after Selma was born, the sprawling Stieglitz family moved to Manhattan to a five-story spacious brownstone at 14 East 60th Street, close to the still unpaved section of Fifth Avenue. The family had a good view of Central Park. The area was still considered outlying territory by wealthy New Yorkers of the time. Today, 14 East 60th Street is a luxurious condominium building.

Edward's wool business was thriving, but of almost greater interest to him than his business were his Sunday afternoon gatherings of artists, writers, and intellectuals. At age seven, the young Alfred became the wine steward for the men and watched intently as they played billiards, which he came to love to play as well. Among those who attended the Sunday gatherings were Joseph Keppler, the caricaturist and founder of *Puck* magazine; Scottish-born John Foord, an editor of the *New York Times*; Howard Carroll, who was to become a *New York Times* Washington correspondent as well as a playwright; and Adolph Werner, a cousin of Hedwig's and professor of German language and literature at City College of New York (then called the College of the City of New York). Werner's interest in literature and education was influential to young Alfred. John Foord had three daughters, and the two families became close, visiting each other in New York and on the New Jersey shore. Barbara Foord and her daughter Maggie are pictured at a large Stieglitz family gathering at Lake George in 1888. It is clear that Stieglitz must have had some affection for the young Maggie, for he photographed her reading, and what seems to be a portrait of Maggie has a prominent place in an 1891 lantern slide of his studio, *My Room at 14 East Sixtieth Street*. Also, tucked into place next to a program for a Metropolitan Opera season that included *The Magic Flute*, *Carmen*, and *Tristan and Isolde*, in one of Stieglitz's voluminous and meticulously made scrapbooks from his student days, was an announcement of Maggie Foord's wedding to Mr. G. Bonner on 28 February 1892. Among those listed as attending were Mrs Edward Stieglitz and Miss Agnes Stieglitz. The saved announcement included details of the bride's cream satin dress and magnificently brocaded train.

In September 1871, Alfred began to attend the Charlier Institute, a French and English school for "Young Gentlemen" on East 24th Street in Manhattan. The school was considered one of the best private schools in the city. An early report card, now in the Philadelphia Museum of Art, shows Alfred to be a good student, although he later recalled his distaste for rote learning and recitation: "At school I refused to memorize, to recite poetry or anything else by heart. My teacher of Elocution and Declamation was in a quandary about what to do. Since I was first in my class in every other subject as well as in conduct, he must have felt he could not give me a zero. So he marked me a hundred. I said this was not fair to others. This was when I was twelve. I have always rebelled against learning anything by heart. I came to have little respect for what might be called academic standards."[6]

Alfred's tendency to venture beyond "mainstream" conventions and his need for attention is also seen in his often-repeated story of the organ-grinder. This story is perhaps best told in his own words and spans several decades:

In 1875 – I remember it as if it were yesterday – one Saturday evening as the family – children, father and mother and aunt – sat down to supper, an organ-grinder began playing the "Miserere" from *Il Trovatore*, the "Marseillaise", etc. I got up and went out and gave him ten cents of my own. I had a dollar a week from my father, for car-fares, etc. The organ-grinder was an Italian with a gray beard, and there was a monkey and a tin cup. The man wanted the monkey to thank me – but I shrank back – I didn't like to be touched. The following Saturday, as we sat down as usual punctually at seven, the organ-grinder once more began the *Trovatore*. I went into the kitchen and asked the cook for a sandwich and a cup of coffee. And when they were ready I went out into the coldish night and gave the organ-grinder the sandwich, coffee, and a dime. He again wanted the monkey to thank me, but I made the Italian (he spoke no English and I no Italian) somehow understand thanks were not necessary. And so every succeeding Saturday night, except in the summer months when we were in the country for ten weeks, the organ-grinder appeared punctually as we sat down. I went regularly to the kitchen to get the sandwich and coffee which were ready and then went out to give the organ-grinder these, with the ten cents. The years rolled by. It was a bitter cold Saturday night in January of 1881 when, as the organ-grinder began the *Trovatore*, out of tune as since the beginning, I got up to go to the kitchen. My mother and father simultaneously said: "Alfred, you look pale. It's a bitter cold night. Don't you think you'd better eat your hot soup before going out?" I went to the kitchen. The soup could wait. The organ-grinder received his hot coffee, sandwich, and dime. He was covered with snow. The monkey had a coat on which also was covered with snow, as was the organ. I returned to the table and ate my soup. My parents said nothing.

Some weeks later my father decided to take the family to Europe for a five years' stay. He was retiring from business at forty-nine. He wasn't a rich man, but well-to-do for the times. He wished to give his children a European education and he wanted to travel and paint. He was a merchant, but had a gift for painting – a love for art and living. We had an open house – painters and musicians and literary folks, as well as some business people frequented our house. As soon as I heard of my father's decision, the organ-grinder came into my mind. And on Saturday evening of that week, I informed the organ-grinder that in about ten weeks the family would be moving out of the house and that we'd be gone for years. I felt he should know. And when the last Saturday came around we said goodbye to each other. It was all as natural to us as the happening of one day succeeding the other.

That was in 1881. And now, thirty-five years later, sitting on the porch in Lake George with my mother, she asked me did I remember the organ-grinder. He had not been mentioned in thirty-five years. Not during the six years that I regularly went out to him Saturday nights leaving the dinner table did any of the children or my parents or aunt or anyone else ever make any kind of remark about the happening. So when my mother thirty-five years later asked me did I remember the organ-grinder, I was a bit startled. She wanted to know why I hadn't listened to her and my father that cold night when they asked me to eat hot soup before going out. I merely laughed and said, "Ma, do you know who the organ-grinder was?" She looked up and said, "Why of course, he was an Italian with a gray beard and he had a monkey." I asked was she sure? She said, "Alfred, there you are with your mystery again." She said she was glad my brother, the doctor, was coming from New York that night. He came weekends to see his family. We children and our families all, most times, summered with my father and mother. She was glad the doctor was coming because she wanted me examined, she said, feeling I might be a bit crazy. Of course I laughed again. I said, "Ma, do you want to know who the organ-grinder was?" She impatiently replied, "There you go again. Why the organ-grinder was an Italian with a gray beard and a monkey." "Are you sure?" I repeated. "Ma, do you want to know a secret?" I asked. "Well, I will tell you. I was the organ-grinder." She said, "No." I said, "Ma, I'm not crazy. I really was the organ-grinder – I never gave to him nor have I ever given to anyone else but myself." For a moment she was stunned. She looked up. After a few moments she said, "Did you know that from the beginning, even when you were eleven?" "Why, of course," I replied. She looked again at me and continued knitting. Both of us remained silent.[7]

That silent alliance between mother and son was perhaps one reason why Stieglitz returned each summer to his family home on Lake George.

LAKE GEORGE

The Stieglitz family made their first visit to the Lake George area in upstate New York in August 1872, staying at the famous Fort William Henry Hotel. When the hotel was opened in 1856 as the first elegant resort on Lake George, the United States included only thirty-one states. The town was then called Caldwell. The beauty of the area had been extolled much earlier in a letter from Thomas Jefferson to his daughter Martha on 31 May 1791, when he wrote:

Lake George is unquestionably the most beautiful water I ever saw; formed by a contour of mountains into a basin 35 miles long, and from 2 to 4 miles broad, finely interspersed with islands, its water limpid as crystal and the mountainsides covered with rich groves of thuja, silver fir, white pine, aspen, and paper birch down to the water edge, here and there precipices of rock to checker the scene and save it from monotony. An abundance of speckled trout, salmon trout, bass, and other fish with which it is stored, have added to our other amusements the sport of taking them.[8]

The hotel was "the destination" for the upper class. Its furnishings were of the latest Victorian mode, and gas lamps lit the rooms. In the 1870s the writer William Cullen Bryant described this magnificent edifice:

The spacious Fort William Henry Hotel, situated upon the site of the old fort of the same name, stands directly at the head of the lake, with a noble expanse of its waters spread out before it. The coach is driven with a sweep and a swirl through the grounds of the hotel, and suddenly turning a corner, dashes up before the wide and corridored piazza, crowded with groups of people – all superb life and animation on one side of him, and a marvelous stretch of lake and mountain and island and wooded shore on the other – such a picture, in its charm and brightness and completeness, as the New World traveler rarely encounters.[9]

In 1909, a devastating fire destroyed the hotel, but in 1910 a simpler, more classic structure was erected. Today, the original ballroom from the 1910 hotel remains; a new hotel similar to the 1910 building opened in 2003.

Billiards was a popular activity at the hotel, as well as visiting the ruins of an old fort that had been destroyed during the French and Indian War. Also popular were boat excursions to Tea Island for afternoon teas. On sunny afternoons patrons of the hotel were rowed to a small tea house on Tea Island about a mile down the lake; it was reported that treasure belonging to General Abercrombie had been buried there in the eighteenth century. It was also thought by some to be the site of a legendary underground tunnel to China, through which tea could be imported without customs dues.

The Lake George area, with its islands, was steeped in history as well as beauty, attracting artists and writers as well as vacationers to its shores. The first white man to see the lake was reported to have been Father Isaac Jogues, a French priest who arrived at the north end of the lake on 29 May 1649, the eve of the festival of Corpus Christi, and thus called the lake, Lac du St. Sacrament. In 1755, the name of the lake was changed to Lake George, named after the English king, George II. In 1874, the writer and photographer Seneca Ray Stoddard, noted for his postcard-like views and descriptions of the Adirondacks and Lake George area, wrote in his illustrated book, *Lake George (Illustrated): A Book of Today*: "It is a little over thirty-three miles long, running north and south, nearly four wide at the broadest place, surrounded by high mountains; drains but little territory, and is fed by brooks from the mountain sides, and springs coming up from the bottom . . . It is said to contain three hundred and sixty-five islands, one for each day of the year; and one accommodating little fellow, who goes and comes every four years, that the twenty-ninth of February need not feel slighted."[10]

Famous was the *Minne-Ha-Ha* steamer that made excursions up and down Lake George. Visitors to Lake George have included Benjamin Franklin, Thomas Jefferson, James Madison, Calvin Coolidge, and Theodore Roosevelt, who first came as a twelve-year-old boy the year before the Stieglitzes did. Both young boys kept journals recording their time there. The young Roosevelt recalled his father reading to him from James Fenimore Cooper's *The Last of the Mohicans*, which was inspired by Lake George.

Lake George was a favorite subject for a number of the Hudson River School and Luminist painters, as seen in Jasper Cropsey's *Dawn at Morning, Lake George* (1868, Albany Institute of Art), John Frederick Kensett's *Lake George* (1853, Williams College Museum of Art), or Martin Johnson Heades's *Lake George, New York* (1862, Museum of Fine Arts, Boston). Other artists such as Winslow Homer depicted combined landscape and genre scenes such as *On the Road to Lake George* (1869, Adirondack Museum), in which three children wave goodbye to a departing stage coach. The Lake George landscape, with its broad vistas, smooth waters, and majestic mountains evoked the elements of the "sublime" that were so important for Americans viewing landscape paintings in the nineteenth century. The many and varied patterns of light, shadow, color, shape, and form that the mountains, water, sky, islands, trees, and rocks provided, also conformed to notions of the "picturesque" sought by nineteenth-century artists.

Stieglitz's photographs of Lake George reinforced the significance of the landscape for artists. His early images tend to be intimate, closely cropped views of the lake and Tea Island, often taken from Oaklawn, his family home purchased in 1886. His later Lake George work became more expansive and reaches toward the abstract, as seen in his *Songs of the Sky* and *Equivalents* series.

Tea Island had a number of owners. In the Stieglitz era, it was owned by the Van Cortlandts from 1872 to 1899; the William Spier family from 1898 to 1908 (William Spier was a prominent businessman and philanthropist from Glens Falls, New York, with international pursuits in South America and Mexico); the Frederich Gates family from 1908 to 1928 (Gates was the close advisor of John D. Rockefeller, becoming the director of the Rockefeller Foundation and president of thirteen corporations controlled by Rockefeller outside the oil business). From 1928 to 1934, the small island jewel was owned by a cousin of Alfred Stieglitz, Eugene Small, who bought the island at the urging of Alfred's father, Edward. Three months after purchasing the island, the Smalls gave it to their daughter, Hannah, for the sum of one dollar. Eugene Small built there a small, picturesque log cabin that pumped water from the pristine lake. (Stieglitz was to take snapshots of the Smalls during their Lake George days that capture spontaneous summer moments of relaxation and leisure.)

The Lake George area was easily accessible. The social elite and wealthy as well as artists could take a steamboat from New York City to Albany, where a train departed to Saratoga Springs, then a resort famous for its waters, gambling, and horse racing. From there a traveler could cover the remaining 27 miles to Lake George by stagecoach through Glens Falls. Well-known families such as the Ochs, the Trasks, the Peabodys, the Tuttles, the Jacobis, or the famous Metropolitan opera star Marcella Sembrich, spent many summers on the shores of Lake George.

The young Alfred explored upstate New York further when, at age nine, he and his father traveled together to the Adirondacks and visited the Catskill Mountain House. The hotel had been associated with the Hudson River School painter, Thomas Cole, whose series of allegorical paintings, *The Voyage of Life* and *The Course of An Empire*, were to have an impact on the American public. It had a magnificent view of the surrounding area. Alfred's balance sheet, jotted on the back of a Catskill Mountain House flyer, and the journal he kept – both now in the Beinecke Library at Yale – reveal his sense of detail and expectation of remuneration for his labours:

10 [cents]	getting blanket
10	carrying book for 1 hour
10	get my and your coat
5	letter
4	buying newspaper

39 cts
Alfred Stieglitz
$3.87 cents of old bill
39 today
that makes
$4.26

During the summer of 1873, Alfred went with several of his friends to have his collection of toy lead horses photographed by a Mr. Irish, a tintyper in Caldwell (the town now known as Lake George). He became fascinated by the "magic" that seemed to take place in the darkroom, as he had been the previous year when his mother took him to be photographed with his brothers and sisters by Abraham Bogardus, a

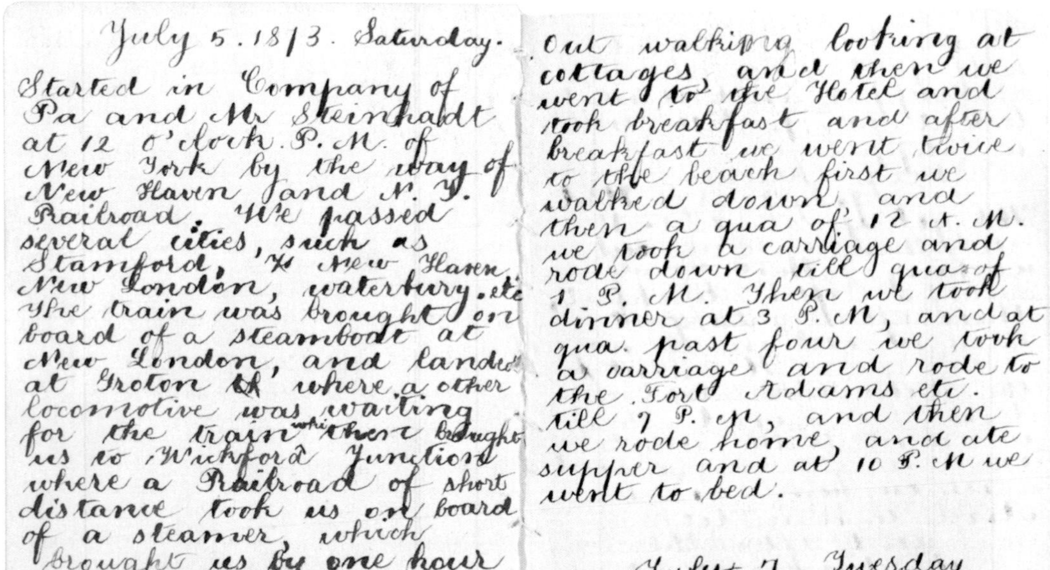
July 5. 1873. Saturday.
Started in Company of
Pa and Mr Steinhardt
at 12 O'clock. P. M. of
New York by the way of
New Haven and N. Y.
Railroad. We passed
several cities, such as
Stamford, New Haven,
New London, waterbury. etc
The train was brought on
board of a steamboat at
New London, and landed
at Groton where a other
locomotive was waiting
for the train which then brought
us to Wickford Junction
where a Railroad of short
distance took us on board
of a steamer, which
brought us by one hour
sail to Newport a 9
P. M. Where we stopped
at the Ocean house and
it was rainning hard
till quarter of 11 then
we went to bed.

July 6. Sunday

We got up out of bed at
half past five A. M.
And we then we went
Out walking looking at
cottages, and then we
went to the Hotel and
took breakfast and after
breakfast we went twice
to the beach first we
walked down, and
then a qua of 12 A. M.
we took a carriage and
rode down till qua of
1 P. M. Then we took
dinner at 3 P. M, and at
qua. past four we took
a carriage and rode to
the Fort Adams etc.
till 7 P. M, and then
we rode home, and ate
supper and at 10 P. M we
went to bed.

July 7. Tuesday

We got up and went
away of Newport to
Boston at 7.20 A. M.
and got to Boston at
qua. to 10 A. M, and
then we took a wagon
and rode out till
half past 11, and then
we went to the
Tremont house and
ate dinner and went
away of Boston to Conway

6 (*facing page*) Alfred's journal entries for 5, 6, and 7 July 1873

7 Unknown photographer, *Alfred Stieglitz and His Father*, 1875

fashionable photographer in New York City. Alfred visited Mr. Irish on several occasions and was somewhat dismayed to see him touching up the photographs with hand-coloring to provide pink cheeks and so on.

There were a number of photographs made of Alfred as a young boy. In one from 1875, perhaps serving as a window into the future, Alfred is shown with a bow and arrow in hand, kneeling behind his father, who is lying on the grass with a book in front of him. Alfred had recently learned archery and lawn tennis and was later to recall: "I soon found that simply to hit a target was meaningless. I wanted to hit what you might call the center of the center of the target ... That has been my concern when making my photographs, in my contact with public and in personal relationships."[11]

Stieglitz continued his interest in the "archer image" when, years later, he had a personal bookplate made, now in the Beinecke Library, for his collection of books with an archer as the primary image. The bow and arrow have had symbolic meanings in many cultures. The arrow has often referred to movement beyond conventional means and has been seen as an imaginary release from the confines of space and gravity. The bow has been seen as a symbol of fate as well as embracing the act of procreation and the search for perfection. The image of the zodiac sign Sagittarius is frequently that of the human part of a centaur pointing his arrow at the stars, suggesting that he is filled with life and oriented toward fulfillment. It would seem that a number of the archer characteristics could well relate to Stieglitz – his drive for perfection, his need to create, and his non-conventional interests. The small 1875 photograph of Stieglitz with bow and arrow and his father was indeed prophetic.

At Lake George, Stieglitz learned to row, swim, and fish and was a noted miniature golf player. He also loved to run. He quickly became a leader among his friends and; as he noted later in life in connection with sports and board games, "I quickly tired of playing games according to the rules that came with them."[12] But despite his interest in exercise, Alfred was viewed as a delicate child, tall, thin with a complex and brooding temperament. For much of his life, as Richard Whelan has noted, "Alfred would suffer terribly from incurable hypochondria, the first cousin of depression . . . As an adult, Alfred clearly had strong manic-depressive tendencies. Afraid he could not be loved for who he was, he resolved to ensure that he would at least be loved for what he did. To that end, he would expend a tremendous amount of energy in pursuit of perfection and the highest ideals."[13]

EARLY LITERARY AND CULTURAL INFLUENCES

As a young boy from approximately 1874 to 1879, Stieglitz collected autographs in small leather albums. Not only did he seek autographs of his friends and family, but he also searched out copies of signatures of those he admired and read about: such figures as Duke Karl August, the patron of the German writer Goethe (Stieglitz greatly admired Goethe); Johann Schadow, a sculptor and teacher; Karl Friedrich Schinkel, whose magnificent neoclassical architecture graced Berlin and other European cities; Julie Rettig, an actress; and Heinrich Schliemann, the archaeologist. On some pages carefully drawn fan or leaf shapes encase the names in a decorative, artistic fashion. On the back page of one album, in carefully rendered letters, is a poignant message from his father, written in New York on 2 May 1874: "Be the master of Truth, Master of Passion. To his son, Edward Stieglitz."[14] In another album there is a questionnaire that is more autobiographical in nature, put together when Alfred

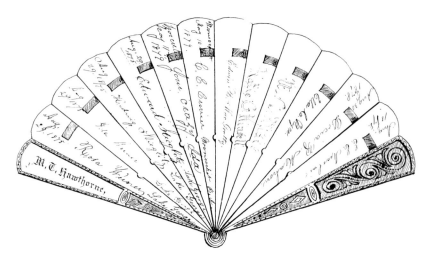

8   Printed image on a leaf from Alfred's autograph album, 1875

was thirteen, recording that his favorite color was cardinalian black; his favorite season, "whenever there is no school"; his favorite non-religious book, "a pocketbook filled with money"; the place where he would most like to live, Lake George; the most admirable traits in men and women, "Honesty and Truth"; his own distinguishing characteristics, inquisi-

9   J. Dessaur, *Stieglitz*, *c*.1875

tiveness and changeableness; the sweetest words, "Father and Mother"; the saddest words, "too late"; and his favorite painters, Fedor Encke, who had lived with the Stieglitzes, and an unidentified "H.L." Another small blue leather volume has signatures from his friends at the Charlier Institute, mostly simple statements, "From a school friend, W. I. Peyser, N. Y., Mar. 11, 1878"; or, "Your friend, A. Wollberg, N. Y. February, 1876". From a very early age Stieglitz seemed to have a need to be connected to others – those close to him and those to whom he wished to be culturally or psychologically connected. In later years, as collector, editor, and gallery director, he had a vast network of connections as he strove to achieve perfection and be the "Master of Truth" that his father had advocated when he was only ten.

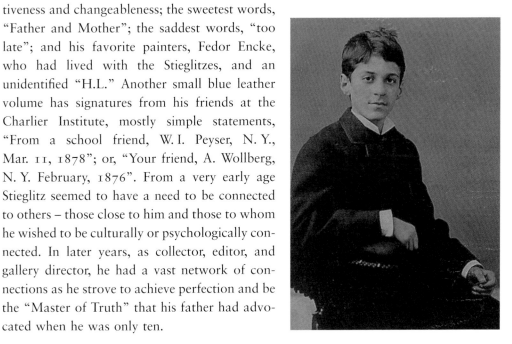

Alfred took the search for truth seriously as a young boy. In 1877, he wrote a letter to his father: "For the past two months, I could not think of anything but the lie I told you ... I read a book in which this story appeared. I then wrote it from memory – I would swear to it that I did not copy it [inserted in pencil with a caret] – and then gave it to you, and tried to make you believe that I wrote it out of my own head ... I would rather bear the severest punishment from you than to tell another lie in my future life."[15]

In 1877, on his thirteenth birthday, Alfred received a *trompe l'oeil* painting, now in the Beinecke Library, in the style of William Harnett by Julius Gerson, a family friend. It was a watercolor of stamped postcards, a Western Union telegram, and the envelope of a letter. The top postcard was addressed to "Mr. Alfred Stieglitz, 14 East Sixtieth Street, New York." Alfred was captivated by the piece and valued it throughout his life. He included it in an exhibition in 1937 at his gallery, An American Place, entitled, *Beginnings and Landmarks*, where it represented a significant part of his past. Although Stieglitz's sense of aesthetics did not tend to advocate "copies," the abstract quality of the montage composition and its layered effects foreshadow Cubist collage experiments. As a "portrait" of Alfred, the piece was perhaps prophetic, for Stieglitz was a prolific letter writer, with a voluminous correspondence throughout his career, for both his personal and professional life.

At thirteen the young Alfred also ran a 25-mile race against himself in the basement of his home in about three-and-a-half hours. As in later life, Alfred loved to have an audience, and staged the event as if it were a record-breaking contest. There was an audience of his friends and younger brothers, all holding stopwatches, pails of water and sponges, and some periodically mopping the sweat from the runner's face.

As a young boy, Stieglitz read voraciously. He was not so interested in fairy tales but he did read books about the American Revolution, books by Mark Twain and Horatio Alger. He read Harriet Beecher Stowe's *Uncle Tom's Cabin* with much interest, and was to go on to read Lord Byron's *Don Juan*, and Shakespeare's *Venus and Adonis*, *As You Like It*, and *The Rape of Lucrece*. Of the American revolutionary heroes, Alfred looked not toward the familiar heroic figure of George Washington, but toward General Nathanael Greene. "Greene's merit in the boy's eyes," as Paul Rosenfeld, a cultural critic and friend and admirer of Stieglitz's, wrote, arose from "the fact that he had broken the British strength down there in the South, and he had lost few men doing so; from the fact he had broken the British strength precisely because he had sacrificed so few lives in his own army. Greene indeed had won no signal victories or their stirring glories. He was too poor in men and ammunitions to risk decisive encounters. But he had invariably returned from unequal engagements with his resources intact."[16] Stieglitz was later to become a little like Nathanael Greene in his continuing fight for photography as a fine art, in his "unequal engagements," advancing and meeting obstacles, trying to keep his limited resources – financial, professional, and personal – intact.

One of the most significant works that Stieglitz first read when he was ten was Goethe's *Faust*, which he went on to read numerous times, seeing the operatic version on many occasions. Stieglitz claims to have been most interested in the characters of Marguerite and the Devil. "Marguerite and the Devil have continued to fascinate me. All thinking men must feel a similar concern about Woman and the Devil. Due to something in the male and something beyond. What Woman feels about the male and the Devil, I do not know. People kill one another because they love one another too much. Jealousy, envy, are always at work, no matter what one does. The result is a constant. Yet everyone claims to be seeking peace."[17] Perhaps it was the purity of Marguerite, or Gretchen's as she is frequently referred to, that so attracted Stieglitz. Despite his insistence on his lack of interest in the character of Faust, he in many ways might be considered a Faustian figure in his continuous striving for perfection – as he worked hours in the darkroom on individual prints or, on the broader level, as he fought for the recognition of photography as a fine art and for the recognition of modern art.

In Part II of Goethe's poem, Faust meets Helen of Troy, who comes to symbolize the "unattainable," "the beautiful," "Woman." In Act IV, a significant image appears that perhaps stayed subconsciously in Stieglitz's mind: a great cloud carries Faust from Arcadia, gently setting him down in high mountain country and then dividing. In his study of Goethe, Henry Hatfield notes: "Faust describes how one part assumes the shape of a woman of classical beauty – Juno, Leda, or Helen – the other a less heroic but lovely form, suggesting 'beauty of the soul,' linked, Faust says, to what is best in him."[18] At the end of Part II, Faust is "saved" from his pact with the Devil, not through conversion, but through a series of metamorphoses. The image of a chrysalis, which appears in earlier sections of the work, is seen again. (It is interesting to note that a number of Georgia O'Keeffe's drawings from her 1915 *Specials* series, which Stieglitz praised highly, particularly numbers 2, 4, 5, and 9, have chrysalis-like forms and suggest metamorphosis.)

At the end of *Faust*, the "eternal womanly" is seen as a symbol of love, purer than Faust can give. The final lines of the piece are spoken by the Chorus Mysticus:

> All earth comprises
> Is symbol alone;
> What there ne'er suffices
> As fact here is known;
> All past the humanly
> Wrought here in love;
> The eternal womanly
> Draws us above.[19]

The poem thus ends with its emphasis on heightened development with the affirmation of love. It is easy to see how Stieglitz was fascinated with the story and how the storyline relates to Stieglitz's life-long interest in "Woman" as an ideal and in particular the women with whom he was associated. The writer and admirer of Stieglitz, Nancy Newhall, noted that the highest praise Alfred could give a man was that "he is as perceptive as a fine woman or a racehorse," and that "women and children, he felt, were like plants and a man should be as a gardener. He should see that each had the light and the soil it needed, and freedom from pests and plagues."[20]

Stieglitz was probably also captivated, perhaps unknowingly when young, by the stylistic elements in *Faust*, such as the alternating play of light and dark throughout the poem. There are rapid changes of night and day, or when Mephistopheles enters the scene the tone of the language may become dark and brooding. The metaphoric elements of dark and light are seen in such lines as these by Mephistopheles:

> Part of a part am I that once was all
> A part of darkness, mother of the light,
> Proud light that seeks a sway imperial,
> Outranking far the ancient realm of night.
> Yet strives in vain, doomed to be cleaving still,
> To forms, embodied, struggle as he will.[21]

The language often evokes a strong sense of emotion, inherent in much Romantic writing and in Goethe's *Sturm und Drang* (Storm and Stress) period. Indeed, Faust at one point states

Feeling is all.
The name is sound and smoke,
Beclouding Heaven's glow.[22]

Faust was to inspire a number of composers and playwrights whom Stieglitz admired, such as Robert Schumann, Franz Liszt, and Richard Wagner, in particular the latter's *Faust Overture*, or Christian Dietrich Grabke's *Don Juan and Faust*, Heinrich Heine's ballet sketch, *Doctor Faustus: A Dance Poem*, Nikolaus Lenau's drama, *Faust*, and Charles Gounod's opera, *Faust*. Stieglitz saw a number of these performances of the Faust story, as demonstrated by the large number of drama and opera programs he carefully pasted in his scrapbooks.

The Faust figure has been seen by some as a key metaphor for modern man struggling to make sense of the experience of modernity. As the writer Marshall Berman has noted,

Modern men and women in search of self-knowledge might well begin with Goethe, who gave us *Faust*, our first tragedy of development. It is a tragedy that nobody wants to confront . . . but that everybody wants to re-enact. Goethe's perspectives and visions can help us see how the fullest and deepest critique of modernity may come from those who most ardently embrace its adventure and romance. But if *Faust* is a critique, it is also a challenge . . . to imagine and to create new modes of modernity, in which man will not exist for the sake of development, but development for the sake of man.[23]

Much of Stieglitz's adolescence appears to have been filled with uncertainty, although he was always a good student in school. In looking back over his life, he noted:

I find the keynote to whatever I have done has been unpreparedness. In reality, the only thing in which I have been actually thorough has been in being thoroughly unprepared . . . I feel that all the unpreparedness running through my life came from my being uprooted, originally from Charlier's, and being out of place in public school and from being again uprooted from City College. The feeling of being unprepared has to do with the fact that while my father was in business he was always talking about getting out of business and about taking the family to Europe. All this was very perfect in a way, very wonderful, but it did not lead to my being thoroughly prepared.[24]

In many ways Alfred may be considered an outsider figure from his early days. His unwillingness to follow rules; his romantic sensibilities, which were sometimes in conflict with the more rational world around him; his German-Jewish heritage, although the family was not particularly religious; his delicate health – all contributed to a sense of being an outsider and unprepared. But feeling unprepared also allowed Alfred to develop a sense of the positive side of adventure and an ability to deal with new situations and new ideas.

Alfred's transfer to public school in September 1877 – Grammar School No. 55 on 20th Street – was in part prompted by Adolph Werner, who wished him to enter City College, which did not take graduates from private or parochial schools. His parents also wanted to appear democratic. At public school, Stieglitz became noted for his mental arithmetic abilities and for his beautiful penmanship. The principal, Mr. Conklin, offered him a job writing the payroll instead of spending time in class. The vice principal, Mr. Meighan, often asked Stieglitz to take over classes for him, and bet a top hat with a Board of Education member that Stieglitz could answer quickly almost any question put to him. Mr. Meighan won his hat. Stieglitz could not be stumped, although there was little interest in how he arrived at the answer. Stieglitz's mathematical abilities were to serve him well when he went on to study chemistry and photochemistry at the university level, making it easier for him to experiment and work with different chemical equations.

In 1879, Alfred entered the five-year program at College of the City of New York, or CCNY as it was known. Edward Stieglitz urged Alfred to become an engineer or a chemist. But by 1880, there was a growing sense of anti-Semitism at the school, and Adolph Werner voiced his disappointment and concern that it was not adopting the larger and more flexible curriculum that existed in many German universities.

Thus, in January 1881, Edward Stieglitz, at the age of only forty-eight, decided to retire and take his family to Europe for at least five years. A frustrated would-be artist, Edward wanted to pursue his hobby of painting while his family experienced European culture. Edward sold most of his share of his profitable imported wool and dry goods business, Hahlo and Stieglitz, for more than $400,000 and invested his profit in the stock market.

*   *   *

GERMANY

On 18 June 1881, the family set sail from Hoboken for Germany. There was Edward, Hedwig, Alfred, Alfred's younger twin brothers, Julius and Leopold, his sisters Flora, Agnes, and Selma, a family servant, and their maiden aunt, Rosa Werner, Hedwig's sister. Sue Davidson Lowe, Stieglitz's great-niece, described the event, as reconstructed from family letters and stories: following the stately carriages carrying the family, "came a string of well-wishing friends bearing baskets of fruit, flowers, and champagne. At the end, the luggage wagon: new Saratoga trunks, footlockers, crates, valises, portmanteaus, hatboxes, compartmented shoe chests, duffel bags heavy with parasols, umbrellas, and walking sticks. At last they were aboard. Father Abraham, with his 'heart nearly broken,' as Hedwig would write Alfred thirty-two years later, 'watched us go from the shore, where no one saw him.' "[25]

The Atlantic crossing may be seen as a turning point in Alfred's life, for it was the route to his discovering his love of photography. On shipboard he met the young Louis Schubart and Joseph Obermeyer who were en route to Europe to meet their parents, who had departed before the boys' schools were finished. Schubart's and Obermeyer's lives were to become closely intertwined with Alfred's, although they were from very conventional upper-middle-class Jewish families and shared little of Stieglitz's artistic interest and unconventional attitudes. Within eighteen months the three were roommates in Berlin. They became business partners at a printing business in New York approximately nine years later. And they became in-laws when Alfred's sister Selma married Lou Schubart, and Alfred married Joe's younger sister Emmeline in 1893.

Following the Atlantic voyage, the Stieglitzs were met by Fedor Encke, the portrait and genre painter, originally from Berlin, who had lived with the Stieglitz family in New York for almost a year in 1877. Edward Stieglitz had planned that his three boys would attend the Realgymnasium in Karlsruhe (today known as the Ludwig Erhard-Schule), because one of Encke's closest friends, the painter Wilhelm Gustav Friedrich Hasemann, was studying in Karlsruhe. Alfred stepped back somewhat to improve his German and to prepare himself for entry into the German university system. The younger girls were to study at Frau Wappenhans's seminary for young women in Weimar, and Flora was to attend a music conservatory to continue her study of piano. Edward, Hedwig, and Rosa, planned to travel while the children were studying, the family as a whole gathering on vacations and holidays in various European cities and scenic rural locations such as Paris, Rome, Venice, Florence, and Zurich.

10   Unknown photographer, *Wilhelm Hasemann*, c.1905

Upon arrival in Germany, the family spent time traveling and had a month of rest in August in the Black Forest resort of Baden-Baden before the boys entered the Karlsruhe Realgymnasium. The twins stayed with the Träutlein family, through whom they took chamber music lessons with the Stieffel sisters, whom the brothers would eventually marry – Julius and Anny, Leopold (Lee) and Elizabeth. Alfred stayed with Professor Doktor Karl L. Bauer, who was a master at the Realgymnasium and noted for his mathematical abilities.

Dominating the city of Karlsruhe was the presence of the Baroque *schloss* and surrounding gardens in the middle of the city, from which radiated a number of streets, like the ribs of a fan. The city, founded in 1715 by Margrave Karl Wilhelm, was modeled to some extent after the Baroque planning of Versailles. Not too far from the spacious English-style park and gardens was the Stadtliche Kunsthalle, which Stieglitz and his family probably would have visited. Artists represented in the collection included Matthias Grünewald, Albrecht Dürer, Peter Paul Rubens, Rembrandt, and Casper David Friedrich. In 1865, a group of poultry farmers in Karlsruhe had purchased a swampy section of land and filled it with geese, ducks, and pheasants. Later deer and other animals were added and the site gradually evolved into a zoo. Thus Stieglitz was able to experience both culture and nature in his Karlsruhe environment.

Studying with Dr. Karl Bauer at the Realgymnasium gave Alfred opportunities for independent study. His classes were small; he was one among eight, aged seventeen to twenty-one, attending class approximately thirty-six hours a week. There was less homework than at CCNY, and in class each boy was given his own individual problems to solve. Alfred seemed to thrive in the independent atmosphere. Indeed, he was chosen to be Dr. Bauer's laboratory assistant. In Dr. Bauer's home, Alfred also experienced a calmer and smaller household than his own. Alfred's

11   The Realgymnasium (Ludwig Erhard-Schule), Karlsruhe.

father had a volatile temperament, while Dr. Bauer was patient and mild mannered at home.

The Stieglitz's friend Hasemann was studying at the Grossherzoglichen Kunstschule as a student of Professor Gustav Schönleber. He spent Christmas and New York 1887 with the Stieglitz family as well as other holidays in the next four years.

Hasemann was becoming known as a fine draftsman, illustrator, and painter of peasant life and native culture in the Black Forest. Born in 1850, in Mühlberg/Elbe, he had studied as a young man with Professor Carl Gussow in Weimar, where he met Fedor Encke. From 1866 to 1872 he continued his studies in Berlin, interrupting his work to serve in the Franco-Prussian War in 1870 as a sanitation worker. In 1878, he traveled to Paris, where he encountered the French Naturalist and Impressionist experiments, and in 1879 he went back to Berlin, where he was introduced to the German painter Adolf von Menzel, who was indirectly to influence Stieglitz. Menzel suggested that Hasemann should spend time in Munich studying with members of the Munich School instead of going to Italy.

The writer J. Nilsen Laurvik in an August 1911 article, "Alfred Stieglitz, Pictorial Photographer" in *the International Studio*, recorded a meeting between Stieglitz and Menzel during Stieglitz's student days, and commented that Stieglitz found the artist somewhat patronizing and not ready to embrace photography as a fine art. But both Hasemann and Stieglitz could well have learned lessons from Menzel and were influenced by his interest in the working class as subject matter equal in importance to upper-class society, as in images such as *Bartiger Arbeiterkopf in Profil* (*Bearded Worker's Head in Profile*) of 1844 or *Karrengaul* (*Carthorse*) of 1844–6 (Berlin, Alte Nationalgalerie). Menzel, Stieglitz, and Hasemann also depicted workhorses in closely cropped compositions.

Menzel also made some cloud studies, such as his 1851 *Wolkenstudie* (*Cloud Study*) (Berlin, Alte Nationalgalerie). Menzel's studies, focusing on the light conditions of sky and clouds, were primarily recorded in his sketchbooks, as were Hasemann's. Stieglitz could well have seen both men's studies, which must have influenced his own interest in sky imagery.

Although Menzel is frequently characterized as the painter of Frederick the Great, some of his work demonstrates Impressionist qualities and an interest in the interplay of light and shadow in formal settings, as in his *The Balcony Room* (1845), where the painter plays with two different levels of perspective as light shines in the room from the outside world. This interest in atmospheric elements also appeared in Hasemann's and Stieglitz's early work.

All three men also dealt in their work with the arrival of the train into contemporary culture. Menzel and Hasemann explored the intrusion of the train into a rural setting, as seen in Menzel's *Die Berlin-Potsdamer Eisenbahn* (*Berlin, Potsdamer Railroad*) of 1847 (Berlin, Nationalgalerie) and Hasemann's *Schwarzwaldtal* (*Black Forest Valley*) (private collection). Stieglitz was to explore the role of the train in modern culture in photographs such as *The Hand of Man* (1902) and *In the New York Central Yards* (1903).

Stieglitz's contact with Hasemann also introduced him to the small southern German town of Gutach, which he first encountered during his month of rest in the Black Forest on his arrival in Germany. Fedor Encke had sent several letters to Hasemann earlier in the spring and summer from Paris, Berlin, and Lichtenthal, saying that he hoped to bring the Stieglitzs to the town, where Hasemann was then living, and the family did visit in August. (A letter dated 15 August 1881, from Hedwig to Hasemann, thanked him profusely for sending a pair of eyeglasses that Edward left behind there.)

Noted for its beautiful landscapes and footpaths into the mountains of the Black Forest, Gutach has traditionally attracted artists. It is the home of the famous Bollen hat, probably dating from the eighteenth century, with colorful balls or pompoms, worn by the women. Typically the hat has fourteen balls, red ones for unmarried women, black ones for married women. Traditional farmhouse architecture with huge sloping thatched roofs and carved wood interiors and exteriors would have marked the surrounding countryside. (Today the Freilichtmuseum Vogtsbauernhof contains a number of restored farmhouses.) The area was devoted to handcrafted objects, in particular carved wooden items such as clocks. The colorful dress served as a reminder of the significance of the Black Forest culture.

Hasemann first came to Gutach in April of 1880 while he was working on illustrations for the novel *Lorle, die Frau Professorin* (*Lorle, the Woman Professor*) by Berthold Auerbach. His early illustrations are romantic and lyrical, with delicate lines and shades of dark and light. From 1882 until his death, Hasemann spent much of his time in Gutach. Around him a small artists' colony began to develop, including Curt Liebich, the sculptor and painter who was to become Hasemann's brother-in-law, Ernst Kielwein, and Fritz Reiss. The artists were attracted to Gutach for its picturesque beauty, its pride and dedication toward retaining its traditional dress and handcrafts, and its lack of industry and technology. Like Paul Gauguin's living alongside Breton peasants and Tahiti natives, these artists saw in the Gutach way of life something purer, more authentic, and more human than could be found in late-nineteenth-century urban life.

Hasemann did not paint simply sentimental portrayals of peasant life, but rather he sought to preserve an aspect of being with an enriched interior life that was represented by the exterior "tracht," a traditional dress that he felt was important, at a time when the beginnings of modernity were being experienced by the world at large. Hasemann's paintings of the Gutach villagers at work and at home were to influence Stieglitz a number of years later when he returned to photograph Gutach in 1894. In the meantime, his intervening visits could not help but be embedded in his psyche.

In 1882, Hasemann completed a watercolor portrait of the young Stieglitz. Edward Stieglitz, who corresponded fairly regularly with his new-found artist friend, praised the work extensively in a letter of 25 May 1882:

12 Wilhelm Hasemann, *Alfred Stieglitz*, 1882.

You have made for my family a very true-to-life portrait of my son –
and you will become a household name for me and my children! I can
see great strides in your creativity, primarily in how you handle color,
and that you have worked in watercolor, which you have seldom done.
So you will go forward my dear, special friend and teacher and will
become part of the row of German artists whose work will be enjoyed
by generation after generation, year after year.

So I say to you good night with much joy and a thankful heart.

Yours truly,

Edward Stieglitz.[26]

Edward Stieglitz was so taken with a postcard that Hasemann sent him with one of his drawings that he asked the artist to send move. For a number of years, Hasemann was to send the Stieglitz family his hand-drawn cards, continuing after the family returned to the United States. (There are approximately forty such cards mounted by the Stieglitzs in a leather album now in the Beinecke Library Collection). Edward also worked on his own drawing skills with Hasemann, producing drawings similar to Hasemann's landscape drawings, but dry and flat in comparison to the richness of the German artist.

During the spring of 1882, Alfred visited Gutach and traveled through the Black Forest while on vacation and on 18 April 1882 he wrote to his cousin:

I made a short trip with an artist by the name of Hasemann through part of the Black Forest. Our principal stay was in Gutach, a small village situated at the beginning of the "Schwarzwald." It is beautifully situated in a valley, which is hemmed in on all sides by mountains of 2000–2500 feet high. On our arrival, I was quite surprised by the beauty of the scenery . . . It was a picture – the whole valley was, so to say, in bloom; the cherry trees that are so plentiful there were bedecked with white blossoms, so that one thought that snow had lately fallen. Not a sound but the monotonous ring of the village church bell and the rippling of a brook was to be heard. It was Easter Sunday, the peasants were just going to church. They were a queer-looking set of people; the woman wearing short black dresses, whose circumference must have measured at least three yards; then what was on their heads? It was a large white hat, covered with immense black balls made of plush or something of the sort. The men were a hand-some lot. Broad shouldered and well built. They wore long velvet coats and yellow and red vests. These were my first impressions of Gutach. As Mr. Hasemann was at home there, I had a splendid chance to become acquainted with the people. I found them to be very agreeable and pleasant company, not at all stupid, on the contrary. Very wide awake. I would like to go on relating, but must stop, for my piano teacher is due in a moment. I enclose one of my pictures, which I have lately had made, the family think them a little too "schwärmerisch."

With best regards to all.

I remain your affectionate,

Alfred.[27]

13   Wilhelm Hasemann, *Gutach*, 14 June 1883.

14   Wilhelm Hasemann, *Gutach*, 19 August 1883

The eighteen-year-old's great attention to detail is here revealed. Alfred's description of Gutach as a "picture" suggests his predisposition for the pictorial and the picturesque, which was to characterize much of his early photographic work. It appears, too, that the young Alfred is breaking some stereotypes of the peasant as "stupid," which will open

15 Postcard from Stieglitz to his sister Flora, 10 April 1882, with a drawing of a Gutach scene by William Hasemann.

the paths that he follows in photographing the lower classes and peasant life in Europe and New York City. It is unclear from the letter whether Alfred is referring to photographs he had taken by someone else or to some he had taken himself. (Schwärmerisch can be translated as fanciful, wild-looking, like a dreamer.) Stieglitz's detailed writing style has some affinity to the naturalism of Zola, whom he admired.

During the summer of 1882, the Stieglitz family spent a good deal of time in Gutach at the Gasthaus Zum Löwen, where a number of artists had stayed when visiting the idyllic setting. Pages from an artists' album from the Gasthaus list approximately seventy artists who had visited. An unidentified photograph shows Hasemann working on a painting of a young woman wearing traditional dress and *Bollenhut*. A small crowd of various ages has gathered around him. This would have been a typical scene of artists working in Gutach.

Before arriving in Gutach, Alfred made sure to add his greeting from Badenweiler to an admiring letter from his sister Selma to Hasemann of 11 June 1882: "Beste Grusse von ihren, kleinen Freund, Alfred Stieglitz"

– "Best wishes from your small friend, Alfred Stieglitz." All of the family seemed to enjoy greatly spending time with Hasemann. In a letter of 3 June from Edward to Hasemann, Edward praised a drawing of Herr Aberle, the owner of the Gasthaus zum Löwen, that Hasemann had given Alfred.

In the fall of 1882, Alfred headed to Berlin to go to university, initially staying with the artist Erdmann Encke, Fedor's older brother and a successful academic sculptor who also worked in portrait photography, but keeping in touch with Hasemann. On 31 October 1882 the young Alfred wrote to Hasemann from Berlin, thanking him profusely for a drawing he had sent:

> My dear Mr. Hasemann,
> How astonished I was to come to the table yesterday morning and find your beautiful postcard. It is a wonderful drawing and made everyone feel good, including Erdmann Encke. He and his wife send you hearty greetings. How I am, you have probably heard already from Papa (who is staying in Gutach) and I can only say again that I am deeply involved in my studies.
> With very best wishes and many thanks,
> your Alfred Stieglitz.[28]

Hasemann hoped to build an Atelierhaus or studio in Gutach and was having trouble making ends meet as an artist. On 14 December 1882, Edward Stieglitz sent him 800 marks on extended loan to use for the studio. The following August 12, Hasemann gave a dedication party for his studio and invited the village folk. From the 1880s until his death in 1913, Hasemann gained much regional and national popularity. In 1887, the Grand Duchess Luise von Baden gave her father Kaiser Wilhelm for his ninetieth birthday a large grandfather clock and asked Hasemann to paint two young women in the native dress of Gutach and Mühlberg. In the same year he was also asked to illustrate, with Edmund Kienoldt, Theodor Storm's novel, *Immensee*.

By 1898, Hasemann had been given the honorary title of professor by the state. Hasemann brought the world to Gutach and Gutach to the world as he attempted to preserve and present a sense of identity that belonged to the Gutach area. In comparison to the Renaissance and Baroque building projects and the growing industry in Karlsruhe, Gutach, just a short train ride away, retained for Hasemann a distinct sense of native German identity. That identity united history, culture, and a work ethic, as well as an all-encompassing sense of community.

Hasemann did not isolate himself in his studio and got to know the village population who greatly respected and admired him. He was also friends with the village pastor, Heinrich Hansjakob, who, like Hasemann, was interested in the preservation of regional traditions and dress. Their mutual interests led to a text by Hansjakob, *Unsere Volkstrachten* (*Our Traditional Dress*) (Freiburg, 1892) and to the formation of a preservation association. Hansjakob also asked Hasemann to illustrate a short story he wrote, "Vogt auf Mühlstein" ("The Governor from Mühlstein"). The Stieglitz family also met the pastor and Alfred sometimes sent a special greeting to him in some of his letters to Hasemann. Hasemann's piercing portrait of Hansjakob, with its simple lines, prefigures some of the photographic portraits Alfred was to take in the early twentieth century of his friends and fellow artists, particularly those taken at his 291 gallery.

Mary Bowles, an English writer traveling to Germany in 1893, described her visit to Hasemann's studio and Gutach, which she noted had existed since 1275 but was never mentioned in Baedeker's travel guides. She wrote: "Fertile fields, fruit gardens, and orchards, diversified with shady nooks, cover the sides of the hills, real old Black Forest houses peep out among them and are dotted through the valley down to its bright rippling river looking southward, the ruined castle at Hornberg stands high up as a crowning point to this picture. It is a little world of happy sunshine."[29] Her article contained several Hasemann drawings, one of his studio, which Stieglitz was to photograph on a return trip in 1894. Bowles described the studio in great detail:

> With sympathetic taste he has built his house in exact resemblance to a Black Forest peasant's cottage, in all its rustic simplicity and beauty of color, the soft dark brown of an old pine cone, with its low many-paned windows, the long upper balcony with the high carved balustrade, the overhanging roof, protective alike from storms in winter and heat in summer, and standing "all in a garden fair." But in the studio itself a surprise awaits us; for though a studio *par excellence* in height and space and its northern light, it is most skillfully combined with the features distinctive of the interior of the peasant's cottage. The large window looks to the north and commands an extensive view down the valley, beautiful alike at all seasons; but, if you stand with your back to this, there are first presented to you the immediate surroundings of the artist, in the lofty space given to the studio proper. Then, cunningly contrived, a portion of ceiling much lower than this, supported by beams and rafters, all add to its effect the very

heart of the peasants' room, the "Gottes Winkel," as he calls it –
"God's Corner." Two sides of it are open to the room and two are
surrounded by the latticed window with its little openings and small
panes of glass. Under this runs a bench, and before that stands the
large table for the family meals; and in the corner itself are small
bracket shelves, holding first the family bible, and, above all, the cru-
cifix. Flowers always adorn these corner windows, and here much of
the household work is done. In summer it is the family resting place,
which in winter is tranferred to the other centre, the great tiled stove,
of some subdued colour, standing a little in the background on one
side. This also has its wide bench running round three sides of it, and
is the comfortable and warm chimney corner, where all gather in the
long winter evenings – the men with their pipes, and the women with
their spinning wheels – to listen to the village gossip and also to what
the German heart holds so dear, the old tales and poems of the Father-
land. Opposite the stove is the steep and narrow staircase leading to
the rooms above and protected by a high balustrade like that of the
balcony. All is adorned by studies of pictures, some already painted
and others to come, while here and there hang some of the pretty ornamented caps of the peasant women and bright bits of their costumes;
while a few good old pieces of carved furniture, black with age,
complete the whole, in perfect harmony with the artist's tastes and
surroundings.[30]

It is perhaps easy to understand how Hasemann's work may have been
subsumed into the National Socialist rhetoric related to homeland and
German nationalism after World War II and how he became relegated
to the stance of sentimental painter of peasant life. But in truth some of
his work contained modern qualities in simple, straightforward compositions, succinct use of line and shape, and the search for a deepened
sense of humanity that Hasemann found in peasant life. The significance
of young Stieglitz's time with Hasemann and of his viewing Hasemann's
drawings and paintings became clear when Stieglitz began to take photographs and particularly when he returned to Gutach with his camera
in 1894.

Arriving in Berlin in the fall of 1882 after having been in Gutach most
of the summer must have been somewhat of a culture shock for the
young Stieglitz. By 1877 Berlin's population had reached one million and
was still growing (by 1905 it was two million). In 1871 it had become
the capital of the newly established state after the Franco-Prussian war,

fulfilling the ambitions of Chancellor Otto von Bismarck. By 1879 electric lamps lit the streets and in 1881 the first telephones were installed. The Baroque era had left its mark, with magnificent palaces such as the Schloss Charlottenburg. But the most significant architecture that would have been prominent during Stieglitz's time was that of Neoclassical origin. The great Brandenburg Gate, modeled after the Athenian Propylaea, was designed by Carl Gotthard Langhans and had been erected from 1778 to 1791. It was crowned by the "Quadriga" – a two-wheeled chariot drawn by four horses and driven by the winged goddess of victory (sculpture designed by Johann Gottfried Schadow). – and framed by a pair of pavilions. Karl Friedrich Schinkel's elegant Neoclassical structures also graced the city: the Neue Wache of 1818, a dignified war memorial and guard house; the Schauspielhaus of 1821; or the Altes Museum of 1830 on the northern edge of the Lustgarten. The museum's interior rotunda, housing antiquities, was designed after the Roman Pantheon. The Schlossbrücke was lined with eight clusters of white marble statues portraying the training and development of a Greek warrior. The Alte Nationalgalerie, which resembled a Greek temple, was designed by Friedrich August Stüler, a disciple of Schinkel, and opened in 1876. There is little doubt that Stieglitz would have visited these places. The Berlin museums had strong collections; the art museums were sometimes seen as an extension of the university. The clean lines and balanced compositions of much of Stieglitz's photography would seem to have some basis in the lines of those Neoclassical architectural forms that he would have experienced as a student.

Alfred stayed for about a month with Erdmann Encke, Fedor's older brother and a successful academic sculptor who also worked in portrait photography. Encke encouraged him to visit museums, Stieglitz being reluctant at first. A painting by Fedor of his brother shows him to be a pensive, thoughtful man. Erdmann's calling card from 1883 shows that his title was "Professor," and he was a member of the Senate at the "Königlichen Akademie der Kunste." There are some remaining photographs from Encke's portrait studio, including some of the young Alfred.

In October 1882, Alfred entered the all-male Königliche Technische Hochschule, which had been formed in 1879 as a result of the union of the Königliche Gewerbeakademie (Royal Vocational Academy or Polytechnik) and the architectural academy. (John Roebling the designer of the Brooklyn Bridge had attended the vocational academy and Ludwig Wittgenstein studied at the Hochschule from 1906 to 1908.) Alfred

16　The Technische Hochschule, Berlin, 2002

entered the mechanical engineering department, the head of which was Franz Reuleaux, who was noted for his engaging personality and wide variety of interests, including philosophy, logic, travel, and literature. (He translated Henry Wadsworth Longfellow's *Hiawatha* into German.) Despite Reuleaux's convincing style, Alfred found it difficult to sit through his classes on mechanical analysis.

But during his first term in Berlin, Stieglitz discovered he could also take courses at the University of Berlin on Unter den Linden. Founded in 1810 at the initiative of Wilhelm von Humboldt, the university was housed in a building that had been constructed in 1753 for Prince Heinrich of Prussia. Its noted scholars include Johann Gottlieb Fichte, George Wilhelm Friedrich Hegel, Max Planck, and Albert Einstein; among its graduates are Heinrich Heine, Karl Marx and Friedrich Engels. Within these Neoclassical halls, there was less structure in the curriculum. Students could choose whatever courses they wished and paid the professors directly. There Alfred took a class with the well-known physicist and physiologist Hermann von Helmholtz, but found the work too complex. (Julius Stieglitz later studied with and received recognition for his work under Helmholtz.)

Stieglitz was thus arriving in Berlin as it was really beginning to blossom in the late nineteenth century, economically and culturally. Although he may have been frustrated by some of the courses he took, he relished the atmosphere of intellectual freedom that he found there. He spent hours reading in his room. He discovered the Russian authors, Mikhail Yuryevich Lermontov, Nikolai Gogol, Alexander Sergeyevich Pushkin, Ivan Turgenev, and Count Leo Tolstoy. He particularly liked Lermontov's *A Hero of Our Times*. He read Alphonse Daudet's *Sappho* and his *Tartarin* series. He then discovered Emile Zola, whose naturalist style greatly appealed to him. Indeed, Stieglitz's own style of writing took on some of Zola's naturalism, as seen in his description of his April

17   The University of Berlin, *c.*1880–1900

1882 visit to Gutach. Stieglitz loved *Madeleine Férat*, Zola's 1868 novel and, on finishing it, stayed up most of the night reading it to his friends, happy to have an audience to share his enthusiasm. Afterwards he read some of Zola's *Rougon-Macquart* series, "the natural and social history of a family living under the Second Empire" as it was subtitled. There were two branches of the family: the Rougons, small shopkeepers and petty bourgeoisie; and the Macquarts, who were poachers, smugglers, and alcoholics. Some of the family rose to the top of society; others sunk to the bottom, victims of heredity and social problems.

For Zola, naturalism involved "Nature seen through a temperament." For the young Stieglitz, whose emotional nature and romantic leanings were a significant part of his personality, the emotional content and naturalistic detail would have been appealing. Paul Rosenfeld, Stieglitz's friend and a cultural critic, commented that Stieglitz was attracted to Zola's "employing fiction experimentally as a means of penetrating to the laws underlying the phenomenon of life."[31] No doubt Stieglitz was also attracted to the writer's description of womanhood. He read *La Faute de l'abbé Mouret* (*The Mistake of Abbot Mouret*), *Une Page d'Amour* (*A Page of Love*), *L'Oeuvre* (*The Masterpiece*), and others in the Rougon-Macquart series. *L'Oeuvre* (1886) was said to be based roughly on the life of Cézanne and the novel caused a rift in the artist's friendship with Zola). Little did Stieglitz know at this point that Cézanne's work would be among the first "modern" European art he

18   Alfred Stieglitz,
Snowscape (Berlin),
1888–90

19 *(facing page)*
Alfred Stieglitz,
Winter (Berlin),
1887

would see a few years later in Paris, and that he would show Cézanne's
work at his 291 gallery. Stieglitz was actually in touch with Zola, asking
him if a good translation of his work from the French existed. A 22 May
1884 postcard from Zola addressed to Stieglitz in French at his apartment on Behrenstrasse in Berlin indicates that Zola knew of no good
translation. Zola commented, too, "Les Américains ne volent toutes mes
oeuvres" – "The Americans do not steal all my works".[32] Most likely
Stieglitz admired Zola's stand for the cause of Alfred Dreyfus, the French
Jewish army officer who was falsely charged with giving military secrets
to the Germans. His famous public letter, "J'accuse" to the president of
the French Republic, became most controversial, and Zola was forced
to flee to Britain until Dreyfus was cleared.

Beginning in the summer of 1888, Zola also began to take photographs, in part to amass material for his future writing projects,
prompted by Victor Billaud, the French writer, poet, and editor, and
Nadar, the photographer, whom he had known since the 1860s. From
1894 to 1902, when he died mysteriously, Zola took thousands of
photographs of family, friends, Parisian life, and life in the country. It is
not known whether Stieglitz actually saw these photographs, but Zola's
and Stieglitz's photographs of Paris shared an eye for detail and careful
composition. Stieglitz's work tended to be more "picturesque," while
Zola's retained the naturalistic details of his novels. Both photographed
wet boulevards – for example, Zola's image of the Place Clichy seen from
the corner of the rue d'Amsterdam, or his Place Prosper-Goubaux and

Avenue de Villiers (1890s), or Stieglitz's *A Wet Day on the Boulevard* (1894) or *Paris* (1894). Both photographed at night, an experimental process at the time. Zola photographed the 1900 World's Fair in several night shots. Stieglitz became noted for his night images of 1897 and 1898 of New York – in particular the Savoy Hotel and *An Icy Night*.

Zola was a defender of photography in his writing. He bought approximately ten cameras during his career and installed three darkrooms in the basements of his various homes. Stieglitz could have seen some of Zola's photographs in Paris, or perhaps through his association with Theodore Dreiser, the American writer who was influenced by the integrity of Zola, who admired the early photographic work of Stieglitz, and wrote about Stieglitz's work. Sitting in his room as a student reading intensely, Stieglitz could not know all of these connections, direct and indirect, but Zola's keen interest in the fabric of life, the struggles in life, and the intensity of a life deeply lived, had an impact on the young Stieglitz, who would often characterize his own life and artistic concerns as a struggle, a fight.

Besides reading Zola, Stieglitz also read and greatly liked the German writer Viktor von Scheffel's *Ekkehard*, which revolved around the significance of the role of "Woman." At the time, Scheffel was a successful and popular historical novelist. Stieglitz's reading seemed to echo what he was perhaps feeling inside and corroborate some of his personal experiences, and to open the door to various modes of creative expression.

Stieglitz not only studied and read for pleasure, but also played cards and billiards, and spent much time at the Café Bauer. He visited horse races and spent many evenings at the theater, attending concerts, ballets, and the opera. Students were able to buy tickets cheaply. In Berlin at the time state theaters were required by city ordinance to make available to students all tickets not sold to the public an hour before the performance. Stieglitz's copious well-kept scrapbooks, filled with hundreds of tickets and programs from his student days and from New York following his return there in 1890, suggest that he went out almost every night of the week, and that he had a variety of tastes, from high opera to vaudeville, from Baroque to Classical to Romantic music.

Scrapbook seven, as an example, contains materials primarily from New York and Berlin, but also from Karlsruhe, Munich, Bayreuth, Heidelberg, Weimar, Bremen, Leipzig, Interlaken, Berne, Lucerne, and Budapest. Pasted on the inside of the cover are portraits of Edwin Booth, an actor, and an unidentified woman, cut from serials. Scrapbook eight,

20 Unter den Linden and Ecke Friedrichstrasse with the Café Bauer, Berlin, 1885

dating from 1888 to 1902, again primarily contains programs from New York and Berlin, but also includes events in Washington, D.C., Bayreuth, Munich, Oberammergau, Vienna, Paris, Biarritz, Bordeaux, and London. In the back of this scrapbook in Stieglitz's handwriting is an alphabetical listing of plays, concerts, and operas, with the places where each was seen and the page number where Stieglitz placed the playbills. Stieglitz carefully attached letters in red, blue, and black to individual pages to complete his listing.

Among Stieglitz's favorite actresses was Eleonora Duse, of Italian origin, who had grown up in a traveling theatrical family, and had spent much time near Venice and Chioggia, where Stieglitz was to travel. Duse was a passionate and sensual actress, performing such roles as Emile Zola's Thérèse Raquin, Nora in Henrik Ibsen's *A Doll's House*, Hedda, in Ibsen's *Hedda Gabler*, and Juliet in Shakespeare's *Romeo and Juliet*. Stieglitz went to see her in numerous performances. Scrapbook eight contains also programs for circus performances, an exhibition of trained animal acts (1894), a benefit concert and ball for the Mount Sinai Nursing School (1891), and an invitation, menu, and newspaper announcement of Stieglitz's marriage to Emmeline Obermeyer in 1893.

The layout of the scrapbooks shows an innate sense of design and of detail, as well as a desire to remember performing arts events. Many of the individual programs are very artistic in nature. For instance, programs from the Comédie Française have strong graphic design elements and also list current books that were recommended for further reading. Stieglitz did not take courses in basic design or graphic design as a photographer might today. But these programs must have enhanced his visual sensibilities and perhaps indirectly contributed to the strong graphic design components in such photographs as *The Steerage* (1907) or *A Decorative Panel*, taken along the Seine in 1894, or to the layout of the periodical *Camera Work*.

Stieglitz attended performances of Shakespeare, Calderón, Goethe, Lessing, Schiller, Ibsen, Echegaray, Wagner, Bach, Mozart, Verdi, Bizet, and others. He attended performances in Paris and Vienna in the spring and summer of 1890 and on 23 July 1890 he attended the lengthy Oberammergau Passion Play, performed once a decade with all the parts played by the townspeople. He attended numerous Wagner operas and saw *Tristan and Isolde* many times, as well as *Tannhäuser*, *Die Meistersinger*, *Das Rheingold*, and *Götterdämmerung*.

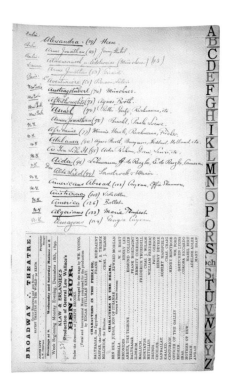

23a, b and c   Pages from Stieglitz's
Scrapbook eight

21 (*facing page left*)   Unknown
photogapher, *Eleanora Duse*, n.d.

22 (*facing page right*)   Playbill from
Stieglitz's Scrapbook eight

Why was Stieglitz so captivated by Wagner? Born in 1813, Wagner was coming to maturity as Stieglitz was born. When Stieglitz was a student in Berlin, Wagner was being hailed by some as a major force not only in music, but in the arts in general. In an address to the Vienna Wagner Verein in 1875, Camillo Sitte, the city planner, spoke of Wagner's work as providing a framework for artistic values in a growing capitalist world, claiming that figures such as his Siegfried provided integrative myths that helped people to deal with the fragmentation of modern life. As the historian Carl Schorske records: "Sitte exalted Wagner as the genius who recognized this redemptive, future-oriented work as the special task of the artist. The world that the rootless seekers of science and trade destroyed, leaving the suffering *Volk* without a vital myth to live by, the artist must create anew. Sitte cited the injunctions of the spirits to Faust [Wagner greatly admired Goethe's Faust]

> You have destroyed,
> The beautiful world, . . . Build it again,
> In your breast rebuild it."[33]

Like Stieglitz, Wagner admired Goethe and Shakespeare. His notion of the Gesamtkunstwerk, – the total work of art that would unite poetic drama, music, the visual arts, and dance – was seen as a way to counterbalance the growing fragmentation of modern man and woman. Indeed, *Camera Work*, the periodical that Stieglitz edited from 1903 to 1917, may be seen as a kind of *Gesamtkunstwerk*, as Stieglitz gathered works from the areas of art, music, literature, poetry, and drama to compile a powerful whole.

Both the narratives and music of Wagner's operas probably appealed to Stieglitz. *Tannhäuser*, for example, is concerned with the triumph of a woman's Christian love over pagan sensuality, and it sets forth the theme of redemption. The setting is medieval Germany. *Lohengrin*, also set in medieval times, involves a knight of the Holy Grail and the role of a woman's love and faith. In *Tristan and Isolde* the theme involves sexual love, where the lovers can be reunited only in death. The writer Ralph Flint later noted that Wagner's *Die Meistersinger* was magical for Stieglitz:

The four-hour flow of that magical work was to him the ultimate in creative art, and it was undoubtedly the Sachs [Hans Sachs, a cobbler-musician] in him that permitted such responsiveness, that kept him spellbound until that climactic moment when the victor's wreath is placed on the cobbler's brow amidst the town's rejoicing. I like Stieglitz best as Sachs and it was the *Meistersinger* note that sounded throughout our long summer at the lake [George]. For my part, he was first and foremost the embodiment of Wagner's greatest creation. Hans Sachs–Sachs the philosopher, the lover of mankind, the advocate of individuality and free expression, the apostle of enduring beauty, of inspirational activity, of art triumphant. Here was the inner Stieglitz, the basic man, the core and substance of a highly enigmatic character, here was the witty, sparkling companion I loved – full bodied, lyrical, wearing naturally with easy grace the laurels belonging to all true devotees of truth and beauty. But this fun-loving, flashing Stieglitz was not always apparent, not easily arrived at, for he could be almost anyone in the long list of Wagner's "dramatis personae."

It often took time and patience to banish the darker side of his nature; as in Wagner's scoring, he could drop down into the depths where only the ponderous croaking of the double basses predominate.[34]

In his operas, Wagner became noted for his musical leitmotifs, which held his structures together, and for developing a chromatic style that allowed for greater expressive qualities in the music. The leitmotif gave Wagner more opportunities to deal with ideas, or links between ideas, such as the unspoken thought of a character on stage. The device can be related to Stieglitz's notion of *Equivalents*, where he linked the visual to ideas or states of emotion. Wagner's chromaticism may be seen to have some analogy to Stieglitz's subtle use of black, white, and grays, of intricate areas of light and shade, which enhanced the expressive qualities of some of his photographs such as *On Lake Thun, Switzerland* (1886), or *Sun Rays, Paula* (1889).

Stieglitz's incorporation of music into his total aesthetic and approach to the visual arts, particularly in his *Songs of the Sky* (begun in 1922–3), is rooted in his early interest in music. From Mozart and early Beethoven, Stieglitz could well have learned to appreciate further the significance of form, in particular the precision of classical form. The Romantic strains of Beethoven, Schumann, Chopin, and Wagner must have fed the emotional yearnings of Stieglitz. And Beethoven's Sixth Symphony, *The Pastorale*, is specifically oriented toward a landscape setting, before, during, and after a storm. Beethoven's Ninth Symphony, with its dramatic final chorus section, asks, in the words of Friedrich Schiller's *Ode to Joy*, for the whole world to come together in an embrace, and appeals for a sense of brotherly love. Music was very much in the air for the young Stieglitz and must be counted as a significant factor in his development.

Stieglitz not only frequented theaters and concerts, he also played the piano in Berlin. He had taken lessons in Karlsruhe, but did not like to follow the exercises his teacher presented. As with games and certain aspects of his schoolwork, Stieglitz wished to operate outside the commonly accepted framework and to follow his own guidelines. He noted that he "was never without a piano. Among my favorite scores were *Carmen* and those of Wagner and Gluck. At times I played Chopin's *Funeral March* or a Tyrolese song. I loved Beethoven, Mozart, Schumann. Although never much of a pianist, I had a passion for music. Oftentimes at night I would sit bare-skinned on the piano stool and play."[35]

Stieglitz's passion for music can be viewed in the larger context of music's connections to the notion of creation and revelation. Some Greek philosophers saw creation as an act of music. By the Middle Ages there was a further concept that the created universe was in a state of music, that there was a perpetual cosmic dance. One early medieval encyclopedist, Isidore of Seville, wrote, "Nothing exists without music, for the universe itself is said to have been framed by a kind of harmony of sounds."[36] By the seventeenth century, René Descartes recognized that the movement of music could inspire movement in the soul and that poetics "like our music was invented to excite the movements of the soul."[37]

This sense of the power of music continued into the late nineteenth century and figured prominently in the Symbolist movement, which greatly influenced Stieglitz. For the Symbolist artist, the work of art was the product of emotion and the inner spirit of the artist, not simply the observation of nature or other aspects of visual reality. Nature could serve as the inspiration for an artistic idea, but the greatest and highest reality lay in the realm of imagination. The Symbolists favored a suggestion of mystery, of metamorphosis. Some, such as Odilon Redon, were attracted to Eastern religions that promoted the idea of a fusion between humankind and nature. Representations of silence and solitude were also seen as ways of entering a deeper spiritual world. Among other Symbolist influences, the writings of Belgian playwright Maurice Maeterlinck were greatly admired by Stieglitz and the photographer Edward Steichen. Stieglitz was particularly interested in Maeterlinck's notion of correspondences among color, sound, and emotional states.

The theory of correspondences was also based on the writings of Charles Baudelaire, who, like Stieglitz, admired Wagner. Baudelaire saw all things as potential symbols of a transcendent reality. Correspondences operated on two levels: between different arts – painting, poetry, and music – and within a single art, where, for example, colour might suggest sound. At the beginning of his poem "La Musique," Baudelaire writes, "La musique souvent me prend comme une mer!" – "Music often carries me away like a sea." Here music is seen as an overpowering, indefinable art. Indeed, the original French suggests sexual connotations of possession. A further line by Baudelaire, "La musique creuse dans le ciel" – "Music burrows into the sky" – suggests both a sense of hollowness and a hallowed divinity, pointing to the ephemeral quality of music, and the possible paradox of experiencing emptiness as well as divinity.[38] Music was seen as a medium with few boundaries, capable of reaching toward a new realm of abstraction. Baudelaire's lines seem particularly apt for Stieglitz's explorations of the sky. The reissue of Baudelaire's *Fleurs du Mal* in 1873 coincided with the essayist Walter Pater's famous words, "All art constantly aspires to the condition of music."[39] Baudelaire, however, was not a proponent of the artistic potential of photography: as noted in his famous 1859 essay, "Photography", he feared the commercial aspects of photography would corrupt art.

In 1872, Friedrich Nietzsche had published the *Birth of Tragedy*, suggesting that music, more than the visual image, is capable of symbolizing a cosmic order. Although God may have been dead for Nietzsche, art was seen as wiser and more philosophical than philosophy, particularly that art associated with Dionysian festivals; and music was seen as more philosophical than language. Beethoven was associated with the Dionysian for Nietzsche. A Socrates who practices music was envisioned as well as an art based on Wagnerian concepts that would reveal the human condition. Nietzsche quoted extensively from Arthur Schopenhauer:

According to all of this, we may regard the phenomenal world, or nature and music as two different expressions of the same thing, which is therefore itself the only medium of analogy between these two expressions, so that a knowledge of this medium is required to understand the analogy. Music, therefore, if regarded as an expression of the world, is in the highest degree, a universal language . . . music is distinguished from all the other arts by the fact it is not a copy of the phenomenon . . . but is the direct copy of the will itself, and therefore represents the metaphysical of everything physical in the world . . . We might just as well call the world embodied music as embodied will.[40]

In song and dance, man was seen to express himself as a member of a higher community. For Nietzsche, the synthesis of Apollonian and Dionysian tendencies in Greek tragedy was an ideal. In other works, Nietzsche made direct reference to dance and saw the art of life as a dance in which the dancer rises to inner freedom and to a rhythmic harmony that surpasses the ordinariness of everyday existence. In *Thus Spoke Zarathustra* (1883–5) he wrote, "I would believe only in a god who could dance . . . when I saw my devil I found him serious . . . it was the spirit of gravity . . . Now I am light, now I fly, now I see myself beneath myself, now a god dances through me."[41] Stieglitz, in his philosophizing and advocacy of the arts, as well as in his own work, could well have been the kind of Socrates whom Nietzsche envisioned. Nietzsche was often referred to by contributors to *Camera Work*, and short excerpts of his writing were published there.

Stieglitz's ability to immerse himself in the artistic culture of Berlin and the larger culture of Europe was due primarily to the generous allowance he received from his father. He recalled his student days in Berlin as

Congenial, free – the freest I have ever experienced. What more could a person want than I had . . . I had no desire to drink or to eat rich food. I harbored no social aspirations and was devoted, above all, to photography. I was crazy about billiards and racehorses, but this neither complicated my life nor interfered with my work. I was interested in Woman, but not in women. I frequented cafés, mainly the Café Bauer, which was open day and night. There were no set times when I had to do anything. If tired, I slept, if hungry, I ate. When I wanted to read, I read. Even at the racetrack in Europe I thrived on the color, the movement, the jockeys on wild, rushing horses, the elements of nature controlled by man. I was excited by the entire picture of life: spectators, participants, comedy and tragedy – all dovetailing, breathing![42]

Besides his scrapbooks, documenting the many plays, concert, and ballets that he attended, Stieglitz also began an album entitled "Erkenne Dich Selbst" ("Know Yourself") dated from 1885 to 1917 in which he and his friends and relatives recorded their likes, dislikes, favorite artists, and so on. It was also referred to as a *Gedenk* album or "idea" album. In the beginning of the album is a quotation from Schiller: "If you wish to know yourself, see what is the driving force in others. If you wish to understand others, look into your own heart."[43] The day after he turned twenty, 2 January 1884, in Berlin, Stieglitz noted the following for his own page, written in German and translated here:

Favorite characteristic in a man – energy and endurance

Favorite pastimes – reading, disputation, rowing

Idea of good luck – to be loved

What profession – to be a millionaire

If you weren't you, who would you be – der Herrgott [the Lord God]

Where would you like to live – Venusberg [from Wagner's opera setting]

What period of time would you like to have lived – time of the myths

Your idea of being unlucky – to have no luck at all

Main characteristic of oneself – fickleness

Favorite writers – Shakespeare, Byron, Bulwer [the Romantic British novelist and poet, 1803–73]

Favorite painters – Rubens, Van Dyck, Angelo, etc. [Raphael was crossed out and replaced by Van Dyck. After visiting Venice Stieglitz later noted he was moved by Tintoretto. He was also charmed by Rubens' *Hélène Fourment*.]

Favorite composers – Beethoven, Mozart, Schumann, Wagner, etc.

Favorite color and flowers – dark red, carnation, violet, rose

Favorite hero in history – Leonidas, Washington

Favorite heroine in history – Joan of Arc, Portia

Favorite character in poetry – Hamlet, Marquis Posa [a character of moral integrity in Schiller's *Don Carlos*, who was both soldier and prophet]

Favorite name – Madeleine, Thea

Figures whom you can't stand in history – Nero, Napoleon III

What faults would you first forgive – human weakness

Insurmountable dislikes – gloomy women

What do you fear most – myself

Favorite food and drink – sugar kisses and love potion

Your temperament – changeable

Others such as Joseph Keiley, photographer and co-editor of *Camera Work*, Louis Schubart, his friend from his student days, Flora and Julius Stieglitz, his sister and brother, and his daughter Kitty, filled out pages with similar categories. When Kitty filled out her page in 1917, one of the last to be written, she noted at the end, "Whoever believes this is a fool with my compliments." (Kitty was nineteen at the time, ready to enter Smith College, her parents' marriage had clearly begun to unravel and her father had met Georgia O'Keeffe.)

It is evident from Stieglitz's entries that, much like many twenty-year-olds in the modern era, he was alternately pessimistic and idealistic, ego-centric, fluctuating in mood and temperament, and interested in sex and Woman. Figures who struggled or were visionary appealed to him. That he was scared of himself suggests that he perhaps had some sense of his own personal power and capabilities, which were to evolve as he matured.

In November of the same year, the young Stieglitz also began a "commonplace book," a collection of quotations from philosophy, literature, and history. The small, leather-bound book, entitled "Extracts, etc." (handwritten by Stieglitz on the first page) contains 143 quotes in German and English. Stieglitz did not seem necessarily to record each quotation in its original language. The selected quotes listed below again show the young Stieglitz vacillating between pessimism and idealism, his interest in the feminine as well as his interest in aspects of self-identity and the role of the individual, and art in the world. A variety of authors were included, such as Aristotle, Shelley, Shakespeare, Byron, George Sand, Goethe, Madame de Stäel, and Schiller. In some instances, no author is given:

"Art is not the study of positive Reality, but rather the free search for an ideal truth." George Sand [recorded in German by Stieglitz]
"It is easier to gain twelve enemies than repress one." Cardinal Richelieu
"God has forgiven Mary Magdelene; men are much harsher." [no author]
"Man is half angel and half beast; one needs only to stir the angel and the beast comes forward." (no author)
"To understand means to forgive." Madame de Stäel
"Love is the torment of one, the felicity of two, and the strife and enmity of three." Washington Irving
"Imagination rules the world." Napoleon I
"Sweet is revenge – especially to women." Lord Byron
"Each person should explain only what he has seen. In this way the world will experience truth." [no author]
"Architecture is the combination of musical forms." [no author]
"To thine own self be true/ And as the night follows day, you cannot be false towards anyone." William Shakespeare

"Fire that is closest kept, burns most of all." William Shakespeare

"Man's heaven, and hell is woman." [no author]

"Jealousy is the view of narrow minds; confidence the virtue of enlarged ones." [no author]

"I hold the world but as the world/ A stage where every man must play a part." William Shakespeare

Alfred had some romantic interests, as seen in his photographs of a mysterious young woman called Paula in Berlin. His great-niece, Sue Davidson Lowe, noted in her memoir of Stieglitz that his romantic search "apparently bore other fruits; he sent the mother of a child he felt he had fathered a stipend for the rest of her life, and thereafter to the child."[44] Whether this is true or simply the stories of an old man to his young impressionable great-niece is unclear.

University discourse in general at this time, whether related to formal courses or informal discussion in *Weinstuben* or cafés, frequently revolved around topics such as Marx's treatises on capital, Charles Darwin's ideas about evolution, Tolstoy's denunciation of the ruling classes and idealization of aestheticism, Dostoevsky's interests in psychological motivations, or Zola's documentary-like novels. Stieglitz was thus in Berlin at a time of lively intellectual and creative thinking.

Walking in Berlin one day in January 1883, as he was returning to his room from a somewhat boring university lecture, Stieglitz saw a camera in a small shop on Klosterstrasse. He bought it impulsively, a short transaction with momentous impact for his future. If Stieglitz actually took photographs in 1882 in Karlsruhe, they are lost, and it is in Berlin that he was "first really drawn to photography, first as a toy, then as a passion, then as an obsession."[45]

At the Technische Hochschule he studied photochemistry with Herr Professor Doktor Hermann Wilhelm Vogel in the department of chemistry and metallurgy. In 1884, Vogel was fifty and well connected to the photographic community in the United States as well as being respected in Europe. The young Stieglitz admired Vogel and spent hours in the photochemical laboratory. Vogel wrote regularly for

24 Klosterstrasse, Berlin, 2002

25   Alfred Stieglitz,
Professor Vogel, 1885

The Philadelphia Photographer, and visited the United States in 1870, 1876, and 1883 to attend conventions of the National Photographic Association. In 1876, Vogel was the German commissioner for the photographic section of the Centennial Exhibition. He became noted for his experiments in orthochromatic photography and established ways of using dyes to give truer color values in a black and white photograph. The January 1873 issue of *The Philadelphia Photographer* included an article sketching Vogel's biography, beginning with his birth on 26 March 1834. Vogel was the son of a small retail grocer in the village of Dobrilitsh, about 16 miles south of Berlin. He entered into the natural sciences upon going to London and pursued his interest in photochemistry. In 1860, he became a teacher at the Berlin Polytechnical Academy. He was awarded the title "Doktor" by the Göttingen University in 1863, helping found a photographic society in 1863. He edited *Die Photographisches Mitteilungen* and introduced photography as a field of study at the Royal Polytechnical Academy in 1865 following the International Exhibition of Photography (the first of its kind in Berlin). He served as juror at the Paris Exposition in 1867, and he traveled to Egypt in 1868 to photograph the pyramids.

Vogel also wrote a book, *The Chemistry of Light and Photography in Their Applications to Art, Science, and Industry*, which was published in New York in 1882 as part of an international scientific series. In his introduction from Berlin in 1874, he noted,

> A new science has been called into being by photography, the chemistry of light; it has given new conclusions respecting the operations of the vibrating ether of light. It is true that these services, rendered by photography to art and science, are only appreciated by the few. Men of science have in great measure neglected this subject after the first enthusiasm excited by Daguerre's discovery had passed away, but seldom is photography mentioned in the textbooks of physics and chemistry.[46]

Vogel's book discussed not only chemical effects, but also techniques for portrait, landscape, and astronomical photography. Despite his scientific emphasis and background, Vogel was careful to note the significance of the eye of the artist. In discussing landscape photography, he stated, "The man having the eye of the artist who knows how to seek the best position will at all times give the best picture."[47] In general, Vogel felt that Americans gave more credence to photography and the advancement of scientific knowledge than Europeans did.[48]

A kindly man with a full beard and often disheveled hair, Vogel took Alfred under his wing. For two years, Alfred assisted him in testing new chemicals and took classes with him. Among the first assignments was a project to photograph a statue of the Apollo Belvedere, partially draped by a black velvet cloth, in such a manner as to show all the modeling on the statue and all the details in the cloth, for frequently photographers would make the light areas too white and shadows too black. Alfred spent weeks on this project, and his results went far beyond the expectations of Vogel, who felt the problem was impossible to solve fully.

Vogel also thought that it was nearly impossible to take a photograph of an outdoor sculpture in which the work of art and the background environment could be equally sharp. Alfred rose to the challenge in photographs such as his 1886 images of Kaiser Wilhelm II's 1877 memorial to Queen Luise, attributed to Erdmann Encke, and of the 1880 monument to Goethe by Fritz Schaper, both located in the Tiergarten in central Berlin. The sculptural details are clear, with emphasis on the classical lines. In each, the background foliage is distinct enough to provide an appropriate frame for the marble forms. The photograph

26   Alfred Stieglitz, (?)*Tiergarten, Berlin, c.*1888

27   Tiergarten, Berlin, 2002

28   Wilhelm Hasemann, *Tiergarten, Berlin*, 1871

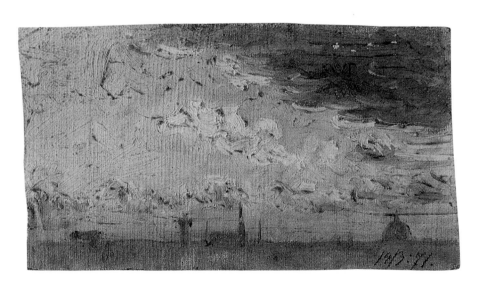

29   Wilhelm Hasemann, *Clouds, Berlin*, 1871

30 and 31 (*left and below*) The memorial to Queen Luise in the Tiergarten, Berlin, 2003

32 (*facing page*) The statue of Goethe in the Tiergarten, Berlin, 2003

of the Queen Luise relief was awarded a certificate in the *Amateur Photographer*'s monthly lantern slide competition in a category for copies of pictures and statuary.

The full-standing sculpture of Goethe must have been a pleasure for the young Stieglitz to seeked the full splendor of the statue. It is perhaps not surprising that he chose to include in his photograph the beautifully sculpted feminine muses seated around the base, representing poetry, drama, and science, one holding a musical instrument. They are accompanied by a cherub-like, winged young male holding a small torch. Stieglitz chose to photograph the muses of poetry and drama along with the full-standing Goethe in an image that remains in the Key Set at the National Gallery in Washington, D.C. (The original sculpture is now in the Lapidarium in Berlin; a copy was placed in the Tiergarten in 1987.)

Not far from these monuments is a large sculpture of a seated Richard Wagner with emotion-filled figures from his operas at his feet, dated 1903, by Gustav Eberlein. In the Luise photograph, Stieglitz chose to depict the base of the sculpture under the large free-standing sculpture of the young queen. The entwined figures in relief that circle the base seem to represent aspects of family life and new love. Stieglitz focused on a young family, where a young soldier appears to be saying goodbye to his small children and wife, who looks pensively up at him. To the left and right young couples embrace. Not far from the Queen Luise statue was a similar statue of Wilhelm II by Friedrich Drahe, erected "to King Friedrich Wilhelm II from the thankful residents of Berlin" in 1849. In another early photograph, probably taken in the Tiergarten, of the Löwen-brücke, Stieglitz has captured the details of the landscape foliage and play of light on the water. Wilhelm Hasemann made an oil sketch of the same subject at a different time of the year, when the leaves have disappeared, and Stieglitz could well have seen this.

As a result of his friendship with Erdmann Encke and another sculptor, Moses Ezekiel, also in Berlin, Stieglitz was asked by other artists such as Franz von Lenbach, Pierre Cot, and Jules Bastien-Lepage to photograph their works. An 1886 photograph of a sketch by Lenbach of the profile of a young girl is clear and precise. Stieglitz's exposure to Bastien-Lepage's images of rural peasant and working-class life could well have influenced his interest in peasant life a few years later.

In his very early years of photography, Stieglitz was probably more interested in the chemical and technical aspects of the medium than in the artistic elements. An 1886 portrait of Vogel taken by Stieglitz shows that he had mastered elements of portrait photography. Vogel, shrouded in darkness, appears all the more powerful as the light falls on his skin and hair. The delicate strands of his graying beard and sideburns are executed in a manner of elegant realism and realistic elegance. Vogel was to many, including Stieglitz, a man to be revered. The photo engages the viewer in a reverent manner as Vogel looks straight into the camera and at the viewer. Stieglitz also photographed a drawing of Vogel by Fedor Encke in the 1880s.

Among the first photographs taken with the new dry plate camera that Stieglitz had purchased on Klosterstrasse was an 1883 collage image of eleven separate photos of Stieglitz himself, taken by Erdmann Encke on several different occasions. The photos, of carte-de-visite size, were arranged on a drawing board. In four photos placed symmetrically at the top and bottom of the group, Alfred is wearing a North African head scarf, a burnous. In the other photos he appears sometimes clean-shaven with a mustache, and sometimes with a full beard. Several of the repeated

33   Alfred Stieglitz, photograph of a collage of photographic portraits of Stieglitz taken by
Erdmann Encke, 1883

images appear to be pairs. Perhaps Stieglitz was looking for his twin or
soulmate-like the relationship he saw between his younger twin
brothers. But Stieglitz also seems to have been trying out different
identities for himself – an "other." In terms of physical appearance, it is
his mustached visage that he chose to wear for the rest of his life with
his tousled hair. So anxious was Alfred to develop this image that he

improvised a darkroom in his apartment rather than waiting to go to school the next day.

Outside, Alfred took photographs of advertising kiosks and the façade of the Technische Hochschule, as well as the plain plaster wall opposite his apartment in various light situations, to practice. He quickly became hooked on photography, and was fortunate that the Technische Hochschule had recently moved to a new building in Charlottenburg, then considered a suburb of Berlin (now easily connected by U-bahn to the central part of the city). The photochemical laboratory was considered state of the art and lit by electric lighting. There were five darkrooms for wet and dry processing, a room for storing finished plates, a room for printing and so on. The laboratory, initially open during the day, extended its hours when Alfred offered to be in charge, allowing him to work well into the night when he chose. Alfred quickly decided he wanted to make a career out of photography and not to study engineering or pursue a PhD as his brother Julius and friends Lou Schuburt and Joe Obermeyer did. (Leopold ended up studying in Heidelberg and became a doctor Schubart and Obermeyer arrived in Berlin probably in the fall of 1883 and, with Alfred, found a place to stay.)

Professor Vogel was impressed with his young student's work and asked him if he could show it to some Berlin artists. They could not believe the pictures were photographs, and asked to meet Stieglitz, who recounted the meeting a number of years later:

"What a pity it is that your photographs are not paintings." That remark rather startled me. What did he mean? I asked him what he meant. He said, "Why, young man, if those photographs of yours had been made by hand they would be art, but not having been made by hand, wonderful as they are, they are not." Then he also added that he wished he had painted what I had photographed. I looked at him in great surprise. I really didn't understand the meaning of it all. "I never felt like photographing anything I ever saw painted," I said. They all laughed, for all seemed to be interested in what was happening. Suddenly I said, "You mean to say that a pair of shoes made by hand is necessarily superior to a pair of shoes made by machine?" What prompted me to say that at that time, I am not quite aware of. It just popped out. The painter said, "No shoes made by machinery can ever be as good as shoes made by hand." Now the shoes I bought in Berlin were hand-made, made to order. The shoes I had bought in America, or my mother bought for me, were made by machine. Then

I added, "But supposing a pair of shoes made by machine were to cost less money than a pair of shoes made by hand, and the pair of shoes made by machine were serviceable and could be had for the amount of money in my pocket and the hand-made shoes were more expensive, what would happen? Would I wait until I had enough money to buy an hand-made shoe if I really needed a pair of shoes?" He looked at me and seemed not to understand. Then I added, "If in time the machine-made shoe would supplant the hand-made shoe because of lesser cost, what then?" He said, "That could never be. A hand-made shoe would always be superior to a machine-made shoe, so a machine-made shoe could never supplant a hand-made shoe." Then I said, "But supposing the shoemakers were forced to compete with the machine-made shoes, what then?" He said, "There will always be apprentices who will love to make shoes. Their kind will never die out, no matter how many machine-made shoes may come into the world." I was really thinking of my photography and also of the painters who were gathered about me. Would what they were doing and what they called art continue to live if what they felt about my photographs were true? Some were willing to give me paintings for a photograph. I didn't want their paintings. I gave them prints gladly. I said, "you keep your art. You need not give it to me in exchange for the prints I have made. I'll gladly give you what I make." I was only too happy to feel that the photographs were wanted and that they meant something to the artists. I did not realize at the time that all men who painted pictures were not artists. Finally I said, "I have a feeling that there will be fewer and fewer hand-made shoes." Why, I didn't exactly know, and as I look back at that evening I realize that both I and the artists were saying something true, but somehow that I "saw" more clearly into the future than he did – something fundamental which was in the machine – and that the machine had come to stay. My camera and lens in a way could be looked upon as a machine, but without the machine and myself being one, that which these artists so admire would not exist. As I got up to go several artists told me I was a genius and that night when I put my head on my pillow I heard those words and all the other things that they had said. I knew that for the most part they did not know what they were talking about. Yet I was not clear why I felt that way. One thing I did know, that I was not a genius – genius to me was Shakespeare and Beethoven and Wagner and Cervantes and such men. I was positive I did not belong in that class. I fell asleep.[49]

Although Stieglitz told this story as an older man, in almost parable fashion, it is clear that as a young man he saw the need for the marriage of art and science, of artistic vision and spirit, and technological or mechanical means. The story reveals also his ability as a raconteur and concern for communicating the power of photography as an art form.

Among Stieglitz's early photographs that give an insight into his life during his student days is an interior, *My Room* (1885–6) and two self-portraits, one at Mittenwald (1884), the other at Freienwalde-an-der-Oder (1886), now known as Bad Freienwalde, a resort town north-east of Berlin. In the interior shot Stieglitz's nickel-plated Columbia high-wheel bicycle dominates the right side of the photograph, his camera equipment just in front of the large wheel. The two mechanical devices that were important to Alfred are well lit by the window light. On the wall appears to be a portrait of the young Stieglitz by Fedor Encke. Stieglitz recalled that "my mother's picture hung in an ornate Swiss-carved wooden frame," but it is difficult to ascertain from the photograph who is in the frame and the figure appears to be a male.[50] The dark furnishings, complete with the dark textured cloth covering the table to the left of the desk, speak of an older, nineteenth-century world. The bicycle, the camera, and streaming light to the right speak of exploration of a new century soon to arrive.

In 1884, Stieglitz photographed himself again with his large wheeled bicycle, a machine of exploration standing in front of a fence in a panoramic, expansive landscape setting. Here Stieglitz's early interest in the interplay of light and dark is evident in the fence posts and the radiating spokes of the bicycle wheel. The lines of the fence foreshadow later, more abstract sunlight and shadow effects, such as those in Stieglitz's *Sunlight and Shadows* showing Paula in Berlin, also titled *Sun Rays, Paula* (1889). The gentle lines of the far hills can also be found later in the hills and horizon line in parts of his *Music* series (1992).

Stieglitz made a number of photographs in Mittenwald, where he and his family spent the summer of 1885. Alfred returned again in the summer of 1886, when he and possibly his brothers and sister Selma hiked through Bavaria and Switzerland. Alfred placed some of his photographs from Mittenwald in a small ($5^{1}/_{2} \times 8^{5}/_{8}$ in.) leather-bound album in which he wrote, "A Souvenir of 'Summer 1886'/to the family."[51] The album contains various images of the town, as well as genre scenes such as *The Truant*, where a young boy stands barefoot with his schoolbag in front of his mother, or *The Harvest, Mittenwald, 1886*, showing a young girl with one hand raised to her brow and the other hand holding

34   Alfred Stieglitz, *"My Room,"* 1885–6

35 (*facing page*)   Alfred Stieglitz, *Mittenwald*, 1886

a long rake. One version of the latter print was placed in a later album Stieglitz compiled in 1895, titled "Sun Prints" (National Gallery of Art, Washington). Accompanying this image, Stieglitz wrote on interleaving tissue in graphite, "One of my earliest attempts at picture-making, Mittenwald 1886." These different versions of the same subject suggest Stieglitz's search for a "perfect" image as he changes the placement of the subject or crops the background to focus further on the strong linear

36   Alfred Stieglitz, *Self-Portrait*, 1886

37   Alfred Stieglitz, *Bavaria (Figure Asleep in a Cemetery)* 1886

elements of the piece – the girl's arms, the long diagonal rake handle, the edges of the triangular section that frames the upper body and head of the young woman. Indeed, the photograph could be easily abstracted to a series of interlocking triangles and this composition enhances the visual interest of the photograph. Stieglitz also captures the subtle changes in texture and color graduation in the gray tones used in his depiction of the surrounding fields.

Stieglitz's interest in strong linear elements is seen further in another image from the souvenir album, *Mittenwald*, where four figures are seated quietly in a rowboat on the still water of the lake, surrounded by mountains. The lines of the lakeside grass and the long oars with their reflections in the water make this more than a genre image of four men rowing. It calls to mind George Caleb Bingham's river paintings or some Luminist paintings. Stieglitz's early genre-like photographs of peasants are also reminiscent of the Munich school of painting, including artists such as Fritz von Uhde, Max Liebermann, or Arthur Langhammer. But

Stieglitz's *The Harvest* group with its varied compositions of the same subject and strong geometric structure, theme and variation, show Stieglitz going beyond the painters' visions. Both *The Truant* and *The Harvest* were later published in a number of photographic magazines; Stieglitz was quickly becoming known internationally.[52]

Other images in the album included a rustic inn set in the Alps and a sleeping tramp propped up against a cross in the village cemetery. Among these early German photographs there is also an image of women doing laundry together at a common village trough. It is marked by the strong verticals of a post, water pump, and four doors, along with the standing women, counter balanced by the horizontal form of the water trough.

Some of Stieglitz's landscape photographs from 1886 appear to have direct relevance to his later work, in particular his *On Lake Thun, Switzerland*, where the stillness of the lake is overpowered by the dramatic movement of the sky. The brilliantly lit clouds foreshadow the clouds from Stieglitz's *Song of the Sky*. Here the Apollonian, the quiet still order of the lake, and the Dionysian, the powerfully moving clouds as part of a Bacchanalian rite, are united in one frame. There are hints

38   Alfred Stieglitz, *On Lake Thun, Switzerland*, 1886

of Wagner in the dramatic sky. The layers of mountains and hillsides lie like silent bodies but have a strong presence as one of the leitmotifs of the piece. In his 1886 *Bavaria* a bank of mist appears in a valley formed by U-shaped undulations of mountains. Here the emphasis is on the barren landforms; a strong rhythmic quality inherent in the mountainous shapes suggests the flow of music.

Stieglitz's other self-portrait of this time, taken in Freienwalde in 1886, also shows him in a landscape, standing in front of leafy foliage ready to take a photograph. This image appeared in a small leather album, stamped in gold with the date 4 July 1886, a time when Stieglitz and some friends were at Bad Freienwalde. In this photograph, Stieglitz stands firmly rooted in nature but clearly focused on the act of taking a photograph. The world of nature and machine seem well married in the figure of Stieglitz and his camera. The photographs in the album are primarily playful shots of Stieglitz's friends cavorting and posing for the camera along the water, or in cavernous settings. In one several of the young men are standing watch as one of the group uses a women's bathroom. Stieglitz's friend, Morris Loeb, wrote a poem that was a spoof on Gilbert and Sullivan's "Three Little Maids from School Are We" from their recently released *The Mikado*. His version began with "Eight little boys from school are we/ Happy that our Country's free . . . / one's taking care of the camera's works;/ outside of the picture he therefore lurks." By the self-portrait Loeb wrote: "Here's the man and his grand machine,/ Which enables these wonders to be seen/ With his right hand placed on his pistol/ He held us attentive to his whistle/ Now then a cheerful expression."[53]

39   Alfred Stieglitz, *Frank Simon "Sime" Hermann*, 1894

Among his friends and traveling companions at this point in time were his brothers, Joe Obermeyer, Louis Schubart and Frank Simon ("Sime") Hermann (1866–1942), whom Stieglitz had known at CCNY also. Hermann was studying in Munich at the Royal Academy. Stieglitz and Hermann were to have reciprocal influences on each other, and at various points

40   Alfred Stieglitz, *Self-Portrait, Freienwalde*, 1886

in the 1890s Stieglitz's photography has some resemblance to Hermann's painting.[54] Hermann later took up photography himself and became a successful amateur. His painting was rooted in Romanticism and Post-Impressionism, with expressive application of color in a very painterly fashion.

ITALIAN JOURNEYS

In August of 1887, Stieglitz, Obermeyer, Schubart, and probably Hermann and Alfred's brothers, set out from Munich with thirty pounds of camera equipment on a photographic journey to northern Italy. A photograph of the travelers shows them to be carefree, ready for adventure.

42   The approach to Bellagio, 2001

41 *(facing page)*   Alfred Stieglitz and his friends, 1887. Stieglitz and one
of his twin brothers are standing at the back (right and left respectively)
and Frank Hermann (left) and Joseph Obermeyer sit on the floor.

On one of the most beautiful lakes in Italy, Lake Como, they stopped
at Bellagio, a small hill town situated on a promontory overlooking the
lake, at the point where Lake Como and Lake Lecco divide. The Romans
called it "Bilacus" (between the lakes). For many years Bellagio had been
a fishing and agricultural community but by the end of the nineteenth
century it had become increasing affluent through the textile and candle-
making industries and tourism. Villas, luxury hotels, homes, and shops
were beginning to spread through the Italian lake area. Approaching the
promontory by boat, Stieglitz would have viewed the enchanting hillside
town from afar with a dramatic vista of the lake and mountains. He was
captivated by it and remained a few days extra to take more photographs. His hotel, the Pensione du Lac, overlooked the magnificent
lake, giving views of the expansive blue of the still waters and the
surrounding mountains. The varied line of the mountain contours and
the hues of green, gray, and blue in both clear and misty weather were
alluring.
    In 1880, the Grand Hotel Bellagio had opened in a building that was
originally the elegant villa of the Frizoni family, with formal gardens,

43　Alfred Stieglitz, *Maria, Bellagio,* 1887

two hundred rooms, thirty salons, a billiard room and reading room. But it was not the luxury or the tourist areas that attracted Stieglitz's photographic eye: it was the simple contours of the stone stairs and the street, the everyday life and people of the town. Not far from his pensione, on the Salita Mella, Stieglitz met a charming sixteen-year-old fruit seller, Maria, her mother, and her brother, Leone. He photographed the demure Maria front on, throwing light on her bodice and dress, which become an integral part of the textures and patterns created by straw baskets, cobble stones, and fruit. A partially cropped onlooker in a top hat gives a sense of formal verticality to the piece as well as suggesting pictorial narrative. In a lantern slide of the same subject, Stieglitz removed the male figure on the right, thereby eliminating some of the narrative quality of the image and concentrating on the figure integrated with shapes and patterns. A few years later, the image of Maria alone appeared in a prominent spot, framed and enlarged in a photograph of Stieglitz's room on 14 East 60th Street.

Stieglitz photographed Leone, Maria's brother, against a mottled stone wall, his hands in his pockets. The bottom horizontal line of his jacket is carefully balanced with the horizontal line of the wall and he directly engages the viewer in his half-man, half-child stance. In another photograph, *Via Fiori Bellagio*, a woman, probably Maria's mother, is nestled among her baskets of fruit, at one with her livelihood and environment. The viewer's eye travels quickly past the fruit seller up well-trodden ancient stone steps to arches above, leading to the light. In a later printed image of 1894 that appeared in the "Sun Prints" album, Stieglitz removed all human presence and concentrated on the architectural forms and patterns, as well as the overriding arch that frames the staircase. The darkened inner arch provides a striking contrast to the light at the top of the stairs leading outward to the unknown. Stieglitz's handling of the various gray tones that are

44 Alfred Stieglitz, *Leone, Bellagio*, 1887

45   Alfred Stieglitz, *Bellagio (Venetian Doorway)*, 1887 (print 1894)

46   Steps at Bellagio, 2001

modulated as they move upstairs into the sunlight is masterful for his early work.

From his veranda at the Pensione du Lac, Stieglitz shot *The Approaching Storm* as he was looking toward the Punta Balbianello, a small peninsular promontory where an elegant villa was located. In his biography of Stieglitz, Richard Whelan writes, "Having hoped for some time "to capture" by photography a gathering storm – a sight "at once overpowering and of potential beauty," he was able to take full advantage of his opportunity in Bellagio because he was well supplied with Vogel-Oberrnetter orthochromatic plates. Using them with a yellow filter, through which it was difficult to see for focusing, he managed to capture the magnificent play of light and clouds over the lake."[55] Here was nature alone; the musicality of its forms is evident.

Another poignant portrait remaining from those days in Bellagio is the *Italian Mason*, with his plaster-speckled clothes. The mason is at once a laborer and a philosopher figure, with gnarled hands and wrinkled skin, but a facial expression suggesting thoughts of a higher realm. Stieglitz's placement of the figure in partial shadow enhances the enigmatic quality of the elderly Bellagio citizen.

Perhaps the most well-known of Stieglitz's images from Bellagio is *The Last Joke, Bellagio* (1887), also known as *A Good Joke*. The photograph was to win first place in the *Amateur Photographer's* Photographic Holiday Work Competition, appearing in the 25 November 1887 issue. It was considered the only spontaneous work in the competition, judged by British photographer Dr. Peter Henry Emerson. The photograph is of children laughing and talking as they gather about a woman who appears to be collecting water. It is closely cropped, focusing on the children, with architectural arches in the background providing a stage set for the image. There is another version of the subject in which a man stands in

47   Alfred Stieglitz, *The Last Joke, Bellagio,* or *A Good Joke,* 1887

48   Alfred Stieglitz, *At Lake Como*, 1887

the background shadows in the upper left corner, overlooking the scene. As the writer Doris Bry has noted, the version with the male figure won the prize. "It is interesting that the print Stieglitz kept from this negative (now in the Key Set at the National Gallery of Art in Washington, D.C.) is not the print that won the prize, but is a later print made in the 1890s. The matting and cropping of the later print, resulting in a much stronger composition than the 1887 presentation, suggests the more discriminating use of space Stieglitz had learned in the intervening years."[56]

Stieglitz combined his interest in landscape and the life of the lower classes in a photograph such as *At Lake Como*, in which a group of women are washing clothes along the lakeside. Although the figures are in focus, the viewer's eye moves quickly from the lower left to the partially cropped sail out on the lake. The arched shapes of the boat's ribs gently balance the curves of the women bending over their wash. Stieglitz's continued interest in the worlds of the washerwomen is seen in two other images, *Washer Women at Riva de Garda* (1887) and an untitled lantern slide (no exact date) of a similar subject. The print of the women at Riva de Garda was not reproduced until 1898 in the *American Annual of Photography*, and then printed again as a gelatin silver print in the 1920s or 1930s. (It was not uncommon for some

49   Alfred Stieglitz, *Untitled (Women Washing)*, 1887

images to be printed a number of years after the image was shot.) It
includes a large area of dark foliage on the trees lining the waterfront,
which dominate the photograph, providing a strong diagonal to the composition but diverting attention from the protruding piers and women
along the water's edge. In the lantern slide image, the viewer is brought
very close to the women. The human presence is important here, but the
women's gestures are frozen in time, in the stillness of the lake. Somewhat like a Luminist paining, this piece focuses on silence and stillness.
The darker right side of the piece seems to represent civilization – the
human forms, constructed walls, a building – and is like a shadow for
the lighter left side of the piece, where the subtleties of a dappled light
effect on the lake and the hazy mountains and sky speak of a mystery
that surrounds and transcends the everyday world – the music of the
spheres.

Stieglitz's images of the washerwomen and the lake scenes may
perhaps also be seen as symbolic, representing purification and
cleansing – a metaphor for Stieglitz's later struggle for the recognition of
photography as a pure art form. The washerwomen are also a continu-
ation of a subject that interested many nineteenth-century painters –
Jean-François Millet, Honoré Daumier, Edgar Degas, and Eugène

50 Alfred Stieglitz, *Woman Washing, Europe*, ?1884–6

51 Alfred Stieglitz, *Lake Garda*, 1887

Boudin. Stieglitz admired Millet, but unlike Millet, Daumier, and Degas, whose laundresses frequently appear burdened with their work, Stieglitz's figures, like many of Boudin's, become an integral part of the landscape.

The world of work is also explored in an image of a young girl cleaning a pot on the Lake Como shore, *Kettle Cleaner, Lake Como, 1887*.

52 Lake Garda, 2001

Here the focus is on the young girl; the lakeshore waters could be anywhere. Stieglitz has caught her at work. She partially glimpses the viewer from under her kerchief. By eliminating all details of the background except the gentle ripples of the lake and wet shores, Stieglitz forces the viewer to concentrate on the crouching form that becomes one with the kettle.

In *The Unwilling Bath* Stieglitz captures a young boy trying to wash a cow. Here the sleek forms of the cow's back make reference to the mountain forms in the background on the far side of the lake. The strong, visual diagonal running from the boy's pant legs to the end of the pier marks the shore's division of the world of humans and animals from the distant, unknown, natural world of the lake, mountains, and sky. *An Idyll* (1887), which draws its title from a literary tradition of poetic descriptions of pleasant rural scenes, seems to glorify the large working steers standing in the sunlight in the rocky soil, their shadows providing a dark counterbalance to their weighty bodies. There is a strong, peaceful quality communicated in the photograph, even though these are hard-working animals. These two images were reproduced in a number of photographic publications such as the *American Amateur Photographer* and the *Photographic Times* in the 1880s and 1890s.[57]

In a number of instances, the working class seems to have provided a path to a purer, more meaningful world for the young Stieglitz. As he wrote in the *Photographic Times* in April 1896: "Nothing charms me so much as walking among the lower classes, studying them carefully and making mental notes. They are interesting from every point of view. I dislike the superficial and artificial, and I find it less among the lower class. That is the reason they are more sympathetic to me as subjects."[58]

53   Alfred Stieglitz, *Kettle Cleaner, Lake Como*, 1887

From Bellagio, Stieglitz, Lou Schubart, and Frank Hermann made their
way to the small fishing town of Chioggia, recommended to them by an
Englishman in Venice, from where it could be reached by a short boat
ride. Chioggia, then as now, is primarily a fishing port on the lagoon.
There is a gritty character to the town with its fish smells, vibrantly

54 and 55   Chioggia, 2001

colored boats, nets, and fishing tackle, alongside Venetian architecture
such as the church of San Martino, in the Venetian Gothic style; the
church of San Giacomo; the church of San Domenico, which houses
Vittore Carpaccio's last known work, *St. Paul* (1520); the house of the
artist Rosalba Carriera; and a long single-story granary, a Gothic building built with porticoes and pillars of Istrian stone and wooden archi-
traves. The beautiful Vigo Bridge (1665), which Stieglitz photographed,
is near the open harbor and crosses the Vena Canal. In an 1889 article
that Stieglitz wrote for the *Amateur Photographer*, he described the
village as "sort of a miniature Venice, consisting like the latter of very
narrow streets, canals, and numberless bridges. But there is a marked
difference in the people of these places. For Chioggia is inhabited by fishermen and their families. A picturesque but rough and unsociable set of
people . . . the only charm of the place lies in the characteristic appearance of its people."[59] Stieglitz also expressed disappointment that he did
not have a flash to photograph the narrow, dark canal and street areas.

His photographs of two of the town's major bridges suggest he was
quick to grasp essential elements of the town's architectural character
and its role as a fishing port. In *On the Bridge, Chioggia* he captures a
group of the town's men chatting on a bridge, the Ponte Cucagna, over-

56　Alfred Stieglitz, *On the Bridge, Chioggia*, 1887

looking some fishing boats. One of the boats, with its large sail, provides
a vertical balance to the chimneys on the buildings behind the bridge.
Stieglitz described how he came to take the photograph:

> Passing out of these dark alleys, we came to the chief canal of the
> place, and as we approached a bridge to cross it, we noticed a crowd

of people who seemed unusually excited. Imagine our surprise to see our Munich friend [Hermann] in the midst of the crowd, vociferously gesticulating and showing unmistakable signs of anxiety. We thought he had gotten into trouble with the people, and hastened to his assistance . . . He tried to cover his embarrassment by assuring us that his object was simply to offer us a good opportunity to photograph the bridge after the style of Passini [an Italian artist, Ludwig Passini, who painted genre scenes]. We had a good laugh at him, but took the picture, the idea having been an excellent one."[60]

The bridge form, with its gentle arched underside, the triangular sail, the repeated rectangles of the shuttered windows on the building behind, give the viewer a pre-Cubist view of the "old world" scene. The darkened foreground of the sterns of the fishing boats in shadow provides a necessary balance and weight to the illuminated bridge. Another version of the same subject, with few variations, illustrates how Stieglitz was deeply thoughtful about the details of his pieces. Here, there are more people on the bridge, many of them looking down toward the water, presenting to the viewer a series of dark hats. Instead of a man leaving the bridge on the right, a man faces the viewer, his elbows on the bridge. There is young boy lying on the top edge, and a man in the center is carrying a barrel raised high in his arms. (In the foreground there is a reflection on the water, providing a lighter triangular area that mirrors the triangle of the limp sail.) The first version seems to work better visually.

The *Stones of Venice, Chioggia* (1887) is Stieglitz's photograph of the Ponte Vigo. His title, taken from John Ruskin's book, *The Stones of Venice*, is indicative of his, as well as Ruskin's, admiration for aspects of Venetian architecture. (Ruskin's beliefs in the importance of handcrafted works and individual craftsmen seemed to influence Stieglitz later, when he came to publish *Camera Work*. And he borrowed a phrase from Ruskin's *The Seven Lamps of Architecture* when he equated the "Secessionist Idea" with the "Spirit of the Lamp" on his Editor's Page.[61])

In *The Stones of Venice*, Stieglitz captures the wide expansive steps onto the bridge, which still exist today, along with the Ponte Cucagna, much as they appeared in Stieglitz's day. A woman, dressed in black, white, and gray, on the steps of the Ponte Vigo, brings a human dimension and sense of warmth to the otherwise cold grays of the bridge. The lions of St. Mark (a symbol of Venice) serve as protectors of the bridge and the woman. The clarity of the boats in the distant water on the

57   Alfred Stieglitz, *Stones of Venice (Chioggia)*, 1887 (print 1894)

horizon line and the figures to the left of the bridge provide a counterpoint to the bridge, which leads off into the unknown. The photograph
is poetic, with a spare grace that seems to mark much of Stieglitz's work.

Another piece perhaps made in or near Chioggia at about the same
time, *Boats*, is, unlike the *Stones of Venice*, filled with shapes, textures,
and a sense of the colorful sails. To
the left, a man sits mending nets   58   Ponte Vigo, Chioggia, 2001
in a small boat. His head is bent,
intent on the task. The multiplic-
ity of textures and "colors" – the
baskets, sails, nets, foliage, water,
wooden masts and booms – is a
feast for the eyes. The repeated triangular forms intertwine in both
positive and negative spaces, and
the play of light and shadow keeps
the eye engaged. The human figure
is small, but a significant part of a
picture that is formally well com-

59   Alfred Stieglitz, *Boats*, c.1887

posed and filled with poignancy, as one might imagine a day in the life
of a fisherman, either at sea or on shore, mending nets.

60   Alfred Stieglitz, (?)*Italian
Fisherman*, 1887

As with the village mason, Stieglitz made a portrait of
one of the fishermen he encountered, capturing in a
close-up format the spirit of the working man. The fisherman's thoughtful eyes and wrinkled skin, his pipe in
hand, suggest a man who thinks as well as toils with his
hands on the open seas. Again, as with the village
mason, there is a special dignity that can be found in
many of Stieglitz's portraits of everyday figures who are
not celebrities nor even artists. In his article, "A Day in
Chioggia," Stieglitz refers to meeting Fiametta, a pretty
Chioggian market girl, whom he photographed. He
notes, "You will notice that she wears a characteristic
dress, that is, an apron worn at the back instead of in
the front, as our ladies wear them, and which can be
drawn up over the head, thus protecting the wearer from
the burning sun, when she has occasion to pass through
the open market place."[62]

Stieglitz recorded photographing a young girl while in
Chioggia, who is probably the subject of his photograph

A Wanderer's Return (1887). This could have been taken anywhere and is filled with a sense of romantic narrative, visual and verbal. As Stieglitz relates, "the landlord told us that the girl whose picture we had just taken was his youngest daughter, who had been enticed away from home, and had but shortly returned, filled with remorse, yet still carrying in her heart the picture of her lover, and dreaming over again the romance of her life."[63] That Stieglitz took this type of photograph and chose to relate the tale as the last sentence of his article, shows his continuing romantic sensibilities, perhaps not at all unusual for a young man of twenty-three (twenty-five when the article was published) in the late nineteenth century.

In 1895, Stieglitz printed a slightly different version of this image to include in his "Sun Prints" album. It shows more of the stone and brickwork on either side of the doorway where the young girl is leaning wearily against the door. A close-up of the girl, *Marina* (1887), set against the brick wall, her shawl wrapped around her shoulders, reveals a dark-eyed, dark-haired, simple beauty whose eyes betray in part some of her inner anxiety. Stieglitz's sensibilities seemed to sense her concerns.

61 Alfred Stieglitz, *Marina*, 1887

62 Alfred Stieglitz, *A Venetian Gamin*, 1887

One other image, *A Venetian Gamin*, dated 1887 in Dorothy Norman's *Stieglitz Memorial Portfolio*, is worthy of mention. (The piece is listed by the National Gallery in Washington, D.C., as being printed in 1894 as a platinum print in another version, processed with mercury, and again in the 1920s or 1930s as a gelatin silver print.) The Venetian child of the street is depicted full length, seated on stone steps in front of a rough stucco wall. His feet are bare, his clothes tattered, and his look is grim, old for his young years. Yet Stieglitz's lens does not judge, nor take pity. In the tradition of Zola, the boy is how he is. Other versions draw the viewer close to the young curly-haired boy, now seated in front of large wooden doors that contrast less with his clothes and give his facial expression greater prominence. This photograph was among twelve submitted to the Photographic Holiday work Competition and caught the judge's eye, although it was not awarded the medal.

Stieglitz's interest in street life and his frequent wandering through various towns and cities is also seen in his mid-1880s photographs, which focus on general street scenes. For example, two albumen prints entitled *Street Scene, Europe*, show large architectural forms that dominate the street. In one, a large arched stone form carefully frames the human activity on the street's edge. In the other, the large mass of the rectangular building serves as backdrop to the street life. The production of albumen prints was relatively new, dating from about 1855. It was a complex process that required a number of steps, but allowed for a wider range of shadows and highlights as well as details, and enabled multiple copies to be made from a single negative.

A more intimate scene is found in *A Nook in Pallanza* (1887), where a seated woman, barely visible, looks shyly out from her seat in the gentle arch of a doorway. The focus is not on the woman but more on the crumbling stonework of the building and the empty horizontal clotheslines, in contrast to the vertical branchless tree on the right. A sense of loneliness and isolation pervades the piece.

Stieglitz's sensitivity to rural life versus town or city life is seen in a late 1887 print, *November Days*, taken on a Bavarian road near Munich. Stieglitz captures a carriage in the vanishing point of the image, which has modern elements in its grid-like form, implied by the trees, their shadows, and wagon ruts in the dirt road. The silhouettes of the leafless tree branches provide a striking contrast with the cloudless sky and the soft texture of the road. This picture appeared in the "Sun Prints" album and won silver medals in Britain and Vienna in 1888 and Milan in 1894. It was reprinted as a gelatin silver print (versus the platinum print of 1887) in the 1920s or 1930s.

63   Alfred Stieglitz, *November Days*, 1887

Some, such as Doris Bry, have considered the photographs Stieglitz made in 1887, particularly those made on his trip to Italy, as "the first cohesive body of work he produced comparable in quality to his late work. They reached and maintained a consistently high level of work, which was widely acclaimed. It is significant that in later life, having lost or destroyed most of his earliest work, Stieglitz had kept prints from these negatives and showed them to represent the earliest stages of his photographic evolution."[64]

THE WORLD OF PICTORIALISM AND RETURN TO NEW YORK

At the end of his 1887 travels, Stieglitz mailed off his prints, including *A Good Joke*, to the *Amateur Photographer* and, as noted, won first prize, two guineas, and a silver medal. Thereafter, Stieglitz was to win many medals and prizes, of which he was proud and kept records in his albums and scrapbooks. The judge of the contest, Peter Henry Emerson, was a significant figure in British photography at the time and may be seen as having influenced Stieglitz.

In the late 1880s in Britain, Emerson and another photographer, Henry Peach Robinson, were at odds with each other concerning the nature of photography and its potential as an art form. Robinson felt that a work of art could be attained by combining multiple photographic negatives to make a composite print. His well-known *Fading Away* (1858), showing a dying girl surrounded by her grieving family, was a combination print from five negatives, forming a picture in stages in what today would be called photomontage. For almost thirty years, Robinson produced at least one combination print for the annual exhibition at the Photographic Society of London. These compositions were also shown in other exhibitions in Britain and on the Continent and came to be described as "pictorial photography". Robinson's book, *Picture Making by Photography*, was popular, and was still being reprinted during the First World War.

Contrary to Robinson's combination techniques, which made Pictorial photography, for some, synonymous with artificiality and often sentimentality, Emerson urged for a return to nature as inspiration. An admirer of Millet and the Barbizon School, Emerson spent many years photographing images of nature in the Norfolk Broads, and published a striking photographic book, *Life and Landscapes on the Norfolk Broads*, in 1886. The book's forty platinotype prints tipped into the book depicted, without ornamentation or aggrandisement, the simple lives of the people who lived among the marshes and lagoons of the Norfolk Broads. This interest in the depiction of everyday folk can be seen to be analogous to that of Stieglitz.[65]

Emerson's lecture, "Photography: A Pictorial Art," delivered to the London Camera Club on 11 March 1886 and published the following week in the *Amateur Photographer*, marked the beginnings of Pictorialism.[65] In 1889 he published his now-famous manifesto, *Naturalistic Photography*, as an attack on artificial picture making. His title page included the lines by John Keats from *Ode to a Grecian Urn*,

'Beauty is truth, truth beauty,' – that is all
Ye know on earth, and all ye need to know.

As a photographer, scientist, and doctor, Emerson became interested in Hermann von Helmholtz's *Psychological Optics* and advocated soft-focus images as part of his theory that the principal object in a photograph should be as sharp as the eye naturally sees it, but everything around it should be slightly out of focus. (Some of his Norfolk Broads images have sharply focused areas.) Emerson looked to painters such as J. M. W. Turner, the Impressionists, and James McNeill Whistler as artists to be admired. Within a year of his publication advocating soft-focus images, however, Emerson reversed his position after Whistler convinced him he was confusing art with nature, and published a black-bordered pamphlet entitled "Death of Naturalistic Photography, A Renunciation," prompted by his belief that the soft-focus movement was becoming too extreme in the hands of the photographer George Davison.

The conflict between Emerson and Robinson also related to economic and social class, Emerson being from an affluent background and Robinson from the bourgeoisie. The notion of amateurism versus professional endeavors that surfaced with such a conflict was to occupy Stieglitz as well.

Emerson also advocated matte platinum (platinotype) printing and photogravure, which Stieglitz by 1892 considered the "prince of all processes."

For exhibition work it is indispensable, and the sooner the New York amateur makes up his mind that, in order to compete successfully with the Englishman, or even with the Philadelphian, in the large exhibitions, he will have to discard all albumen paper, glazed aristotype (that *bête noire* for every fine-feeling eye), etc., and turn to either kallitype paper or still better, to that prince of all processes, the platinotype . . . let me assure you that many of my prize photos, all of which are still in as perfect condition as on the day they were made, were turned out inside of fifteen minutes, including printing, developing, fixing, washing, and mounting![66]

Stieglitz and Emerson corresponded after Stieglitz was awarded the medal and into the 1930s, although over the years they did not always agree with each other. Emerson asked Stieglitz to translate his book into German in 1888. Stieglitz initially agreed but the project was never realized. Stieglitz was upset when Emerson published his *Death of Naturalistic Photography*, but acknowledged the role that Emerson had in proclaiming the potential of photography as an art form. He favorably reviewed an American edition of *Naturalistic Photography* in *Camera Notes* in October 1899, and in *Scribner's Magazine*, described Emerson as a man to whom Pictorial photography "owes more than to any other man."[67] And Emerson's words, "There is a poetry of photography as there is of painting and literature . . . the ones who see deeply, they are the poets"[68] had a strong resonance for Stieglitz.

In general, the Pictorialists saw the elevation of the photograph to the status of art object as a primary goal. Beauty and nuance took precedence over fact, and a personal vision was emphasized. The emphasis on individuality of expression and aesthetic quality allowed for a variety of approaches to Pictorialism. Manipulation of the image was frequent – through scratching, drawing, blurring, and tonal adjustment. The gum bichromate process was particularly popular and became a specialty of the French photographer Robert Demachy. From 1886 to about 1912, Pictorialism had its proponents in both the United States and Europe. Photographers such as Anne Brigman, Frederick Evans, Theodor and Oscar Hofmeister, Gertrude Käsebier, E. J. Constant Puyo, Heinrich Kühn, the young Stieglitz, and Edward Steichen were to adopt various approaches to Pictorialism. Subjects of common interest on both sides of the Atlantic included the nude, with allegorical and erotic dimensions; the female figure as a study in beauty or as mother; children at play or at home; pictures of innocence and purity; the landscape with its infinite variety of subtle and subdued tones and shapes; and literary or sacred themes, such as F. Holland Day's series of the Christ figure.

In July of 1888, Stieglitz interrupted his European sojourn to return home with his brothers for his sister Flora's wedding to Alfred Stern, a manager of a wine business. As the brothers entered New York harbor they saw the Statue of Liberty for the first time, and soon thereafter saw the grand Queen Anne home, Oaklawn, that Edward Stieglitz had purchased for his family in 1886. Overlooking beautiful Lake George, the mansion stood strong with its gables, turrets, and large veranda. In 1891 Edward enlarged his holdings even further and bought an old farmhouse on the hill across the road and the surrounding 63 acres, in part to end the pig-sty aromas that on occasion drifted down to Oaklawn. It was this farmhouse that Georgia O'Keeffe and Stieglitz were frequently to occupy.

That summer, Hedwig and Edward Stieglitz tried to do some matchmaking by inviting the family of their friend, the editor John Foord, to Oaklawn, hoping that Foord's daughter, Maggie, and Alfred would become a couple. Although the two were friends, nothing further came of the relationship. Maggie is seen, as previously noted, in a large group family portrait that Stieglitz took on the veranda that summer, which reveals the extent of Stieglitz's large family. This, along with the ambience of Oaklawn, the hill, and Lake George, would draw Stieglitz back year after year. (Oaklawn today is a luxury condominium and hotel, The Quarters at Four Seasons Inn, but much of the shell of its original exterior is still evident.)

Stieglitz took a number of photographs of his family that summer and a significant image of clouds, dated as approximately 1888 in a 1975 exhibition at George Eastman House Rochester, New York, could also have been taken at Lake George, showing Stieglitz's interest in clouds from an early stage. It is not as abstract as his later *Equivalents*, but it does show only the clouds, with no landscape to ground the image and give perspective to the skyscape so that the viewer is floating with the clouds. It is reminiscent of some of the painterly cloud studies by the British Romantic painter John Constable, recording different cloud formations at various times of the day. Here was a beginning step toward Stieglitz's later *Equivalents*.

At this time, Edward tried to convince Alfred he needed to get a job in some area of business, such as the printing industry. However, Alfred and his brothers returned to Berlin in October.

64   The Quarters at Four Seasons Hotel (formerly Oaklawn), Lake George, 2002

65   Alfred Stieglitz, *Oaklawn*, photograph on a postcard from Edward Stieglitz to Wilhelm Hasemann, December 1903

*   *   *

66   Alfred Stieglitz, *Oaklawn, Lake George*, 27 August 1897

68 (*facing page bottom*)   Alfred Stieglitz, *The Parlor at Oaklawn, Lake George*, 1907

67 (*above*)   Alfred Stieglitz, *The Stieglitz Family at Oaklawn, Lake George*, 1888. *Top row:* Ernest Werner; Theresa Werner; Riekchen Dietz Werner, Hedwig Werner Stieglitz, Julius Stieglitz; *second row:* Ida Werner Small; Herbert Small; Minnie Friedman (or Franny Einstein); Edward Stieglitz; Sarah Werner Stieglitz; Selma Stieglitz (Schubart); *between rows, left:* Jane Werner; *right:* Arthur Werner; Flora Stieglitz (Stern); *bottom row:* Leopold Stieglitz; Agnes Stieglitz (Engelhardl); Flora Small (Lofting); Edward Werner; Rosa Werner; Barbara Foord; Maggie Foord (Bonner)

 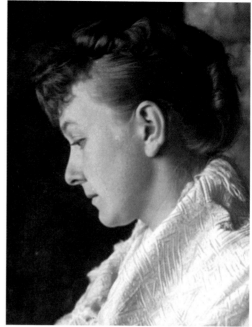

69 Alfred Stieglitz, *Listening to the Crickets*, 1891

70 Alfred Stieglitz, *Maggie Foord*, c.1888

71 Alfred Stieglitz, *Untitled (The Dock at Lake George)*, 1890s

72 Alfred Stieglitz,
Meeting of Day and Night,
Lake George
(Moonset/Dawn), 1896

74 (*below*)   Alfred Stieglitz, *Clouds*, *c.*1888

73 (*facing page top*)   Alfred Stieglitz, *Evening, Lake George*, 1890s

75 (*left*)   Alfred Stieglitz, *Lake George*, c.1895

76   Alfred Stieglitz, *Untitled (Lake George)*, c.1890

77   Alfred Stieglitz, *Equivalent (Clouds)*, 1924 or 1926

A RETURN TO EUROPE

During the summer of 1889, Alfred worked on preparing for a large jubilee exhibition in Berlin, sponsored by the Deutsche Gesellschaft von Freunden der Photographie under the management of Professor Vogel, celebrating the fiftieth anniversary of the birth of photography. The exhibition contained four sections: artistic photography by amateurs from all over the globe, judged by a jury headed by Erdmann Encke; scientific photography; photomechanical reproduction; and apparatus and chemicals, for which Alfred was a judge. Alfred won a silver medal and a prize for technical excellence given by the Steinheil camera and lens company. Joe Obermeyer also exhibited his photographic work taken in Italy. Stieglitz was to write about the exhibition: "It was the first exhibition of the kind ever held in Germany and was the first time that the

78   Cover and page from the catalogue of the jubilee exhibition in Berlin, 1889

— 47 —

30. Hedinger, Oberstlieutenant, Berlin W., Kurfürstenstr. 99. *Treppenpodest l.*
3 Fischverkäufe in Zandvoort, Holland.
2 Zoolog. Garten, Pfauen.
2 Klein Machnow, Hühner.
1 Atelier des H. Prof. Scarbina.
1 Oelbild Charles Hognet.
3 Momentbilder: Frauen-Chiemsee.
3 Berninagruppe Pontresina.
1 Fischer aus Zandvoort.
3 Fiscnerboote (Pinken) aus Zandvoort.
1 Vergrösserung: Pinke aus Zandvoort.

31. Stieglitz, Alfred, Berlin, Kaiser Wilhelmstrasse 44. *Treppenpodest r.*
(No. 1—14 incl. sind Platin-Aristodrucke nach meinem eigenen noch nicht veröffentlichten Verfahren. Die Bilder sind ohne Ausnahme unretouchirt und alle mit Steinheil Aplanat 19″, Stegemann Camera u. Vogel-Obernetter Eosinsilberplatten aufgenommen. Der Effect im Bilde 21 ist nur durch Tonen erzielt worden. D. Ausst.)
1. Die Heimkehr. 2. Im Sommer. 3. Portrait (im Freien aufgenommen). 4. Italienische Typen. 5. Jung Amerika. 6. Am Comer See. 7. Mürren (Schweiz). 8. Bellagio's „Maria". 9. Ochsen (Stie). 10. Bei Venedig. 11. Beleuchtungsstudien. 12. Kleine Hände. 13. Chioggia (bei Venedig). 14. Wasserscheu (Comer See). 15. Studienkopf (im Freien). 16. Nach dem Regen (Schweiz). 17. Herrannahendes Gewitter (Comer See). 18. Träume. 19. Zum ersten Male photographirt. 20. Leone (Italien). 21. Abendstimmung (Amerika).

32. Sack, Eduard, München, (Wien 1888 prämiirt). *Treppenpodest.*
1. Landschaftliche Studien.
2. Kostümstudien (Platinotypien).
3. Reproduktionen.

83. Lunden, A., Schloss Deurne bei Antwerpen in Belgien. *Augenblicksbilder. Treppenpodest.*

84. Robinson, H. P., Vice-Präsident der Photogr. Gesellschaft von Grossbritannien. Winwood, Tunbridge Wells, England. Fröhliche Fischermädchen.

85. W. W. Winter, Midland Road in Derby, England.
a) Mein Mütterchen! †
b) Der Versmacher und sein Opfer. †
(Trockenplatten, entwickelt mit Pyrogallus-Ammoniak, Druck Platinotypie).

German public could be introduced to the work of the amateurs, German and foreign, who play such an important role in the art and science of photography."[69] In the catalogue, Stieglitz stated that his images were not retouched, and only one, *Abendstimmung (Amerika)*, was toned.

A photograph taken at the exhibition by Stieglitz shows the extensiveness of the show. It is interesting to note that many of the images appear to be simply framed, and are a marked contrast to the heavy classical architecture of the exhibition hall.

That same summer, Stieglitz also photographed a young woman, Paula (probably Paula Bauschmied), ostensibly a young prostitute with whom he was romantically involved. His now famous *Sun Rays, Paula,* also exhibited as *Study in Light and Shade* and *Sunlight and Shadow,*

79   Alfred Stieglitz, *Jubilee Exhibition, Berlin: Main Hall,* 1889

was exhibited and published widely. The piece is remarkable for the abstract qualities of sun and shadow that pervade the image. Paula is leaning over her writing table, dressed in middle-class finery, much like a classic nineteenth-century genre painting. But the play of light and shadow brings it into the modern world. On the back wall, well lit, are some of Stieglitz's photographs: two images of *The Approaching Storm,* which had been recently published in *Die Photographische Rundschau,* flank images of Paula, two of her bedecked in white, one the reverse of the other from the same negative.[70] Another image of Paula is placed at the bottom of the montage on the wall. She is lying on the bed, suggesting a sense of intimacy with Stieglitz. Paula's portrait in a white hat is also tucked into the mirror on the writing table. A small studio card, a portrait of Alfred himself, is tacked next to the photographs with three

80   Alfred Stieglitz, *Sun Rays, Paula*, 1889

beribboned hearts. *Sun Rays, Paula* is not only a portrait of Paula, but also, indirectly, a portrait of Stieglitz himself, whose life was temporarily entwined with Paula's. The two birds in the cage may be seen as love birds, entrapped in circumstances that made a permanent relationship impossible, in some way mirroring the relationship of Alfred and Paula. The bars of the birdcage also complement the "bars" in the room, formed by the shadows on the wall. Stieglitz's photographs of Paula in white seem to suggest a wish to identify her with notions of purity and innocence. His *Approaching Storm* photographs, framing this image of innocence, mark the uncertainty and drama of Alfred's life – his continuing personal in-security about women, searching for a perfect figure, and his uncertainty about his career, whether business as his father wished, or photography as Alfred hoped. The photograph is also about photography – about light and shadows, using photographs within a photograph. Stieglitz has organized line, form, light, and shadow to express both feeling and a delight in the interplay of formal elements, particularly light and shadow.

Unlike Paula, Alfred's sister Flora had traveled the expected route for young women of her day of marriage and starting a family. But on Valentine's Day 1890 she delivered a stillborn child and three days later she died of blood poisoning. Upon

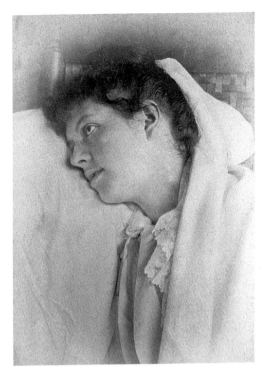

81   Alfred Stieglitz, *Paula*, 1889

hearing the news, Alfred was grief-stricken. To assuage his grief and feelings of helplessness, he immersed himself in his work. He traveled that spring to Vienna to study at the Graphische Lehr und Versuchsanstalt, studying under Josef Eder, and became a member of the Wiener Club der Amateur Photographen. In June of 1890, Stieglitz photographed a young woman lying on a pillow of sticks in an open field. Entitled *Weary*, it has some affinity in subject and form to artists of the Karlsruhe School, whose work was characterized by a "mechanical" Impressionist style.

82   Alfred Stieglitz, *Weary*, 1890

Another 1890 print, *Sunlight Effect*, shows a young peasant girl in profile, closer to the viewer, seated on a grassy knoll holding flowers. Barefoot, with the sun shining on her dress and the grass around her, she seems to represent a rural life filled with purity. Unlike *Weary*, this image

quickly draws in the viewer through the effect of the sunlight. The photograph was also titled *In Full Sunlight*. In a similar photograph of around 1890 Stieglitz explores sunlight effects, as a young girl bends over, picking flowers in a field, with a basket at her side. The sunlight and shadows falling on the various textures and patterns of the basket, the young girl's clothes, and plant life, are equally as significant as the young girl, whose face is not seen.

83 Alfred Stieglitz, *Peasant*, c.1890

Stieglitz's interest in the world of peasant and lower-class life was not limited to the human form, but extended to the workhorse. In *Before the Tavern* (also called *A Hot Day* when reproduced in W. I. Lincoln Adams' *Sunlight and Shadow: A Book for Photographers Amateur and Professional* in 1897), a team of dark workhorses is lined up in front of a tavern. Stieglitz's interest in horses also relates to his avid interest in racing. Horses were to appear later in several of his New York City shots, such as *The Terminal* (1893), *Winter Fifth Ave* (1893), *The Street-Design for a Poster* (1900), *Excavating New York* (1911), an untitled image of three horses (1911), and some Parisian shots from 1894. The horse stood for strength and power but, as a work beast, was bound to the constrictions of man's world.

84 Alfred Stieglitz, *Lago di Misurina*, 1890s

In August 1890, Stieglitz took some vacation days from his laboratory studies to travel to Cortina d'Ampezzo, a tourist town located at the base of the Dolomite mountains in Italy, and Sterzing in the Tyrol near Innsbruck, Austria. A self-portrait taken in Cortina finds Stieglitz lying on a large stone staircase, a

85 Alfred Stieglitz, *Self-Portrait, Cortina, c.*1890

young traveler at rest. In an 1892 article, "Cortina and Sterzing," Stieglitz described his journey to these locations. He referred to his disappointment with the rainy weather, and how excited he was to see the clouds breaking: "Away I rushed with my camera, inasmuch as I wanted one picture at least. What a delightful spot on earth! Picturesque and grand at the same time. The sun having come out in full force, I was enabled to get a fine view of the village of Cortina."[71] Stieglitz recorded traveling to Lago di Misurina, about two hours away, five o'clock in the morning. There he saw "a magnificently situated lake, surrounded by gigantic mountains, grand in their outline. The light was somewhat too glaring to get a view of the lake, but I managed to get a fine view of some of the mountains, which were about 3 miles distant from where I stood. Returning to Cortina, I met a crowd of peasants working in the fields; the result gives one an idea of the beauty of the surrounding country."[72]

The Dolomites are often considered the most distinctive mountains in Italy. Formed by mineralized coral, the pale rocks have been carved and sculpted by the effects of sun, rain, and ice. Often the peaks appear rose pink in the dawn sunlight. Stieglitz sought this effect on his early morning journey. His photograph of Lago di Misurina captures some of that light effect with a slight reflection at the water's edge. In his composition, Stieglitz placed the curved roadway winding through the broad plain on a slight diagonal, suggesting the strong diagonals of Japanese prints, which had recently become popular in Europe.

The Last Load, taken near Cortina, depicts peasants loading hay, with mountains in the background. Focusing on the hay, rather than on individuals, the image depicts the men as if they were frozen in time, choreographed in a workers' chorus, set in the beauty of the surrounding

86　Alfred Stieglitz,
The Last Load, 1890

countryside. In his article on Cortina, Stieglitz also noted the number of pumps available for washing linen and dishes in the streets; such washing was not done in the home.

On his way back to Vienna, Stieglitz stopped in Sterzing, the Tyrolean town famous for its narrow, winding streets.

The following morning was bright, and no trace of rain was to be seen when I arrived in Sterzing, a small quaint village situated near Franzen-feste. Having heard of the queer streets in that place, I determined upon "skipping" a train and looking around. The streets are exceed-ingly picturesque, and the houses are the queerest bits of architecture my eye ever struck. The interior would be a real "strike" for painters like Defregger and Grützner [specialists in paintings of quaint inte-riors]. Unfortunately I had no flash light with me, and it was much too dark to try to photograph the interiors without; hence that plea-sure was postponed to some future date. Upon my way to the train I passed through a street (!) remarkable for its width. All my photos were taken with a Steinheil Aplanat 19, on orthochromatic plates, without a yellow screen . . . Note – the paper used for prints 2, 5, 6, 7, 8 is a new one and not in the market yet. The red one may not please everyone, but my artist friends consider it "fine" especially for certain effects.[73]

Stieglitz was evidently experimenting in both content and technique on his visit to Sterzing. *A Street in Sterzing, the Tyrol* beautifully cap-tures the play of light and shadow on the "queer" forms of the archi-tecture and winding streets that attracted Stieglitz. Indeed, the image looks like a scene from a German Expressionist stage set in a movie such as *Dr. Caligari* made approximately thirty years later.

The summer of 1890 Alfred also traveled to south-west France, having won £25 in the *Amateur Photographer's* contest for a traveling studentship. Peter Emerson sent a special letter of congratulations to Stieglitz, the last of their correspondence for twelve years: "I congratu-late you on the scholarship – Bravo! We are all winning around here and soon everybody will be a naturalist. I hope to see you working on the *American Amateur Photographer* when you get back [Emerson knew Stieglitz was reluctantly returning to the United States owing to his sister's death] . . . I hope you will get a publisher in Germany."[74]

In south-west France Stieglitz spent a couple of weeks in Biarritz, St. Jean de Luz, Arcachon and the Ile de Ré. Charles Hastings of the *Amer-ican Amateur Photographer* had written to Stieglitz on 7 August 1890,

87   Alfred Stieglitz, *A Street in Sterzing, the Tyrol,* inscribed 1887 but probably 1890

"We shall be glad of views of general interest, beach views, promenades, bathing customs. The photographs should be large. We must of course leave the selection of views to you, only reminding you that the negatives are required more for commercial purposes than as examples of art photography . . . views of general interest should include cathedrals, castles, ruins, and public buildings of interest."[75] Because Stieglitz had to give up his negatives, there are few surviving images from this trip.

Biarritz, close to the Spanish border, provided Stieglitz with an opportunity to explore extensive beaches and the charming resort town, "discovered" by Empress Eugénie and Napoleon III in the mid-nineteenth century. The beaches of Biarritz extend past two cliff areas, and from the

88   Alfred Stieglitz, *Untitled (?Biarritz)*, *c.*1890

promenades in the heart of the town there are steep drops to the ocean, where the sea frequently rages against the jagged rocks. The coastal road winds up and down the cliffs before arriving in St. Jean de Luz, a lively Basque town and important fishing port. Narrow Basque houses covered by overhanging red-tile roofs dot the town, which was noted as the setting for the wedding of Louis XIV and the Infanta Maria Theresa of Spain in 1660, which took place in the great Basque church, St. Jean Baptiste, with its glittering seventeenth-century altarpiece.

One of the surviving images taken by Stieglitz at Biarritz is a quiet beach scene, *At Biarritz 1890*, where two small groups of beach-goers, sitting under colored parasols, look out to figures cavorting in the gentle surf and to two large rocks, sculpted by the waves. In the center is an artist painting the view. The image is reminiscent of Boudin's beach scenes, such as his *Fashionable Figures on the Beach* (1865), set in Trouville. Unlike Boudin, though, who concentrates on the finery of the Second Empire figures, Stieglitz presents figures who are not elegantly dressed as they parade the beach but are caught up in watching the world of nature. Perhaps more important than the type of dress in the photograph, are the parasols of diverse colors and patterns, their round, solid shapes counterbalanced by the verticals and horizontals of the open-backed wooden chairs that face the viewer. Stieglitz later published one of Boudin's paintings, *The Old Basin at Dunkirk* (1903), in *Camera Work*. He also photographed a *Cloud Study in Biarritz* on this trip.[76]

In Arcachon, just south of Bordeaux, Stieglitz would have seen Europe's largest sand dune, overlooking the vast Atlantic coast, and strolled the shores of the Arcachon basin. On the Ile de Ré, he would

89   Arcachon, 2002   90   Ile de Ré, 2002

have found an island of white houses, green shutters, hollyhocks, fishing boats, salt marshes, and vineyards. Until the end of the nineteenth century, the island was a major source of salt for the mainland. It has a dreamlike quality and has attracted a number of artists, including, during the nineteenth century, Honoré Patureau, Gaston Roullet, Eugéne Fromentin, William Barbotin, and Jean-Franck Baudoin.

Mid-Ocean, which shows only the ocean's whirling waters and the white spray of breaking waves, was perhaps taken on this trip.[77] Unusual for Stieglitz at this time was his concentration on the water alone, bringing the viewer close to the rushing waves. As clouds were to become

91   Alfred Stieglitz, *Mid-Ocean*, from *Sunlight and Shadow*, 1897

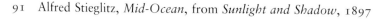

later, waves appear to be a kind of "equivalent" for Stieglitz's inner emotions as well as a descriptive image of the ocean.

NEW YORK

At the end of the summer, in September 1890, Stieglitz returned to New York, leaving his Berlin schooldays behind. He was reluctant to leave in many ways – he was beginning to find a place for himself in Germany. But, still affected by his sister's death and his mother's desire to have her children close by, he made the long journey back to the United States.

The city Alfred returned to was, in many ways, very different from the city he had known. Much of New York was lit by electricity, making nightlife more plausible; Madison Square Garden was under construction; one of the first skyscraper-like buildings, the Manhattan Life Insurance Building, would be completed in 1893. The area near the Stieglitz's family home was becoming more gentrified as the more affluent moved uptown. McKim, Mead, and White completed the Renaissance design for the Metropolitan Club in 1893 across from the Stieglitz house on East 60th Street. In the art galleries, visitors were seeing the grand portraits of John Singer Sargent, the rural peasant scenes and genre paintings of Bastien-Lepage, or the academic nudes of Adolphe-William Bouguereau, the latter a popular representative of French salon painting. The wealthy Havemeyer family had begun to collect paintings by Corot, Manet, Degas, and Courbet, and these works would eventually become part of the collection of the Metropolitan Museum of Art in New York.[78]

At first Alfred had a hard time adjusting to life in the United States. He was lonely; there were no cafés; the streets seemed dirty. A number of years later (25 November 1926), he told Herbert Seligmann, his gallery assistant, that he cried himself to sleep every night. As Seligmann recorded, there were three things that gave Stieglitz hope for life in the United States: the fact that Eleonora Duse, one of Stieglitz's favorite actresses, performed in New York in *Camille*; that such comedians as Joseph Weber and W. C. Fields performed in New York; and the presence of the streetcar horses he had seen and photographed in such images as *The Terminal* (1893). Seligmann also noted that Stieglitz related a story of how Duse wanted to meet him on what was to be her last journey to the United States. Stieglitz refused, replying " 'Duse is going to die. She will never leave America alive.' And Duse did die in the West.

The same thing happened in the case of three other people who asked to meet Stieglitz."[79] The tale suggests something of Stieglitz's egocentrism, which became more pronounced with age, as well as the trusting manner of his admirers and disciples, who accepted the story.

But Seligmann also articulates much of what came to concern Stieglitz in New York, in particular his fight for the worker, not so much in the socialist, Marxist sense, but in the sense of promoting honest, direct work that came from the soul, whether as an artist or a laborer in the fields. "The chief objective before him always was the fight for the true sensitive and selfless worker, particularly in America. The foe was commercialism and its accompanying indifference to quality; its snobbism, its hypocrisy, and its disregard for the spirit sacrificed to the predominance of mass production criteria."[80]

Upon his return home, the old billiard room in Stieglitz's parents' home at 14 East 60th Street became his studio. In an 1891 photograph, some of Stieglitz's favorite visual images are carefully displayed on or near the fireplace, which serves as a focal point. Among the images are enlargements of his photograph *Maria, Bellagio*, portraits of his father and mother, a photograph of Rubens's *Helena Fourment* with a fur coat, and a portrait of Maggie Foord. There are also two skulls on the mantel, and numerous images of women tacked in a sheaf on the door to the right. Primarily faces, these probably show actresses, friends, and models. Clearly the predominant subject is "Woman" – women who are young, old, nude, clothed, shown in various poses. The emphasis appears to be on youth and a beguiling gaze. The two skulls add a vanitas quality to the photograph, suggesting the inevitable passage of time, and ultimate decay of youth and all things beautiful.

92   Central Park, New York, near East 60th Street, 2002

From 1890 to 1895, Stieglitz acquiesced to his father's wishes that he become involved in business. At the urging of John Foord, the Stieglitz's family friend and editor, he took a job at the floundering Heliochrome Company, a printing company in lower Manhattan on Fulton Street that was working on a process of color photographic reproduction. Alfred, with his photographic and chemical experience, was seen as someone who could assist in the three-color processing and thereby salvage the company's failing revenues. Stieglitz also convinced his Berlin roommates Joe Obermeyer and Lou Schubart to join him. But the business world and Stieglitz did not mix well and approximately five years later Stieglitz left his position.

Shortly after arriving in New York in 1890, Stieglitz renewed his connection with Frederick Beach, the editor-in-chief and founder of the *American Amateur Photographer*, as Emerson had suggested. In 1891, Stieglitz joined the Society of Amateur Photographers, of which Beach had been the first president from 1884 to 1888 and of which Stieglitz was president from 1890–1. Collaborating with the Photographic Society of Philadelphia and Boston Camera Club, the New York Society hoped to promote the exhibition of photography, encouraging artistic and scientific excellence. At an 1891 exhibition, Alfred won a medal and, inspired, went on to write a passionate article, "A Plea for Art Photography," for the 1892 annual, *Photographic Mosaics*:

> Simplicity, I might say, is the key to all art – a conviction that anybody who has studied the masters must arrive at. Originality, hand-in-hand with simplicity, are the first two qualities which we Americans need in order to produce artistic pictures. These qualities can be attained only through cultivation and conscientious study of art in all its forms. Another quality our photographs are sadly deficient in is the entire lack of tone. These exquisite atmospheric effects which we admire in the English pictures are rarely if ever seen in the pictures of an American. This is a very serious deficiency, inasmuch as here is the dividing line between a picture and a photograph.[81]

Unlike some of Stieglitz's earlier writing, this article focused more on aesthetic, as opposed to technical concerns. Several years later Stieglitz was to write further on "Simplicity in Composition" in a contribution to a book, *The Modern Way of Picture Making*, 1905. By simple, Stieglitz seems to have meant bold, direct, and perhaps daring, and he cited Whistler's *At the Piano* (1858–9) as an example of good composition. Further, Stieglitz made an analogy to music – "Just as in music we find that the simpler the theme, the more thorough must be the knowledge of the musician in order to compose acceptable variations thereon, so, in fact in every art this rule obtains . . . Those modern Pictorial photographs that have attracted so much attention . . . their keynote is simplicity in arrangement and the true rendering of tonal values."[82]

Stieglitz began to hone his writing skills and share his aesthetic concerns with a wider public by writing fairly regularly for the *American Amateur Photographer*, and by the spring of 1893 he was offered a position as editor, which he agreed to take without salary, since he was still working at the printing company, now known as Photochrome.

As editor, Stieglitz attempted to secure ties with British photographers. In particular, he sought to make contact with a group known as the Brotherhood of the Linked Ring, by asking the noted photographer George Davison to contribute regularly to the magazine. Davison's photographs, in their blurred, evocative style, alluded to both Symbolism and Impressionism. The Linked Ring had been formed in 1892 when Davison, Henry Peach Robinson, and thirteen others resigned from the Photographic Society of Great Britain to form a group devoted to the "development of the highest form of Art of which Photography is capable. Those only are, in the first instance, eligible who loyally admit artistic capabilities in photography, and who are prepared to act with a spirit of LOYALTY."[83] The implied symbolism of the linked rings is seen quickly on the information sheet for prospective members or "postulants," where Loyalty and Liberty are referred to as the "devices" of the group. Stieglitz was elected to membership on 26 October 1894, remaining a member until 1909, and was awarded a special medal in 1924. The yearly juried photographic salon in London sponsored by the Linked Ring was seen as significant in Alfred's eyes. This transatlantic link that Stieglitz forged via Davison helped to give artistic photography a firmer foundation upon which to build.

Shortly after seeing Eleonora Duse in one of her performances in 1893, Stieglitz met up with his friend and fellow photographer William B. Post at the Society for Amateur Photographers on George Washington's birthday. Post was marveling at his new hand-held camera, which held 4-by-5-inch plates that Kodak had developed in 1889. He offered to loan the camera to Stieglitz, who quickly accepted and immediately went out into the snowy weather and stood for three hours (as he later claimed) on the corner of Fifth Avenue and 35th Street. His now famous photograph, *Winter, Fifth Avenue*, is a testament to his tenacity in getting the photograph he sought and to his technical versatility – he printed it as a photogravure, in two carbon prints, and later as gelatin silver prints in the 1920s or 1930s. In the latter prints, the viewer becomes somewhat distanced and in one of then the horizontality of the scene is emphasized in contrast to the verticality of the earlier versions. A photogravure appeared in *Camera Work* on 12 October 1905. The large carbon print,

93   Alfred Stieglitz, *Winter, Fifth Avenue*, 1893

$14^5/_8 \times 10^5/_8$ inches, was inscribed on the back: "This photograph is the basis of so-called 'American photography' shown in every important exhibition since then."[84] In the large carbon print and in subsequent prints the railroad ties do not appear, indicating the negative was retouched by Stieglitz.[85]

Stieglitz recounted the taking of this photograph in an article he wrote, proclaiming the virtues of the hand camera:

In order to obtain pictures by means of the hand camera it is well to choose your subject, regardless of figures, and carefully study the lines and lighting. After having determined upon these, watch the passing figures and await the moment in which everything is in balance; that is, satisfies your eye. This often means hours of patient waiting. My picture *Winter, Fifth Avenue* is the result of three hours' stand during a fierce snowstorm on 22 February 1893, awaiting the proper moment. My patience was duly rewarded. Of course, the result contained an element of chance, as I might have stood there for hours without succeeding in getting the desired picture. I remember how, upon having developed the negative of the picture, I showed it to some of my colleagues. They smiled and advised me to throw away such rot. "Why, it isn't even sharp, and he wants to use it for an enlargement!" Such were the remarks made about what I knew was a piece of work quite out of the ordinary, in that it was the first attempt at picture making with the hand camera in such adverse and trying circumstances from a photographic point of view. Some time later the laugh was on the other side, for when the finished picture was shown to these same gentlemen it proved to them conclusively that there was other photographic work open to them during the "bad season" than that so fully set forth in the photographic journals under the heading, "Work for the Winter Months." This incident also goes to prove that the making of the negative alone is not the making of the picture. My hand camera negatives are all made with the express purpose of enlargement, and it is but rarely that I use more than part of the original shot. Most of my successful work of late has been produced by this method. My experience has taught me that the prints from the direct negatives have but little value as such. The hand camera has come to stay – its importance is acknowledged. A word to the wise is sufficient.[86]

Winter, Fifth Avenue along with *The Terminal* (1893), were to become significant images for Stieglitz. Many years later he retold the taking of the two images in a more impassioned tone, recorded and published in Dorothy Norman's *Twice a Year* in 1938:

> There was a great blizzard. I loved snow, I loved rain, I loved deserted streets. All these seemed attuned to my own feeling.
>
> During the blizzard I stood at the corner of Thirty-fifth Street and Fifth Avenue with Post's hand camera. I had been watching the lumbering stagecoaches appearing through the snow: the horses, the

drivers, the driving snow – the whole feeling – and I wondered could what I felt be photographed.

The light was dim – at that time plates were "slow," and lenses were also "slow," but somehow I felt I must make a try. Wherever there was light, photographing was possible, – that is what I had discovered in 1884 in the cellar of the Polytechnic when I made a photograph of a still dynamo lighted by a 16 power electric bulb, exposing over twenty-four hours and getting a perfect negative. That was an event that took my professor's breath away when he heard what I had done.

Yes, where there was light there was the possibility of making a photograph. Finally I ventured to make a photograph of the blinding snow and the stagecoach with its horses and its driver coming towards me.

I went to the Society of Amateur Photographers, of which I was a member, and developed the negative. I was terribly excited. I showed the still wet negative to the men. They all laughed and said, "For God's sake, Stieglitz, throw that damned thing away. It's all blurred and not sharp."

And I replied, "This is the beginning of a new era. That negative is exactly what I want." And when, twenty-four hours later, I showed them the lantern slide made from this negative there was great applause and none would believe that it was made from the negative they had told me to throw away.

The next day I walked the streets, and found myself before the old Post Office. The Third Avenue street railway system and the Madison Avenue car system had their terminal down there. Naturally there was snow on the ground. A driver in a rubber coat was watering his steaming horses. There seemed to be something related to my deepest feeling in what I saw, and I decided to photograph what was within me.

These two pictures, *Winter, Fifth Avenue* and *The Terminal (Street car Horses)*, became internationally famous. They still hold their own and now they are regarded as classics.

I bought myself a camera similar to the one of Post's and then began my series of New York pictures. I had in mind doing one hundred photographs – that is, to do one hundred different phases of New York – to do them as supremely well as they could be done and to record a feeling of life as I felt it. Maybe in that way to establish photography in its true position in the realm of plastic expression.

But somehow this series that was clearly in my mind never was fully realized. The struggle for true liberation of self and so of others had become more and more conscious within me and before I realized it I was editing magazines, arranging exhibitions (demonstrations), discovering photographers and fighting for them. In short, trying to establish for myself an America in which I could breathe as a free man.[87]

The later commentary is the voice of an old man, proud of himself, self-absorbed, seeing himself as continuing to fight for his cause. But it also reveals much of the core of Stieglitz's passionate concerns and ways of working – his striving for perfection, his willingness to take risks, his wish to publicize his work, his use of lantern slides, and his interest in series. And, as was frequently the case, there is an emphasis on the struggle for liberation and freedom of the spirit.

Shortly after the turn of the century, Stieglitz began frequently to use a Graflex, a hand-held, single-lens, reflex camera that came in various sizes to accommodate different-sized plates. He used Goerz Double Anastigmat lenses with different-sized cameras, depending on the occasion. His devotion to Graflex was such that he included a letter of his to the company praising the camera in a Graflex advertisement that appeared in *Camera Work*.

The hand camera allowed Stieglitz to roam the city and more easily take a variety of images. His blizzard image gives heroic stature to the horse-drawn carriage and driver. The horses force their way through the driving snow to the viewer. Stieglitz seems almost to equate himself with the horses and driver. As they struggled through uncontrollable elements, so, too, did Stieglitz feel alone and somewhat adrift in a storm in his beginning days of fighting for the cause of photography. Stieglitz's other shots, taken during and shortly after the same storm, continue to celebrate the role of the horse and carriage as it ventures out into the empty snowy streets. *The Blizzard, New York* and *Winter, New York*, the latter title comprising three different compositions, appear like frames in a movie. In *Winter, New York*, the storm has subsided; there is less concentration on the elements and Stieglitz has widened his perspective to include more of the city environment, including a commercial sign for the Union Tobacco Company.

In these New York photographs, unlike his earlier European photographs, Stieglitz set himself the task of photographing in difficult weather conditions. But the snow also gave a certain Picturesque or Romantic quality to his images. Beyond this Romantic emphasis, however, Stieglitz placed nature and civilization side by side, for in a number of his photographs where snow appears, it takes up approximately half the content of the image.

The Terminal shows man and nature again, but here the emphasis is on man and his horses, dealing with the cold and snowy weather. Again, perhaps Stieglitz identified with the driver, struggling, watering his horses, caring for them, as Stieglitz cared for photography and later for the artists he fostered at his 291 gallery. Later in life, Stieglitz commented about this photo: "A driver I saw tenderly caring for his steaming car horses in a snow-covered street came to symbolize for me my own growing awareness that unless what we do is born of sacred feeling, there can be no fulfillment in life."[88] Like *Winter, Fifth Avenue*, this image was printed in a variety of formats – photogravure (two), carbon print, and gelatin silver print (two in the 1920s and 1930s), indicating Stieglitz's continuing interest in the image. One photogravure appeared in *Camera Work* in October 1911. A larger photogravure shows more of the neo-classical post office building, its columns and pediment reflecting in some ways the window bars and roof lines of the horse car, giving more stature and dignity to the vehicle, its horses, and driver.

94 Alfred Stieglitz, *The Terminal*, 1893

95   Alfred Stieglitz, *Untitled (New York City)*, *c*.1890

96   Alfred Stieglitz, *Old New York*, 1892

Over the next four years, Stieglitz continued to roam the streets of
New York as he photographed various weather conditions, men at work,
Central Park, Madison Square Park, various street scenes, a young
girl getting a drink of water, or architectural settings. Many of the
photographs give the viewer a sense of New York on a human scale – a
place where every day people live, work, and stroll the streets. There is
no sense of an overpowering city. Stieglitz has frozen in time moments
of humanity through his artistic vision.

It is perhaps no surprise that some of Stieglitz's photographs of New
York were chosen to accompany an article, "The Twentieth-Century
City," by John Corbin, published in March 1903 in *Scribner's Magazine*.
A number of Stieglitz's photographs are well suited to Corbin's words.
Although in some instances the writer focused on the more affluent
dimensions of the city, he noted:

> What our American cities most need to render them beautiful is an
> artist who will body forth to our duller eyes the beauties already there
> ... The clean dull grays are a joy in themselves as they merge with
> infinite graduations into profound darkness at the end of side streets,
> or leap into porcelain whiteness around the twin arc lights on Fifth

97   Alfred Stieglitz, *Untitled (New York City)*, 1890s

Avenue. The most casual eye may find delight in noting how softly building fades into building in the heart of the town, and with what rich variety of tone the smoke of steamers and factories on the waterfront merge in the surrounding gray . . . Most beautiful of all are the flurries of snowflakes, in which the commonest city sights loom vague and mysterious.[89]

Corbin goes on to compare New York to Chicago, and suggests that New York can remain "the 'Metropolis' and its life is as likely to grow almost daily in the richness and variety as in the harmony and proportion."[90] Corbin even talked about an improvement of the position of women, and in more general terms stated: "The life here is the life of a present that looks out to a future infinite in the variety of its possibilities."[91]

In some of his New York scenes, such as *West Street, New York* (1893), Stieglitz explores the reflective qualities in the wet streets and melted snow. In this image, the prow of the ship intersecting with the tall street light forms a strong triangle, which is, in turn, re-

98 (*above*) Alfred Stieglitz, *Shades of Night*, 1890s

99 Alfred Stieglitz, *Untitled (Central Park)*, 1890s

100   Alfred Stieglitz, *West Street, New York*, 1893

flected on the water in the street. Stieglitz further explored formal qualities in his *Five Points, New York* (1893), the crowd of dark-suited men,
their backs to the viewer, forming a large moving block of shades of gray
and black, in contrast to the sign, "Clothing House," in the lighter open
air above. An untitled photograph of the 1890s is a close-up of a small
group of men, their backs again to the viewer, gazing at some kind of
market stalls. Two young boys in lighter
shirts interact at the right. It is the shape
and form of their hats and suits that are
of interest, as well as the moment of
their day that Stieglitz has captured on
film.

101   Central Park, New York, 2002

A set of photographs from the
Herbert Small Collection is representative of some of Stieglitz's street photographs from the 1890s. A number of
them are shot in and near Madison
Square Park in lower Manhattan,
located where Broadway and Fifth

102 (*right*) Alfred Stieglitz,
*Untitled (Clock, 12 o'clock
Noon)*, 1896–9

104 (*facing page top*) Alfred
Stieglitz, *Untitled (Woman
Crossing the Street)*, 1896–9

105 (*facing page bottom*) Alfred
Stieglitz, *Untitled (Horse-drawn
Trolley)*, 1896–9

103 (*below*) Alfred Stieglitz,
24 Hours after the Fall, 1896–9

Avenue cross at 23rd Street and near the New York Camera Club, to which Stieglitz belonged, at 3 West 29th Street, where he did much of his processing while he was living uptown.

The small collection of photographs dates from approximately 1896 to 1899, a number of them having more complex compositions than his work of the early 1890s. There is, for example, a view of the *Dress Parade* on Fifth Avenue on Easter Sunday, a tradition begun in the late 1860s; a view of hansom cabs lined up along the edge of Madison Square; a photograph taken along 23rd Street looking back to Madison Square Park; a view looking up Fifth Avenue from 30th Street, near what became Stieglitz's 291 gallery and also the site of a later photograph, *The Street Design for a Poster* (1900–1); a site near the Photochrome Engraving Company; and an image of the great temporary arch erected on 23rd Street for the Dewey Day celebrations of 30 September 1899. In the 23rd Street view, Stieglitz has carefully used the verticality of the double street lamp to bisect the street's breadth, providing a central point of balance between the building façades on either side of the street. In the shot taken near the Photochrome Engraving Company, a large New York clipper clock dominates the left side, marking the passage of time, reminding the viewer there is a past, present, and future in the city. The delicate, open ornamentation of the clock provides a counterpoint to the solid forms

106   Alfred Stieglitz, *An Impression*, or *The Asphalt Paver*, 1892

of the building façades on the right. Of these pictures, the photographic historian Peter Bunnell has written, "[they] reflect a style characteristic of Stieglitz's work at this time ... That is, the oblique angle of view with a strongly weighted one-sided balance, various triangular forms throughout the composition, and a basic architectural structure established in the image by the buildings themselves, with the human subjects interacting in a kind of stage setting."[92]

In contrast to photographs that feature some aspect of human activity in the larger New York City stage set, are those photographs Stieglitz took of Central Park, where there is little or no sense of man or woman, except in the distant buildings. A more Romantic world of nature dominates. An example is *A Winter Sky, Central Park* (1894), where it is the sky and the lone, tall tree that dominate the image. One small human figure stands to the right, gazing at the tree, calling to mind the paintings of the German Romantic painter Caspar David Friedrich, who painted several lone trees, adding a small human figure to provide scale and stress the power of nature. Stieglitz may well have seen Friedrich's work in Germany. The distinct Gothic spires of Stieglitz's New York also recall Romantic paintings that idealize Gothic architecture. Two images showing snowy roadways only hint at a human presence and focus on tree branches and the path in the road.

Like the British painter J. M. W. Turner, who was interested in the effects of snow, steam, and fog in his paintings, Stieglitz studied the atmospheric effects of steam in pieces such as *The Asphalt Paver* (or *An Impressionism*) (1892–3), *The Rag Picker* (1892–3), and *The Street Paver* (1893). Most pronounced is the steam effect in *The Asphalt Paver*, which was printed both as a photogravure and as a gelatin silver print. The tones of the photogravure wrap the asphalt paver in a blanket of warmth, whereas the gelatin silver print, printed in the 1920s and 1930s, distances the viewer from the asphalt paver and the atmosphere is cool. In both versions the misty smoke of the machinery is typical of many early Pictorialist photographs, which celebrated soft-focus and atmospheric effects. It could be likened to an

107 Alfred Stieglitz, *The Rag Picker, Centre Street, New York*, 1892

Impressionist painting or piece of music. But it is more than an Impressionist piece and more than the dream world of a Symbolist painter. And therein lies a certain irony in the beauty of these pieces: their beauty lies in the song of the earth, work, and of a newly emerging city. The strong, dark diagonals in *The Rag Picker* are counterbalanced by the vapors of white steam rising in the distance. In each of the images, Stieglitz has brought dignity to the tasks depicted. The viewer does not pity these figures; they are seen as an integral part of New York's emerging stage set.

EMMELINE AND FURTHER EUROPEAN TRAVELS

Stieglitz's return to New York brought not only increased pressure to enter the business world, but also pressure to get married. In early photographs such as *The Intermission* (*circa* 1887), probably taken in Munich, where a young woman model lies nude in an odalisque position next to a painter with a pipe and stein of beer, or *A Study*, published in *the American Amateur Photographer*, February 1893, where a young woman with long wavy hair looks provocatively at the camera, Stieglitz is clearly interested in sex and sexuality. He eventually suc-

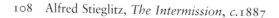

108   Alfred Stieglitz, *The Intermission*, *c.*1887

cumbed to convention in marrying Emmeline Obermeyer, the younger sister of Joe Obermeyer and the daughter of a wealthy brewery owner, thereby capable of bringing some financial security to Stieglitz's life. Edward Stieglitz had been financially hurt by the panic of 1893 when the New York Stock Exchange plunged.

Nine years younger than Stieglitz, Emmeline, or Emmy as she was known, was captivated by him. But that deep admiration was not reciprocated, although Stieglitz developed some fondness for her in the early days of their engagement and marriage.

They were married on 16 November 1893 in Sherry's, a fashionable restaurant on Fifth Avenue, and spent their first night in the newly opened Savoy Hotel, at 59th Street and Fifth Avenue. Stieglitz claimed later that the marriage was not consummated that first night, nor for at least a year, and that he sublimated his energies into his work and into playing the piano. Emmy was reported to have disliked his passionate interpretations of Wagner and Beethoven so much that Stieglitz chose to have the piano removed from their home.

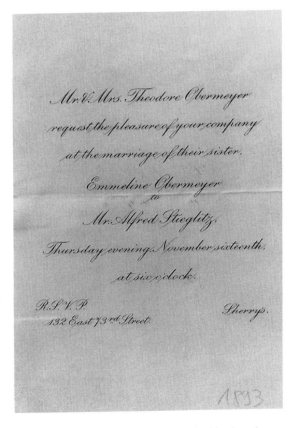

Alfred and Emmy's union is a sad tale of a marriage that should never have been. Emmy was a conventional young woman, anxious to fit into the mores and manners of upper-middle-class society. She would probably have loved to have been perceived as, for example, one of John Singer Sargent's society women.

In the early days of their marriage she tried at some points to please Alfred, and he took a number of photographs of her at Lake George, but there is never any of the intensity or sensuality that exists in the photographs that Stieglitz took of Georgia

109 Invitation to the wedding of Alfred and Emmeline, 1893

O'Keeffe or other women, such as Rebecca Strand and Dorothy Norman. Emmy is seen lying in the grass on Tea Island or tying her shoes before

110 Alfred Stieglitz, *Emmy on Tea Island at Lake George, c.*1893

111 Alfred Stieglitz, *Emmy at Lake George, c.*1893

112   Alfred Stieglitz, *Emmeline Obermeyer Stieglitz and Flora Stieglitz on the Porch at Oaklawn*, n.d.

113   Alfred Stieglitz, *Emmy on the Porch at Lake George*, c.1893

a tennis game or on the dock of Lake George. It was soon clear that she did not understand or have patience with Alfred's artistic interests.

On 5 May 1894, Emmy and Alfred set sail on the French ship, the *Bourgogne*, for Europe on their delayed honeymoon. Frank Hermann accompanied them. Alfred hoped to take photographs and meet various European photographers. Emmy hoped for glamorous shopping excursions and society parties. It was difficult to find points of compromise.

On board ship Alfred began photographing soon after departure. One of the passengers on board, a lively looking

114   Alfred Stieglitz, *The Bourgogne, Le Havre, May 14/94*, 1894

young woman, Lotte Linthicum, appears in a number of the photographs, both alone and within a group. In one group shot a couple, along
with Emmy and Lotte, are posed on large coils of rope. The diagonal
lines of the ship's rigging and the vertical lines of the flagpole provide a
structure for the figures. The large, dark smoke stacks stand in strong
contrast to the white of the ship's railing and to the billowing smoke
softly wafting above. The open waters and expansive sky, stretching
outward give the subjects and the viewer a sense of freedom and of
plein air.

In Europe, Emmy and Alfred traveled to Paris, Switzerland, and Italy.
In Italy they visited Milan, where Stieglitz saw the International Photographic Exhibition in which he was one of four American exhibitors,
and Venice. They also visited Austria and Germany, stopping in Gutach
and Stuttgart; the Netherlands, visiting Katwyk and then Rotterdam; and
Belgium. They ended their tour in London. Emmy was happiest in Paris,
the great city of light, with its grand Eiffel Tower, completed just five
years before.

In Paris, Alfred took several now well-known photographs in which
reflections on the wet pavement are the subject of approximately half the
image. In many ways these photographs are similar to such Impressionist paintings as those Camille Pissarro and Gustave Caillebotte,
painted in Paris. But through the photographic medium, Stieglitz travels

115   Alfred Stieglitz, A *Wet Day on the Boulevard, Paris,* 1894 (print 1897)

beyond Impressionism to focus on the patterns on textures, light, and shadow on the wet pavement. *A Wet Day on the Boulevard, Paris* is shot at the intersection of Boulevard des Italiens and Rue Scribe. As with a number of his images, Stieglitz made prints as a photogravure and carbon print. The lush tones of the carbon print captured the evanescent qualities of the light, water, and shadows. Inscribed on the back of the print, some years later, by Stieglitz was "This print is the original that opened the way for so-called 'Rainy Day' pictures."[93] In other images of the same street he cropped his image to study different aspects of the scene. The photograph was published internationally in numerous publications, such as the *Photographic Times*, *International Studio*, *Sunlight and Shadow*, *New York Tribune*, and *Photographisches Centralblatt*.

Stieglitz's image includes a corner of the Old England Store, a long-established British store that Emmy would have loved and that still exists today. Its slightly bowed façade and windows are part of a rhythm of curves found in the umbrellas, the kiosks, and the arch forms across the street. Around the corner from the Old England Store was the Grand Hotel at 12 Boulevard des Capucines, with its eight hundred rooms, built in an elegant Beaux-Arts style. The hotel hosted numerous evening galas, performances, and concerts. In 1896 the great Sarah Bernhardt was to appear in an acclaimed performance. It seems likely that Alfred and Emmy would have visited for at least an evening or to take tea.

One of Stieglitz's photographs of Paris shows the prominence of the Eiffel Tower on the skyline, as the viewer looks down the Seine. Large cumulus clouds fill the sky, as boats head down the river. Stieglitz raises questions about the balance of nature and culture, and of nature

116 The Old England Store, Paris, 2002

and technology as he sees the urban world having a greater impact on society in places such as Paris, where, in this image, commerce is suggested by the boats and buildings along the river's shore.

In *On the Seine, Near Paris* (1894), *Goats Outside Paris* (1894), and *Homeward* (1894), a small flock of goats lies along the roadway on the bank of the Seine. In the distance is the city. In *Near Paris*, the large

117   Alfred Stieglitz, *The Eiffel Tower*, 1894

receding triangular form in which the goats lie is flanked by the triangular shape of the Seine, which borders the city – boats, buildings, and smoke stacks. To the left is a row of trees that separates another receding roadway and more buildings. The rhythmic repetition of the trees, the ordered composition, the contented goats – variety within a unity of form – suggests the peaceful coexistence of nature and culture, this particular roadway with trees and goats appearing to lead to culture.

In 1903–4, Stieglitz made a later photogravure of this subject on beige, thin, slightly textured Japanese paper and called it *A Decorative Panel*. The term "decorative" no doubt refers to the growing interest in the decorative motif as a significant element, with obvious simplification or repeated patterns allowing Art to speak more clearly to the public realm. The critic Georges Lecomte had given a speech in 1892 where he stated

118   Alfred Stieglitz, *On the Seine – Near Paris*, 1894

his thesis: "The concern for decorative beauty is the distinctive mark of our epoch in the history of Art."[94] He added "Fénéon talked of Pissarro treating Nature as a reportoire of decorative motifs . . . The key terms here – 'decoration,' 'ornament,' 'synthesis,' even 'style' . . . are called on to do the magic work, which Modernism still believed possible, of soldering together the aesthetic and the social."[95]

One image, *Along the Seine*, shows only man and nature, without reference to the city: Stieglitz focuses on goats butting horns as their weary caretaker lies asleep on the roadside. Other Parisian images, such as *Going to Pasture*, where a herd of sheep block the roadway, or *In the Suburbs of Paris*, where a small, lone figure tends his garden, or *Sketching in the Bois*, tend to be more pastoral, leaving the city behind. The artist sketching in the Bois du Boulogne on the outskirts of Paris may well be Frank Hermann, who accompanied Stieglitz on his photographic excursions.

One of Stieglitz's photographs, *The Card Players*, was shown in the first exhibition that exhibited photography as art, sponsored by the Photo Club of Paris at the Durand Ruel Gallery in January 1894. The staged image shows Stieglitz, Hermann, and a third friend dressed in period costumes, emulating a large tapestry on the wall behind them. They have new identities and, costumed, they become an integral part of an extended tapestry that continues to the pattern of the carpet on the floor. Stieglitz liked games such as billiards and board and card games, particularly if he could set the rules, which in a sense he has done in "setting the stage" for this photograph.

Through his Paris connections, Stieglitz eventually became friendly with Robert Demachy, whose work was to appear later in *Camera Work*. Pictorialist in style, Demachy gained a reputation for his portraits, his landscapes with horses, and his studies of Breton peasants and villages. Through the years the two men carried on an extended correspondence.

From Paris in 1894, Stieglitz and his wife traveled to Lake Lucerne. His photographs, such as *Lake Lucerne* (1894) or *Twilight* (1894), showing a steamer coming across the lake, its a dark billowing smoke contrasting with the clouds, previews his later *Hand of Man* (1902), where the smoke of the train dominates the photograph. But instead of focusing on the railroad tracks and evidence of the machine as its primary subject, the Lucerne image places a "hand of man" in the center of a pristine lake; the still lake and its surrounding land and skyscape are the main subject of the photograph, enveloping the man-made.

Turning from the lake shore, Stieglitz photographed the mountains. Images such as *From the Höheweg Interlaken* (1894), *Landscape (Mid Ice and Snow)* (1894), or *The Jungfrau Group* (1894) show his ongoing interest in the plunging V shapes of the mountain forms and the sky above the landscape – and are forerunners of his *Songs of the Sky* and

119   Alfred Stieglitz, *Landscape (Mid Ice and Snow)*, 1894

120   Alfred Stieglitz, *The Jungfrau*, 1894

Equivalents. The plunging V forms were to appear in a number of Georgia O'Keeffe's paintings, and the dappled cloud forms in *Landscape (Mid Ice and Snow)* were seen many years later in O'Keeffe's *Sky Above the Cloud* series from the 1960s. The thrusting V shapes and the rising mountains suggest the great crescendos and decrescendos in the work of Wagner or late Beethoven. The layers of darks, grays, and whites are like the groups of sound masses moving in space that the Parisian-born composer Edgard Varèse advocated. (Varèse moved to New York during World War I and knew Stieglitz.)

121 Alfred Stieglitz, *Mountain Bridges*, 1894

122 Alfred Stieglitz, *Grindelwald Glacier*, 1894

Although terrified of heights, Emmy did go with Alfred on one of his photographic excursions to see the spectacular Jungfrau mountain group from Murren, but became so nervous she could not continue, and by one account, claimed that he was trying to murder her![96] Stieglitz did photograph Emmy on the *Höheweg*, where she appears very nervous and anxious.

Besides the magnificent landscape views of the towering mountains, Stieglitz also took close-up images in the mountains, such as his *Mountain Bridges*, or his images of the Grindelwald glacier. The arches of mountain bridges are photographed in front of the rocky crevices. The brickwork of the human bridges seems fragile in relation to the massive rock formation. Here nature is depicted as somewhat formidable, but able to be tamed and traversed. The viewer is brought close to the fissures and crevices of the Grindelwald glacier, being perched edge of a powerful mass of ice, frozen in time. This proximity creates a forceful impression of texture, the abstract play of line, the pure forms that make up the glacier. Here Stieglitz seems to be searching later for his *Equivalents* – forms, shapes, expressions of thoughts or emotions rather than simply descriptions of nature. These last three images, like a number of Stieglitz photographs, were made into lantern slides, allowing him to project them at a public gathering and present his work in a dramatic fashion in a kind of theater performance.

VENICE

Arriving in Venice later that summer, Stieglitz photographed a combination of genre and cityscape scenes, capturing one or two figures crossing bridges, lying on steps, or leaning against lamp-posts. In *The Two Fashions, Venice* (1894) he photographed a fashionable young woman

123 Alfred Stieglitz, *The Two Fashions, Venice*, 1894

124   Alfred Stieglitz, *Venetian Scenes (A)*, 1894

near the top of some steps and a poor woman with a shawl, below. However, they are framed visually together within the shadows cast on the steps. Titles such as *Gossip, Venice* show a continued interest in a sense of narrative; the viewer wonders what the gossip is, who these people are. In these images Stieglitz's figures are set on a Venetian architectural stage – near the Piazza San Marco at the Ponte della Paglia, or next to the Procuratie Vecchie, or at a Venetian well on the Campo dei Santi Giovanni e Paolo. As in his 1887 photographs, there are scenes of women doing laundry, or laundry hanging along the side of a canal. Stieglitz also photographed the great doors and towering Corinthian capitals of the grand church of Santi Giovanni e Paolo, and the simpler, but elegant doorway of the Palazzo Soranzo van Axel.

The basilica of Santi Giovanni e Paolo – or San Zanipolo, as the Venetians call it – is a striking building. The church was dedicated to the two brother saints, John and Paul, martyrs in Rome in the fourth century. The building was worked on for almost two centuries before its con-secration in 1430. Its Italianate monastic Gothic façade looks imposing from the open piazza, with its two heavy pilasters, a central rose window, and a large "eye" on either

125 (*above*)   Alfred Stieglitz, *Church Entrance, Santi Giovanni e Paolo*, 1894

126 (*left*)   Santi Giovanni e Paolo, Venice, 2002

side. In tabernacles rising above the crown of the façade are statues of St. Thomas of Aquinas, St. Dominic, and St. Peter the Martyr. On the pinnacles are an eagle, symbolizing St. John the Evangelist, the Eternal Father, and the Lion of St. Mark. The portal that Stieglitz photographed was built with six columns brought from the island of Torcello and carried to the church in 1459. It was said that the capitals of these had been sculpted by Bartholomeo Bon, the frieze by Master Domenico de Firenze and the cornice by Magister Luce.

The open doors in the photograph invite the viewer inside. The interior with its numerous burial monuments, has been called the Pantheon of the Doges. The massive building speaks of Venetian history. Much of the sculpture was made by members of the Lombardo family. Its plan, a Latin cross, with nave, single side aisles, and five polygonal apses, plus ten enormous columns supporting the arcades, is overwhelming. Stieglitz's photograph, although of the exterior, captures the monumentality of the building and, through its open door, implies a large interior space. The doorway, which is decorated with Byzantine reliefs, is one of the earliest Renaissance architectural features in Venice.

Inside, Stieglitz would have seen not only many sculptural monuments, but also magnificent Venetian paintings, such as Giovanni Bellini's multi-paneled *Polyptych of St. Vincenzo Ferreri* (1464) or Giovanni Battista Piazetta's *The Glory of St. Dominic* (1727). Indeed, one of the female figures depicted in profile on the *Pieta* panel of the polyptych has some affinity with a later photograph by Stieglitz of a young woman in profile, entitled *Portrait – "An Arrangement,"* where evening light forms a kind of halo around the young girl's head. Like the Renaissance figure, Stieglitz's figure is simply presented, with a plain dark dress and open neckline. In the Piazetta painting, figures with musical instruments are seated in the clouds, combining musical and sky imagery as Stieglitz chose to do many

127   Alfred Stieglitz, *Portrait – "An Arrangement,"* from *Burr McIntosh Monthly*, April 1907

years later. The Campo dei Santi Giovanni Paolo has also been known as the Field of Marvels and it is one of Venice's most famous squares in terms of its art and history. The Dominican Fathers had it paved in 1592.

Close to the church is a large statue of the mercenary leader Batolomeo Colleoni sculpted by Leonardo's master, Andrea del Verrocchio. The statue has a strong sense of power and movement. Just behind it is

128   Alfred Stieglitz, *A Venetian Well*, 1894

a sixteenth-century well-head, richly decorated with *putti*, which Stieglitz photographed, juxtaposing the *putti* with the young woman drawing water from the well. Here the sacred and the secular are well integrated.

Facing the basilica is the Scuola Grande di San Marco, one of six grand colleges or confraternities founded for charitable purposes in the thir-teenth century. Its beautiful decorative façade was designed by Pietro Lombardo with his sons. Inside the Scuola, Stieglitz could have seen the large cycles of paintings *The Miracles of St. Mark* by Jacopo Tintoretto and *The Preachings of St. Mark* by Gentile Bellini. Visiting other Venet-ian sites, Stieglitz could also have seen a number of eighteenth-century Venetian *vedute* paintings by artists such as Giovanni Canaletto and Francesco Guardi, from which he might have learned lessons in the subtle variations of light at various times of day depicted by the skilled painters.

Stieglitz and Emmy stayed at the celebrated and fashionable Hotel Danieli on the Riva degli Schiavoni. (Before their arrival, Stieglitz had been careful to send Hasemann a postcard giving him the Venice address.) Built in the fourteenth century, the Danieli, with its deep pink façade, had become famous as the site of the first opera performed in Venice, Monteverdi's *Proserpina Rapita* in 1630. The building had

129   Alfred Stieglitz, *Venice*, 1894

become a hotel in 1822 and had hosted such guests as Balzac, Dickens, Ruskin, Wagner, and Debussy. From the Riva degli Schiavoni there was a beautiful view across the lagoon to the island of San Giorgio Maggiore. Here, as in other places Stieglitz visited, he consciously and unconsciously absorbed lessons of history and art history that would serve him as a foundation to forge his own pathway.

The nearby Ponte della Paglia, which Stieglitz photographed, may have derived its name from the boats (*paglia*) that once unloaded cargoes of straw and was rebuilt in 1847, replacing a 1360 bridge. Close by was the Bridge of Sighs, built in 1600 to link the Doge's Palace with the new prisons. According to legend, the bridge's name was derived from the sighs and anguished lamenting of prisoners on their way to the state inquisitors. The Riva degli Schiavoni was also one of the

130   Alfred Stieglitz, *A Venetian Canal*, 1894

131   Alfred Stieglitz, *A Venetian Canal*, 1894

132   Alfred Stieglitz, *Venice*, 1894

city's most famous promenades, which must have pleased Emmy. The hotel's central location made it easier for Stieglitz to explore the city.

Perhaps the most striking of Stieglitz's Venetian photographs are his canal images, which explore the alluring Venetian architecture and the reflective waters of the canals. In these images he plays with such dualities as light and dark and the solidity of the buildings versus the fluidity of the waters, and with the concepts of growth and decay inherent in much of Venice's very nature. The boats on the canals or the hanging laundry suggest a human presence. A number of the canal scenes inspire reflection, drawing the viewer into a mysterious Venetian world. Two images of the same canal show how Stieglitz could crop an image and have two equally arresting photographs.

GUTACH

That summer, Alfred and Emmy arrived in Gutach, Germany, to visit Hasemann in late July 1894. Stieglitz and his twin brothers had been disappointed not to be able to attend Hasemann's wedding to Luise Lichtenberg in September of 1889. Stieglitz seemed happy to be bringing Emmy to Gutach. He had also recently seen one of Hasemann's paintings, *Edle Reiser*, in Munich, and referred to it in a postcard of 18 June

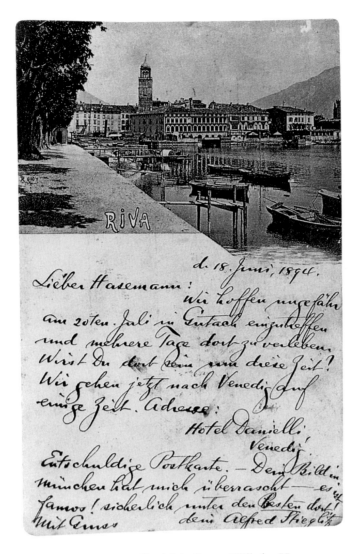

133   Postcard from Alfred Stieglitz to Wilhelm Hasemann,
18 June 1894

1894 to Hasemann, as being the best there, telling him that it was famous![97] The painting shows a farmer instructing a young boy in the art of plant grafting as they are standing in the open hills.

Stieglitz described Gutach as a place where

Stories are told in fairy tales . . . the inhabitants have taken something of the sunshine and the odor of the pines into their souls, making them cheerful simple natures ever willing to assist, entering into the spirit of the artist, and the smallest gratuity prompts the willing spirits to

134 (*above*) Alfred Stieglitz, *Pride of the Black Forest*, 1894

135 Gutach, 2002

long hours of posing. The many artists who frequent this famous town and the fact that it lies far off the beaten track of globe-trotters and summer excursionists explains the simplicity and readiness to oblige of these simple people. The town itself offers every possible variety of subject. Mountains, even the snow-clad ones of the Alps in the distance, beautiful vistas in the pine woods, farming scenes, for these people are distinctly agricultural – everything that the artist could desire, and no tall factory buildings with their modern rectangular lines of bricks and windows to disturb, no railroads with smoky locomotives to dim the pure atmosphere, and all these ever changing, presenting a new and varying view at every turn, changing with each season of the year, with every change from lowering storm to noble inspiring sunshine. Trees, flowers, wheat fields, mountains and valleys, rushing streams and babbling brooks, a waterfall here and there to add variety, willing models in their quaint caps and medieval costumes, what more can the artist or photographer desire than unlimited time and an inexhaustible supply of plates and lenses.[98]

Stieglitz and his wife were welcomed by the Hasemanns. Their week-long stay was later pronounced as one of the high points of their trip in a letter from Edward Stieglitz to Hasemann of 1 February 1895. (Edward also commented that he hardly ever drew or painted anymore, but that Lake George provided him with much happiness.) While in Gutach, Alfred and Emmy spent time with two other artists, Curt Liebich and Fritz Reiss, and their wives. A group photo taken by Stieglitz includes Liebich, the Hasemanns, the Reisses with their young daughter Gertrud, Emmy, and Marie Lichtenberg, Luise Hasemann's sister.

136 Wilhelm Hasemann, *In der Dorfgasse*, 1891

Stieglitz's photographs taken that week in Gutach have similarities to some of Hasemann's paintings. In some instances there is similar content and composition, as in Stieglitz's *Gutach Children* and Hasemann's *In der Dorfgasse*, or in Stieglitz's *The Old Mill* and Hasemann's mill images. Sometimes Stieglitz pushes the photographic spectrum beyond the point where painting could easily go, exploring light and shadow effects in pieces such as *Sunlight*, where a young Gutach girl is collecting water. In a larger version of the same subject, *At the Pump, Black Forest*, Stieglitz included the surrounding countryside and part of a typical Gutach barn. In both versions the sunlight and shadow effect become the main subject and the young girl becomes secondary.

Stieglitz seems to have captured the spirit and pulse of this rural community. *A Gutach*

137 (*right*)　Alfred Stieglitz, *The Old Mill*, 1894

138　Alfred Stieglitz, *Gutach*, 1894

139　Alfred Stieglitz, *Farm Scene at Gutach*, 1894

Peasant Girl shows a young peasant girl holding her bucket, standing shyly at the barn door, her workboots suggesting her labors. Stieglitz's photograph exhibits a touching tenderness, showing a reticent child who knows hard work but is beautiful in her simplicity. The photographer Paul Strand thought this portrait was the finest photograph Stieglitz ever

140 Wilhelm Hasemann, *Peasant Girl*, 1890s

141 (*below left*) Alfred Stieglitz, *Gutach*, 1894

142 (*below right*) Alfred Stieglitz, *Gutach Peasant Girl*, 1894

made. There are men and women harvesting, seemingly proud of their work. Or there is the old woman spinning, in a series of four photographs that show her working from a variety of angles. In this series, *The Old Woman with Spinning Wheel*, also titled *Wrinkles*, the woman's face is not visible at all. More important is her work, the work of many years, as suggested by her worn, bony arms.

143   Alfred Stieglitz, *The Village Philosopher*, 1894

One of Stieglitz's most poignant portraits from his Gutach visit is that of *The Village Philosopher*, depicted in profile, his hand at his chin, leaning over a book. Stieglitz has captured an air of pensive thought. *The Village Philosopher* was photographed in Hasemann's studio, suggesting the association of art and deep contemplation. Stieglitz shot the elderly man on full focus, leaving the background in soft focus to emphasize his profile, the wrinkles in his shirt and face bringing a certain rhythm to the piece. A number of Hasemann's drawings and paintings also show close-ups of the Gutach village folk – a man with his pipe, an old farmer, a man in profile. Indeed, *Der Alter Bauer* or *Old Farmer* is a painting with contemplative qualities similar to *The Village Philosopher*. Both include a window and vase of flowers, but the painting contains elements of Romanticism and nostalgia, rather than the universality inherent in Stieglitz is image.

Stieglitz's photograph of Hasemann's studio shows the painter working at a table with two of his images of young women in the traditional dress of the area. The carved wood of the easels, chair, and shelves was typical of the houses around Gutach. Rather than photographing Hasemann close-up, Stieglitz chose to photograph him at work, as an integral part of the other objects in his studio. Indeed, the paintings occupy a larger presence in the photograph than Hasemann himself. The portrait seems fitting, for Hasemann was devoted to his work and did not appear to be a flamboyant character, but rather one who wished to be integrated into the life and work of the village of Gutach.

144 (*above*) Alfred Stieglitz, *Black Forest Studio*, 1894

145 Hasemann's studio building, Gutach, 2002

146 Alfred Stieglitz, *Group Portrait in Gutach*, 1894. *Left to right, standing:* Wilhelm Hasemann, Marie Lichtenberg; *seated on bench:* Curt Liebich, Emmeline Stieglitz, Luise Hasemann, Frau Reiss; *seated on grass:* Fritz Reiss and his daughter, Gertrud.

147   Alfred Stieglitz, *Early Morn*, 1894

Although some of Stieglitz's photographs of peasants, particularly those in Gutach, have been said to show the influence of the Karlsruhe School painters, whose members used somewhat Impressionist techniques, Stieglitz frequently brought a new candor and freshness to his images. For example, in his *Harvesting, Black Forest, Germany*, also titled *Early Morn*, the figures are an integral part of the landscape composition – the woman bending with the grasses, the man leading the viewer's eye back to the hazy cloud cover. The woman's rounded back is mirrored by the turning wheel in the background. As in a well-choreographed dance piece, there is both stillness and motion, and the viewer also becomes caught up in a sense of the musical movement of sunlight flickering on the wheat.

By including figures in a number of his early landscape photographs, in contrast to some French nineteenth-century experiments in landscape, where the figure has disappeared, Stieglitz suggests the idea of landscape being anchored in human life, a concept later developed by John Binkerhoff Jackson, a landscape advocate: "The true and lasting meaning of the word landscape: not something to look at, but to live in; and not alone but with other peoples."[99] Many of Hasemann's landscapes are also frequented by people as both primary and secondary aspects of the paintings.

Stieglitz would have probably seen some of Hasemann's sketches and earlier works in his studio and certainly spoken with him about his drawings and paintings. Their interests appear to have intersected in several areas: Hasemann's oil sketches of the sky and clouds from the 1890s certainly have some affinity with Stieglitz's interest in the sky and clouds in both his early and late work. Although Hasemann did not necessarily articulate any concept of "equivalence" as Stieglitz later did, he did experiment with light and color in his sketches in a modern, semi-abstract manner that is quite spontaneous and was not simply interested in a descriptive image.

Like Stieglitz, Hasemann was also concerned with the increased role of technology and machines in society at large and with the intrusion of the train into the natural landscape around Gutach. A drawing, *Hopfgarten*, and painting, *Schwarzwaldtal*, show a train arriving into the idyllic landscape. In the painting the train is not too intrusive and is small in comparison to the mountainous terrain. But in the 1876 drawing, the train is much closer to the viewer and utility poles dominate the landscape. The composition of the drawing, its placement of the train tracks and utility poles, prefigures in some ways Stieglitz's later photographs dealing with the train, such as *The Hand of Man* (see page 206), in which Stieglitz placed the vertical poles on the opposite side of the image.

Stieglitz seems to have mentally stored some of Hasemann's influence, drawing upon it, perhaps indirectly or subcon-

148 (*above*)   Wilhelm Hasemann, *Hopfgarten* (near Weimar), 1870

149 (*right*)   Alfred Stieglitz, *The Letterbox*, 1894

sciously, in his later years. But he may in turn have influenced some of the artists who were working in Gutach. As an example, Stieglitz's photograph *The Letterbox*, showing two young girls posting a letter, may well have inspired a later postcard that Curt Liebich drew, depicting one young girl, instead of Stieglitz's two, posting a letter. Liebich's composition is the reverse of Stieglitz's, with the young girl on the right. Liebich and Reiss would have probably seen Stieglitz's photographs of Gutach, since Alfred sent approximately twenty photographs to Hasemann to share with Liebich and Reiss, which he refers to in a letter of 9 January 1895:

> My wife and I think often of Gutach and would like to return soon. It is much prettier there than this dirty city, where everything depends on money . . . this month we moved into our own home, which is quite comfortable.
>
> I would like to have bought a picture from you last summer, but did not have the money. We sent you some photographs today. Keep what you like, and share the others with Reiss, Liebich, and so on. I will send more . . . let me know if Reiss or Liebich would like certain images.
>
> Don't you want to paint a winter landscape scene with snow? We have spoken about this.
>
> My wife sends many greetings to you.
>
> Your friend,
>
> Alfred Stieglitz[100]

Emmy and Alfred left Gutach to head for Stuttgart. In subsequent letters to the Hasemanns from Alfred and other members of his family, it is clear that that week meant much to Alfred personally and for his photographic work. He wished to return to Gutach and wrote to Hasemann in 1896 from Lake George: "From a photographic standpoint, my '94 trip was very successful. I must return once again to Gutach. We think often about the pleasant time we had there together with you."[101] Lizzie Stieglitz, Leo's wife, wrote to Hasemann in 1899 from Karlsruhe: "Remember me to your dear wife – through Alfred and Emmy's enthusiastic stories, I feel as if I know you all. Most friendly greetings from Lizzie Stieglitz."[102] In the same letter Lizzie refers to gifts Edward has asked her to bring to Hasemann's young children – an elaborate silver place setting for each child – and to Aunt Rosa Werner's death on 11 April 1899.

150 Alfred Stieglitz,
Stuttgart Market, 1894

In Stuttgart, Alfred photographed the open market place, which was typical of many European towns. In these photographs it is the human inclusion that is important. And in one, Stieglitz provides the viewer with a bit of humor – rare for him – photographing the large rear end of a woman bending over to gaze at the market goods.

KATWYK

On that summer journey, Stieglitz and Emmy also visited Antwerp, the Hague, Amsterdam, and Katwyk, a small fishing village on the coast, about an hour from Amsterdam that was another haven for photographers. Stieglitz later wrote to Hasemann: "Here [Katwyk] was a place abundant with all types of things to photograph – perhaps richer in photographic motifs than Gutach, except that there were no mountains. Otherwise everything was there. In spite of the rain and stormy weather, I took many photographs, and will send you some from New York."[103]

He noted in his letter that he would send some photographs of Katwyk to Hasemann from New York.

With its low-slung, white houses stretching along a wide, sandy beach, Katwyk offered open vistas and a hard-working fishing community as subject matter. In an article Stieglitz wrote with Lou Schubart extolling Gutach and Katwyk, he elaborated further upon his response to the coastal beauty of the small fishing village:

> As Gutach lives off its land, Katwyk lives off the ocean fishermen and their boats, and the houses built to resist rude storms, are the themes here on which artists frame their poems and the people are like the phase of nature that surrounds them. Immense in stature, hardy, brave beyond belief, stoical from long habit, seeing brother, father, son, and husband leave on their perilous fishing trips far out in the North Sea, not knowing when or whether at all they will return, welcoming them with a simple handshake, no embrace, no tender kiss for the return-ing hero, for hero he is. The homecoming is saddened by the shadow of the next departure with all its risks and all its uncertainties. The boats which these hardy fishermen use look as if they could weather any storm and outlive any of their masters, yet ten years is considered a long life for them and the beach is strewn with what were but a few years ago staunch vessels, built of hardest oak, and ribbed with knots and sinews of steel.
>
> The way these boats are landed on their return is not the least inter-esting of the many novelties that Katwyk presents to the observer. The strand is constantly patrolled and watchful eyes scan the sea. We observed one man for two long days with spyglass to his eye, stand-ing motionless, trying to pick out on the horizon one particular sail. Who knows what the weary vigil meant to him, but no change of expression told the tale. A sail came in sight, the watcher withdrew to his home – no smile, no expression of relief – that watch was to him, no doubt, one of many. The boats approach; it is high tide; brave men on horseback rush through the surf, far out till only the head of the horse remains out of water. The rider returns with the anchor-rope; he plants the anchor deep in the sand; then strong arms warp the boat as high up on the beach as they can, the tide recedes, and our vessel, with its load of men and fish, lies high and dry. The next tide floats her and she leaves again. So day after day, one unending monotony. The whole village is out of doors to greet the coming fleet, but the men in one group, the women in another – always separate, always serious and silent.

The dunes lie quite high at Katwyk, and from the land side the ocean is not visible. It is on these dunes that the nets are spread to dry, and it is a remarkable sight to see the women outlined against the horizon bending over their work mending the rents. There is one peculiarity about these people that made our work somewhat difficult at first. A superstition exists among them that to have their portraits taken is to sell their souls to the Evil One. A group of women and children seated on the sands gave promise of some fine pictures, but at the first click of the shutter they started to their feet, and with pale and frightened faces left the spot. After that every time they saw us with our cameras they eyed us with suspicion . . . in fact they seem to enjoy posing for the painters who visit Katwyk; and it was only after a friendly artist explained to them that we were not there to make portraits, but to make pictures (even though we used no canvas or colors), that they would allow us to use them in our work. There were, of course, the difficulties which a stranger unacquainted with the language must expect, but these were soon overcome and are not sufficiently impor-tant to be dwelt upon . . . When the photographer has made all the pictures he can and has left his work still uncommenced, for Katwyk is inexhaustible, he has but to travel for fifteen minutes to find the green fields, romantic windmills, and shepherds with their flocks, which serve as inspiration for the grand pastoral pictures of Israels and his followers.[104]

Stieglitz seems to have been inspired by the hearty, seafaring folk of Katwyk, painting verbal pictures of them mending nets. He and Lou seemed to have overcome language barrier and native superstitions about portraiture, demonstrating a willingness to try to understand those they were photographing rather than photographing with a superior or "colo-nial" attitude. Today the spare coastline, sandy dunes, and single church spire remain much as they did in the late nineteenth century.

Stieglitz refers to the painter Jozef Israels, whose pastoral genre scenes and compassionate portraits of Dutch peasants were quite popular in the Netherlands in the nineteenth and early twentieth centuries. Associated with the Hague School of peasant genre painting, Israels was often called the Dutch Millet. Before coming to Katwyk, Stieglitz had probably seen a reproduction of one of Israels' paintings, *The Bashful Suitor*, repro-duced in the September 1891 issue of *Sun and Shade*, which featured photographic reproductions of paintings and photographs. Israels was a Chevalier of the order of Leopold and had been elected to the Legion of

Honor, and was described as "so good, so human, so melancholy, with a bit of sentimentality. He harmonizes colors; it speaks under his brush, the language of suffering things."[105] *The Bashful Suitor* depicted a young boy and girl in traditional dress walking slowly through a field. There is a simplicity and directness in both the content and composition that would have appealed to Stieglitz.

Stieglitz may have met the prolific painter German Grobe, who painted in a somewhat Impressionistic style, with a heavy impasto. Grobe's images included land- and seascapes, with an emphasis on the human presence within the scene. He came to Katwyk almost every summer for fifty years, beginning in 1888 and was there the summer of 1894, when Stieglitz visited, as was the German Impressionist Max Liebermann. Katwyk, like Gutach, was to become a kind of artists' colony by the early twentieth century.

J. M. W. Turner had come to Katwyk in 1817 and created several drawings. Other artists of Stieglitz's era who were inspired by the raw beauty of the coastal town and the sturdy villagers included Jan Toorop, Paul Hermans, and Olof Jernberg as well as a number of Americans: George Henry Boughton, Stephen Salisbury Tuckerman, and Melbourne Hardwick. Like Stieglitz, these painters were captivated by the boats, the shoreline, the long stretch of beach, the rhythms of the sea, and the lives of the fishermen at sea and of those left behind, waiting for the return. A number of the painters favored a soft focus, Impressionist brush strokes, and a palette that reflected the tones of the earth, sea, and sky. The atmospheric effects of the fog, the changing light on the water, and the contours of the boats and beach dunes all contributed to the artists' works.

The subjects of Stieglitz's Katwyk photographs are similar to those of such painters: boats near the shore; the peasant women working, watching, and waiting for the return of the boats; and village scenes. But although he used elements of soft focus in his works, Stieglitz's figures are solitary and well-defined, and are frequently depicted outside in the expanse of the surrounding environment. Many of his Katwyk images stress the horizontal and the vast panorama of the sea and beach.

As well as land- and seascapes, Stieglitz's photographs include close-up portraits of the townspeople, particularly some of the women at work: a woman hanging up laundry, a woman mending nets, a woman sewing, a woman walking through the windy streets with two small children. Stieglitz asserted that his favorite picture was that of *The Net Mender*, showing a woman in profile seated alone and adorned with a

151 Alfred Stieglitz, *The Net Mender*, 1894

traditional white bonnet in the middle of an open field, mending her
husband's nets. Her dark dress and white cap are well integrated into
the landscape. She appears at one with the flat Dutch countryside, which
is met by a vast slightly cloudy sky that serves as a soft-focus frame for
the woman's face and upper body. In addition to the carbon print, *The
Net Mender*, Stieglitz made a smaller platinum print of the same image,
entitled *Mending Nets*, also dating from 1894.

It is a most difficult and unsatisfactory task to single out one of my
pictures as a favorite. But you insist, and so it must be done. Possibly,
if I have any preference, it may be for *Mending Nets*, as it appeals to
me more and more, and time is the true test of merit. Then, too, the
picture brings before my mind's eye the endless poetry of a most picturesque and fascinating lot of people, the Dutch fisher folk. What
artistic temperament does not delight in studying them and portraying them either in art or literature! *Mending Nets* was the result of
much study. It expresses the life of a young Dutch woman: every stitch
in the mending of the fishing net, the very rudiment of her existence,
bring forth a torrent of poetic thoughts in those who watch her sit
there on the vast and seemingly endless dunes, toiling with that

seriousness and peacefulness that is so characteristic of these sturdy people. All her hopes are concentrated in this occupation – it is her life. The picture was taken in 1894 at Katwyk. Taken on an 18-by-24-centimeter plate, with a Zeiss lens. The exhibition prints used are enlarged carbons, as the subject needs size to express it fully.[106]

For Stieglitz this was a song of life; the young woman is firmly rooted into the earth and the sky. She is comfortable in both spheres.

In *Wash Day, Katwyk*, Stieglitz used a white sheet being hung to dry as a frame for a young Dutch women, contrasting with the stripes on her shirt. The vertical stripes are balanced by the horizontal stripes of wood in the background. In *Dutch Study* Stieglitz moved indoors, concentrating on the play of light and shadow on a seated woman in front of a wood wall. The intensity of her expression as she stares at the camera draws the viewer to her visage, wanting to know her life story.

One of Stieglitz's best-known images from Katwyk, widely published and exhibited, was *Scurrying Home*, printed in three different versions from the same negative – in photogravure, platinum, and silver gelatin prints. One photogravure was entitled *The Hour of Prayer* and has some similarities to a Dutch genre painting. Two women with their backs to the viewer, dressed in heavy overcoats with white bonnets and wooden clogs, appear to be making their way against the wind through a muddy field to a church in the distance. The church with its unusual spire looms on the flat horizon. The platinum print, a quarter the size of the photogravure, shows more of the negative: a wall to the left of the church and a tower far away to the right of the women. In this version, the tower and the church frame the women's heads, and they appear more distant from the viewer. A house appears between the two women – a detail that does not appear in the photogravure. The gelatin silver print was made approximately twenty-five years later and includes a manor – a dark form, except for its sunlit roof, that appears on the horizon to the left of the church. In this version the women appear even smaller in the windswept landscape. In one version, entitled *Scurrying Home*, there appears to be a secular destination, although the triangular relationship

152   Katwyk, 2002

153   Alfred Stieglitz, *Scurrying Home*, 1894 (print *c.*1897)

between the women, the church, and the manor house implies the role of both sacred and secular in the lives of these women.

Stieglitz's photographs of the boats, beach, and sea at Katwyk are both explorations of formal, aesthetic elements, particularly triangular relationships, in a composition, and narratives of lives revolving around the sea. He shows the town's women *Watching for the Return*, standing in their clustered black dresses and white bonnets on the shore on a windy, cloudy day. He shows the boats landing, the men and women in separate groups. His frequent emphasis on the horizontal orientation of the image places the viewer at the water's edge, sensing the vastness of the sea stretching into the distance. Sea and sky become closely aligned in the horizontal panorama.

Stieglitz's images of single boats without clusters of townspeople tend to draw the viewer's eye to formal geometric relationships, as seen in *The Incoming Boat*, *Unloading*, and *At Anchor*. In *Unloading*, of which there are two versions, a fishing boat is being unloaded, silhouetted against the sky and water. A slight movement is reflected in the shallow waters. The stark contrast between the boat and the surrounding seascape invites the viewer to focus on the language of forms – positive and negative triangular shapes, for example – in the ship's jib and furled mainsail. There are strong references to a language of pure form, close to music, where form and matter have been closely identified with each other. There is an optical music of triangular shapes in particular, reverberating against each other and across space and time. As Walter Pater wrote in 1873, "It is the art of music which most perfectly realizes this artistic ideal. This perfect identification of matter and form."[107] An image such as this is important for its subject matter. But it is also important for its forms, which have been freed from the material world; form and content are united in a kind of pure perception. In one version of the image a young girl bends over a net at the water's edge, while a single figure standing further out in the water appears to be directing a wagon approaching the fishing boat. In a slightly different version, the human presence is diminished. The young girl and standing solitary figure are gone; a horse-drawn cart is approaching the boat.

Another well-known Katwyk image depicts the prow of a boat at anchor, its boom, lower sail, and rigging forming varied triangles. The prow of the boat points toward two women talking nearby at the water's edge. Entitled, *Gossip, Katwyk*, the photograph focuses on narrative and formal elements. The women stand firm, their hands on their hips, forming small triangles that balance the ship's forms and one of the

154   Alfred Stieglitz, *At Anchor, Katwyk*, 1894 (print 1920s or 1930s)

155   Alfred Stieglitz, *Gossip, Katwyk*, 1894

women looks toward the ship. The strong horizontal elements of the beach, water, and sky, serve as a well-integrated backdrop for the women and ship. The small lantern on the boat seems to light the image symbolically. Joseph Keiley, Stieglitz's friend and fellow photographer, was to write in 1899 about this piece:

> Attention is called to the almost perfect composition of this picture. It presents two Katwyk women, who have stopped in their stroll along the beach, have fallen into the natural attitude of their class and stood a while gossiping, catching upon their shoulders the weak, waning light of the setting sun, their united forms casting a long, faint shadow upon the sand. The figures tone in wonderfully with the splendid background of sea and sky, and bring sea, sky, and sand together into a perfect picture, whose horizontal and perpendicular lines are relieved and balanced by the curved and angular one of the sail, tackle, hull, and boom.[108]

Despite Keiley's somewhat patronizing comments about the women and their class, he well describes much of Stieglitz's artistry in this spare but elegant composition.

Stieglitz continued his exploration of sky and water, moving inland and photographing *A Dutch Waterway*, also titled *On the Dykes*. On a quiet waterway contained by long grasses on either side, a small single-sail boat travels down wind. There is a gentility and peacefulness to the image in contrast to the images of the open seas. The man in the boat seems at one with his environment. It is interesting to note that Hasemann, although not in Katwyk, made a few sketches of boats with similar compositions to some of Stieglitz's photographs, such as *Lastkahn auf der Elbe*, where the triangular forms of the boat's rigging are significant elements of the drawing.

156 Alfred Stieglitz, *On the Dykes*, 1894

Leaving Katwyk, Alfred and Emmy traveled to the Hague and Amsterdam, where Stieglitz saw some works by Rembrandt, which he described as having impressed him greatly and as being "fantastic." In a letter sent to Hasemann from London before he left for New York City at the end of the summer, Stieglitz wrote: "From Antwerp, we

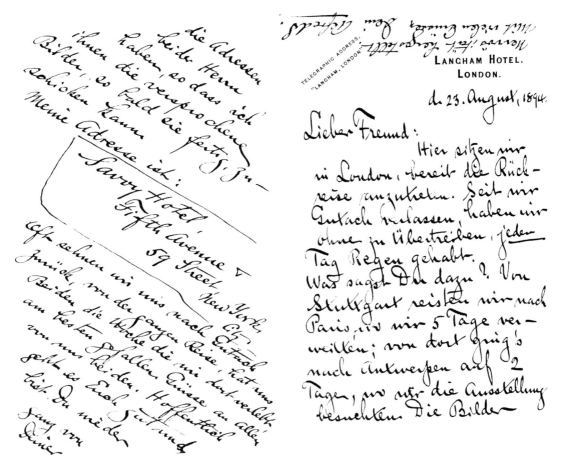

157   Part of a letter from Alfred Stieglitz to Wilhelm Hasemann, 23 August 1894

traveled to the Hague. The Rembrandts were impressive and colorful. We didn't really know Rembrandt's work before seeing it in Holland. From New York, I have just received news that the cards sent from Reiss and Liebich brought much joy to my family."[109]

The photograhs Stieglitz took on that 1894 summer trip were to remain important to him, and he returned to a number of them some twenty years later to reprint them in gelatin silver, sometimes retaining the same image, sometimes altering it. The photographs show his continuing interest in exploring a formal interpretation of the image. That formal interest became most clear in the Katwyk photographs. The summer trip also spawned Stieglitz's first successful rainy-day photographs.

THE CAMERA CLUB AND *CAMERA NOTES*

Soon after returning to New York in the middle of September 1894, Stieglitz was unanimously elected to the Linked Ring membership, along with Rudolph Eickemeyer. They were the first American photographers to be so honored. His summer visit to London had helped secure the election, and Stieglitz saw this as a stepping stone to help him further the cause of photography in the United States.

At this time there were two photograhic clubs in New York: the Society of Amateur Photographers on 38th Street (incorporated 1884) and the New York Camera Club on Fifth Avenue, (incorporated about 1889). The critic Sadakichi Hartmann noted, "I found both societies as good as dead. There was no vitality in them. Photography was merely a pastime to them, and all they had to show were innumerable portraits, transcripts of nature, views, and snapshots such as is in the power of almost anyone to produce. Of course there were some men with higher aims . . . Also the financial condition of the two clubs . . . was none of the best."[110] In 1896, Stieglitz pushed for the amalgamation of the two groups to become the Camera Club of New York. He accepted the vice-presidency of the organization, although he was offered the presidency. He also became chairman of the publications committee and obtained a seat on the exhibitions and lantern slide committees.

The lantern slide had been particularly useful in enabling group show-ings of members' and other amateurs' work. As a result of the Society of Amateur Photographers' efforts to attract critical reviews of members' works and to see what similar groups in other parts of the country were doing an organization called the American Lantern Slide Exchange had emerged. The lantern slide, originally an image painted on glass, had become popular in the mid-nineteenth century with the slide projector popularly called a magic lantern. In the 1850s, such images became pho-tographic with the use of albumen or collodion coating on one side. The coated side was then protected with a second piece of glass of the same size (usually about $3^1/_4 \times 3^1/_4$ inches) taped to the first piece. From a social perspective, the medium of the lantern slide allowed photogra-phers to come together and critique each others' work. Such showings had on element of performance and theatricality. Stieglitz, with his love of theater and his impresario qualities, would have thoroughly enjoyed such events, particularly those he orchestrated. He became a master of the early lantern slide. Many of his most famous early views, such as *Winter, Fifth Avenue* and *Icy Night*, were first displayed in lantern-slide format at the Camera Club. He also wrote an extensive article, "Lantern Slide Compensating Cover Glasses," in the *American Amateur Photographer* in February 1899.

In April of 1897 Stieglitz proposed to expand the official organ of the club to a larger publication for subscription to the public. Each member would get a free subscription. *Camera Notes*, with its high-quality layout and graphic design and Stieglitz as editor, premiered in July 1897 and was immediately successful. (In 1896, Stieglitz had resigned from the *American Amateur Photographer* because of a dispute over copyright issues.) Of particular note were the magnificent photogravures that filled each issue of *Camera Notes*, which had a print run of approximately one thousand copies.

Theodore Dreiser, the Mid-western journalist and novelist, wrote of the Camera Club, "The spirit of the Camera Club is compounded of a warm enthusiasm for the beauty and the sentiment of the world. And in accordance with the very strength of this feeling it has become a beneficent influence among those who love beauty in photography. Not strange, then, that it is dominated by men of more or less poetic inspiration."[111]

Much of Dreiser's article is illustrated by Stieglitz's photographs, and the writer gives high praise to Stieglitz's untiring labors and exemplary work:

> Stieglitz is not only vice-president of the club, but the founder and editor of its distinguished organ ... He spends the major portion of every day in the rooms of the club. His influence on development is not so much understood as felt. No man has done subjects more widely apart in conception and feeling and none has done better. He has no speciality and apparently no limitation ... His attitude toward the club has come to be the club's attitude toward the world. He openly avows that he has planned to accomplish three things: first, to elevate the standard of Pictorial photography in this country; second, to establish an annual national exhibition, giving no awards, but whose certificate of admission should be prizeworthy above all medals; and third, to establish a national academy of photography.[112]

Stieglitz had a magnetism that attracted such other photographers as Clarence White, Gertrude Käsebier, Joseph Keiley, and Frank Eugene. With these colleagues he was to form a power base within the club. Those members who did not subscribe to Stieglitz's ideas or brand of Pictorialism were at times indignant and Stieglitz was expelled from the club in 1908 – the same year that Paul Strand joined at the age of seventeen. But in those intervening years, Stieglitz gathered around him and encouraged some of the most creative photographers in the United States, helping to organize exhibitions, writing letters and articles, and publishing *Camera Notes*.

Each issue of *Camera Notes* was an art object itself, with its finely printed photogravures, well-designed layout and range of articles and text. The first issue in July 1897 announced its mission:

> With this number the *Journal of the Camera Club* takes unto itself a new name, a new dress and a different scheme of publication. It has been deemed advisable to enlarge the scope of the official organ of the club in several ways. First, as to regularity of issue. It has been hitherto a kind of comet, flashing occasionally into view at unexpected intervals, but will now become an orderly planet making complete revolutions four times a year. Secondly, to make it more acceptable to our members, possibly to reach a class outside the membership, and to stimulate them to artistic effort, it is proposed to publish with each number two photogravures representing some important achievement in Pictorial photography; not necessarily the work of home talent, but chosen from the best material the world affords.
>
> In addition to this feature, articles of interest, illustrated by halftone prints, will from time to time appear. In the case of the photogravures the utmost care will be exercised to publish nothing but what is the development of an organic idea, the evolution of an inward principle; a picture rather than a photograph, though photography must by the method of graphic representation. Thirdly, while *Camera Notes* will continue the work of the former journal of recording the proceedings of the Camera Club in the most faithful way, it is intended to take cognizance also of what is going on in the photographic world at large, to review new processes and consider new instruments and agents as they come into notice; in short, to keep our members in touch with everything connected with the progress and elevation of photography.[113]

The magazine, measuring about $10^3/_4$ by $7^1/_2$ inches, had a green cover with an Art Nouveau sunflower design in black. Within the text was printed on heavy-stock glossy paper in a standard typeface with halftone illustrations, not necessarily related to the articles. But it was the meticulously printed photogravures and theoretical articles that distinguished the magazine. As the writer Christian Peterson stated in 1993:

The imagery of *Camera Notes* typified the emerging aesthetic of American Pictorial photography, which was characterized by accessible subject matter, soft-focus effects, and simplified composition. Pictorialists used a relatively limited number of subjects, easily identifiable by the general public. Avoiding anything that was topical, political, or controversial, they concentrated on figure studies, landscapes, and genre scenes. In their interest in distinguishing their images from ordinary photographs, Pictorialists purged their pictures of all detail and extraneous elements. By simplifying the scene and softening the focus, they produced evocative and mysterious – hence artistic – images.[114]

Thus *Camera Notes* came to include such photographs as F. Holland Day's *Ebony and Ivory* (July 1898) and *An Ethiopian Chief* (October 1897); Charles Berg's *Magdalen* (January 1899) and *Odalisque* (January 1900); Ernest Ashton's *Evening Near the Pyramids* (October 1898) and *A Cairene Café* (April 1901); Robert Demachy's *Raven* (January 1898) and *Study in Red* (July 1898); Rudolph Eickemeyer's *The Dance* (October 1900) and *Vesper Bells* (January 1898); Gertrude Käsebier's *The Manger* (July 1900) and *Blessed Art Thou Among Women* (July 1900); Clarence White's *Spring* (October 1899) and *Telephone Poles* (April 1901); Frank Eugene's *Portrait of Alfred Stieglitz* (January 1901) and *La Cigale* (April 1900); Edwards Steichen's *Landscape* (January 1901); and Stieglitz's own work. During the years of *Camera Notes'* publication, from 1897 to 1903, Stieglitz published twenty-two of his own images, two of which appeared twice. He included both his American and European photographs, as well as some experiments based on work with Joseph Keiley. In the April 1900 issue, an experimental process, an "Improved Glycerine Process for the Development of Platinum Prints," is described, followed by illustrations showing step-by-step examples of Stieglitz deleting details and background from the image of a seated woman to arrive at a final *Vignette in Platinum* in two colors, showing only a close-up of a three-quarter view of the back of the woman's head, a slight profile, and shoulders. A few tendrils of her upswept hair fall spontaneously on her neck. This example is followed by a second, *Experiment in Mercury and Oxalite*, showing a lovely young woman in profile, with a pearl necklace and white-collared V-necked dress, her romantic pose rendered in shades of black, gray, and purple that suggest painterly tones.

In addition to *Camera Notes*, Stieglitz published a number of the photographers' images in a special green-bound album with the gold Camera

Club insignia on the front in a limited edition of 150 copies. Entitled
American Pictorial Photography, the album was published for *Camera
Notes* and printed by the Photochrome Engraving Company.

Stieglitz also had a portfolio of his own work – twelve photogravures
on paper in a fairly large format of 14 × 27 inches and titled *Picturesque
Bits of New York and Other Studies* – published by the Russell Company,
with a foreword by the photographer Walter Woodbury. The images
were beautifully presented, toned in blue, green, sepia, and so on. The
portfolio included European and American images, such as *A Venetian
Canal*, *Scurrying Home*, and *Spring Showers*, *The Sweeper*. Stieglitz
made his own transparencies for the photogravure plates and oversaw
the entire printing process. These large photogravures in portfolio presentation helped establish the role of the photograph as an independent
work of art. This project was thus particularly important to Stieglitz. He
gave a copy of the portfolio to the Camera Club library, to which he also
gave numerous technical and fine art books. The volume was favorably
reviewed in *Camera Notes* in the January 1898 issue.

As editor of *Camera Notes*, Stieglitz allowed some of the text of the
magazine to articulate ideas contrary to his, but in general his opinions
dominated the editorial direction of the visual and verbal inclusions in
Camera Notes. The following quote from an 1898 issue, illustrates the
strength of opposing views:

> A growing and very dangerous tarantism has innoculated the club, and
> it appears that nothing is artistic that is not *outré*, nothing beautiful
> that is not "bizarre" . . . This fad for muddy, fogged, bombastic, indis-
> tinguishable, unguessable monstrosities will soon pass away, and we
> will recognize that a photograph to be artistic need not be hideous.
> But in the meantime cannot the editors of *Camera Notes* preserve us
> from them? Their production may be glossed over as mere senile ine-
> briety, but their reproduction is a heinous crime.[115]

That Stieglitz's strong positions provoked strong opposition is perhaps
not surprising. There was frequently little space for a middle-ground
response to Stieglitz's positions.

Besides compelling visual reproductions, *Camera Notes* provided a
record for and reviews of the events and exhibitions sponsored by the
Camera Club as well as other exhibitions of Pictorial photography. A
significant series of exhibitions reviewed in *Camera Notes* consisted of
four Philadelphia Photographic Salons held at the Pennsylvania Academy
of Fine Arts from 1899 to 1902. Unlike the Camera Club shows, which

focused on members' works, the juried Philadelphia salons included what was considered the best artistic photography from throughout the country. The extensive critiques in *Camera Notes* about the Philadelphia salons were written by Joseph Keiley.[116] In the January 1899 issue, he discussed ten Stieglitz works in the Salon:

The maker of these pictures had the artist's keen human sympathy and a correct appreciation and love of what is interesting and beautiful in nature; such qualities as enable Balzac and Stevenson to get so near to the heart of humanity and to thrill with immortal life the pages of their books; such qualities as enabled Frans Hals and Jules Breton to preserve for all times the Dutch burgomasters and the Breton peasants. The quick sympathy and keen eye of the artist has felt the full human charm of such scenes as *Scurrying Home* and *Gossip*, and has caught in an instant what it would have taken the painter hours, if not days, to obtain; and yet, technically, as to composition and the like, these pictures are almost faultless. On the other hand he has appreciated the local feeling and artistic possibilities of such subjects as *Winter*, *Fifth Avenue*, and *Reflections*, *Night*, and that too, when such things were held to be photographically impossible; and after patiently waiting and watching for the right moment has caught on his plate the conception of his brain. Today, when night pictures are more or less common, one remembers the great surprise and interest excited by Alfred Stieglitz's night picture exhibited in the London Salon of 1895. It was, as nearly as I have been able to ascertain, the first night picture taken or exhibited, and one of the most picturesque ... *Mending Nets*, which to me is one of the greatest of Mr. Stieglitz's pictures, should have been differently framed and printed to have enabled the casual observer to appreciate its real values. Indeed, several other pictures of his should have been shown. No one realizes this more thoroughly than does Mr. Stieglitz himself, but his services to photography in another line, services for which every lover of the art owes him a profound debt, have prevented his enjoying the luxury of giving the time to his own photographic work that would be necessary for the proper interpretation of his negatives. None of his friends but regrets that he is not doing more work with his camera and plates; and none but appreciates the extent of the sacrifice that he makes in not doing so. He is the exponent of realism in photography.[117]

30. **Summer, An Impression**, P.D. 1894
   London Salon, 1895

31. **Watching for the Return**, Ph. 1894
   London Salon, 1896

32. **At Lake Como**, P.D. 1887–1899
   Gold Medal, Buda-Pesth, 1889

33. **On the Dykes**, Ph. 1894
   London Salon, 1895

34. **Maria, The Fruit Girl**, P.D. 1887
   Silver Medal, London, 1888

35. **A Portrait**, P.D. 1885
   This platinum print was made by Mr. Stieglitz in 1885, and was one of the very first made in Germany.
   Silver Medal, Joint Exhibition, New York, 1891
   Bronze Medal, England, 1891

36. **An Icy Night**, C.E. 1898

37. **Mending Nets**, C.E. 1894–1899
   This picture, says Robert Demachy, in his review of the Paris Salon, 1898, is of a rare poetry, the effect of atmosphere being wonderfully rendered. Attention must be called to the truthfulness of the white note of the bonnet against the sky, for we have often found occasion to criticise the falseness of the relation between the tone of the sky and the whites of linens or of walls in photography.
   London Salon, 1897
   Silver Medal, England, 1894

38. **Winter, Fifth Avenue**, C.E. 1893–1899
   Considered the first successful attempt at pictorial winter street photography.
   Of this picture the art critic, Hartman, has observed: "It is a realistic expression of an everyday occurrence of metropolitan life under special atmospheric conditions, rendered faithfully, and yet with consummate art."
   Silver Medal, New York, 1894
   Silver Medal, Vienna, 1896

39. **Gossip, Katwyk**, C.E. 1894–1899
   Attention is called to the almost perfect composition of this picture. It presents two Katwyk women, who having stopped in their stroll along the beach, had fallen into the natural attitude of their class and stood a while gossiping, catching upon their shoulders the weak, waning light of the setting sun, their united forms casting a long, faint shadow upon the sand. The figures tone in wonderfully with the splendid background of sea and sky, and bring sea, sky and sand together into a perfect picture, whose horizontal and perpendicular lines are relieved and balanced by the curved and angular ones of the sail, tackle, hull and boom.
   Silver Medal, New York, 1898
   London Salon, 1896

40. **A Decorative Panel**, C.E. 1894–1895
   "Royal" Medal, London, 1896

41. **Gossip, Venice**, C.E. 1894–1899

42. **Gossip, Venice**, BI.G. 1894–1898
   The same subject as No. 41, but printed in 1898, in bichromate of gum.
   London Salon, 1898

158   Pages from the catalogue of the Camera Club exhibition of Stieglitz's photographs, 1899

In 1899, Stieglitz also exhibited eighty-two of his works at the Camera Club, from 1 to 15 May. Joseph Keiley wrote a brief introduction and catalogue entries for the exhibition, carefully noting the medals won by individual pieces at international exhibitions, along with formal descriptions of selected works. *Gossip, Katwyk* appeared on the cover.[118]

While Stieglitz's work contained more elements of realism than that of some of the photographers included in the issues, there was also a consistent emphasis on subjectivity, individual intuition, and expression in his work. The emphasis on intuition no doubt had some connection with the work of French philosopher Henri Bergson, who saw the world as a process of creative evolution that can be viewed in two different modes – intellectually and intuitively – as described in his book, *Creative Evolution*. For Bergson, the intellectual mode dealt with the rational, ordered, and external objects of life. Intuition dealt with the inner core of life – the spirit, the irrational. Through intuition it was possible to

transcend the facts and events of everyday life. Dallett Fuguet, photographer, writer, and editorial associate for *Camera Notes*, wrote in the
January 1902 issue, "To know how to bring out our negative is science;
to know how to bring out your self is Art. Develop and develop and
develop – yourself."[119]

Not all articles in *Camera Notes* related to photography. Indeed,
Stieglitz, feeling photographers should study the other arts and aesthe-
tics, included articles on Impressionism, Symbolism, genre painting, and
portraiture. William Murray was probably the editorial associate who
contributed most to *Camera Notes*. After Murray left the journal,
Stieglitz relied more on critics from outside the Camera Club, such as
Charles Caffin, Sadakichi Hartmann, and the artist–teacher Arthur
Wesley Dow.

Dow's emphasis on harmonious design and beauty, as found in
Japanese decorative and spatial principles, was to find resonance in the
work of both Stieglitz and Georgia O'Keeffe, who studied with Dow at
Columbia Teachers' College, where Dow taught from 1903. The reserved
native New Englander studied with Gauguin in Brittany, and was curator
of Japanese art at the Museum of Fine Arts in Boston. (In 1924, the
Boston museum, then one of the most conservative in the country, took
on a collection of twenty-seven Stieglitz photographs, thereby helping to
advance the recognition of photography as an art form.)

Dow's well-known book of 1899, *Composition*, proposed a more decorative and abstract approach, more open to interpretation, than the
strict academic exercises normally used in teaching drawing and painting. His approach emphasized structure rather than imitation. He felt
that music was a key to the other arts, and that the spatial arts might
be called visual music. Dow's notion of filling space in a beautiful way
inspired many of his students and readers. In his writings, he quoted
Hegel, saying, "Wood, stone, metal, canvas, even words are in themselves dead stuff. What art creates upon this dead stuff belongs to the
domain of the spirit and is living as the spirit is living."[120]

Stieglitz's last issue of *Camera Notes*, in July 1902, contained a vale-
dictory statement signed by him and his four editorial associates:

Recent events within the Camera Club of New York have made it
incompatible with the ideas and principles for which we have striven,
that we should continue to conduct this magazine. The official policy
of the club, as indicated by the deliberate nominations of a new Board
of Officers avowedly out of sympathy with the policy so long main-

tained by *Camera Notes*, makes it incumbent on the Editor and his associates, in justice to the desires of the club as expressed by the nature of its nominees, to leave the new management with a free hand to inaugurate and shape its own policy, unhampered by the convictions to which we are so uncompromisingly pledged.[121]

Juan Abel, the Camera Club's librarian and one of Stieglitz's editorial assistants, was appointed editor in May 1902. Although Abel respected Stieglitz, he chose to turn to a more conservative graphic design for the journal, based on principles of the Arts and Crafts Movement, and to a more moderate content. His tenure was short-lived; his last issue was December 1903. It featured a photograph of Abel's *Early Morning in the Catskills*, showing the mountains cloaked in clouds and a rising fog, which bears some resemblance to Stieglitz's much later sequence, *Music – A Sequence of Ten Cloud Photographs*, the first of which appeared in 1922. Stieglitz certainly would have seen Abel's image, although Abel's piece depends more on atmospheric effects than the subtle forms suggesting musicality in Stieglitz's piece.

Christian Peterson has noted that in Stieglitz's five years as editor of *Camera Notes*:

> There was no question as to the magazine's first-place position among American photographic periodicals. It included the most insightful articles and the best photographic illustrations available from throughout the world. Its outstanding photogravures, taken as a set, embody this country's first cohesive argument for photography as a fine art . . . The journal, in fact, stands as a monument to an idealized attempt at introducing strict aesthetic standards to a mass audience. Such a union will never be achieved, but in *Camera Notes*, it was given its best photographic incarnation.[122]

As Joseph Keiley noted, Stieglitz's own photographic work of the 1890s and early 1900s was hindered somewhat by the amount of time he devoted to writing and being an editor. However, he did produce some significant images during the 1890s in the United States. A number of portraits presented classical frontal studies in character and detail: for example, that of his father (1894); Moses Ezekiel, (1894) an American-born sculptor who had studied in Berlin and lived with the Stieglitz family in New York City and Lake George; and Mr. Randolph (1895), a New York bookseller who also had a summer home in Lake George. Stieglitz's ability to capture facial details, strands of hair, and wrinkles as the light falls on his subjects' faces, set against dark backgrounds, gives the viewer a sense of direct contact with the subject: their eyes meet the viewer's. These portraits were well published and exhibited.

In January 1895, Stieglitz had a serious case of pneumonia and spent some time in Rockledge, Florida, where he captured the tropical foliage in distant and close-cropped views. More casual family photographs were also taken at Lake George in 1895. In one, Emmy poses alone, walking into the woods, her head turned in profile to catch Stieglitz's and the viewer's eye. It is a photograph that is well composed and executed, with the smooth texture and light shadows on Emmy's dress serving as contrast to the dark foliage behind and leaf-strewn ground. But it lacks the intensity that many of Stieglitz's portraits contained.

159   Alfred Stieglitz, *Emmy at Lake George*, 1895

160   Alfred Stieglitz, *September*, c.1897

In a piece entitled *September*, probably taken in 1897, Stieglitz experiments with painterly, pictorial means. There is no human presence here. Rather the haystacks and trees loom as singular figures in a stark but muted landscape. Although there are details in the grass, Stieglitz has eliminated extraneous details that would take away from the dominant vertical forms. The vertical emphasis in this and other works recalls chordal emphasis in composers such as Wagner and Beethoven

Perhaps the most significant images from the late 1890s are Stieglitz's night photographs, some of which appeared in *Camera Notes*, where he captured the glow of city lights reflected on wet pavement or freshly fallen snow. In 1897 and

161   Alfred Stieglitz, *Reflections: Night, New York*, 1897

1898, he produced a number of images, some printed later in the 1920s and 1930s. Some of his most striking night scenes were shot from Grand Army Plaza at Fifth Avenue and 59th Street, looking east across the wet pavement to the Savoy Hotel, where he and Emmy had been living since their marriage. His 1897 photograph *Savoy Hotel, New York* is a nocturnal study of the interplay of light, shadow, and reflection. It is both cityscape and landscape, the strong silhouette of a lone tree dominating the image.

Although Stieglitz preferred to reproduce his night scenes as lantern slides, feeling the luminosity was better presented in this medium, he did make some prints in 1897, and again in the 1920s and 1930s. His platinum prints were tinted with yellow dye, which adds a melancholy air to the image. Paul Martin had worked on night photography in Lon-don before much of Stieglitz's work was done, but Stieglitz later claimed that he had been the first to experiment successfully with the genre. In the *American Annual of Photography and Photographic Times Almanac* for 1898, he wrote an article discussing the introduction of life into nocturnal scenes: "We believe that this branch of photography [night photography] opens up certain possibilities that have not as yet been attempted. We refer to the introduction of life into these scenes. The illustrations to this article are the first experiments made by the author in this time, and he is fully convinced that they are but the first steps to a most interesting field of work."[123] By reducing the exposure time to less than a minute rather than a half-hour, Stieglitz was able to capture a human presence in some of his night images. In the Savoy Hotel image he has included a driver atop a horse-driven carriage in front of the hotel.

In *Icy Night* (1898), forked trees lining a snow-covered street become almost human, their limbs stretching upward, to frame a solitary tree in the distance. Here nature is almost more predominant than elements of the city: the city lights serve to illuminate natural structures. In several versions of an image entitled *A Foggy Night, New York* (1898), Stieglitz used tall, black forms of forked trees to contrast with the fog, the dim silhouettes of horses and carriages, and the faint glow of the city's lights. His focus on the verticality of the trees suggests a city that still has some reverence for nature.

162   Alfred Stieglitz, *Icy Night*, 1898

Stieglitz's nocturnal scenes are in many ways like musical nocturnes, a genre particularly popular with Romantic composers such as Chopin, whose highly expressive themes evolved a dreamy Romantic atmosphere.

KITTY AND EMMELINE

The same year that Stieglitz was experimenting with night photography, he also celebrated the birth of his first and only child. Katherine "Kitty" Stieglitz was born on 27 September 1898, shortly after the couple had moved to a new apartment at 1111 Madison Avenue between 83rd and 84th streets. With the assistance of Emmy's family money, the couple was able to afford a cook, a chambermaid, and a governess. Stieglitz had feared having children, knowing that Emmy's mother had suffered from melancholia or post-partum depression after Emmy's birth. (Stieglitz did not know that this condition can skip a generation, and that his own daughter, following the birth of her son in 1923, would suffer sever post-partum depression, from which she never recovered, and would be institutionalized until her death in 1971.) Although Alfred was no model father, he was at least initially devoted to his daughter and photographed her frequently, both alone and with her mother. Emmy was a nervous mother and wanted to conform to the conventions of the day, while

163 and 164 (*above and facing page*) Alfred Stieglitz, prints from Photographic Journal of a Baby, 1900

From the Photographic
Journal of a Baby
1902

Alfred Smith

165   Alfred Stieglitz, *Baby being fed by Emmy*, 1899

166   Alfred Stieglitz,
Katherine, Lake George,
1899

Alfred wanted to make a photographic record of his baby's growth and development. Emmy discouraged him, often asking him to leave the baby alone.

Alfred was most interested in the concept of a cumulative portrait and composite record. Despite Emmy's protests, Stieglitz continued to photograph his daughter, sometimes obsessively, waiting for the "right" gesture or expression he wished to capture. He photographed Kitty intermittently until about 1902 and then more irregularly into Kitty's teen years. Once she went to Smith College, from in Massachusetts where she graduated in 1921 before marrying Milton Stearns in 1922, there is little photographic record of her by Stieglitz. But the photographs that Stieglitz did take over a period of years, when viewed together, are more than just the snapshots that many parents take of their children, particularly their first-born. With his ability to focus intensely and intently on his subjects, Stieglitz provides a rich record of his daughter's growing up. Many of the images are close-up, direct, sometimes soft focused. They allow the viewer to enter Kitty's world and to share in her experience – watching ducks feed, holding a butterfly net, smelling flowers on a spring

167 (*above left*) Alfred Stieglitz, *Kitty with Mother*, 1902

168 (*above right*) Alfred Stieglitz, *Kitty Stieglitz holding a Book*, 1904

169 (*right*) Alfred Stieglitz, *Family at the Beach*, 1900

171 Alfred Stieglitz, *Spring*, 1901

170 *(left)* Alfred Stieglitz, *Steichen and Kitty*, n.d.

172 (*top left*) Alfred Stieglitz, *Kitty and Emmeline*, c.1905–6

173 (*top right*) Alfred Stieglitz, *The Swimming Lesson*, 1906

174 (*above left*) Alfred Stieglitz, *Kitty holding a Plant*, n.d.

175 (*above center*) Alfred Stieglitz, *Kitty*, 1908

176 (*above right*) Alfred Stieglitz, *Katherine Stieglitz*, 1910

177 (*above*) Alfred Stieglitz, *Katherine Stieglitz*, 1910

178 (*above*) Alfred Stieglitz, *Kitty in Profile*, 1912

179   Alfred Stieglitz, *Kitty Stieglitz*, 1907

day, having a swimming lesson – conveying something of the wonder and delight of a small child.

Less cheerful is a 1905 portrait of her that was reproduced in *Camera Work*, where Kitty stands before a nursery-rhyme figure who holds a knife, from *Three Blind Mice*, whose tails were cut off with a carving knife. Dressed in a lovely white dress, embroidered at the neck and sleeves, and holding a book, Kitty is a picture of innocence and unknowing in front of the violent image. Her father suggests a sense of foreboding for what may come in the future for his child. The Mother Goose figure could also be read as part of a child's integrating fairy-tale and nursery-rhyme violence into an interior mindscape to be dealt with like many childhood fears.

180   Alfred Stieglitz, *Katherine*, 1905

Particularly beautiful are the autochromes Stieglitz took of his daughter. He began to experiment with this procedure of producing color images with Edward Steichen and Frank Eugene in 1907. The subtly colored images frequently show Kitty with her long wavy hair, often tied with a large ribbon, well dressed and holding flowers, leaves, or a plant. Stieglitz's association of his daughter with blooming plant forms suggests the traditional analogy between the female and the life cycles of nature.

Stieglitz's photographs of Kitty were widely published and exhibited and praised by critics such as Charles Caffin for their originality of concept. Caffin, in his 1901 book *Photography as a Fine Art*, included a number of photographs of Kitty alone and Kitty with Emmy, along with other Stieglitz photographs such as his Katwyk *At Anchor*, *An Icy Night*, or *The Net Mender*, in a chapter entitled "Alfred Stieglitz and His Work." Caffin notes at the end of the chapter:

He [Stieglitz] excels in studies of human subjects, and in his best examples attains a realism that is no bare record of facts, but the realization of a vivid mental conception. When he sets his figures in a scene, they become part of it and one with it in spirit. He puts them there because he has seen that they belong to it. His sentiment, never degenerating into sentimentality, is always wholesome and sincere, and his pictures have the added charm of handsome arrangement and of simple and controlled impressiveness. In his hands, the "straight photograph" in the broadest sense of the term, is triumphantly vindicated.[124]

That Caffin and Stieglitz chose to publish images from the "Photographic Journal of a Baby," as part of a book advocating photography as a fine art, suggests that these photographs had more importance than might be expected. In 1900, the "Photographic Journal of a Baby," was exhibited as a series in London.

Stieglitz's photographs of his daughter may also be viewed in the context of other photographs of children at the time. In the early part of the twentieth century, a number of Pictorial photographers such as F. Holland Day, Clarence White, Gertrude Käsebier, and Edward Steichen, chose children as a subject, quite often their own or their friends' children. As the art historian George Dimock has noted, these children, for the most part

> were portrayed as beautiful, well dressed, secure, happy and beloved. They also embodied a romantic ideal of childhood in keeping with Pictorialism's ambitions to achieve the spiritual in art . . . The Pictorialist child embodied the defining characteristics of the "priceless child" in whose name the Progressive reform movement fought to abolish child labor. In Pictorialist iconography, children remained, for the most part, safely ensconced within the sumptuous, if often darkened interior of the bourgeois home. When they ventured outdoors, it was invariably to bucolic nature or to a carefully tended garden. Their principal activities consisted of posing with their mothers, reading or just holding a book, and playing children's games. They came before the camera as deeply treasured, carefully nurtured members of an intact nuclear family . . . The adults who attended them were invariably benevolent and attractive.[125]

Kitty and Emmy were not only subjects for Alfred; they were also photographed together by Gertrude Käsebier and Clarence White. Indeed, Emmy appears at her loveliest with her baby Kitty in her arms in the intimate embrace of mother and child captured by Gertrude Käsebier. Steichen made a number of photographs of Kitty and her father about 1904–5, as well as one of Emmy and Kitty in 1904. Stieglitz photographed other children besides Kitty, including a tender embrace

181   Alfred Stieglitz, *Lou Schramm and Daughter*, ?1890–94

182   Alfred Stieglitz, *Untitled (Georgia E. with Teddy Bear)*, ?1916

between his friend Lou Schramm and daughter and a number of charming autochromes of his niece, Georgia Engelhard from 1912 to 1913. The golden-haired six-year-old is photographed outdoors with flowers or her dolls. In several of the color images, a red shawl – the red of passion – is contrasted to the delicate skin tones of the little girl.

A counterpoint to the Pictorialist depiction of "priceless children" were the photographs taken by Jacob Riis and Lewis Hine, who sought to expose slum conditions in New York and exploitation of children in the workforce in the early twentieth century. Hine's children are depicted in factories, on the street, dirty, in ragged clothes. He was a pioneer in documentary photography, his photographs representing social work where these of the Pictorialists represented camera work.[126] Hine emphasized social responsibility while Stieglitz emphasized individual freedom. But the Pictorialists' children were widely published and reproduced. Like some of Norman Rockwell's paintings of nostalgic family scenes in the 1950s, these children were in many ways ideals and perhaps represented the "way we never were."

Stieglitz's concept of a multifaceted portrait such as that of Kitty was significant, and may well have had some of its roots in the newly evolving cinematic medium, which allowed subjects to be seen more easily over time in moving pictures. Stieglitz was to comment a number of years later: "To demand the portrait that will be a complete portrait of any person is as futile as to demand that a motion picture be condensed into a single still."[127]

183   Kitty Stieglitz, *StillLife*, n.d.

Kitty was in many way as conventional as her mother, although she showed artistic leanings, making drawings and paintings as a young child and receiving some art instruction from Max Weber, an artist befriended by Stieglitz. Kitty's still-life paintings combine Cézanne-like geometric forms with a refreshing Matisse-like sensibility with vibrant colors. Weber praised her work, and Stieglitz actually showed some of them at his 291 gallery along with other children's works. But Kitty was to major in chemistry at Smith College, taking a general art history class in her senior year. She did take a few courses at Columbia in studio art following her graduation *cum laude* in 1921.

Growing up at 1111 Madison Avenue, Kitty was surrounded by a variety of visual images. Among the pictures in her family living room were reproductions of two recent paintings by Franz von Stuck, a founder of the Munich Secession: *Die Sünde* (*Sin*) (1893), depicting a femme fatale with a piercing gaze and serpent around her bare shoulders, which provoked much discussion in turn-of-the-century Munich; and *The Kiss of the Sphinx* (1895), which shows a full-breasted creature digging her bloody claws into the back of a kneeling naked man whom she is embracing. There was also a version of Arnold Böcklin's *Island of the Dead* (1880), in which a coffin accompanied by a ghostly figure is brought by boat to the island of the dead, with vaulted cliffs and looming cypress trees. Each of these paintings has erotic and Symbolist dream-like qualities, suggesting a concern for exploring subjective experience as distinct from contemporary reality. Böcklin seemed to bestride the antique and modern worlds, using classical figures but evoking a surreal subjectivity that was subtly anxiety provoking. These somewhat dark, somber images must have been intimidating for a little girl, and even for her mother, Emmy, who probably barely tolerated the works. Also in the apartment was a reproduction of a portrait of the actress Eleonora Duse by Franz von Lenbach, showing the actress holding the artist's child. In the bedroom was a reproduction of Rubens' painting of his wife, Helena Fourment, in a fur robe, which Stieglitz had seen in Vienna in 1882; that same reproduction was also in his East 60th Street room.

In contrast to such images were Stieglitz's own photographs, in particular *The Net Mender*, printed and framed in a large format. In his biography of Stieglitz, Richard Whelan has noted that the paintings reproduced in Stieglitz's home "represent Alfred's ideal women – in pointed contrast to Emmy. (A self-portrait shows Alfred seated beside a framed print of *The Net Mender*, exactly as many nineteenth-century photographic portraits included a framed portrait of a departed loved one.) To hang those three pictures on the walls of his home – where they would taunt his wife, who must have intuited their significance, was nothing short of sadistic."[128]

In Kitty's early years, and in the early years of Emmy's marriage to Stieglitz, there was considerable correspondence between Stieglitz, his wife, and his daughter when any of them was away from the other. Emmy's letters are friendly, factual descriptions of her social and daily activities while on vacation in Europe or the United States, and reflect the world of a young woman of the upper middle class who is materialistic, has leisure time, and the economic means to do much of what she wishes. If Kitty was with her, frequently there would be a brief message in a child's handwriting, sending loving greetings to her father. The letters from Emmy to Stieglitz reveal in some instances the unraveling of their marriage, as Emmy struggles to understand why they are misfits and how the marriage does not work.

In 1899, she wrote to Alfred that she was worried about the baby taking food and not drinking milk, "I am at my wit's end..." on 5 February 1904:

> All is well...Kitty and I miss you very much. Kitty is quite herself again – weighs 57³/₄...I skated two hours this morning and in the afternoon called on Lizzie. I found it was Flora's birthday and sent your mother and Amanda there. When you get back, you must photograph Dinky Hoff as she really is a lovely-looking child and I am sure she would make a fine picture...How much I wish you back you cannot think. Keep well and come home soon. With a big hug and kiss. Ever from Emmy. Lots of kisses from Kitty. She was on the ice with me this morning.

At the bottom of a November 1910 letter, Kitty wrote, "I have just come home from Beatrice Stern's. We had a good lunch and enjoyed ourselves very much. Miss you very much and will miss you more tomorrow at dinner. Come back as soon as you can. With love from Kitty."

On 28 August 1913, Emmy wrote from Europe, "Am glad that you are playing tennis and swimming but got the blues as you always seem to get sporty when I am not there. Still it's good for you and I guess that's the main thing." 25 April 1914 (from the Elberon Hotel, New Jersey): "Your letter this morning was strange. No moonlit night is anything to me if mosquitoes are around and in this little difference between you and me lies the whole trouble. You are always dealing in semi-abstract things while the small but real things of life mean most to me. Your praising the war condition makes me sad . . . you write so little of Kitty. Is she ill? After all she is my greatest interest – and the war and all else seem secondary. No, I don't think of coming down. I can manage . . . Good-bye, Alfred. Kiss Kits for me." On 21 August 1914 Emmy describes how nervous she is, suggesting that perhaps she should go to Lennox Hospital. 27 August 1914: "I would like cleared up by what means you say you could not let things go on as you did for years – Do you mean the European trips or what? [she talks of becoming less extravagant, having fewer servants] . . . Why make me so wretched and make me more morbid and fearsome than I am already? You certainly don't help me with your disposition, as you're nothing but gloomy." 19 September 1916: "I'm sorry Kits is blue . . . I will get her something in Boston . . . I miss it when I can't play golf . . . did you see my first attempt at photography I sent Kitty?"[129]

Surviving letters from Stieglitz to Emmy and Kitty are few. One, written on 7 February 1919, relates to the break-up of their marriage:

Dear Emmy,
Before your going to Northampton [the location of Smith College] I wish to express again, that as soon as you return and are ready, I'll be only too glad to go over your financial affairs with you . . . you know I want to help you . . . because of Kitty and because you are a human being, and because if anyone understands you, I do. Therefore, I may be able to give you something if you will let me give it in my own way. I don't know what I'll be able to give you, but I know that out of the chaos of our own particular little circle, something fine must evolve, even if it isn't that particular thing you may have in your mind. Don't be too hopeless. Chaos to me has always signified Hope. And Peace – Good will . . . Together we [he has referred to Georgia O'Keeffe, with whom at that time he was living] may all help one another – perhaps many heartaches. I have no particular plan in mind. I merely want to

minimize your suffering. And minimize also Kitty's and mine. And also
Miss O'Keeffe's. Give my love to Kitty and remember both of you are
much more on my mind than you can see . . . I wish to make life bear-
able for all of us, devoid of animosity and mutually helpful. It is in
my power to accomplish that – I, too, need help. –
Alfred.[130]

It seems clear that neither Alfred nor Emmy understood each other.
Kitty's childhood must have been affected by her parents' strained relationship. Her numerous cards and letters to her father, though, indicate
her love and adoration for him. She was devastated at the break-up of
her parents' marriage and in the years following there is limited contact
between father and daughter. When his daughter was institutionalized,
Stieglitz appeared to send only occasional cards and boxes of candy on
holidays to Kitty and her husband, Milton Sprague Stearns, and son,
Milton, Jr. The following excerpts from correspondence give some sense
of Kitty's early relationship to her father.

In 1904, Kitty was learning to write and trying to write in German
when she sent her father a Happy New Year's card: "WIE GEHT ES DIR?
GRÜSS VON KITTY" (How are you? Greeting from Kitty). On 14
December 1907, she wrote to her father, "Dear Papa, Miss you very
much. I think Mama misses you, too. Tell me how you like Mr. Kühn's
house [the photographer, Heinrich Kühn]. Hope you are well. Clara
[Kitty's governess] sends her love . . . tell Mr. Kühn I thank him for that
pretty bunch of flowers. You know what I mean, that pretty bunch of
roses. Love from your loving little Kitty Stieglitz." 3 July 1909:
"I wonder what you are doing in Munich? I can see Mr. Eugene [Frank
Eugene, the photographer] and Dr. Raab [Fritz Raab, an amateur painter,
photographer, and doctor practicing medicine in the United States and
Austria]. My cold is all gone, not a speck left . . . with love from your
little Puppy." In June 1911, in a letter addressed to her mother and father,
who were in Europe, Kitty spoke of long walks at Lake George, of
picking leaves, of printing postcards, and was upset with her parents for
only sending "postals" and "Papa sometimes nothing." On 24 November 1917 she wrote to her parents, "Oh, it's such fun to not only know
you are independent, but really feel you are, and I am feeling it now.
Had three classes this morning." On 24 July 1918, Kitty wrote from
camp to her father, speaking of her concerns about meeting Georgia
O'Keeffe at Lake George as if she were taking Emmy's place as her
mother. She talks of the need to be sensitive to her mother's feelings

but also tries to be sensitive to her father's feelings. She ends the letter, "I love you father, dear. Remember that – Kitty."[131]

On 7 April 1919, Stieglitz wrote to Kitty,

Dearest Kitty,

I don't seem able to grasp it – one idea has been uppermost in my mind since I left you. Why is it that I seem invariably to hurt you with what I say – When you are the last person in the world I wish to hurt ... and why is it you seem to hurt me likewise as I seem to hurt you. And I know that for twenty-five years your mother had no friend like I was her friend – no matter what appearances to the contrary ... perhaps I'm all wrong in all the things I feel – I sometimes question that I'm really living – Always your devoted father – [adds] Yet perhaps I don't know what a friend is, nor what a Father is, or a husband is. Yet I may have no right to claim anything – perhaps I'm all wrong in all the things I feel so frequently. You make me question whether I'm really living.[132]

In 1919, Stieglitz addressed Kitty in the form of a book dedication which eventually became a story, published as "Who am I?" about twenty years later in *Twice a Year*. Stieglitz spoke of the power of faith, born of beauty, saying that he had begun the book before World War I, which brought suffering, and that now they were in a new era. "This book is for you – is for all those seeking Light, Truth – it is a book born of my Faith – That Faith is stronger than ever – nothing can shake it."[133]

On 11 August 1919, Kitty sent her father her grades: Bible, A–; German, A–; History, B+; Physics, B+; Chemistry, B–; Hygiene, B. On 27 June 1922, she wrote to her father from the Samoset Hotel in Rockland, Maine, how wondrously happy she was, having just been married: "We were married at 9:15 A.M. Thursday last. No one was there except Ray Skilton, whom we picked up on the way to the minister's house, who was Unitarian." She describes a happy trip to Ogonquit, Maine, and gives her father her address at 15 Park Vale Avenue, Allston, Massachusetts. This was probably one of the last letters she wrote to her father, and she described herself as "wondrously happy."[134] It is perhaps understandable why her parents were not at her wedding, that their marital difficulties were too difficult for Kitty to handle. Emmy, as convention would suggest, sent out formal announcements of the wedding on 22 June 1922.

Stieglitz's photographs of his daughter, from shortly after her birth to her college years, were not only significant in their own right, but also provided a conceptual foundation on which Stieglitz could build the composite portrait he took of Georgia O'Keeffe, beginning in 1917. Kitty is often depicted as a "priceless child" of the Pictorialist era, but she is also sometimes depicted with a directness and intensity that tells us she is not "a" child but "the" child and the only child of Stieglitz. In many of the O'Keeffe photographs, particularly the early ones, much of that directness and intensity is transformed into a lover's passion.

Stieglitz's relationship with Emmy and Kitty, although it continued into the twentieth century, was grounded in the nineteenth century, and it is with them a chapter of Stieglitz's life is closed. The latter part of the nineteenth century had provided Stieglitz with a variety of influences and experiences that were to provide a basis for his life and work in the twentieth century. The turn of the century was to bring new ventures and concerns for thirty-six-year-old Stieglitz.

Part 2

THE TWENTIETH CENTURY

I hear the voice of the sound I love, the sound of the human voice;
I hear all sounds running together combined, fused or following;
Sounds of the city, and sounds out of the city – sounds of the day and
   night; . . .
The heav'e' yo of stevedores unloading ships by the wharves – the refrain
of the anchor lifters; . . .
The steam-whistle – the solid roll of the train of approaching cars; . . .
I hear the violincellos ('tis the young man's heart's complaint;) . . .
I hear the chorus – it is a grand opera;
Ah, this indeed is music! This suits me.

Walt Whitman, "Song of Myself"[1]

184 Alfred
Stieglitz, *Spring
Showers, New York,*
1900–1

NEW YORK: A NEW CENTURY

The date 1 January 1900 was New Year's Day, a new century, and Stieglitz's birthday. In many of his photographs taken in New York in the early years of the new century, Stieglitz captures the city as an emerging urban center. He depicts ferryboats, skyscrapers, railroad tracks, steam, smoke, and other aspects of the urban scene. His images celebrate the openness and possibilities of a new age, including urban life. While some of his European photographs, although often formally innovative, celebrated tradition and a more rural way of life, his early New York photographs seem to marry nineteenth-century Romantic world views with a faith in twentieth-century progress.

The year 1900 was to be important for Stieglitz as the beginning of his relationship with Edward Steichen. (Steichen changed the spelling of his first name from Edouard to Edward in about 1918.) In May of that year the twenty-one-year-old Steichen, a painter and photographer originally from Luxembourg whose family had immigrated to Michigan, arrived in New York on his way to Paris to study painting. He stopped by the Camera Club, at the recommendation of Clarence White, to meet Stieglitz, who was hanging a members' show there. Stieglitz was most impressed with Steichen's work and his optimistic spirit. He bought three photographs from Steichen for five dollars each and told Emmy at dinner that night, "I think I've found my man."[2]

Steichen had been working in Milwaukee as an apprentice at the American Fine Art Company, a lithographic firm that supplied posters and display cards for the brewers, flour mills, and packing houses in and around Milwaukee. At the same time he had been studying figure drawing with two Milwaukee artists, Robert Schade and Richard Lorenz. He began to take photographs in 1895 and saw issues of *Camera Notes* and reproductions of Clarence White's work, much of which was rooted in a Symbolist aesthetic at the time. Steichen began to correspond with White and submitted photographs to the Chicago Salon of 1900, for which White was a juror. Much impressed with the caliber of Steichen's photographs, white encouraged him to meet Stieglitz. The meeting marked the beginning of a close relationship for nearly fifteen years.

Steichen and Stieglitz were to collaborate on two extended endeavors that had a major influence on modern art in America: the quarterly *Camera Work*, beginning in 1903, and the Little Galleries of the Photo-Secession, established in 1905, later to be called 291 after the location at 291 Fifth Avenue. Steichen's two years in Paris from 1900 to 1902 had brought him into contact with artists such as Auguste Rodin, Pablo Picasso, Constantin Brancusi, Paul Cézanne, and Henri Matisse, whose work would be shown, in some cases for the first time in the United States, at 291.

Stieglitz's own photographs at the turn of the century in New York reflect Japanese design principles such as those espoused by Arthur Dow, as well as a Symbolist aesthetic. The snowy scene in *The Street – Design for a Poster* (1900–1), also titled *The Street, Fifth Avenue*, finds Stieglitz returning to the site of an earlier 1890s photograph looking up Fifth Avenue from 30th Street. The silhouette of a horse and part of its carriage is balanced by a tall lone tree that thrusts upward, its leafless

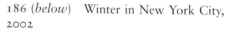

185   Alfred Stieglitz, *The Street – Design for a Poster*, 1900–1

186 (*below*)   Winter in New York City, 2002

branches providing decorative linear elements in the background. The snowy atmosphere gives the piece a dreamlike quality. Yet there is an intimacy to the scene, as if the viewer were there walking to meet the cloaked figure.

Stieglitz shows the New York of the smaller neighborhoods of lower Manhattan, where there is a human dimension, with brownstone dwellings and horse and carriages on the street. This is the "old" New York, rooted in the nineteenth century, much different from the New York of later Stieglitz's photographs where the buildings, in their abstract, geometric configurations, speak of a coldness that is part of the rise of technology and urbanization in New York City in the twentieth century. In those later photographs, the human presence is gone.

In some of these turn-of-the-century photographs the quality of touch seems important. It is as if the viewer can reach out and touch the snow, the wet streets, the figures. As Stieglitz noted, "The quality of touch in its deepest sense is inherent in my photographs. When that sense of touch is lost, the heartbeat of the photograph is extinct."[3]

Spring Showers (1900–1) has a Japanese-like composition and a sense of the human presence in the city. The photograph, taken on Madison Avenue and 23rd Street, may be seen as both a cityscape and a landscape. The city buildings are shrouded in mist. One lone tree stands in a protective cage dwarfing a street cleaner. The tall vertical format is the reverse of the traditional horizontal landscape format. Stieglitz printed several versions of this piece. In one, the street cleaner stands between two trees. The verticality of the background building is totally lost in the mist. A variant of this image without the street cleaner is *Tree in Snow*, probably taken at Madison Square Park, showing a

187 Alfred Stieglitz, *Rockefeller Center from the Shelton Hotel, New York City,* 1935

188 Alfred Stieglitz, *Tree in Snow, New York City,* 1900–2

delicate tree with a protective cage, photographed after a slight snowfall. The tree's branches are barren, but a small flock of birds is perched on them. In the misty background, city buildings and a carriage appear. On two lantern slides, it is possible to see how Stieglitz has masked the

189   Alfred Stieglitz, *Snapshot, From My Window, New York City*, 1902

190   Alfred Stieglitz, *Snapshot, From My Window, Berlin*, probably 1904

slides to place the birds and tree in the center of the image, thereby emphasizing the continuing role of nature in the city and a sense of balance between the man-made and the world of nature.

A vertical emphasis and use of strong linear elements is also seen in Stieglitz's *Spring Showers, The Coach* (1899–1901). The well-constructed composition recalls some of the lessons of Arthur Wesley Dow in his 1899 book, *Composition*. And the atmospheric effects of the rainy day and shadows on the wet pavements, recall James McNeill Whistler's *Harmonies* and *Nocturnes*. Looking south from his window at 1111 Madison Avenue, where he lived with Emmy from 1898 to 1918, Stieglitz's photograph was taken on a Sunday afternoon and provides a slight aerial, angular perspective. He seems to concentrate on the linear elements of the composition: the intersection of the streets, the right-angled picket fence, the vertical lamp-post, the diagonals of the tree branches, the shadows of the buildings on the street. That spare geometry is balanced by the suggestion of human activity: the trolley car and the small figures crossing the street. Two years later, Stieglitz photographed a smaller scene from the window, just after snow had fallen. The tree is filled with "snow blossoms" and more of the height of the buildings is shown. Further emphasis on linearity is found in the tracks in the snow. The diagonal emphasis in both images taken from his window calls to mind the Japanese prints that were popular at the time.

Stieglitz published one of his snow images, *Snapshot, From My Window, New York* (1902), in *Camera Work* on 20 October 1907, with *Snapshot, From My Window, Berlin* (probably 1904). The juxtaposition of the two images from the "old" and "new" worlds suggests that Stieglitz's emotional ties at this point still belonged to both worlds. The Berlin image was shot on a rainy day. The foliage in the foreground, as well as the trees lining the street, show a city where nature still has a role, which Stieglitz chose to emphasize. The trees, along with the imposing façade of the Gothic cathedral that dominates the left side of the image, speak of a continuing Romantic presence that was part of nineteenth-century German culture and was embedded in Stieglitz's psyche. That he chose to emphasize the Gothic structure suggests his continued interest in the "old world." By juxtaposing the old and new worlds in *Camera Work* he may have hoped to suggest a harmonious balance of the two worlds, and certainly showed "compartments" or periods in his own life. Both snapshots stress an angularity in the intersection of two streets, viewed from above, and both contain a human presence – the passerby in the street. The New York scene, shrouded in snow, has more atmospheric and decorative elements, as if Stieglitz felt freer to experiment in the new world, although the Berlin photograph was actually taken later.

While he continued to take photographs, Stieglitz was also heavily engaged in Camera Club and *Camera Notes* activities as well as other exhibition work in 1900. Conservatives in the Camera Club began bickering with Stieglitz and others about his orientation, so much so that he resigned as vice-president in 1900, refusing to lower his standards. As previously noted, in 1908 he was actually expelled from the club, prompting some members to resign in protest. Shortly thereafter he was reinstated, but promptly resigned of his own accord.

The Art Institute of Chicago, in conjunction with the Chicago Society of Amateur Photographers, held a major Salon from 1–18 April 1900, consisting of 118 juried works selected from among 900 entries. Stieglitz assisted his colleague, the photographer William B. Dyer, in organizing the show.

At the same time, the Boston-based photographer, F. Holland Day, was competing with Stieglitz to become the chief promoter of fine art photography, and was hoping to claim Boston as the seat of American photographic experiments and exhibitions. For an 1899 Society of Arts and Crafts photography exhibition in Boston, Day had chosen two Stieglitz photographs, *Night in Union Square* and *Mending Nets*, to be in the show. Stieglitz admired Day's Symbolist and Pictorial photographs and had published several in issues of *Camera Notes* as recently as October 1899.

Stieglitz's initial affinity with Day is evident in their choice of similar subject matter in the late 1890s. Photographs by Stieglitz, Day, and Clarence White of a young girl in an exotic long dress with fringed shawl placing a wreath on the shoulders of a garlanded statue suggest the three were taking photographs of this subject at about the same time, 1897. Stieglitz had described Day's 1898 show at the New York Camera Club as "the most remarkable one-man exhibition yet shown" in that series.[4] But he wanted nothing to do with an American Association of Pictorial Photographers based in Boston, in which Day invited him to participate. Stieglitz wanted the limelight for himself.

Stieglitz felt threatened when Day organized a major show at the Royal Photographic Society in London entitled *The New School of American Photography* in 1900. Touring to Paris the following year, the show attracted young Pictorialist photographers such as Alvin Langdon Coburn and Edward Steichen, who described it as "a bombshell exploding in the photographic world of London . . . It was a red flag in the face of the public, and the press had a holiday making fun of it."[5] The young Steichen, naive about the politics of exhibitions and photography, could not understand why Stieglitz and Joseph Keiley were not included in the show, and wrote to Stieglitz on 19 October 1900, wondering how a show of the New School of American Photography could be complete without their presence. Day, however, was greatly to inspire and motivate Steichen, teaching him the value of experimentation.

The London exhibition did draw much critical attention, as Steichen noted. The painter James McNeill Whistler attended and particularly admired Clarence White's *Girl with a Pitcher*. In New York, despite his opposition and his behind-the-scenes efforts to derail the show, Stieglitz ran Robert Demachy's positive review in *Camera Notes* on 1 July 1901. However, Stieglitz's editorial in the same issue attacked the quality of the show, even though he had not actually seen it. "It comprises the work of many photographers of all schools," Stieglitz wrote. "Many of the prints were actually unfinished, or what are termed 'seconds,' that is, prints not up to exhibition finish. Hence, much of the unfavorable criticism."[6]

The rivalry between Day and Stieglitz eventually excluded Day from Stieglitz's sphere of influence and the circle of artists for whom he served as advocate and friend. Day refused to be included in any issues of *Camera Work* that Stieglitz was to edit between 1903 and 1917.

Stieglitz's curatorial and organizational skills were rewarded on the international level in 1901, when he was invited to select works for the International Exhibition in Glasgow. That same year, American photographers had already been selected for a number of places in the Photo Club of Paris and London's Linked Ring Salon. The Glasgow show was significant since it was the first time a major international exhibition had given photography a place equal to the other arts in the fine art section. Stieglitz picked prints made from 1881 to 1900 that to him represented various types of experiment in the American school of photography.

THE PHOTO-SECESSION

Stieglitz was continually striving for an association of photographers, a "Secession" group that would be free of the restrictions he found to be imposed by other salons and that could promote advanced Pictorial photography. At the turn of the century, those working in Pictorial photography besides Stieglitz included Edward Steichen, Gertrude Käsebier, Clarence White, Alvin Langdon Coburn, Frank Eugene, Joseph Keiley, F. Holland Day, Eva Watson-Schütze, Charles Berg, Mary Devens, and William Dyer. These photographers sought beauty, "spirit," and formal elements within a photograph that would appeal to the emotions of the viewer. In general, there were two main currents under the Pictorial umbrella – those who favored a straight, unmanipulated, or unretouched image, such as Stieglitz, White, and Coburn, and those who favored a more painterly approach, such as Steichen and Eugene. Or there were those, such as Gertrude Käsebier, who lay somewhere in the middle. As time went on, photographers such as Stieglitz and Steichen were to turn away from what they came to see as the aesthetic excesses of Pictorialism. Painting was no longer a model; rather there was an interest in the accuracy, clarity, and detail that the medium of photography could achieve, rendering a true recording of reality as viewed by the photographer. (By the early 1920s, the straight aesthetic had come to influence

By JAMES C. SAVERY

A brief sketch of a movement that has raised photography to the
dignity of a fine art, with illustrations by some of
its most prominent workers

"SUNLIGHT"
Clarence H. White, New York

191   The first page of an article on the
Photo-Secession by James Savery, published
in *Burr McIntosh Monthly*, April 1907

documentary photography in the United States and Europe, and embraced the clean, clear lines of Modernism.)

On 17 February 1902, the Photo-Secession was formally born, with Stieglitz as its founder, modeling his group after the principles of European secessionist groups of the time. Indeed, that same year Gustav Klimt completed his large-scale mural project celebrating Beethoven's Ninth Symphony at the Vienna Secession as part of a transformation of the secession building under the direction of architect Josef Hoffmann to celebrate Max Klinger's giant statue of Beethoven. The Viennese artists strove, like a number of secessionist groups, to provide in art a surrogate religion offering refuge from certain aspects of modern life.

Stieglitz, too, could be said to have had the fervor of a religious zealot, believing that art might take on certain aspects of religion. A number of years later, he noted, with a sense of lament, "But my experience covering over fifty years, in my own country has shown me that those who are seemingly the most 'wildly enthusiastic' about art really do not care for it when put to the test. With such people art is mainly a topic of conversation. Or it is a medium for gambling, or it is a fetish. There is little genuine humility and wonder before the manifestation which we know by the name of art. And all true art is a religious manifestation."[7]

In founding the Photo-Secession, Stieglitz asserted that it was a "rebellion against the insincere attitude of the unbeliever, of the Philistine, and largely exhibition authorities."[8] Stieglitz conceived of the organization as a revolutionary one, with a select membership: "Progress has been accomplished only by reason of the fanatical enthusiasm of the revolutionist, whose extreme teaching has saved the mass from utter inertia . . . The Secessionist lays no claim to infallibility, nor does he pin his faith to any creed, but he demands the right to work out his own photographic salvation."[9] In the prospectus, he described the group's purpose: "To hold together those Americans devoted to Pictorial photography; to exhibit the best that has been accomplished by its members or other photographers; and above all to dignify that profession until recently looked upon as a trade."[10]

In a lengthy treatise written in 1903 at the request of the editor of *Camera Craft*, Stieglitz revealed his insistence on certain standards and wish to remain in control of what was shown:

> Like all secessions the Photo-Secession is but an active protest against the conservatism and reactionary spirit of those whose self-satisfaction imbues them with the idea that existing conditions are akin to perfection, and that the human race cannot improve upon the attitude and accomplishments of the good old days. This stick-in-the-mud policy, this complacent self-satisfaction, this belief that the standards of yesterday must be the standards of all time to come, this spirit which Matthew Arnold characterizes as Barbarism and Philistinism, has been the bane of all efforts towards "Sweetness and Light." The object of the Photo-Secession is not, as is generally supposed, to force its ideas, ideals, and standards upon the photographic world, but an insistence upon the right of its members to follow their own salvation as they see it, together with the hope that by force of their example others, too, may of their own free will see the truth as we see it. This hope can never be realized by weakly accepting standards in which we have no faith, nor by compromise, which never yet has satisfied either party to a question. If the way we have chosen leads nowhere we have but fooled ourselves; but if ours is a path towards Truth, then it argues but a weak faith on our part willingly to follow any other.
>
> Our attitude is not one of pique or envy, nor do we intend to hold aloof from photographic activities that display an earnest desire for improvement, although it has been forced upon us to insist upon our own standards in so far as our own pictures are concerned. The sham of so-called high standards and the exploitation of the names of painters, known and unknown, who have been induced to pat photography patronizingly upon the head, the ministration to the vanity of individuals, the substitution of in judicious praise for honest criticism, the complacent acceptance of the mediocre as perfection, all have injured photography and have forced the issue. Those who charge us with an unwillingness to take part in exhibitions that are not run under our own direct or indirect management speak without knowledge. During the past year, the first of the organized existence of the Photo-

Secession, we have not declined a single invitation to contribute to exhibitions great or small throughout the world – Turin (Italy), St. Petersburg (Russia), Photo Club of Paris Salon (France), Wiesbaden Art Gallery (Germany), L'Effort (Belgium), Hamburg (Germany), Toronto (Canada), Denver (Colorado), Minneapolis (Minnesota), Cleveland (Ohio), Rochester (New York) – each has received a collection of the work of the Photo-Secessionists, assembled often under great difficulties and inconvenience. It has been our policy to refuse none whose earnestness we were assured of. It is true that certain conditions were first insisted upon in order that no action of ours could be construed as a compromise with our principles. We demanded, first, moral assurance of the good faith and high intentions of the management of all such exhibitions whose previous history was not sufficient guarantee of their endeavor; second, the right to send a collection that would be accepted as a whole without submission to a jury; third, that such collection be hung as a unit and catalogued as "Loan Exhibition of the Photo-Secession"; fourth, that the shipping expenses be borne by those who had extended the invitation. We have yet to hear that any of the societies mentioned had found aught to regret in their acceptance of our seemingly high-handed and dictatorial demands. The standards by which the Photo-Secession selected the work of its members that went to make up these collections was in each case far more severe than that of the jury of the respective exhibitions, and it was no doubt because of these high standards that our work attracted the attention it did. It must not be understood that membership in the Secession denies the right of the individual to exhibit personally at any exhibition. On the contrary, the individual is free to follow their own light, yet insist upon our right to do likewise. ALFRED STIEGLITZ, DIRECTOR OF THE PHOTO-SECESSION.[11]

The Secessionists were not without their critics, and a controversy erupted shortly after its inception over the hanging of photographs at the 1904 St. Louis World's Fair. The organizers of the fair felt photography should be hung in a liberal arts building, not a fine arts building. Stieglitz found himself in conflict with one of the organizers, J.C. Strauss, a St. Louis photographer who tried to ameliorate the situation, but not in a manner to Stieglitz's liking. Finally, the Seccession agreed to support the exposition if at least one photographic print, selected by the National Jury of Artists, would hang in a fine arts building.

The year 1902 also saw Stieglitz helping organize on important exhibition at the National Arts Club in New York. Founded in 1898, at the initiative of the writer Charles de Kay, the club was to be a place for exhibitions, publications, initiatives, and social events for those involved in the arts. Stieglitz was invited by de Kay to show his photographs at the club to further the recognition of photography as a fine art. But Stieglitz convinced de Kay that a large group photographic exhibition would better achieve his aim. With the help of photographers Charles Berg and F. Benedict Herzog, who had joined the National Arts Club, Stieglitz chose the entries, although the catalogue cover for the exhibition, *American Pictorial Photography*, says it was arranged by the Photo-Secession.

The show opened on 5 March 1902 in the midst of a blinding snowstorm. A number of years later, Steichen recalled the event,

> In those days, New Yorkers had plenty of what it takes to leave the softer comforts of after-dinner hours and go out in a snowstorm for their art education. Transportation was by shoe leather, street cars, and hansom cabs. New Yorkers came that night to find out what the shouting was for and to hear what Alfred Stieglitz had to say about it. The chronicles have it that the audience was distinguished and had an international flavor, for there came not only New Yorkers, like Richard Gilder, editor of the *Century Magazine*, but also the Duke of Newcastle and Sir Philip Burne-Jones.[12]

The show was the first exhibition for the Photo-Secession as a group. In a letter of 15 March Stieglitz followed up on a conversation with Gilder about the possibility of having a number of the Photo-Secession prints published in the *Century Magazine*.[13]

The art historian William Homer notes that, although the show was significant in its promotion of photography as an art, "the quality of work in the National Arts Club show did not entirely live up to the ideals that Stieglitz had publicly professed. To put it plainly, more than a few inferior photographers participated . . . Stieglitz was so eager, it seems, to defend the idea of photography as an art that he was willing at least in 1901 and 1902 to accept every possible effort in that direction, even mediocre examples."[14] But with the show, Stieglitz had effectively declared secession from the Camera Club. And after reviewing the exhibition in *Camera Notes* in July 1902 as a departing statement, Stieglitz resigned his editorship.

Stieglitz's 1902 collaboration with the National Arts Club did not occur again, although some of Stieglitz's work appeared in a 1908 exhibition of contemporary art organized by J. Nilsen Laurvik, a fellow

Photo-Secessionist. In that exhibition, paintings by members of the Ashcan School, such as Robert Henri, John Sloan, George Bellows, and Georg Luks, hung next to Photo-Secessionist works that included photographs by Stieglitz, Clarence White, Gertrude Käsebier, Joseph Keiley, and Frank Eugene. It is interesting to compare paintings such as Robert Henri's *Snow in New York* (1902) (National Gallery of Art, Washington, D.C.) with Stieglitz's 1893 *Winter, Fifth Avenue*, or the composition of George Bellows' *Blue Morning* (1909) (National Gallery of Art, Washington, D.C.) with Stieglitz's 1904 *Going to the Start*, the post-and-lintel forms of the foreground architecture sharply defining the composition in similar ways in each piece. A few years later, in 1911, Laurvik was to write of Stieglitz and the Ashcan school, "His *Winter, Fifth Avenue*, made in 1893, created a sensation, not only in photographic circles, but in the world of art, and blazed the way for a whole school of painters who set themselves the task of depicting the streets and life of New York."[15]

The years 1902 and 1903 brought forth several of Stieglitz's most well-known photographs – *The Hand of Man* (1902), *Snapshot, In the New York Central Yards* (1903), and *The Flatiron* (1903). In the first two images, Stieglitz photographed oncoming trains. *The Hand of Man* was

192   Alfred Stieglitz, *The Hand of Man*, 1902

193   Alfred Stieglitz, *In the New York Central Yards*, 1903

made from the back of a train as it pulled into the freight yard at the Long Island City railroad station in Queens, while *In the New York Central Yards*, also titled *The Railroad Yard, Winter*, was probably made from a 48th Street footbridge crossing over the railroad yard at Grand Central Station. In both images the curvilinear train track as well as the vertical and horizontal utility poles and lines form strong linear elements in the composition, while thick billowing smoke dominates the upper half of the image. In the winter scene the white of the snow, along with the white cloud of smoke, seems to purify the image, while the dark-gray smoke cloud in *The Hand of Man* rises in contrast to the lighter grays and whites of the cloudy sky in the background. The art historian Weston Naef has noted, "*The Hand of Man* is one of the earliest works in which Stieglitz makes contradiction and duality the stated intent of a picture. The title establishes a poeticizing context that recalls the Symbolism

194 Alfred Stieglitz,
The Flat-iron, 1903

prevalent in art and literature around 1900, yet it also alludes to photographs as the product of a machine and to the eternal dialogue between the handmade and the mechanical."[16]

Stieglitz worked on this image using a variety of approaches for almost three decades: in 1903 he made a small photogravure for the first issue of *Camera Work*; in 1910 he made a larger photogravure on slightly textured Japanese paper; in October 1911 it appeared again in *Camera Work*; and he made a gelatin silver print in the 1920s or 1930s. In the latter print, soft gray and atmospheric areas are replaced by a greater sense of clarity in the sky's clouds and definition of the separate train tracks, whose silver tops are caught in the light.

In both photographs of the oncoming train, the viewer is prompted to consider the role of the railroad in contemporary life and its place in the American landscape and cityscape. *The Hand of Man* also refers to the built environment, and the iron and steam vehicles that were new to American life, pondering what these inventions might bring to American culture. Both photographs raise questions about the beauty and horror of technology.

Stieglitz's oft-reproduced photograph of the Flatiron Building shows him exploring a precarious balance between the built environment and the world of nature. Designed by Daniel H. Burnham and Co. from 1901 to 1903, the Flatiron Building was, at 307 feet tall, considered one of the first skyscraper structures in New York. Located at 175 Fifth Avenue, it was shaped to fit the triangular island centered between Fifth Avenue, Broadway, and 23rd Street in Lower Manhattan. Officially called the Fuller Building after its owner and builder,

195   The Flatiron Building as seen in a postcard of 1905

196   The Flatiron Building, 2002

the George A. Fuller Company, it soon became known as the "Flatiron" because of its narrow, triangular shape. Of particular concern to the engineers was the need for braces to counteract the wind sweeping against the twenty-one-story structure on an exposed site. Popular postcards of the early twentieth century show women near the unusual-looking structure with their skirts billowing in the wind and exposed ankles. The building contained numerous Beaux-Arts details with sculpted faces, lions' heads, foliage, and other ornamentation on the detailed façade. Above the three-story limestone base, the mid-section was richly decorated with white terracotta. A projecting cornice crowns the building, emphasizing the triangular shape. Some found it beautiful, some ugly. Alfred's father, Edward Stieglitz, was among those who found it ugly.

John Corbin wrote, shortly after the building was completed:

> The observer, with his eye on the northward edge of the Flatiron Building, called it an ocean steamer with all Broadway in tow. Another . . . compared it to a medieval campanile . . . there are times when it seems one of the most striking monuments of modern civic architecture – a column of smoke by day, and by night, when the interior is lighted, a pillar of fire . . . this twentieth-century giant, whether ugly or beautiful, stands on the threshold of vigorous new life and of vast architectural possibilities.[17]

Stieglitz was captivated and recalled in retrospect his passion for the new building.

> One day there was a great snowstorm. The Flatiron Building had been erected on 23rd Street, at the junction of Fifth Avenue and Broadway. I stood spellbound as I saw that building in that storm. I had watched the building in the course of its erection, but somehow it had never occurred to me to photograph it in the stages of its evolution. But that particular snowy day, with the trees of Madison Square all covered with snow, fresh snow, I suddenly saw the Flatiron Building as I had never seen it before. It looked, from where I stood, as if it were moving toward me like the bow of a monster ocean steamer, a picture of the new America that was in the making. So day after day for several days, while the snow was still covering Madison Square Park, I made snapshots of the Flatiron Building.
>
> One of these pictures I enlarged. That is, I had a photogravure made from the original negative, in fact, two photogravures, different sizes,

both enlargements of the original negative, and proof pulled under my direct supervision. One enlargement was to be inserted into *Camera Work*; the other one was larger, about 11 × 14 inches. This larger photogravure was one of a series of large prints I had in mind to be made for a portfolio, to be called *Fifty Prints of New York*. This series that I had in mind was never completed. I always permitted my own photographic work to be sidetracked by other affairs having to do with photography – affairs that needed constant attention: *Camera Notes*, the Camera Club, *Camera Work*, the Photo-Secession, 291, and so on.

When I look back to those days, when the Flatiron Building in the snowstorm, and in various lights, was such a passion of mine, I think of my father who met me one day while I was standing in the middle of the Fifth Avenue thoroughfare, photographing it. He said, "Alfred, how can you photograph that hideous building?" I remember my reply, "Why Pa, it is not hideous. That is the new America. It is to America what the Parthenon was to Greece." He was horrified. He had not seen the steelwork as the building had gone up, as it had started from the ground, and had also partly started from the top. He had not seen the men working as I had seen them. He had not seen the seeming simplicity of that, to me, amazing structure, the lightness of the structure, combined with solidity.

He did admire the photograph I had made when I showed it to him. He remarked, "I do not see how you could have produced such a beautiful thing from such an ugly building." And when I saw the Flatiron Building again, after many years of having seen other tall buildings in New York City suddenly shooting into the sky, the Woolworth Building and then still others, the Flatiron Building did seem rather ugly and unattractive to me. There was a certain gloom about it. It no longer seemed handsome to me; it no longer represented the coming age. It did not tempt me to photograph it. What queer things we humans are. But the feeling, the passion I experienced at that earlier time for the Flatiron Building still exists in me. I still can feel the glory of those many hours and those many days when I stood there on Fifth Avenue lost in wonder, looking at the Flatiron Building.[18]

Stieglitz chose to photograph the grand Flatiron Building in the background, while elements of nature – the snow-clad trees, the snow-covered ground, the tall, dark Hiroshige-like forked tree – dominate the foreground. The triangle formed by the forked branch mirrors the shape of the building and frames the towering structure. There is a slight human

197   Alfred Stieglitz, *Going to the Start*, 1904

presence, with several small figures walking in the park, dwarfed by the trees and the building. Although the Flatiron is in the background, the viewer can still sense the beauty of the detailed façade. The photograph emphasizes a decorative, harmonious whole as man-made structure and the world of nature balance each other. The building does not seem like an office building in an urban center. Rather there is a sense of wholeness and idealism in the photograph that speaks not of commercialism or materialism, or of any of the chaos that is part of urban and modern life, but of harmony, peace, and an aesthetic spirit, set in a moment of silence.

Stieglitz was not the only photographer captivated by the towering Flatiron structure. Edward Steichen, Alvin Langdon Coburn, and later Bernice Abbott also photographed the building. These photograhers tended to be more concerned with the building as a part of city life: the building dominates their photographs more fully and the viewer is more aware of traffic on the city street.

A photograph taken a year later, *Going to the Start* (1904), also titled *Going to the Post, Morris Park* when printed in 1910 in a large photogravure format, shows Stieglitz's continued interest in strong linear elements. The T shape of the viewing stand frames and divides the view of the racetrack, focusing the viewer's eye on the curve of the track and the jockeys to the left. The contrast of the dark foreground forms with the gray tones of the race heightens the drama.

CAMERA WORK

Since his resignation from *Camera Notes*, Stieglitz had dreamed of another periodical. January 1903 marked the birth of that dream, *Camera Work*, the now famous periodical that promoted modern art and photography through both its text and visual images. The first issue was actually published 15 December 1902, but dated January 1903. Its title was taken from the notion of photographers as "camera workers." As the writer Andrew Roth noted in 2001,

> Consummately intellectual, deeply connected to the avant-garde tendencies of a remarkable age . . . *Camera Work* was exceptional in the history of the medium in that it used photographic imagery as the stimulus for investigations of time and space, nature and culture, art and life. Stieglitz and his circle always debated broad aesthetic and philosophical issues, as well as more specific questions about pictorial form, content, temporality, and audience within the area of the single photographic frame. As a result, *Camera Work* and all the pictures, essays, exhibitions, and book works that it spawned, were predicated on the supposition that the image itself was a potent "site" for exploration – that the metaphorical meanings of the world were "immanent" within photographs of the most commonplace subjects.[19]

A mission statement appeared in the first issue:

> Photography being in the main a process in monochrome, it is on subtle gradations of tone and value that its artistic beauty so frequently depends. It is therefore highly necessary that reproductions of photographic work must be made with exceptional care, and discretion of the spirit of the original is to be retained, though no reproductions can do justice to the subtleties of some photographs. Such supervision will be given to the illustrations that will appear in each number of *Camera Work*. Only examples of such work as gives evidence of individuality and artistic worth, regardless of school, or contains some exceptional feature of technical merit, or such as exemplifies some treatment worthy of consideration will find recognition in these pages. Nevertheless, the Pictorial will be the dominating feature of the magazine.[20]

Thus, individuality, artistic and technical merit, and the Pictorial were to be watchwords of the magazine, along with meticulous care taken with reproduction processes. Form and content were to be united as the magazine became an art work itself.

Stieglitz was editor, and his associate
editors (with their years of service) were
Dallett Fuguet (1902–17), Joseph Keiley
(1902–17 – his name continued on the
masthead even after his death in 1914),
John Francis Strauss (1902–10), John
Barrett Kerfoot (1905–17), and Paul Burty
Haviland (1910–17). The graphic design
was based, in part, on the designs of
William Morris and the Arts and Crafts
Movement. Set in heavy black text with red
introduced in the first heavily ornamented
letter, each article had wide margins,
making every page visually pleasing. Each
of the fifty issues was bound in a gray–green
paper cover with the title and edition
printed in a lighter gray. The photogravures
were reproduced from original negatives,
separated from the text by blank pages, and
given prominence at the front of each issue.
Even the advertisements were graphically
interesting, and primarily related to the
field of photography – lenses, papers, and
so on.

Camera Work was intended to be a quarterly, with an annual subscription rate of
four dollars, or two dollars for a single
issue. Initially, the publication was greeted
with much enthusiasm, with 1000 copies of
every issue being printed and approximately 650 subscribers. By 1917, when
publication stopped, only 500 copies of
each issue were being produced and there
were only 36 subscribers.

198 (*top*)   Alfred Stieglitz, *Nearing Land*,
1904

199 (*left*)   Graflex advertisement in *Camera
Work*, April 1907

In general, *Camera Work* served a variety of purposes. It served as a forum for aesthetic and critical discussion of art and photography. It also served as publicity and documentation for the Photo-Secession and Stieglitz's 291 gallery, which opened in 1905 and was itself a work of art. "Most of all," according to the curator Pam Roberts, "it was the autobiography of the creative life of one man, its editor, financier, and inspiration. A man who got things done. A man variously known as a despot, a dictator, a guru, a prophet, and a messiah. Alfred Stieglitz."[21]

Initially many of the texts of *Camera Work* were rooted in Symbolist thinking but gradually the magazine became an advocate of Modernism and modern art. As a student in Berlin, Stieglitz had certainly been exposed to the Symbolist aesthetic that was flourishing in Europe at the end of the nineteenth century.

Of particular importance to Stieglitz and the group of artists and writers linked to *Camera Work* was Symbolism's emphasis on dance and music. For example, the Symbolist poet Stéphane Mallarmé saw dance as the art of the future because it alone could translate the transient, fleeting, or abrupt element of human existence to a higher reality.[22] Mallarmé's aesthetic views were set forth in an essay, "Music and Literature," published in *La Revue Blanché* in October 1894: "Using the most elemental and elementary of means, [the artist] will try (for example) the symphonic equation of the seasons of the year, the habits of a sunbeam or a cloud. He will make one or two observations analogous to the undulant heat, or to the inclemencies of the changing climate, which are the multiple sources of our passions...nature exists; she will not be changed."[23] *Camera Work* also often included references and excerpts from the writings of Friedrich Nietzsche, who placed a strong emphasis on music and dance, particularly in *The Birth of Tragedy* (1872), which saw the music of Dionysian festivals as a liberating force that serves to present wisdom by revealing the very heart and soul of nature and human passions.

Maurice Maeterlinck's notion of correspondences between color, sound, and emotional states also interested Stieglitz and his circle and excerpts from Maeterlinck's writings were published in *Camera Work*. Charles Baudelaire's belief that the objects of the material world symbolized a transcendent reality accessible particularly to the artist was also influential. Correspondences between the different arts, a synthesis of the arts, a belief in the relation between form and sensation were all key Symbolist ideas and led to a focus on music. Music was identified with inspiration and stimulation of the imagination. Pictorial composition was frequently described in terms of musicality, which was considered an important manner of expressing beauty. The emotional quality of a work of art was communicated through its poetic qualities, musicality, and visual content. Stieglitz's later series of photographs, *Music: A Sequence of Ten Cloud Photographs*, *Songs of the Sky*, and *Equivalents*, were clearly rooted in Symbolist thought.

Another source of Symbolist thought that in turn had an impact on Stieglitz and his circle was psychoanalysis. The Symbolist exploration of dream states as a way to penetrate the spiritual was clearly influenced by Sigmund Freud, who began his studies of dreams and the unconscious in the 1880s. His *Interpretation of Dreams* (1900) had a great impact on both Europeans and Americans. The physicist and philosopher Ernst Mach, a contemporary of Freud's, emphasized the significance of colors, shapes, and sounds for concepts of transformation and the formulation of a sense of identity and of the ego: "When I say the ego cannot be saved, I mean that it resides in man's perception of everything and every event, that this ego is a part of everything we feel, hear, see, and touch. Everything is ephemeral, a world without substance that consists only of colors, shapes, and sounds. Reality is in perpetual movement, it is changing reflections. What we call the ego is crystallized in this interplay of phenomena. From the instant of our birth to our death, it is in a permanent state of transformation."[24] In a similar way, Steiglitz hoped, through photography and the other visual arts, for some aspect of transformation in his viewers and readers.

Related to Symbolism was Synthetism, a movement founded by Émile Bernard and Paul Gauguin around 1888, in which visual elements were reduced to unmodeled areas or color, similar to Japanese prints, in order to achieve a synthesis of form and color. A number of Synthetists also believed in the correspondence between exterior forms and subjective states.[25] Synthetism also tended toward simplification. Stieglitz can be seen as a kind of Synthetist in his interest in simplifying his photographic compositions, in his synthesis of form and of areas of black, white, and gray (equivalent to the color of the painters), and in his interest in the relation between exterior forms and interior states – his notion of "Equivalents."

The influence of figures such as French philosopher Henri Bergson took Stieglitz and *Camera Work* in a modern direction. Bergson's view of time in his 1907 book *Creative Evolution* (an extract of which was published in *Camera Work* in October 1911) as a continuum in which there are no definite fixed objects, found expression in the images of simultaneity and dynamism of Cubism, Futurism, and their offshoots, as well as in visual pieces that referred to music, an art of time, and painting, an art of and in space. Bergson's *élan vital*, or life-force, and his exaltation of the intuitive and instinctive over the rational, provided a sense of freedom for post-Victorian artists and intellectuals. Edward Steichen greatly admired him and Mabel Dodge (later Mabel Dodge Luhan), influential through her salons, translated Bergson's concept of the *élan vital* to the power of sexuality. Dodge became friends with both Stieglitz and Georgia O'Keeffe and was a catalyst in bringing together a variety of vibrant and interesting people. She also contributed to *Camera Work*.

In his book, *Camera Work: A Critical Anthology*, Jonathan Green divides the fifty issues of *Camera Work* into four major periods:

> Consolidation, 1903–7, a time of transition from *Camera Notes*; Expansion, 1907–10, the development of the Little Galleries of the Photo-Secession, *Camera Work*s' initial contact with modern art, and major exhibits of the Photo-Secession; Exploration, 1910–15, when *Camera Work* and the Little Galleries were vitally concerned with the radical new art movements of Fauvism, Cubism, and Futurism; and the final period, 1915–17, when *Camera Work* offered an effective summation of the interests and activities of the preceding twelve years by publishing photographic tributes to Stieglitz and Paul Strand.[26]

Issues from the first period included articles by George Bernard Shaw, Maurice Maeterlinck, Sadakichi Hartmann (frequently writing under the pen-name of Sidney Allan), Joseph Keiley, Dallett Fuguet, and Charles Caffin. *Fin-de-siècle* concerns with beauty were addressed, and the notion of inner spirit, important for both the Symbolists and Secessionists, was frequently mentioned. Many of the articles were rooted in Symbolism. In these early issues the photogravures were printed on Japanese tissue paper and then placed on color mounts. A highlight of this first period was the reproduction of Edward Steichen's photographs taken using a new color process, the Lumière autochrome, one of the first publications of this new process.

A comic and witty element was woven into many of the early issues, described by Jonathan Green as "an integral facet of the critical, skeptical intelligence that animates *Camera Work*. Expressed in the early issues through fable, aphorism, and jest, it will mature in the later numbers into sophisticated irony and caricature. It will be transformed in the writing of Benjamin de Casseres and caricatures of Marius de Zayas into a scathing Dadaistic attack on American civilization."[27]

THE A B C OF PHOTOGRAPHY.

H stands for Hypo, a salt Jesuitical —
Apparently lamb-like, but subtly mephitical.
    If posterity's going
    To look at your showing,
Believe me, you can not be too hypo-critical.

I 's the Impressionist.   Gee!
What a glorious world this must be
        When your eyes don't quite track,
        And when everything black
Is all purple and pink filigree !

J is Judge Lynch, to whose court we assign
The judging of niggers and prints.   I opine
        That you'll readily know,
        When he's helped hang a show,
By the number of dead ones you see on the line.

K is the Kodaker spry,
From whose interrogative eye
        Gleams the rage of the glutton,
        As, finger on button,
He watches his chance to let fly.

L is the Landscape immense,
With a tree, and three cows, and a fence,
        Which is *l'art à l'Anglais.*
        Why — but then I dare say
That I'm temperamentally dense !

M is the Model, whose beauty
To record is a positive duty ;
        For her torso and thigh
        Are a dream.   But my, my !
Her face is best kept on the Q. T.

N is a Nuance, a brand-new affair
About half-way betwixt and between a split hair.
        I don't think I've heard
        Who invented the word,
But his royalties ought to be mounting for fair.
                                J. B. KERFOOT.

38

200   "The ABC of Photography" from
Camera Work, October 1906

Issues from the second period, 1907–10, recorded and reviewed three important photographic exhibitions of Photo-Secessionist work: at the Carnegie Art Galleries in Pittsburgh in 1904, at the Pennsylvania Academy of Fine Arts in Philadelphia in 1906, and at the Albright Knox Gallery in Buffalo in 1910. The period also marked the birth of Stieglitz's 291 gallery. Critics such as Caffin and Hartmann began to emphasize elements of American society and art, always pushing the power of photography. *Camera Work* became an important vehicle for publicizing the European art that was being shown, sometimes for the first time, at Stieglitz's galleries.

During *Camera Work*'s third period, the periodical began to include reproductions of other art media besides photography. For example, in issue 29, four caricatures by Marius De Zayas were reproduced, and in January 1911, Rodin's drawings of dancers were reproduced. The list of contributors to these issues, both artists and writers, is impressive. Many were attracted to the spirit of experimentation that the periodical espoused. Thus writers such as William Carlos Williams, Mina Loy, Waldo Frank, Paul Rosenfeld, Djuna Barnes, and Gertrude Stein, and artists such as Max Weber, Gabrielle and Francis Picabia, Oscar Bluemner, Paul Burty Haviland, Marius de Zayas, and Wassily Kandinsky were among the many contributors.

There was a revolutionary fervor at the root of some of the articles, many of which referred to connections between art, the visual arts, and music. For example, Sadakichi Hartmann, noted in discussing the work of Rodin, that "in our age, music is the grand source of instant inspiration" and that "form . . . becomes musical when special stress is laid on the surface treatment or the juxtaposition of light and shade, and the broader and more diffused juxtaposition is, the finer the musical exhalation is apt to become. In the *Balzac,* form is felt rather than seen. It is orchestration by the blending of planes – and by the vibration of light on those planes to produce a vague atmospheric effect."[28] Edward Steichen's photographs of Rodin and his sculpture achieved some of this same musical sensibility. Bluemner wrote that music in contrast to art "was soaring skywards and revealing heavenly perspectives of beauty and emotional expression."[29] Charles Caffin compared Matisse and the modern dancer Isadora Duncan, saying each was exploring a vital, primitive spirit. Of Isadora's dance performance, he wrote, "It was a revelation of beauty so exquisite, that it brought happy, cleansing tears. Bravo, Isadora!"; of Matisse, "he is but blazing a path, that as yet he does not himself know how to coordinate with the rhythm and melody of nature."[30] The controversial 1913 Armory Show, which brought many modern European art works to New York for the first time, sparked further support of the avant-garde and helped to validate *Camera Work* and 291 in their espousal of various new experiments and explorations.

World War I marked the final period of *Camera Work* and, along with rising costs and inadequate support, forced the demise of the beautiful magazine. Among the last issues, number 47 included a collection of statements solicited by Stieglitz testifying to the significance of his 291 gallery, for a variety of individuals. In the later years of *Camera Work*, it was clear that Pictorial photography was losing its ground, supplanted by more Modernist trends. Stieglitz devoted the last issue of *Camera Work* to Paul Strand, whose work exhibited clean, precise Modernist lines in both images of the city and everyday objects. His photographs brought the viewer closer to a Modernist world of abstraction.[31]

During the course of publication and in the years thereafter, Stieglitz was continually concerned that complete sets *Camera Work* should be in significant public institutions. He wrote to Mr. McIntosh, the Royal Photographic Society's secretary and librarian,

> I feel that by hook or crook the Royal must have a complete set of the publication which is really part of my life blood. But I do hope you will impress your members with the fact that destroying the completeness of *Camera Work* in any way is robbing the society of a genuine and valuable asset in more sense than one. The publication is doing Trojan work for the "Cause" and it has been instrumental in winning over some of the bitterest opponents of photography not only in this country buy in the rest of the world.[32]

Shortly after the first issue of *Camera Work* appeared, Alfred returned to Europe from May to October 1904 with Emmy and Kitty. For a good deal of the time Alfred was sick and he remained at the Berlin clinic of Dr. Boas for most of June while Kitty and Emmy went to Stutttgart to visit elderly relatives.

The winter and early spring of 1904 had been difficult for Stieglitz. He had overseen the production of two issues of *Camera Work*, produced a limited edition set of five of his photogravures, and with Keiley, Coburn, and Steichen, had mounted major exhibitions of the Photo-Secession at the Corcoran Gallery in Washington, D.C., and the Carnegie Art Galleries in Pittsburgh. He also had problems with two of his *Camera Work* contributors, Roland Rood and Sadakichi Hartmann. Rood objected to Stieglitz's wanting him always to support the Secessionist group. The two men momentarily healed their rift, but two years later further problems resulted in Rood leaving the magazine. Hartmann, that spring, had begun to criticize Stieglitz in some of his writing. Keiley sided with Stieglitz. Hartmann and Stieglitz did not really reconcile with one another until seven years later, when Hartmann resumed writing regularly for *Camera Work* until its demise in 1917. But the effect of these conflicts on Stieglitz's nerves required him to rest for close to a month.

Stieglitz did visit the Photo-Secession show in Dresden (one of six exhibitions he had arranged abroad). There at the Grosse Kunstausstellung, he saw large-scale photographs by Heinrich Kühn, Hans Watzek, and Hugo Henneberg. (In 1906 he exhibited their painterly, gum-bichromate prints at his gallery.) In July he accompanied Dr. Boas to Igls bei Innsbruck in Austria, where he worked with Frank Eugene. Dr. Fritz Raab, a family friend and a painter and photographer as well as a doctor, was in Igls too.

While in Austria, Stieglitz also photographed with Kühn. In a photograph such as *Landscape, the Tyrol* the painterly qualities of the print reflect the influence of Henneberg, Kühn, and Watzek. Stieglitz later wrote of the three photographers in the January 1906 issue of *Camera Work*, "The artist is compelled to deal both with nature and his material in order to create something new that is neither nature in the

201   Alfred Stieglitz, *Landscape, the Tyrol*, 1904

ordinary sense nor mere material. Nature and art – art and photography! There are very few ... who understand the connection existing between those terms."[33] The gently bending trees in the photograph seem almost alive, swaying on the hillside as if on a stage, with a bank of clouds as backdrop. In later cropped images such as *Dancing Trees* of 1922, a dance motif is more clearly articulated.

While working with Kühn, Stieglitz also photographed a farmer, *Ploughing*, and *Horses*, a close-up of two workhorses, one black, one white. *Ploughing*, with its painterly, Pictorial, soft-focus tones, lauds the working farmer, but its layers of gray tones lift the viewer past man and nature into the world of art. The sturdy black and white horses, harnessed for work, seem almost human in their close proximity to the

202   Alfred Stieglitz, *Ploughing*, 1904   203   Alfred Stieglitz, *Horses*, 1904

viewer. It is unclear if Stieglitz intended there to be any specific symbolism in the contrast of the white and black steeds, but they could be read as elements of light, purity, or innocence versus darkness, death, and foreboding. *Horses* appeared in the October 1905 issue of *Camera Work*. A photogravure of the same image was made about five years later with its texture enhanced by Stieglitz by placing sandpaper on the print and running it through a printing press.

In 1904 Stieglitz also photographed Sophie Raab (possibly the daughter of Dr. Raab) in at least three different versions, all depicting her spontaneous expression as if she were in conversation with the photographer. She is shown from the shoulders up, the soft curls of her hair pulled back, her head tilted, wearing a jaunty hat, with the background in very

204   Alfred Stieglitz, *Miss S. R.*, 1904

soft focus, making the photograph more intimate than some of Stieglitz's earlier portraits. Titled simply, *Miss S. R.*, or *Portrait, S. R.*, her be-guiling image was reproduced in *Camera Work* in October 1905 and January 1913, as well as being published in other sources, both in the United States and Europe.

From late August until early October 1904, Stieglitz was in London, where he attended an opening of a Linked Ring Salon and various other exhibitions. He talked to the photographers J. Craig Annan, Frederick H. Evans, Alvin Langdon Coburn, and Alfred Horsley Hinton about the possibility of Linked Ring units in other countries, of which he would serve as over all director. He also had lunch with George Bernard Shaw, who was an amateur photographer as well as a playwright, to talk about promoting photography. The London visit was not entirely successful since Stieglitz became ill and was ordered by the doctor not to talk! This was certainly a dilemma for the gregarious and articulate Stieglitz. Kitty and Emmy were also sick and their trip home had to be postponed by three weeks. Coburn and his mother accompanied the Stieglitz family home. Stieglitz was not to see any of the British photographers again.

*   *   *

291

Back in New York, the year 1905 became important for the founding of the Little Galleries of the Photo-Secession at 291 Fifth Avenue, later known as 291. With the help of Steichen, who had earned enough money to move to a larger studio apartment across the hall, Stieglitz signed a one-year-lease for a small studio and two adjoining rooms behind it to serve as exhibition space for the Photo-Secession group. The gallery would be a headquarters for all Secessionists and have frequent exhibitions of both Europeans and Americans, open to the public without change.

Steichen's decoration of the gallery was primarily in earth tones, influenced by designers such as the Vienna Secessionist architect Josef Hoffmann and the Scottish architect Charles Rennie Mackintosh. The main room was in olive tones, with a burlap wall covering in a warm olive gray, while pleated canvas olive–sepia hangings, behind which was storage, hung below a shelf that ran around the room.[34] The smaller room was covered with a natural-colored burlap on the walls, accented by white and yellow rectangular hangings. A little hallway, also serving as exhibition space, was decorated in gray–blue, soft almond, and olive–gray.

205 Alfred Stieglitz or Paul Strand, the building at 291 Fifth Avenue, 1917

In the main room a few Japanese vases adorned the shelf, and on a burlap-covered table in the center of the room there frequently sat a large, circular, brass bowl filled with flowers or leafy branches, bringing the world of nature inside. The bowl's circular handles hung from lion-like fixtures, perhaps symbolizing courage and exploration in a sometimes jungle-like culture. The bowl reflected to some extent the golden disk that became the gallery's logo. The literary critic and photographer John Kerfoot explained the golden disk in an issue of *Camera Work*: "In our sun whirl there is one planet which has a moon that is turning the other way, and if it be strong enough and last long enough sooner or later the whole mighty wheel of light will return and follow that one little moon."[35] Works were hung in simple frames.

The decoration of the gallery was such that a number of Stieglitz's installation shots of gallery exhibitions were not simply documentary records: they were also interior landscapes, and many showed a new precision and elegance in the interplay of objects, light, and space, just as notes might be combined in a musical score. The earth tones of the gallery rooms, along with the line of the horizontal shelf, provided the viewer with an initial sense of stability and balance. An installation shot of a Picasso and Georges Braque exhibition in 1915 shows Stieglitz's

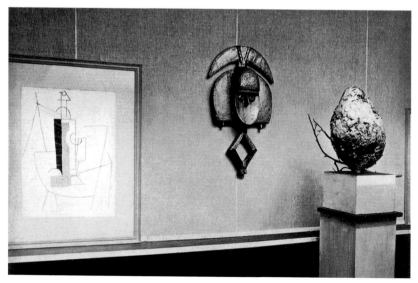

juxtaposition of a wasp's nest with drawings and an African mask. The image reflects Stieglitz's continuing interest in music and dance: the African mask suggests dance rituals and rites, and the Cubist drawings display stringed instruments. The rounded brass bowl, a vessel of reception, holds fresh foliage and provides a contrast to the rough-textured wasp's nest, yet it possesses the same curvilinear form. Another installation shot – of the *Primitive Negro Sculpture* exhibition of 1914 – shows the same brass bowl, this time filled with dry foliage. In the composition

207a (*left*) Alfred Stieglitz, *Primitive Negro Sculpure* exhibition, installation view at 291, 1914

206a (*facing page top*) Alfred Stieglitz, installation view of the Kühn, Henneberg, Watzek exhibition at 291, 1906

206b (*facing page bottom*) Alfred Stieglitz, *Picasso/Braque* exhibition, installation views at 291, 1915

207b (*left*) Alfred Stieglitz, *Brancusi* exhibition, installation view at 291, 1914

208 Alfred
Stieglitz,
installation views
of a Nadelman
exhibition at 291,
December 1915

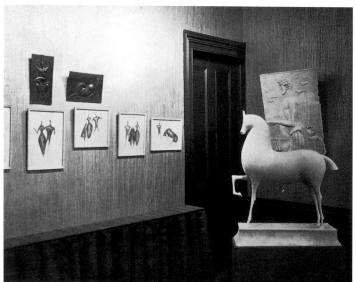

of this photograph, sculptural objects invite the viewer to dance with them.

On the evening of 25 November 1905, the Little Galleries of the Photo-Secession officially opened – with little fanfare. There were one hundred prints, representing thirty-nine Secessionist photographers. "Little" referred not only to the size of the rooms, but also to notions of simplicity, informality, and a small, working community. Like many new or different artistic modes of expression, this show was panned by conservative critics. Charles Fitzgerald of the *New York Evening Sun* wrote, "the vanity of these people is unbelievable. The fopperies displayed in their work, their eccentric frames, the whimsical flourishes in which they habitually indulge, and their incurable gravity – all these are but symptomatic of their essential frivolity."[36]

But there were many who found their way to that small room with the large artistic spirit. Stieglitz estimated that there were approximately fifteen thousand visits the first season, and that he made approximately $2800 from the sale of sixty-one prints, many of which were Steichen's. That first season included: an exhibition of French photography organized by Robert Demachy; a Gertrude Käsebier and Clarence White show; a show of the work of British photographers David Octavius Hill, J. Craig Annan, and Frederick H. Evans; a solo Steichen exhibition; and an Austrian–German show of Heinrich Kühn, Hugo Henneberg, and the late Hans Watzek.

Stieglitz found himself staying at the gallery all day and continued his promotional work over his almost daily round-table lunches at the Holland House, an elegant hotel at Fifth Avenue and 30th Street, a half-block from the gallery. Emmy had given Alfred money from her own family income to help finance the group lunches, perhaps with some hope that she might still win Alfred's love and approval.

In the spring of 1906, Steichen moved back to Paris with his family, hoping to devote more time to painting and his own personal work in photography instead of being caught up in the portrait business. Stieglitz remained in New York to continue his "battle" for the "cause" of photography as art, but was becoming disillusioned by rifts within the Secession group and conservative forces that appeared to be taking charge of the Linked Ring.

On a cold December day in 1906, when Stieglitz was feeling particularly discouraged and disgruntled, a young twenty-eight-year-old woman named Pamela Colman Smith arrived, unannounced at 291. She asked whether Mr. Stieglitz was in. Stieglitz replied, somewhat rudely, "No, I'm not."[37] But despite his initial mood, Stieglitz was quickly intrigued by the young artist who had been living in London. He agreed to show her work, and from 5–22 January 1907, her drawings were shown at 291. This was the first non-photographic exhibition at 291 and the beginning of a new path showing modern art in America. Stieglitz defended his decision to show an artist in a non-photographic medium in an article in *Camera Work*: "Exhibitions of drawings in black and white and color by Miss Pamela Colman Smith . . . marked not a departure from the intentions of the Photo-Secession, but a welcome opportunity of their manifesting. The Secession is neither the servant nor the product of a medium. It is . . . the spirit of the lamp of honesty . . . and when these pictures of Miss Smith's, conceived in this spirit and no other, came to us . . . we but tended the lamp in tendering them hospitality."[38]

Colman Smith's work was described as pictured music and a number of her pieces bore musical titles, such as her watercolor *Beethoven Sonata, No. 11*, (1907), with crescendos and decrescendos typical of many Beethoven pieces. Other titles included *Beethovenesque*, and *The Devil's Sonata*. She described her pieces as "just what I see when I hear

music – thoughts loosened and set free by the spell of sound. When I take a brush in hand, and the music begins, it is like unlocking the door into a beautiful country. There, stretched far away, are plains and mountains and the billowy sea, and as the music forms a net of sound, the people who dwell there enter the scene."[39]

Colman Smith had been a student of Arthur Wesley Dow, who had written in the introduction to his book *Composition*, "music . . . [is] in a sense the key to the other fine arts, since its essence is pure beauty."[40] Dow repeatedly emphasized the notion of synthesis and of filling a space in a beautiful way through composition and construction, not through imitation. With Colman Smith's synthetic abilities and her emphasis on musicality, it is no wonder that Stieglitz was immediately drawn to the free, flowing qualities of her work.

209   Pamela Colman Smith, *Beethoven Sonata, No. 11*, 1907

In her book on Colman Smith, Melinda Boyd Parsons describes how the world that the artist created, with its spatial ambiguities, was rooted in contemporary views of reality: "Late nineteenth-century philosophers like Schopenhauer had asserted the relative and subjective nature of human perceptions of the world. If Pamela's paintings were not an intentional embodiment of this philosophy, they certainly reflected Schopenhauer's definition of reality as relative to our subjective perceptions. This was recognized by her contemporaries and admirably formulated by the American writer Benjamin de Casseres, who was a follower of Schopenhauer."[41] De Casseres praised Colman Smith in the July 1909 issue of *Camera Work*, where he described her as "a blender of visions, a mystic, a symbolist, one who transforms the world she lives in by the overwhelming simplicity of her imagination."[42] Stieglitz actually showed her work three times at 291, and although she disappeared from the mainstream of twentieth-century art history, she is important as a catalyst in Stieglitz's decision to mount non-photographic exhibitions.[43]

Among the significant non-photographic exhibitions at 291 were: drawings by Rodin, January 1908; drawings, lithographs, and water-colors by Matisse, April 1908; during the 1908–9 season, caricatures by the Spaniard Marius de Zayas, oils by Alfred Maurer, watercolors by John Marin, and paintings by Marsden Hartley – all first exhibitions by these artists. In 1909–10, there were second exhibitions of works by Rodin and by Matisse, and shows by new artists Arthur Carles, Arthur Dove, and Max Weber. In the early years of the gallery, Steichen's presence in Paris allowed him to make initial contact with many of the European artists that came to be shown at 291.

Other works shown for the first time in the United States included Cézanne's lithographs of *The Bathers* (1910); Cézanne's watercolors (1911); paintings and drawings by Henri Rousseau (1910); Picasso's Blue Period work and early Cubist drawings (1911); Francis Picabia's studies for larger paintings (1913) and paintings (1915); Brancusi's first one-man exhibition anywhere (1914); African Negro Sculpture (1914); and the work of Gino Severini (1917). Of particular note were John Marin's watercolors in 1912, 1914, and 1915. He showed works by children, including his own daughter's work, marking an emphasis on sponta-neous, direct, and honest expression. The last show at 291 was the work of Georgia O'Keeffe from 3 April–14 May 1917. Stieglitz had already shown her work in 1916 in group shows, after O'Keeffe's friend, Anita Pollitzer, had secretly brought Stieglitz some of O'Keeffe's drawings, of which he pronounced, "Finally, a woman on paper."[44]

The gallery was, for Stieglitz, a community of kindred spirits, of artists and critics who as individuals contributed their special talents. Collec-tively they formed a significant whole that affected the course of modern art in America. The gallery was also an aesthetic laboratory, marrying to some extent art and science. In 1910, it was stated in *Camera Work* that, "It should be remembered that the Little Gallery is nothing more than a laboratory, an experimental station, and must not be looked upon as an art gallery in the ordinary sense of the word."[45] As Geraldine Wojna Kiefer noted in her book on the scientific aspects of Stieglitz's work, "The Little Galleries, having been defined as laboratories, Stieglitz was the man whom both the gallery-going public and the Secessionist circle expected to take the helm as laboratory director. And having had ten years of experience in scientific laboratories he had designed and directed (the Photochrome Engraving Company and the Camera Club of New York) Stieglitz was now ready to undertake this new and distinctly novel assignment."[46] Stieglitz's ideas about science may be likened to those of Ernst Mach, who saw the basis of science as a rich, sensuous experience that should be felt and described before it was explained scientifically. Mach had written, "The play of the imagination around what is experienced or seen, this 'poetry' of life, is the first elevation rising above the everyday, above the breathless bearing of the burden of life ... let us therefore consider this poetic imagination that competes and modifies everything experienced."[47]

A sampling of responses to Stieglitz's query, "What is 291?" for the January 1915 issue of *Camera Work* reveals the gallery's impact for those who frequented or were touched by its small set of rooms. William Zorach wrote:

> I rode up in the tiny elevator and entered the little gallery. The quiet light was full of a soothing mystic feeling and around the room, and on the square under glass in the middle of the room, I looked at what I now know were Matisse drawings. I was all alone and I stood and absorbed the atmosphere of the place and of the drawings. They had no meaning to me as art as I then knew art, but the feeling I got from them still clings to me and always will. It was the feeling of a bigger, deeper, more simple and archaic world. I stood long and absorbed 291 – the quiet, peaceful little room, the strange and wonderful life revealed to me and the square-faced, bushy-haired man with penetrating eyes that swayed in and swayed out of the doorway. I left feeling I had seen something living, something that would live with me, and that has lived with me. For now after an absence of three years I have visited 291 very often and to me it is a wonderful living place palpitating with red blood – a place to which people bring their finest and that brings out the finest that is within all those that come in actual contact with it.

J. B. Kerfoot: "But 291 is greater than the sum of all its definitions. For it is a living force, working both good and evil. To me, 291 has meant an intellectual antidote to the nineteenth century; a spiritual preparation for the twenty-first; and withal, a glorious training camp and practice ground for eclecticism."

Marius De Zayas: "291 not an Idea, nor an Ideal, but something more potent, a Fact, something accomplished, being of a nature, although perfect, by no means final or conclusive, but much to the contrary . . . 291 magnificent school for Autobiography and – caricature."

John Weichsel: "A cosmos-reflecting dewdrop, returning to each one of us his illumined specter – is 291 to me. Diverse images of life are here focused side by side."

J. N. Laurvik: "291 – a human vortex."

Emil Zoler: "The philosophy – if any – of 291 is vivisectional. The psychology is perfectly clinical . . . To me 291 is what the perfect beautiful spring is to the wayfarer who drinks of its live living elements, which water refreshes, strengthens, enhances, and exhilarates life. It receives and welcomes with the same innocence, confidence, trust, hope, and purity, the same realism with which the child accepts as it sits and listens with an alertness of its own."

Arthur B. Carles: "291 is the one place where people gather that has never become a disappointment. And to be welcome is to have a friendship that nothing can spoil . . . As long as 291 lasts I'll always feel that an open road to the world of artists is accessible."

Eugene Meyer, Jr.: "An Oasis of real freedom . . . A test. A solvent. A victim and an Avenger."

Arthur Dove: "It has grown and outgrown in order to grow. It grew because there was need for such a place, yet it is not a place . . . This seems to be 291, or is it Stieglitz."

Marsden Hartley: "A pure instrument is certainly sure to give forth pure sound. So has this instrument of 291 kept itself as pure as possible that it thereby gives out pure expression."[48]

Despite its magical powers to some, the gallery was not without opposition from traditional and more conservative forces in the New York art world at the time. The critic Thomas Craven blasted 291 as a "bedlam of half-baked philosophies and cock-eyed visions," where Stieglitz "shrewdly managed to hold the position of arbiter, to maintain a reputation for superior acumen." Craven also called Stieglitz "a Hoboken Jew without knowledge or interest in the historical American background."[49]

As a result of his interaction with a variety of artists, Stieglitz came to collect a number of significant art works, photographs, and works in

other media. He had begun to collect photographs in 1894 and by 1910
had acquired approximately 650 prints, 580 of which eventually became
part of the Metropolitan Museum of Art's collection in New York.
(Stieglitz gave the museum 400 works in 1933, and the museum received
the rest as a bequest in 1949, three years after his death). Stieglitz's selections for his collection were diverse and represented a variety of subjects
and styles. Artists such as Edward Steichen, Gertrude Käsebier, Adolph
de Meyer, Ansel Adams, and Elliot Porter were well represented.

Of the non-photographic works Stieglitz collected during the 291
years, highlights included lithographs by Henri de Toulouse-Lautrec
drawings by Matisse, Picasso, and Picabia, a Severini Futurist oil painting and drawings, and a Brancusi sculpture. But as the art historian
George Heard Hamilton has noted:

> Stieglitz was not a dealer in the strict sense of the word. Having a
> private income, he did not depend upon his galleries to show a profit,
> nor did he, in the usual manner, claim a stipulated commission for
> each work sold. Rather he acted more as an agent for his artists, as
> their private banker, finding sympathetic patrons, often arranging that
> the price to be paid should suit the patron's purse – provided always
> that the latter seemed to truly understand and want the work in ques-
> tion – and then holding the funds received until the artist needed them.
> Therefore it would seem proper to consider the works remaining in
> Stieglitz's possession as objects that he kept from preference, not from
> necessity.[50]

Stieglitz was possessive of the artists and art works that he showed.
Indeed, in some instances, the artists and their works were almost like
Stieglitz's children – perhaps a replacement of his own daughter in later
years as their relationship deteriorated and Kitty was ultimately institutionalized. Stieglitz was particularly close to the artists who came to be
known as his inner circle – John Marin, Marsden Hartley, Arthur Dove,
Charles Demuth, and, of course, Georgia O'Keeffe.

Upon Stieglitz's death, his collection of art works and photographs
was divided among various American art museums. In addition to the
Metropolitan Museum, works were given to the Art Institute of Chicago,
the National Gallery of Art and the Library of Congress in Washington,
D.C., the Philadelphia Museum of Art, and Fisk University in Nashville.
Stieglitz's own photographs were divided among eleven institutions, with
the Key Set going to the National Gallery of Art.

*   *   *

THE STEERAGE

Stieglitz not only was a collector, gallery director, and editor and writer in the early years of the twentieth century, but he also continued to take his own photographs. Perhaps one of the most famous and most significant photographs of his career is *The Steerage*, taken in 1907. It may be seen as a breakthrough photograph in both its metaphoric qualities and use of formal elements.

In the spring of 1907, Stieglitz and his family sailed to Europe on the large ship the *Kaiser Wilhelm II*. The photograph was taken on that trip. In 1942 Stieglitz described taking the photograph in "How *The Steerage* Happened" for *Twice a Year*:

Early in June 1907, my small family and I sailed for Europe. My wife insisted upon going on the *Kaiser Wilhelm II* – the fashionable ship of the North German Lloyd at the time. Our first destination was Paris. How I hated the atmosphere of the first class on that ship. One couldn't escape the *nouveaux riches*.

I sat much in my steamer chair the first days out – sat with closed eyes. In this way I avoided seeing faces that would give me the cold shivers, yet those voices and that English – ye gods!

On the third day out I finally couldn't stand it any longer. I tried to get away from that company. I went as far forward on deck as I could. The sea wasn't particularly rough. The sky was clear. The ship was driving into the wind – a rather brisk wind.

As I came to the end of the deck I stood alone, looking down. There were men and woman and children on the lower deck of the steerage. There was a narrow stairway leading up to the upper deck of the steerage, a small deck right at the bow of the steamer.

To the left was an inclining funnel and from the upper steerage deck there was fastened a gangway bridge that was glistening in its freshly painted state. It was rather long, white, and during the trip remained untouched by anyone.

On the upper deck, looking over the railing, there was a young man with a straw hat. The shape of the hat was round. He was watching the men and women and children on the lower steerage deck. Only men were on the upper deck. The whole scene fascinated me. I longed to escape form my surroundings and join those people.

A round straw hat, the funnel leaning left, the stairway leaning right, the white drawbridge with its railings made of circular chains – white suspenders crossing on the back of a man in the steerage below, round shapes of iron machinery, a mast cutting into the sky, making a triangular shape. I stood spellbound for a while, looking and looking. Could I photograph what I felt, looking and looking, and still looking? I saw shapes related to each other. I saw a picture of shapes and underlying that the feeling I had about life. And as I was deciding, would I try to put down this seemingly new vision that held me – people, the common people, the feeling of ship and ocean and sky and the feeling of release that I was away from the mob called the rich – Rembrandt came into my mind and I wondered would he have felt as I was feeling.

Spontaneously I raced to the main stairway of the steamer, raced down to my cabin, got my Graflex, raced back again all out of breath, wondering whether the man with the straw hat had moved or not. If he had, the picture I had seen would no longer be. The relationship of shapes as I wanted them would have been disturbed and the picture lost.

But there was the man with the straw hat. He hadn't moved. The man with the crossed white suspenders showing his back, he too, talking to a man, hadn't moved, and the woman with the child on her lap, sitting on the floor, hadn't moved. Seemingly no one had changed position.

I had but one plate-holder with one unexposed plate. Would I get what I saw, what I felt? Finally I released the shutter. My heart thumping. I had never heard my heart thump before. Had I gotten my picture? I knew if I had, another milestone in photography would have been reached, related to the milestone of my *Car Horses* made in 1893. and my *Hand of Man* made in 1902, which had opened up a new era of photography, of seeing. In a sense it would go beyond them, for here would be a picture based on related shapes and on the deepest human feeling, a step in my own evolution, a spontaneous discovery.

I took my camera to my stateroom and as I returned to my steamer chair my wife said, "I had a steward look for you. I wondered where you were. I was nervous when he came back and said he couldn't find you." I told her where I had been.

She said, "You speak as if you were far away in a distant world," and I said I was.

"How you seem to hate these people in the first class." No, I didn't hate them, but I merely felt completely out of place.

As soon as we were installed in Paris I went to the Eastman Kodak Company to find out whether they had a darkroom in which I could

210   Alfred Stieglitz, *The Steerage*, 1907

develop my plate. They had none. They gave me an address of a photographer. I went there.

The photographer led me to a huge darkroom, many feet long and many feet wide, perfectly appointed.

He said, "Make yourself at home. Have you developer? Here's a fixing bath – it's fresh."

I had brought a bottle of my own developer. I started developing. What tense minutes! Had I succeeded, had I failed? That is, was the exposure correct? Had I moved while exposing? If the negative turned out to be anything but perfect, my picture would be a failure.

Finally I had developed and washed and rinsed the plate. In looking at it, holding it up to the red light it seemed all right, and yet I wouldn't know until the plate had been completely fixed.

The minutes seemed like hours. Finally the fixing was completed. I could turn on the white light. The negative was perfect in every particular. Would anything happen to it before I got to New York?

I washed it. No negative could ever receive more care, and when the washing was finished, I dried the negative with the help of an electric fan. I waited until it was bone dry, and when it was completely dry I put the glass plate into the plate holder which originally held it. In that way I felt it was best protected. I could not remove it from that place till I had returned to New York. I had sufficient plate holders with me to permit myself that luxury – or, should I say, that insurance?

I wanted to pay the photographer for the use of his darkroom, but he said, "I can't accept money from you. I know who you are. It's an honor for me to know you have used my darkroom."

How he happened to know me I couldn't understand. Later on I discovered that my name was written on a package which I had left in his office while in the dark room.

And when I got to New York four months later I was too nervous to make a proof of the negative. In making the negative I had in mind enlarging it for *Camera Work*, also enlarging it to eleven by fourteen and making a photogravure of it.

Finally this happened. Two beautiful plates were made under my direction, under my supervision, and proofs were pulled on papers that I had selected. I was completely satisfied. Something I not often was, or am.

The first person to whom I showed *The Steerage* was my friend and coworker Joseph T. Keiley, "But you have two pictures there, Stieglitz, an upper and a lower one," he said.

I said nothing. I realized he didn't see the picture I had made. Thenceforth I hesitated to show the proofs to anyone, but finally in 1910 I showed them to Haviland and Max Weber and de Zayas and other artists of that type. They truly saw the picture, and when it appeared in *Camera Work* it created a stir wherever seen, and the eleven by fourteen gravure created still a greater stir.

I said one day, "If all my photographs were lost and I'd be represented by just one, *The Steerage*, I'd be satisfied."

I'm not so sure that I don't feel much the same way today.[51]

The writer Allan Sekula has read Stieglitz's account of his taking of the photograph as "pure symbolist autobiography," suggesting that Stieglitz "Invented himself in pure Symbolist clichés. An ideological division is made: Stieglitz proposes two worlds, a world that entraps and one that liberates . . . The photograph is taken at the intersection of the two worlds . . . The photographer marks a young man in a straw hat as a spectator, suggesting this figure as an embodiment of Stieglitz as subject. The possibility of escape resides in a mystical identification with the other . . . the final Symbolist hideout is in the imagination . . . Stieglitz comes back to his wife with a glass negative from the other world."[52] Sekula sees *The Steerage* as going beyond significant form and formal qualities, prefiguring Stieglitz's more explicit use of metaphor in his later work, in particular his *Equivalents*. For Sekula, "Stieglitz's career represents the triumph of metaphor in the realm of photography."[53]

Stieglitz did not exhibit or publish the work until it appeared in *Camera Work* in October 1911. *The Steerage* was also published four years later in both deluxe and regular editions of the newly established *291* periodical. As a large photogravure, many have interpreted the photograph as an image that memorialized the New York immigrant experience, just as Lewis Hine did in his Ellis Island series. But in truth, this is an image that was taken on the way to Europe, not to the United States. It does depict a lower-class experience with an elegant composition that draws on Cubist elements, and speaks of Stieglitz's wish to escape the constrictions of his upper-class upbringing and the expectations of his wife Emmy. Stieglitz himself noted, "You may call this a crowd of immigrants . . . To me it is a study in mathematical lines, in balance, in a pattern of light and shade."[54] Stieglitz beautifully used a gangplank, large column, and ladder to form the basis of his geometric exploration. Picasso is reported to have very much liked the photograph, appreciating its Cubist elements. (Having completed *Les Demoiselles d'Avignon* in 1907, by 1911 Picasso was well advanced in his experiments in analytical Cubism, along with Georges Braques.)

Both *The Steerage* and Picasso's 1907 *Les Demoiselles d'Avignon* mark significant junctures in early twentieth-century art and photography: Picasso's piece opened the way to Cubism; Stieglitz's photograph contained proto-Cubist elements and was not only a social document but, as Sekula suggests, a metaphor, created through the unification of Stieglitz's humanist view and his formalist values.

During the summer of 1907, Stieglitz had his first introduction to the art of Cézanne, whom he did not initially appreciate, commenting, "Why, there's nothing there but empty paper with a few splashes of color here and there."[55] It seems somewhat ironic that Stieglitz would respond this way after beginning to explore geometric forms in *The Steerage*.

AUTOCHROME AND OTHER EXPERIMENTS

The summer of 1907 was noteworthy because of the recent appearance of autochrome plates, developed and manufactured by the Lumière brothers from 1904 in Lyons, France. The autochrome process allowed for the production of very subtle color images with soft outlines. Autochromes were positive transparencies on glass plates, not prints. They were meant to be viewed via projection or held up to the light. Like the daguerreotype process, the autochrome process did not produce a negative from which prints could be made. Stieglitz had actually been interested in color processing for a number of years, while he was at the Photochrome Engraving Company. The company had hoped Stieglitz would develop a three-color process for printing half-tone illustrations in color. Stieglitz developed a three-color process, but the company was competing with a process already developed by William Kurtz of New York and Ernst Vogel, the son of Stieglitz's admired Professor Vogel in Berlin. The January 1894 issue of the *American Amateur Photographer* had actually contained a color reproduction printed by the Photochrome Company of a hand-colored platinum print of Stieglitz's photograph, *The Last Load*, which he had shot in Cortina. In Steichen's first exhibition at 291 from March to April 1906, he also included some experimental color photographs made by exposing three black and white negatives through blue, green, and red filters. The negatives were then superimposed on each other and printed with red, blue, and green gum bichromate.

In 1907, Steichen had seen an autochrome demonstration in Paris, and during that summer Stieglitz, Steichen, Frank Eugene, Alvin Langdon Coburn, Heinrich Kühn, and Adolph de Meyer all worked intensely on experimenting with the new color process. Stieglitz worked with Eugene in the Bavarian town of Tutzing, in August. A poignant autochrome image of Alfred and Kitty was made in Tutzing by either Stieglitz or Steichen or both. Seated on a bench, Stieglitz, with his camera, looks intently at his nine-year-old daughter, who holds a bouquet of flowers in her lap with one hand, her other hand gently resting on her father's camera, thereby linking the camera with the world of nature and with her. In this association, she, in some ways, serves as a young muse. The autochromes that Stieglitz produced that summer, both in Europe and back in the United States, are primarily portraits – including Dr. Raab,

211   Alfred Stieglitz, *Oaklawn*, 1910

212   Alfred Stieglitz, *Frank Eugene*, 1907

213 Alfred Stieglitz, *Dorothy Schubart*, 1915

214 Alfred Stieglitz, *Alfred and Emmeline Stieglitz*, 1910

Frank Eugene, Dorothy Schubart, Sophie Raab, Hedwig Stieglitz, Emmy, and *Two Men Playing Chess*. They are, in general, delicate studies in the interplay of light and color.

Stieglitz was so impressed with Steichen's experiments, including a portrait of Bernard Shaw, that he published three of Steichen's autochromes in the April 1908 issue of *Camera Work*. In an article entitled, "The New Color Photography," in October 1907, Stieglitz described his return trip to New York, equating the marvels of "marconigraphing" (wireless telegraphy) at sea and listening to a player-piano to "looking at those unbelievable color photographs! How easily we learn to live on former visions! . . . The Lumière process, imperfect as some may consider it, has actually brought color photography in to our homes for the first time, and in a beautifully ingenious, quick, and direct way."[56] When he returned home from Europe he also sent out a press release inviting the press to view the new autochrome pro-cess at an exhibition at 291 on 27 and 28 September, indicating it was the first time images made from this process would be shown in the United States.

Stieglitz's enthusiasm for the autochrome process was short-lived, not more than two years. But in November 1907, he did attempt to obtain a commission to photograph President Theodore Roosevelt in color, which was

New York, September 26th, 1907.

To the Press:—

    Gentlemen:—

        Color photography is an accomplished fact. That this is actually true will be demonstrated at an exhibition, reserved exclusively for the Press, in the Photo-Secession Galleries, 291 Fifth Avenue, on Friday and Saturday, September 27 and 28, between the hours of 10 and 12 A.M. and 2 and 4 P.M.

        Mr. Alfred Stieglitz, having just returned from Europe, has brought with him a selection of color photographs made by Eduard J. Steichen, Frank Eugene and himself.

        They will demonstrate some of the possibilities of the remarkable Lumière Autochrome Process, only recently perfected and placed upon the French market. These pictures are the first of the kind to be shown in America. You are invited to attend the exhibition.

        Yours truly,

        Alfred Stieglitz.

        Director of the Photo-Secession.

215   Statement to the Press by Alfred Stieglitz, 26 September 1907, announcing the exhibition of autochromes by himself, Steichen and Frank Eugene,

never realized. Steichen was commissioned in early 1906 by the popular *Everybody's Magazine* to take photographs of President Roosevelt, William Howard Taft, Roosevelt's secretary of war, and Robert La Follette, a progressive United States senator from Wisconsin, for an article by Lincoln Steffens, "Roosevelt, Taft, La Follette on What the Matter Is in America and What to Do About It," for the 18 June 1908 issue. Steichen was to receive $500 per portrait. On 26 March, prior to the portrait sittings scheduled with Steichen on 1 April, Stieglitz wrote a letter suggesting that the president perhaps be photographed in color by Steichen. Early in 1909, Stieglitz exhibited autochromes and black and white photographs by Alvin Langdon Coburn and Adolph de Meyer at 291. Steichen's autochromes were the only photographs shown during the 1910 season at 291.

Moving away from his autochrome experiments in late 1907, Stieglitz in December collaborated with Clarence White on an experimental series of photographs that attempted to demonstrate the flexibility of the camera in producing painterly images. These included a number of evocative portraits of Mabel Cramer, a model and friend of the San Francisco photographer Arnold Gentile, and a woman identified as Miss Thompson that are dream-like, soft focused and find their roots in Symbolist painting. Four of the pieces – *Experiment 27*, *Experiment 28*, *Miss Mabel C*, and *Torso* – were reproduced in *Camera Work* in July 1909. The negative of the torso of Miss Thompson, with its subtle lighting, was made in gaslight and initially printed on waxed platinum paper. The collaborative efforts of the two men involved experimenting with lenses and the materials upon which the negatives were printed. They tried different papers and produced various print types such as platinum, gelatin silver, and gum bichromate over platinum. Some were straight prints; some were soft focused and highly nuanced. Some were signed with a special decorative monogram, designed from Stieglitz and White's combined initials. Unfortunately, White and Stieglitz stopped speaking to each other in 1912. Stieglitz returned eighty-four negatives and seventy-five prints to White. He kept fourteen for himself.

In 1908 291 almost closed completely. Steichen was heading back to Paris. Stieglitz told his friend that, because of fatigue and increased rent, he would have to close down 291. Steichen helped him pack up – and then, almost miraculously, a new patron appeared in the person of young Paul Burty Haviland, a French-born descendant of the wealthy Haviland China Company in Limoges, which did business in both the United States and France. Haviland had seen the recent Rodin exhibition at the gallery

with his brother, the artist Frank Burty Haviland, who later exhibited at 291 in 1914. Haviland took a three-year lease on the rooms that
had been part of Steichen's studio at 293 Fifth
Avenue and offered them to Stieglitz who,
always proud, resisted, and argued that the
rooms were even smaller than those of 291.
Others, including Steichen, Coburn, and
George Bernard Shaw, convinced Stieglitz to
accept the offer. After considerable coaxing,
Stieglitz finally conceded and the new space
officially adopted the name 291, by which the
little Galleries of the Photo-Secession had been
known, even though the official address was
293 Fifth Avenue. Stieglitz was better able to
help finance 291 when, on his father's death on
24 May 1909, he inherited $10,000; he drew
$700 annually from that money to help run
291. Whatever grief Stieglitz felt at his father's
death, he kept to himself.

216 Alfred Stieglitz, *Paul Haviland*,
1914

Paul Burty Haviland was to become a key figure in Stieglitz's life,
helping with *Camera Work*, working to facilitate exhibitions, especially
those of work originating in France, and learning to take photographs.
A 1914 portrait of Haviland taken by Stieglitz shows him as a man with
a strong presence, well dressed, with piercing eyes and long slender
fingers, holding a cigarette. He is standing looking straight at the viewer,
in front of a painting, most likely one by his brother such as *Fortifica-
tion*, shown at 291 in April and early May 1914.

NEW YORK, 1910–1911

The most significant of Stieglitz's photographs taken on his own in the
first decade of the century were perhaps those he took in 1910 and 1911
in New York. These photographs speak of transits – arrivals and depar-
tures to and from New York – and of new buildings, in short, man-made
elements forming an architectural stage with backdrops of water and sky.
In contrast to the cold geometry of his later photographs of New York
City buildings, many of these still contain the suggestion of a human
presence and a sense of a developing modern city. There are titles such

217   Alfred Stieglitz, *Old and New New York*, 1910

as *The City of Ambition*, *Old and New New York*, or *Two Towers –
New York*. *Old and New New York* is a view looking east from 34th
Street and Fifth Avenue. A figure in the front, perhaps the artist Max
Weber, appears to be looking at an old brownstone building, while in
the background the scaffolding of new construction rises like a specter
far above the older buildings. In *The City of Ambition* industrial smokestacks, with their billowing smoke, rise in white splendor in contrast to

218   Alfred Stieglitz, *The City of Ambition*, 1910

the dark buildings, up into the cloudy sky, joining nature and industry. The flag on the top of the towering Singer Building appears as a proud pinnacle on the modern building. *Two Towers – New York* shows the towers of Madison Square Garden and the Metropolitan Life Building, looking south from a snow-covered stoop. But it is the snow-covered branch next to the stoop and the man in the bowler hat that catches the viewer's attention. The towers are distant, perhaps not yet fully integrated into the daily life of the Madison Avenue residents.

219   Alfred Stieglitz, *Two Towers – New York*, 1911

Other 1911 images show scenes of excavation and construction –
Excavating, New York, *Construction, New York*, and *Horses, New York*.
In these the emphasis is on labor – horse and manpower. In *Construction, New York* and *Horses, New York*, the atmospheric effects of the
steam and snow add an element of mystery to the contrasting dark, solid,
laboring men and animals. Stieglitz's *Self-Portrait* of 1911 is a study in
both the excavation and construction of an identity, as Stieglitz turns to
his own image. His face is shrouded in a mysterious darkness, from which

220 Alfred Stieglitz, *Excavating, New York*, 1911

221 (*below*) Alfred Stieglitz, *Lower Manhattan*, 1910

222 Alfred
Stieglitz, *City
Across the River*,
1910

223 Alfred
Stieglitz, *The
Mauretania*,
1910

224   Alfred Stieglitz, *Self-Portait*, 1907 or 1911

he emerges, intent, serious, looking directly at the viewer. The dark cavernous background seems to have its roots in a Symbolist aesthetic, but
the clarity of his facial features and his spectacles speak of modernity. In
the context of the city images, Stieglitz, like the modern buildings, is
emerging into the daylight.

225   Alfred Stieglitz, *The Aeroplane*, 1910

The thirty-sixth issue of *Camera Work* in October 1911 contained
a number of these 1910–11 images. The issue, with its sixteen photogravures, was a kind of retrospective of Stieglitz's work from 1892 to
1910. The only other plate was a reproduction of one of Picasso's drawings, the original of which had been shown at 291 the previous April
and which was associated in the magazine with an excerpt from Plato
detailing a dialogue between Socrates and Philebus. Socrates refers to the
beauty of things "straight and round, and the figures, formed from them
by the turner's lathe, both superficial and solid, and those by the plumb
line and angle rule, if you understand me."[57] An emphasis on the geometric is also seen in several of Stieglitz's photographs in the same issue.
There is *The Ferry Boat*, in which white foreground cylinders on the pier
are balanced by the dark smokestack and other geometric shapes of the
boat. Or there is *The Mauritania*, in which similar white cylinder shapes,

226   Alfred Stieglitz, *A Dirigible*, 1910

here pier posts, are balanced by the four smokestacks of the large *Mauritania* in the background.

Among Stieglitz's other prints in the issue, were *The Hand of Man*, *Spring Showers*, *Excavating, New York*, *The Aeroplane*, *A Dirigible*, and *The Pool – Deal*. The photographs of a dirigible and aeroplane were shot just a few years after the Wright brothers' experiments. He captured the significance and wonder of flight, showing each of the aircraft dancing overhead, the new airborne technology silhouetted in grandeur against the sky and clouds. These images may be seen as harbingers of *Songs of the Sky* and the *Equivalents* series, although in the later pieces there is no reference to technology: the viewer is asked to confront the pure forms and any emotion they evoke, without the interference of outside elements such as the aeroplane. Stieglitz's photograph of the pool at Deal Beach, New Jersey, where he and his family often vacationed,

227   Alfred Stieglitz, *The Pool – Deal*, 1910

emphasized the linear elements and geometry of the platform overlooking the pool. The swimmers seem to be secondary to the architecture of the platform and background building.

In the same October 1911 issue, Benjamin de Casseres wrote an article, "The Unconscious in Art, "which suggests a manner in which Stieglitz's photographs might be read, or in which Stieglitz may have wished them to be read: "There are aesthetic emotions for which there are no corresponding thoughts, emotions that awaken the unconscious alone, and that never touch the brain . . . Imagination is the dream of the Unconscious . . . the roots of him [the artist] lie deeper than his personality. The soul of the genius is the safety vault of the race, the treasure pocket of the Unconscious soul of the world. Here age after age the secretive God stores in dreams. And the product of genius overwhelms us because it has collaborated with the Infinite."[58]

Besides photographing intently in 1910, Stieglitz also worked hard to promote the Photo-Secessionist cause. His letter of 10 October, 1910 to F. J. Mortimer, editor of *Amateur Photography*, voicing his concern about lack of acknowledgment for the reproduction of Anne Brigman's photographs from photogravures in *Camera Work*, serves as an illustration of his sharp tongue and sometimes combative rhetoric. But always he stuck to his cause, pushing for recognition and revolt against academic standards. "You, Mr. F. J. Mortimer, are a signal example of what Secessionism does not stand for."[59]

Stieglitz also worked tirelessly on an International Exhibition of Pictorial Photography in Buffalo, arranged by the Photo-Secession. With close to six hundred works, the exhibition sought to "Sum up the development and progress of photography as a means of pictorial expression . . . In view of the comprehensiveness of this historical survey, the excellence and scope of the work of each individual represented here, and the evidence of the present-day vitality of Pictorial Photography, this exhibition at the Albright Art Gallery aims at something more than has ever been attempted heretofore in any previous exhibition."[60] The works were hung by Stieglitz, Paul Burty Haviland, Max Weber, and Clarence White. The catalogue cover was designed by Weber.

Shortly after the opening, Stieglitz sent a night telegram to Emmy from Buffalo: "Exhibition fine one of the best weather beautiful leave for Niagara Monday morning expect to be home Tuesday morning love kiss to Kitty."[61] Stieglitz was clearly well pleased with the exhibition and feeling positive about his work and life around him. The show was highly praised in the January 1911 issue of *Camera Work* by Charles Caffin, Joseph Keiley, and Sadakichi Hartmann. Keiley commented on the exhibition's overriding of the jealous tendencies of individuals, saying that it had a golden glow, raised above the earth. He described Stieglitz's photographs in the show as "symphonic and aggressive, sure of touch and fertile of fancy."[62] And Hartmann noted the significance of the spirit of the exhibit: "Like the delicious odor in some mirrored cabinet that lingers indefinitely for years, this spirit will not fade. It will be remembered long after individual efforts have lost their immediate usefulness. The few masterpieces will remain, the rest will be forgotten, but the spirit will continue to remain an active force, and produce fresh impressions of light and tone, of form, and of grace."[63]

Stieglitz also sponsored a very successful exhibition of Marius de Zayas' work at 291 that same year. Having first met the Mexican immigrant in 1907, Stieglitz had given him his first show at 291 in 1901. It had failed to attract the attention of New York's fairly conservative press. But the 1910 exhibition, in terms of critical response and attendance, was a highly successful event. De Zayas arranged on a stage approximately sixty free-standing cardboard caricatures, mounted on wood, of prominent New Yorkers strolling up and down Fifth Avenue near the

Plaza Hotel. The figures were dubbed "The Boulevardiers." The exhibition was described as a "social satire" in the accompanying brochure, but de Zayas' ridicule was seen as gentle and entertaining. Among those depicted were Theodore Roosevelt, Cornelius and Alfred Vanderbilt, Ethel Barrymore, John Jacob Astor, "Diamond Jim" Brady, Mrs. H. Payne Whitney, and William Merritt Chase. Sadakichi Hartmann praised the show, and its underlying message: "In the harmless form of a puppet show, he unrolls a whole epopee, every page a human life told in a swift and summary way, a protest against the monstrous stupidity of conventions, parades, and badges, and the hypocrisy of morals – a wonderful synthesis of the grandeur and shame of the large city."[64] Unfortunately, there is no trace of the original piece.

De Zayas left for Europe in October while the show was still up. There he established contacts with some of the artists who were later to show at 291. Of particular importance was the development of his friendship with Picasso and his discovery of African art. De Zayas emphasized the importance of "primitivism" for Modernism and proposed an exhibition of African art at 291 which was mounted in 1914. In 1916, De Zayas published a book on the relation of primitive art to modern art, *African Negro Art: its Influence on Modern Art* with photographs by Charles Sheeler. Although de Zayas' writings would be considered racist in many ways in the twenty-first century, he pointed to the significance of feeling, sensation, and abstract form, which he saw as inherent in African art – all areas of interest to Stieglitz and some of his circle. He wrote, "It is certain that before the introduction of the plastic principles of Negro art, abstract representations did not exist among Europeans. Negro art has reawakened in us the feeling for abstract form; it has brought into our art the means to express our purely sensorial feelings in regard to form, or to find new form in our ideas."[65]

Stieglitz's 1915 portrait of de Zayas, probably taken at the Modern Gallery, a more commercial offshoot of 291, pictures de Zayas standing between two African masks and Picasso's 1904 *The Frugal Repast*. De Zayas in turn did a number of caricatures of Stieglitz. His 1910 ink drawing of Stieglitz appeared in the July 1912 issue of *Camera Work*. Faceless, Stieglitz's figure becomes dissolved into the page. The caricatures became increasingly abstract as de Zayas became influenced by Cubism and by an object called a "soul catcher" that he had seen in the British Museum in 1911, consisting of paired circles of vegetal materials on a wooden stick. De Zayas hoped to develop abstract caricatures based on spiritual interpretations of various individuals. The cover of the

March 1915 291 periodical consisted of one of these abstract caricatures of Stieglitz. Unfortunately relations between Stieglitz and de Zayas soured soon after the opening of the Modern Gallery, which de Zayas spearheaded. Stieglitz could not countenance any notion of competition. The two men were never close friends again, although they continued to respect one another and conduct various business transactions.

THE LAST EUROPEAN TRIP, 1911

Through de Zayas, Stieglitz had his own opportunity to meet Picasso when he returned to Europe for the last time during the summer of 1911 and de Zayas took him to Picasso's studio. That summer Stieglitz appeared to appreciate fully the experimental European moderns such as Cézanne, Matisse, and Picasso.[66]

Stieglitz's initial weeks in Europe with his wife and daughter found him frustrated as he tried to accept Emmy's and thirteen-year-old Kitty's wishes. Late in July, Stieglitz visited Frank Eugene in Munich. He wrote to Haviland on 6 August from Lucerne of some of his frustrations:

My dear Haviland,
I was very glad to get your letter and to hear that you were having a few days off. I imagined that our famous government by Interference had been keeping you busier even than you had expected. I hope that when finally we have all been made righteous by law, we shall all receive our special little halos from those in charge of Washington. In my opinion the U.S. is undergoing a silent revolution and the big majority of people have no suspicion of it. As for your bit of news about the "new" place [291], I fully understand the situation. Don't let the matter worry you, 291 has as many lives as the proverbial cat and will right itself. Fortunately we never made any official announcement in *Camera Work* or elsewhere so we have no public explanations to make. We are still in Lucerne and shall remain a while longer. It is not exactly my ideal of a place but the weather is propitious for swimming and rowing and being out of doors generally and so Lucerne gives Kitty and all of us a chance to get some much needed exercise. Although still warm, the weather is well-nigh perfect. We have no plans except that we are booked for Paris, 11 September. None of us will regret when our "vacation" is over and we are back again in New York. An aimless gadding about for a few months gets on anyone's

nerves. I hope B. S. [probably a typo for S. B., Sarah Bernhardt] will make a great hit in London; it is certainly her chance. From America I've had a few letters from Keiley, one from Marin, one from Fuguet; otherwise not a word, except from Phillips, who is actually turning out some work. Let me have the Secession notes when you can.

All wish to be remembered to yourself, Wolf and Kupper; also to the W. H.'s,

Your old,

Stieglitz[67]

Thus Stieglitz arrived in Paris on 1 September 1911 and for three weeks, with the help of Steichen and de Zayas, luxuriated in the Modern art that he saw. The three men visited the art dealers Galerie Bernheim-Jeune and Ambroise Vollard. With Steichen, Stieglitz went to meet Matisse in Issy-les-Moulineaux, and visited Brancusi's studio. He tried to buy a Matisse painting from Matisse, but found the piece promised to a Russian patron. He was inspired by his visits to the Louvre and salons such as the Salon des Indépéndants and the Salon d'Automne. Just six years earlier the Salon d'Automne had exhibited early Fauve pieces that had sparked controversy. Shortly after his visit to Paris, Stieglitz wrote a letter to the editor of the *New York Evening Sun*, urging the Metropolitan Museum to show Cézanne and Van Gogh: "I firmly believe that an exhibition, a well-selected one, of Cézanne's paintings is just at present, of more vital importance than would be an exhibition of Rembrandts . . . The study of Van Gogh is nearly equally essential, if not quite so."[68]

Stieglitz's own photographs from that summer visit to Paris are in part characterized by their oblique-angled viewpoint from above, unlike his 1894 Paris photographs. He titled some of the 1911 photographs "snapshot," emphasizing spontaneity, a simplification of form and subject. In one, *Snapshot, Paris* (1911), the viewer looks down upon a man, sitting on a pile of logs, holding the bridle of his dappled work horse as it pulls a carriage. The carriage is cropped; only the dark form of the man is seen from the rear. The round ends of the logs are repeated in the cur-vature of the street's cobblestones. In one version of the images, the soli-tary man is seen from an angle, partially in profile, with a small dog silhouetted in front of him. Another snapshot is taken from slightly above street level, watching a young woman approaching on a wet street. One 1911 Paris image is taken from the upper story of a building looking down along a long narrow street. The human traffic is small; the simple

228   Alfred Stieglitz, *Snapshot, Paris*, 1911   229   Alfred Stieglitz, *Snapshot, Paris*, 1911

building forms seem to dominate the image. In general these later Paris images have a tighter composition, and the viewer is drawn more quickly into the scene.

RETURN TO NEW YORK: THE ARMORY SHOW

Back in New York, Stieglitz turned to spontaneity and simplified forms in his 1912 exhibition season with works by Matisse and Arthur Dove, and a special exhibition of art by children aged two to eleven, which included work by his daughter, Kitty, and his niece, Georgia Engelhard. Kitty submitted a watercolor of a street scene with a church and other buildings. An article in the *Sunday New York Daily Tribune* referred to the child artists as "The Future Futurists – Things Artistic Revealed to Babes That are Hid from the Wise and Prudent."[69] The *New York Evening Sun* also reviewed the show, quoting Stieglitz's theory of giving a child a brush and leaving him or her alone. The reviewer went onto discuss the work of the Photo-Secession in general, seeing it as a revolt against authority in art, in fact against authority in everything, "and as a reflection of the social unrest of the whole country."[70] For Stieglitz, "the great geniuses are those who have kept their childlike spirit and have added to it breadth of vision and experience."[71]

Modern art was to receive much greater attention in New York with the advent of the famous Armory Show, held at the Sixty-ninth Regiment Armory at Lexington Avenue and 26th Street, from 17 February

230 "The Future Futurists," newspaper clipping from the *Sunday New York Daily Tribune*

to 15 March 1913. Visitors thronged the show, staring wide-eyed, some seeing European modern art for the first time. It traveled subsequently to Boston, Philadelphia, and Chicago. The historian Milton Brown later termed it "the most important single exhibition ever held in America."[72] When the show opened, it was the equivalent of a modern-day "blockbuster," with approximately 1300 works representing over 300 artists from the United States and Europe. Approximately 290,000 people attended the show in New York, Chicago, and Boston.

The chief organizer of the exhibition was the patron Arthur B. Davies, who had become president of the newly formed Association of American Painters and Sculptors, formed in 1911 for the purpose of organizing annual exhibitions. Davies pushed for the display of modern art. Stieglitz was asked to help but declined to be directly involved, although he promised to loan works from 291 artists and agreed to be listed as an honorary vice-president of the exhibition. Claude Monet, Odilon Redon, Mabel Dodge (the New York socialite whose salons were becoming increasingly well known), and Mrs. Jack Gardner (whose house became the Gardner Museum in Boston) had also agreed to serve as honorary vice-presidents. The show included works by the Post-Impressionists Cézanne, Van Gogh, Gauguin, Bonnard, Vuillard; the Cubists Picasso and Braque; the Fauves Matisse, André Derain and Maurice de Derain Vlaminck; and a few pioneer American Modernists, such as artists from "the Eight" and the Ashcan School, who offered a challenge to the traditional American realist academic tradition, as did Stieglitz's 291 exhibitions. There were a few German Expressionists, including Kandinsky, but the Italian Futurists were excluded.

Praise as well as great despair were expressed by the critics and general public. Marcel Duchamp's *Nude Descending a Staircase* was ridiculed by many as representing the incomprehensibility of the new modern art. Arthur Davies stated that the purpose of the show was to show the new modern art "so that the intelligent may judge for themselves."[73] However, the Armory Show soon came to be taken as a defense of Modernism, which was associated with incompetence, immorality, conspiracy, revolution, and anarchy. Arguments for and against the show were based on philosophical as well as aesthetic grounds. Critics such as Kenyon Cox, Frank Jewett Mather, Jr., Edward Daingerfield, and Royal Cortissoz viewed the exhibition not only as an attack on traditional art, but also as an attack upon the order of the world in general. Cox wrote that "the real meaning of this Cubist movement is nothing else than the total destruction of the art of painting,"[74] while Mather wrote, "laymen may well dismiss on moral grounds an art that lives in the miasma of morbid hallucination or sterile experimentation, and denies in the name of individualism values which are those of society and life itself."[75]

However, defenders of Modernism such as the critic Hutchins Hapgood felt that modern art was significant as a way to reach the depths of human experience through the instinctive use of form and abstract expression. The artist Arthur Dow praised the principles of Modernism, claiming that modern art was important for its revolutionary energy. To those who decried revolution, the critic Christian Brinton responded that the development of Modernism was an evolutionary rather than a revolutionary process. To accept this new art was to begin to accept changes in society in general, for the new forms suggested a new way of seeing where the freedom of the individual and his inner instinctual perceptions had come to the fore. Meyer Shapiro described the Armory Show as marking "a point of acceleration" in a revision of the image of the past.[76] No longer was there an absolute reality and set of laws in art and philosophical thinking. Rather there were a myriad of ways of looking at and sensing form, space, color, and content in a work of art.

Although the Armory Show did not bring a complete acceptance of modern art, it did bring an exposure to new ways of thinking and seeing. There were converts to the new art, such as the collectors Duncan Phillips and Katherine Dreier, and new galleries began to show contemporary art. More artists turned to abstraction and semi-abstraction. In its emphasis on the individual spirit, the show marked a further change in the relationship between art and culture and institutions and large organized groups. In the past, in Europe, the church, state, or aristocracy had served as patrons of the arts. By the twentieth century modern art, received little organized support from such groups. It seemed particularly difficult in a growing machine age for the public to deal with individual inner freedom and spirituality. Thus, support for young struggling artists experimenting with new forms was difficult. It remained for proponents of modern art, such as Alfred Stieglitz, to offer some of these artists both monetary and spiritual support. The art historian H. H. Arnason has noted that "The most important single factor, aside form the Armory Show in the birth of the modern spirit, was Alfred Stieglitz, who in his small gallery at 291 Fifth Avenue showed many European pioneers and championed American experimentalists."[77]

From the Armory Show, Stieglitz purchased Kandinsky's *The Garden of Love* (*Improvisation Number 27*) of 1912 (Metropolitan Museum of Art, New York) for $500. He had recently included in *Camera Work* an excerpt from Kandinsky's 1912 book *Concerning the Spiritual in Art* emphasizing the role of inner necessity and spirit to be expressed through art. Stieglitz hoped to mount a Kandinsky exhibition at 291, but this never happened. He formally photographed his Kandinsky painting in 1913, and the photograph is now in the Key Set at the National Gallery of Art in Washington, D.C. Stieglitz also purchased works by Cézanne, Alexander Archipenko, and the sculptor Manuel Manolo, a friend of Picasso's. His only American purchase was a drawing by Arthur Davies.

At the same time as the Armory Show, Stieglitz chose to show about thirty of his own photographs at 291, mainly photographs of New York taken from 1893 to 1912. He seemed to want to put his work to the test by measuring it up against the modern works at the Armory. His photographs were well received. Even the more conservative Royal Cortissoz wrote favorably: "The Photo-Secession Gallery is filled with photographs by Mr. Alfred Stieglitz. It is interesting to see them there, but we cannot forbear noting that any worker with a camera might have claimed admission for his prints at the Salon of the Independents [the Armory Show]." Cortissoz went on to describe Stieglitz's "delightful breadth of mind, his enthusiasm for liberty and all those who fight for it. Mr. Stieglitz has been an exemplary pioneer . . . His liberality is a noble trait, and there is no better occasion than this one for offering it a public tribute."[78]

*   *   *

PICABIA, WEBER, WALKOWITZ, AND BLUEMNER

Among the works in the Armory Show that particularly appealed to Stieglitz were the paintings of the thirty-four-year-old French painter, Francis Picabia, who had come to New York for the controversial show. Four of his large, colorful Cubist abstractions were included. Picabia visited 291 frequently and he and Stieglitz quickly became friends. Picabia's wife, Gabrielle Buffet, and Picabia, who had studied music and singing, also became friends with Stieglitz and contributed to *Camera Work*. Stieglitz showed Picabia's work from 17 March to 5 April 1913, and then again in 1915.

Picabia's show at 291 opened two days after the closing of the Armory Show. His watercolor studies recorded his responses to New York. A number of Picabia's works shown at 291 in both 1913 and 1915 had their basis in the realms of music and dance, such as *Chanson Negre I and II* (*Negro Song I and II*) (1913), *Danseuse étoile et son école de danse* (*Star Dancer and her School of Dance*) (1913), and *Danseuse étoile sur un transtlantique* (*Star Dancer on a Transatlantic Liner*, private collection, Paris) (1913). The star dancer (*danseuse étoile*) was the popular dancer Stacia Napierkowska, who was *en route* to the United States when the Picabias met her. Picabia noted in his introduction to the catalogue of his first 291 show, "I improvise my pictures as a musician improvised music . . . creating a picture without models is art . . . We moderns, if you think of us, express the spirit of the modern time, the twentieth century, and we express it on canvas the way great composers express it in their music."[79] Picabia's abstract watercolor, *La Musique est comme la peinture* (1913–17), was shown at the 1917 Society of Independent Artists exhibition in New York.

Picabia's theories were taken up by a curious New York press. In a 1913 interview with Hutchins Hapgood, Picabia declared, "Art resembles music in some important respects. To a musician the words are obstacles to musical expression . . . the attempt of art is to make us dream, as music does. It expresses a spiritual state. It makes that state real by projecting on the canvas the means of producing that state in the observer."[80] The expression of this spiritual state resonated well with Stieglitz and his circle.

On his 1913 visit to New York, Picabia also met Marius de Zayas and this resulted in a rich interchange between the two artists. De Zayas was instrumental in bringing Picabia's new large abstractions to New York for his 1915 exhibition at 291 and his caricatures began to take on more abstract, geometric qualities following his meeting Picabia. A caricature of Picabia was published in *Camera Work* 46 in 1914.

When Picabia returned to New York in 1915, he helped de Zayas, Paul Burty Haviland and Agnes Ernst Meyer, a wealthy patron who had been a reporter for the *New York Morning Sun* before her marriage, with the publication of the new periodical, *291*. There the public saw for the first time Picabia's newly evolving Dada style. The periodical became a proto-Dadaist statement and a number of issues were sent to France. The magazine was short-lived, with eight single issues and two double issues. The cover of the March 1915 issue was de Zayas' caricature of Stieglitz, *291 Throws Back its Forelock*. A double issue had as its basis *The Steerage*; Stieglitz paid for it and had it printed under his direction. Approximately three hundred proofs of the large photogravure were pulled on Imperial Japan paper for a small deluxe edition.

Two of Stieglitz's photographs of Picabia in 1915 show him in front of two of his paintings that were shown at 291 in 1915: *Mariage Comique* (*Comic Wedlock*) of 1914 (Metropolitan Museum of Art, New York) and *C'est de moi qu'il s'agit* (*This Has to Do with Me*) of 1914 (Museum of Modern Art, New York). In the photographic portraits, Picabia appears at one with the biomorphic and organic forms of his paintings. The curves of his body's outline and the gray tones of his suit flow with the lines and shapes of his paintings. Picabia left New York in the summer of 1916 to go to Barcelona but returned in 1917, when he published three issues of his magazine *391*, a solo production that was circulated among different members of the Stieglitz circle.

Picabia, like a number of artists and intellectuals, was also interested in theories relating to the "fourth dimension." This signified an ideal or higher-dimensional reality, best attained by means of new spatial perceptions based on tactile and motor sensations, such as those experienced via music and dance. For some, a new space would be created that denied the clear-cut three-dimensional approach of traditional academic paintings, suggesting instead the possibility of a new fourth dimension. Fourth-dimension theories were also introduced to the Stieglitz circle by Max Weber, who was a close friend of Stieglitz's until about 1911 and who also made several paintings with music as their basis. The Stieglitz circle became further imbued with fourth-dimension theories through the arrival of Mabel Dodge and through the young architect Claude Bragdon, who had written *A Primer of Higher Space* (*The Fourth Dimension*) in 1913. Georgia O'Keeffe and Stieglitz became friends of Bragdon when they moved into the Shelton Hotel in 1925, where

Bragdon had lived since 1924. He had long been interested in corre-spondences between art and music, as had Stieglitz, and had attended a legendary color organ performance of Alexander Scriabin's piece called *Prometheus: The Poem of Fire* in March 1915 at Carnegie Hall.

Weber's somewhat egocentric personality, along with his espousal of fourth-dimension theories, did lead to some dissent among Stieglitz's associates at 291, and ultimately to his break with Stieglitz in 1911. The developing tensions were fictionalized in a contemporary short story by Temple Scott in the December 1910 issue of *The Forum*. Based on the Stieglitz circle's frequent lunches at the Holland House, not far from 291, the story presents Weber in the character of Weaver as the sole believer of the fourth dimension. Various personalities who were associated with Stieglitz are recognizable in the tale: Finch (Stieglitz), Seaman (Marin), Weaver (Weber), Hardy (possibly J. Nilson Laurvik), Cockayne (pos-sibly Benjamin de Casseres), and Church (possibly Charles Caffin).

Friendly with Max Weber and also exhibiting at 291 was the Russian-born Abraham Walkowitz, who became noted for his drawings and sketches of Isadora Duncan. Walkowitz, who had met Duncan at Rodin's studio in Paris, made more than five thousand drawings and sketches of the famed dancer, capturing her graceful movement in linear lyricism. His curvilinear elements in some of the almost abstract images suggest the spiraling and curved lines of some of O'Keeffe's early work. It was Walkowitz who persuaded Stieglitz to show children's art in 1912 and to show O'Keeffe's work in 1916. In 1916, Stieglitz made several autochromes of Wal-kowitz, capturing the young artist's serious, intellectual ex-pression. In two black and white photographs of the same title taken by Stieglitz the same year, *Shadows in Lake*, Stieglitz and Walkowitz appear as dancing shadows, with leaves, water, and sunlight coalescing in sparkling patterns of light and shadow. The sunlit areas appear as staccato notes in a musical composition. In one, the bow of an old wooden boat

231 Alfred Stieglitz, *Abraham Walkowitz*, 1916

232 Unknown photographer, *Alfred Stieglitz and Friends at Mount Kisco, 1912. Left to right:* Paul Burty Haviland, Abraham Walkowitz, Katharine Nash Rhodes, Mrs. Alfred Stieglitz, Agnes Ernst Meyer, Alfred Stieglitz, J. B. Kerfoot, and John Marin.

with its painter, reflected in the water, provides a stage set for the dancing figures.

When Walkowitz's work was shown at 291, *Camera Work* praised it as "the manifestation of a man who has given expression to a spirit of freedom that he has found in his contact with society."[81] Arthur Hoeber in the *New York Globe* presented a quite opposing viewpoint, calling Walkowitz "as weird as the worst of them."[82]

In 1915, Stieglitz gave the German-born Oscar Bluemner his first one-man show in the United States. Bluemner had first started frequenting 291 about 1909 or 1910, and had been so influenced by the 1911 Cézanne exhibition there that he gave up his career as an architect and chose to travel around Europe studying the latest avant-garde art works and turned to painting himself. Bluemner, too, was captivated by the relationship of the visual arts and music or, as he noted, "the musical color of fateful experience."[83] Further, based on his study of Chinese and Japanese aesthetics, Bluemner believed there to be a relationship between landscape elements and various states of human emotion. He wrote, "My idea fully established: colors like music can excite moods and express emotions, are psychic agents or stimuli."[84] Bluemner's intense colors and forms, his strong suns, moons, and other nature forms were to influence O'Keeffe and other artists of the Stieglitz circle such as Arthur Dove, who made his own series of intense suns and moons. Stieglitz's 1915 portrait of Bluemner focused on his large eyes, gazing directly at the viewer with his pipe in his mouth, his tie slightly askew.

PORTRAITS AND OTHER PHOTOGRAPHS AT 291

In general, Stieglitz's portraits of the early twentieth century are close-ups of his subjects – not celebrities but friends, artists, writers, and those in his immediate environment, including the elevator operator. His portraits begin to show much depth and intensity, attempting to reveal his subjects' inner being, to portray truly as the Latin root *protrahere* meaning to draw forth, suggests. Stieglitz hoped to draw forth qualities from beneath the surface of his subjects. He would often wait with his subject for the right "living" moment. As the photographer Yousuf Karsh later noted, "All I know is that within every man and woman a secret is hidden and as a photographer it is my task to reveal it if I can. The revelation, if it comes at all, will come in a small fraction of a second with an unconscious gesture, a gleam of the eye, a brief lifting of the mask that all humans wear to conceal their innermost selves from the world. In that fleeting interval of opportunity, the photographer must act, or lose his prize."[85] (Karsh photographed O'Keeffe in 1956.)

Konrad Cramer, a painter inspired by Kandinsky and the Cubists, described being photographed by Stieglitz in 1914:

The equipment was extremely simple, almost primitive. He used an 8 × 10-inch view camera, its sagging bellows held up by pieces of string and adhesive tape. The lens was a Steinheil, no shutter. The portraits were made in the smaller of the two rooms at 291 beneath a small

skylight. He used Hammer plates with about three-second exposures. During the exposure, Stieglitz manipulated a large, white reflector to balance the overhead light. He made about nine such exposures, and then we retired to the washroom which doubled as a darkroom. The plates were developed singly in a tray. From the two best negatives he made four platinum contact prints, exposing the frame on the fire escape. He would tend his prints with more care than a cook does her biscuits. The finished print finally received a coat of wax for added gloss and protection.[86]

233   Alfred Stieglitz, *Konrad Cramer*, 1914

234 (*above left*)   Alfred
Stieglitz and Edward
Steichen (print by
Stieglitz), *John Marin*,
1911

235 (*above right*)   Alfred
Stieglitz, *Marsden Hartley*,
c.1915

236   Alfred Stieglitz,
Alfred Maurer, 1915

237 Alfred Stieglitz, *Marie Rapp*, 1913   238 Alfred Stieglitz, *Marie Rapp*, 1916

There is a clear transition from Stieglitz's soft-focus 1911 portraits of the critics J. B. Kerfoot and J. Nilson Laurvik, or from the dark, moody portraits of John Marin, Marsden Hartley, Joseph Keiley, and Arthur Dove of the same year, to the more intense frontal, straight portraits of 1914–15. In the later portraits, subjects such as Paul Burty Haviland, Konrad Cramer, Charles Demuth, Alfred Maurer, Charles Caffin, and even Kitty Stieglitz, are photographed in front of art works at 291, either their own or other's work, thereby emphasizing the interplay between the subject, the art work, and the photographer. Frequently the formal elements in the art work being photographed become an integral part of the person being photographed – such as the outlines of Kitty's hat mirroring the hair lines on the charcoal Picasso drawing, *Head of a Woman* (1909, Metropolitan Museum of Art, New York), behind her.

The intensity and sense of trust in many of the portraits suggest that Stieglitz connected with his subjects and had developed some kind of relationship with them. Among those he photographed in 1914–15 were two women, Marie Rapp and Katharine Rhoades. Marie Rapp, a young voice student, had come to 291 in 1911 as Stieglitz's secretary and stayed

239   Alfred Stieglitz,
Katherine Nash Rhoades,
1916

240 (*facing page left*)
Alfred Stieglitz, *Emil Zoler*,
1917

241 (*facing page right*)
Alfred Stieglitz, *Leo Stein*,
1917

there until 1917 when the gallery closed. She is photographed as an alluring, innocent young woman in various forms of dress – with a large bow
in her hair, in a lace-collared dress, in a sailor dress, or swathed in a
black fur-collared coat, standing in front of Picasso's drawing as Kitty
did. There is a tenderness and wistfulness in her face that Stieglitz
captured and that draws the viewer to the young woman. She later
married George Boursault, the son of a member of the Photo-Secession.
Stieglitz photographed the couple and their young child, Yvonne,
informally when they came to visit him and O'Keeffe at Lake George in
the early 1920s.

The young painter and poet Katherine Nash Rhoades contributed to
both *Camera Work* and *291*, and had her paintings exhibited along with
those Marion H. Beckett at 291. Stieglitz's portraits of Rhoades depict
a sophisticated and theatrical young woman with transparent layers of
dress, far more provocative than Marie Rapp. Rhoades's gaze is
enigmatic and does not always directly engage the viewer. But both Rapp
and Rhoades seem to have inspired Stieglitz to capture their individual
expressive qualities.

By 1917, some of Stieglitz's portraits taken at 291 show him experimenting with hand gestures and the gaze of his subjects and he began to

photograph Georgia O'Keeffe. In one photograph she looks upward.
Another shows, in a similar pose, the painter Emil Zoler, who helped
Stieglitz install various exhibitions at 291. In one photograph of Zoler,
the painter has one hand raised, the other on his hip. In two photographs
of 1917 of O'Keeffe, only her hands are photographed, against one of
her paintings. In another, her hands are just above her waist, gently
touching the long V-shaped neckline of her dress. Or Leo Stein in 1917,
whom Stieglitz had met with Edward Steichen in 1909 in Paris, is shown
with his hands on his hips, a book tucked in the crook of his elbow.

These gestural elements add a theatrical air to the portraits and depart
from more traditional portrait poses. Hodge Kirnon, the elevator operator at 291, was photographed on several occasions. In one instance he
is holding a copy of *Camera Work*; in another, he is lightly grasping his
right suspender strap. His long, black, hands draw the viewer's eye to
his long, oval face. Hodge's perceptions of 291 were included in the
Camera Work issue of July 1914, devoted to "What is 291?": "I have
found in 291 a spirit that fosters liberty, defines no methods, never
pretends to know, never condemns, but always encourages those who
are daring enough to be intrepid, those who feel a just repugnance
towards the ideals and standards established by conventionalism."[87]

242   Alfred Stieglitz, *From the Window of 291*, 1915

243   Alfred Stieglitz, *From the Back Window of 291, Snow-Covered Tree, Back Yard*, 1915

Stieglitz also made a number of photographs from the back window at 291, some of them at night. From these 1915 photographs, it seems that Stieglitz has left behind much of the world of Pictorial photography, where details were suppressed and hard lines toned down. An image such as *From the Back Window, 291, Snow-Covered Tree, Back Yard* (1915) focuses on a snow-covered tree after a storm. It is the clarity of the patterns of light and dark that are striking. Here is nature with city buildings dimly shown in the background. But more than nature, the photograph is an abstract pattern. The building-block qualities of other 291 back-window images recall the work of Cézanne and early Cubist paintings. In some, Stieglitz has used the snow to provide geometric planes that contrast to the darker building shapes. In the night scenes the rectangular windows lit from within form alluring visual grids or singular spotlights on the darkened façades of the buildings. In most of this series nature has little presence; rather the layers and steps of building forms emphasize an urban life and a city that is expanding and growing upward. In a letter to R. Childe Bayley, English photographer and editor of *Photography*, of 1 November 1916, Stieglitz described his recent photographs, emphasizing "straight" photography:

> I have done quite some photography recently. It is intensely direct – portraits, buildings from my back window at 291, a whole series of them, a few landscapes and interiors. All interrelated. I know nothing outside of Hill's [David Octavius Hill] work which I think is so direct and quite so intensely honest. It is all 8 × 10 work. All platinum prints. Not a trace of hand work on either negative or prints. No diffused focus. Just the straight goods. On some things, the lens stopped down to 128. But everything simplified in spite of endless detail.[88]

STIEGLITZ'S INFLUENCE

Much has been written elsewhere about the individual artists who frequented the 291 gallery, whom Stieglitz supported emotionally and often financially – in particular Marin, Dove, Hartley, O'Keeffe, and Demuth. Stieglitz helped each of them find their own voice. They in turn, helped feed his ego in their devotion to and faith in him and his work. They also served as subjects for his own photographic work.

Writing in 1942, the author Henry Miller described the relationship between John Marin and Stieglitz:

> People are often irritated with him [Stieglitz] because he doesn't behave like an art dealer. Of course the fact is he isn't an art dealer. They say he is shrewd, quixotic, unpredictable. They never ask themselves what would have happened to Marin or O'Keeffe or the others if their works had fallen into other hands. To be sure, John Marin might have received more money for his work than Stieglitz was ever able to secure for him. But would John Marin be the man he is today? Would he be painting the pictures he is painting in his seventy-second year? I doubt it. I have witnessed with my own eyes the process of killing an artist off, as it is practiced in this country. We have all witnessed the rise and fall of our great "successes," our transitory idols! How we love them! And how quickly we forget them! We should thank God that a man like Stieglitz is still amongst us, demonstrating every day of his life the constancy of his love. The man is a perfect marvel of endurance, of fortitude, of patience, of humility, of tenderness, of wisdom, of faith. He is a rock against which the conflicting currents of wishy-washy opinion strike in vain. Stieglitz is unmovable,

unalterable. He is anchored. And that is why I have the audacity to picture him sitting in his little office undismayed by the crumbling of the world about. Why should he tremble in the presence of the enemy? Why should he run away? Has he not been surrounded and beleaguered by enemies all his life? Not strong ones, either, but mean, insidious, petty, cunning ones who strike in the dark when one's back is turned. Our own enemies – the worst there can be. The enemies of life, I call them, because wherever a tender, new shoot of life raises its head they trample it down. Not deliberately always, but thoughtlessly, aimlessly. The real enemy can always be met and conquered, or won over. Real antagonism is based on love, a love that has not recognized itself. But this other kind, this slimy, crawling hostility that is evoked by indifference or ignorance, that is difficult to combat. That saps the very roots of life. The only person who can cope with it is a wizard, a magician. And that is what Stieglitz is, and Marin too. They are constantly fecundating each other, nourishing each other, inspiring each other. There is no more glorious wedlock known to man than this marriage of kindred spirits. Everything they touch becomes ennobled. There is no taint anywhere. We reach with them the realm of pure spirit. And there let us rest – until the enemy comes.[89]

The writer and educator Harold Rugg saw Stieglitz as an artist and teacher:

> He is important because he integrates the twofold role of the artist and the teacher in one personality. In an economic period in which it was practically impossible for the true artist to secure an audience and earn a competence, Stieglitz has, in spite of obstacle piled on obstacle, maintained high integrity as a creative artist and a teacher of Man-as-Artist . . . Stieglitz has served his battled era first by a life of creative expression . . . by using a mechanical instrument to lay bare the moving life beneath the surface of organic natural things . . . and second to help the artist to become articulate and to clarify his meaning of life and its portraiture.[90]

Artists, too, spoke of Stieglitz in poetic and laudatory terms. Here is John Marin, who described Stieglitz and 291:

> This spirit place took, cared for, and nourished by this man.
> This spirit had to be fought for offensively and defensively
> For this spirit had its reasons for existence
> From there being surrounding opposing spirits . . .

To realize such a place –
A very tangible intangible place was and is this man's dream.[91]

Marsden Hartley wrote:

> Mr. Thomas Craven, in his latest book, would have the world believe that Mr. Stieglitz has done more evil than good, and that some of us aesthetic "snobs" have "gone to the dogs" because of our interest in eclectic notions . . . quibbling must however be left to the quibblers. Stieglitz will tell you, and he has said it a thousand times, that the 291 idea was never meant to be anything but an experiment, "laboratory" is his favorite word . . . This little room has become to some of us . . . an enormous room . . . it let a few personalities develop in the way they believed in, and find the way to develop of themselves.[92]

Or there were the words of Charles Demuth:

> Lighthouses and fog – a lighthouse and many fogs. There really aren't many lighthouses and fog – seems to be always rolling in from most distinguished shores and seas.
>
> Lighthouses are fixed, sometimes they seem to have moved but they really haven't . . . Lights in lighthouses sometimes wink, and I've seen them myself twinkle.
>
> But you said you were writing about writing about Stieglitz.
>
> Well, I am writing about Stieglitz – here, this is what I have been doing – writing about Stieglitz![93]

And Arthur Dove recalled: "There was never any compromise in the introduction of ideas, which had been introduced one after another for the first time in America . . . When asked what Stieglitz means to me as an artist, I answer: everything . . . I do not think I could have existed as a painter without that super encouragement and the battle he has fought day by day for twenty-

244 Alfred Stieglitz, *Arthur G. Dove*, 1915

five years. He is without a doubt the one who has done the most for art in America."[94]

Samples from Dove and Stieglitz's correspondence from 1914 to 1917 illustrate aspects of their close relationship. Dove lived in Westport, Connecticut, from 1910, shortly after the birth of his only child, William Dove. He was still able to visit 291 frequently since Westport was only about an hour's train ride from New York City.

Westport, Conn.
19 October 1914

My dear Stieglitz,

I have been trying to answer your question ever since your letter came but found it rather difficult to express satisfactorily my ideas. Your request that as little reference be made to yourself as possible makes it doubly difficult. One might almost say that Stieglitz is 291.

It will seem fine to see you all again and I hope to get in shortly after the first, but have so many responsibilities now that there is very little time left. I have been doing some work, however, and hope to do much more this coming month or two.

The question "What is 291?" leaves one in the same position in explaining it as the modern painter is in explaining his painting. The modern painting does not represent any definite object, neither does '291' represent any definite movement in one direction, such as, Socialism, suffrage, and so on. Perhaps it is these movements having but one direction that makes life at present so stuffy and full of discontent.

There could be no 291 ism. "291" takes a step further and stands for orderly movement in all directions. In other words it is what the observer sees in it – an idea to the (nth) power.

One means used at 291 has been a process of elimination of the non-essential. This happens to be one of the important principles in modern art; therefore 291 is interested in modern art.

It was not created to promote modern art, photography, nor modern literature. That would be a business and 291 is not a shop.

It is not an organization that one may join. One either belongs or does not. It has grown and outgrown in order to grow. It grew because there was a need for such a place, yet it is not a place.

Not being a movement, it moves. So do "racehorses," and some people, and "there are all sorts of sports," but no betting. It is more interesting to find than to win.

This seems to be 291 or is it Stieglitz?

This is as little reference to you as I can seem to make. With best wishes for the whole year.

As ever

Arthur G. Dove

Stieglitz's earliest surviving letter to Dove seems restrained, even impersonal, compared with the tone of later communications. It is one of only a handful of letters in the correspondence with Dove, that are typewritten – presumably by Marie Rapp, the 291 secretary:

291 Fifth Ave., New York

5 November 1914

My dear Dove,

I thought I had written to you immediately upon receipt of your delightful letter and MS. But somehow or other I seem not to have, so Marie says when I asked her. I can imagine that you are hard at work. Nevertheless I hope you will manage to get into town soon and let me see what you have done or are doing in the way of your painting.

There is a wonderful show on now by Negro savages. It will be open until 27 November. It is possibly the most important show we have ever had.

The fellows are all back. Hartley is the only one not here. He is still in Berlin.

The 291 number is really going to be a wonder. Your contribution is very fine. I like it immensely.

With greetings,

Your old

Stieglitz

N.B. Haskell [American painter and illustrator] just sent a corker too. He is still up in Maine.

A letter to Dove from Stieglitz dating from two years later is much warmer in tone:

291 Fifth Ave., New York

28 December 1916

My dear Dove:

Here is a check for you: One Hundred and Fifty Dollars. Is it enough? If not wire me and I will send more at once . . .

I am glad you like the Walkowitzes and Hartleys and I am sure you are going to like the Marins. That means pleasure for the few of us at any rate. Real pleasure. And a great pleasure primarily for me.

Maurer was in this morning and brought me his very latest. Undoubtedly a development and I am mighty glad of it. I think later on I will give him a chance to see his work on the walls.

Night before last I was examining the things of yours I have at home. They wear splendidly. And they mean more to me today than they ever did. All of them.

Heartiest greetings,
Stieglitz[95]

The beacon in a lighthouse, the director of a wonderful laboratory, the maker of a spirit place, Stieglitz was for many larger than life. His detractors saw him as a rabble-rouser, a disturbing revolutionary, an opinionated young crusader who brought nothing good to American culture, and later as a cranky old man. For some, Stieglitz was "a restless and ruthless man, with hair-tufts his ears like a fawn, and a face like Socrates." And he "exercised an increasingly dictatorial sway over his stable of painters. He showed their works, lectured them about eternal values, and doled out their money at whim. Your were either for him or against him."[96]

Stepping beyond a cult of personality, though, Stieglitz did provoke discussion and use of a new visual language in both photography and the other fine arts, as Bram Dijkstra has noted:

When Stieglitz began to exhibit the work of European artists at 291, he did so because he recognized that their interest in the autonomous significance of the materials of the objective world was similar to this own. He realized that he could teach the American artists how to truly see a thing in terms of its volumes, outlines, and planes, by pointing to the details of Cézanne's, and later Picasso's, analysis of the visual and tactile properties which constitute an object. Stieglitz, of course, had long ago made the discovery that the spatial and structural relationships between objects, their textures and their forms, when emphasized properly and removed as much as possible from an extraneous, contextual environment, can come to represent in their freedom from anecdotal reference, experiences which touch upon the most profound pre-rational, and therefore otherwise indefinable emotional source of man's actions. The qualities in Stieglitz's prints were similar to those emphasized by the new painting, and it is therefore altogether appropriate that his photograph, *The Steerage*, made in 1907, the year of

Les Demoiselles d'Avignon, should have elicited Picasso's adoring approval.[97]

Writers such as William Carlos Williams were influenced by the new shapes and forms they found at 291. Williams' own style in the early part of the century came to have Cubist' elements. He worked in close association for a period of time with Alfred Kreymborg, who was also influenced by experiences at 291, and was to write such lines as:

> two blue-grey birds chasing
> a third struggle in circles, angles,
> swift convergings to a point that bursts
> instantly!
>
> "Spring Strains"[98]

Like a Cubist painter, Williams often fragmented his forms. His famous poem "The Great Figure," depicting a fire engine with its golden figure 5 passing quickly down Ninth Avenue, was to serve as inspiration for Charles Demuth's painting *I Saw the Figure Five in Gold*. Demuth's painting is both a tribute to Williams and a testament to the rich interdisciplinary experimentation that grew out of Stieglitz's galleries. The painting contains poetic, Cubist, and cinematic allusions in its form and content.

Other writers who were to have a close association with Stieglitz, particularly in the 1920s were Sherwood Anderson and Hart Crane. In 1915, Theodore Dreiser published his novel *The Genius*, which described the rise and fall of a young painter, Eugene Whitla, whose first successful urban subjects resemble those treated by Stieglitz in his early photographs of New York from the 1890s and the first decade of the twentieth century. Dreiser's words could well describe the young Stieglitz and works such as *Winter, Fifth Avenue* (1893) or *Savoy Hotel* (1898):

The city appealed to [Eugene], wet or white, particularly the public squares. He saw Fifth Avenue once in a driving snowstorm, under sputtering arc lights and he hurried to his easel that morning to see if he could not put it down in black and white. He turned to the last reproduction, which was that of Greeley Square in a drizzling rain. Eugene by some mystery of his art had caught the exact texture of seeping water on gray stones in the glare of various kinds of lights ...Eugene's dealer, Mr. Charles, called the work "a symphony in grey," and saw that everything Eugene "touched seemed to have romance and beauty, and yet it was real and mostly grim and shabby."[99]

The allusion to the symphonic qualities in the work by Dreiser recalls the Symbolist aesthetic espoused by a number of the artists and writers frequenting 291, and suggests the influence of Whistler with his painted symphonies and harmonies. The musical allusion also recalls the words of Kandinsky: "Color is the keyboard, the eyes are the hammers, the soul is the piano with many strings . . . musical sound acts directly on the soul and finds an echo there since music is innate to man."[100]

Some of the critics who frequented 291 were also influenced by the Symbolist aesthetic. Of particular importance was Paul Rosenfeld, who was steeped in Symbolist literature and influenced by the work of Kandinsky. Rosenfeld, a music and art critic, became a primary interpreter and promoter of Stieglitz's work and that of the artists in the Stieglitz circle during the late 1910s and early 1920s.

Like a number of critics, he found a kind of magic in the work of the Stieglitz circle and saw artists as heroes who descended into the mind to then express their vision of reality.

Born of émigrés to the United States, Rosenfeld had been sent to a military academy in Poughkeepsie, New York, after his pianist mother died when he was ten. He tended to be rebellious about many things, even at Yale, where he was an undergraduate, and the Columbia School of Journalism. As a young graduate who was Jewish and interested in the arts, he was unsure of what he wanted to do or what he could do. A fellow Yale graduate, the cellist and writer Waldo Frank, introduced him to Stieglitz in around 1915. Rosenfeld quickly became a devoted follower and Stieglitz became a surrogate father to the young Rosenfeld, whose father had died in 1908.

In his *Port of New York*: *Essays on Fourteen Moderns*, a series of essays published in 1924, Rosenfeld celebrated a number of American artists and writers whom he admired. He wrote tributes to American moderns including Albert Pinkham Ryder, Van Wyck Brooks, Carl Sandburg, Marsden Hartley, William Carlos Williams, Margaret Naumberg, Kenneth Hayes Miller, Roger Sessions, John Marin, Sherwood Anderson, Georgia O'Keeffe, Randolph Bourne, and Alfred Stieglitz.

In the chapter devoted to Stieglitz, Rosenfeld made numerous musical allusions: "Snaps from the hand camera and plates from the large camera all are infinite rhythms of warm sensuous light, choral symphonies and dances of the sunpour. The tiny scale between black and white is distended in these prints to an immense keyboard of infinitely delicate modulations. Black and white become capable of registering in strong and subtle relations a universe of ecstasy and dream and anguish . . . the more recent photographs are three-dimensional polyphony."[101]

The writings of critics Sadakichi Hartmann and Charles Caffin also reflected Symbolist tendencies. Hartmann, influenced by the Belgian writer Maurice Maeterlinck, who talked of the soul as a hidden inner core and the importance of the depths of the human inner spirit, wrote such words as "Mystery seems to consist largely of a concealment of actualities, of depriving the words to a certain extent of their literary significance or of investing them with pictorial and musical qualities."[102]

Or Caffin, interested in elements of a universal spirit, wrote in *Camera Work*, "If painting is to maintain a hold upon the intelligence and imagination, as music does, and possibly poetry, and to grow in touch with the growing needs of humanity, it must find some fundamental motive other than the appearances of the world . . . If it is to keep itself in living competition with the superior impressiveness of modern music . . . it must take on something of quality, which is the essence of music – the abstract. It is here that it may learn of the Oriental ideal as exemplified in Japanese art."[103]

Rosenfeld and Waldo Frank were to become apostles of a new American art, advocating the work that artists such as those in the Stieglitz circle had given to the American people, although their language was rooted in European Symbolism and aestheticism. In *Port of New York*, Rosenfeld emphasized, "we have taken root," we can find a "fundamental oneness with the place and the people in it," claiming that these artists conveyed a "religious sense" and a "gift of life."[104]

Frank and Rosenfeld began to call for a national American culture, but still believing in the role of European influences and European modernism. In his 1919 book, *Our America*, Frank wrote of the newly emerging New York and of the role of Stieglitz: "In the nervous tension of New York, the mutterings of American unrest have risen to a shriek. But also they have become the voice of Order. New York lies between invading Europe and America. A frontier city. And a self-conscious one. Here, if anywhere, you must look for the leader and the critic . . . There is one place and one man in whom the creative meanings of these worlds meet, as not elsewhere, in the city. The man is Alfred Stieglitz. Possibly, the place is Alfred Stieglitz also. We shall see."[105]

Stieglitz photographed the two men in the 1920s, capturing a sense of their different personalities: Rosenfeld more of an aesthete, frequently dressed in a jacket and tie with a carefully maintained mustache and limpid eyes; Frank with thick, sometimes unruly hair and volatile, intense emotions.

As the 1920s approached, Stieglitz, too, tended to show the work of American artists. Although he would not forget his European roots he increasingly directed his attention to American shores as he looked back to his birth in Hoboken, a prosperous middle-class town that could be viewed as a typical eastern American heartland. In the catalogue to a 1921 exhibition of his own work he declared, "I was born in Hoboken. I am an American. Photography is my passion. The search for Truth my obsession."[106]

Stieglitz was indeed obsessed with a search for truth, which for him lay in the realm of the spirit and in fighting for the cause of photography as a fine art. That passion and his obsessive search was not to leave him even in old age. His statement of a widening circle of self-consciousness – from his small birthplace, to his being an American, to the world of photography, to a larger, universal search for Truth – may be seen as an ongoing affirmation of life's journeys and struggles, suggesting that a search for Truth was an "inner necessity."

Among those frequenting 291 was the composer and photographer Ernest Bloch. Born in Geneva, Switzerland, in 1880, Bloch had come to the United States in 1916. He found himself stranded in New York after the concert tour of a dancer for whom he was conducting failed. While at a New York hotel, his overcoat was stolen; Waldo Frank lent him his and thus began Bloch's introduction to the Stieglitz circle. A few weeks later, Bloch's just-completed First Quartet was performed in New York to much acclaim. Paul Rosenfeld became a champion of Bloch's and introduced him to Stieglitz. In an essay on Bloch for *Camera* magazine in 1976, Evic Johnson wrote: "Both Bloch and Stieglitz were romantics with a dramatic style in an increasingly cerebral, anti-romantic time in art. They felt a bond of understanding. Indeed, it appears that Stieglitz was encouraged to begin his series of cloud photographs not only because of a remark in a letter from Waldo Frank that his fine portraits were due to a hypnotic power over his sitters but also because of his friendship with the composer Ernest Bloch."[107]

Bloch did not compose a symphony called "Clouds" after seeing Stieglitz's series of photographs *Music, A Sequence of Ten Cloud Photographs*, but he did write a short impressionist piano piece in 1922, "Poems of the Sea," and worked on his Piano Quintet. Stieglitz saw Bloch as a kindred spirit, as is evident from his letter of 1 July 1922 from Lake George after Bloch had seen the cloud photographs:

My dear Mr. Bloch,

Have you any idea how much it meant to me to have you feel about those photographs as you did – To have you see in them what you do – And to know that what you express I understand. And feel is true. – It was a memorable hour. A very rare one. There is much – very much – that you are suffering – physical and otherwise – that has been my lot, too. – It's all necessary for "foolish" people like ourselves I have to presume. Sometimes one wonders, though, must one go through torments over and over again to gain greater clarity – a still deeper sympathy – a greater unity? If it could be otherwise, I suppose it would be otherwise.

Yours gratefully
Alfred Stieglitz.[108]

Bloch's own photographs had some affinity with Stieglitz's early European photographs, comprising landscapes, images of peasant life, and portraits. One of his musical compositions, *Five Sketches in Sepia* (1923) clearly refers to the visual arts and sepia-toned photographs.

Paul Strand solicited Bloch's input when he served as guest editor for *Manuscripts* in 1922 and wished to report on the current state of photography as a fine art. Bloch's letter of response to Strand included eloquent praise of Stieglitz and his work:

In his [Stieglitz's] marvelous work, I see for the first time in history a man, a thinker, a philosopher, using the camera and all its resources to express himself fully and completely like a painter uses brushes and colors or a musician uses sounds . . . He has not only photographed things as they seem to be or as they appear to the "bourgeois," he has taken them as they really are in the essence of their real life and he sometimes accomplishes the miracle of compelling them to reveal their own identity . . . as if all their potentialities could emerge freely; and this is the greatest Art because all signs of technique have disappeared for the sake of the Idea.[109]

Stieglitz, for much of his career, sought to understand the idea of photography, first in scientific and functional terms while studying with Hermann Vogel, and later through aesthetic, formal, and expressive explorations. He noted in a 1914 letter to W. Orison Underwood, a Boston amateur photographer and member of the Photo-Secession, "I had felt that you might have some conception of my methods in trying to establish, once and for all, the 'meaning' of the 'idea' of photography. I have proceeded in doing this in an absolutely scientific way . . . And

245   Alfred Stieglitz, *Lake George – Music No. 2*, 1922

possibly the greatest work that I have done during my life is teaching
the value of seeing. And teaching the meaning of seeing."[110]

Rosenfeld, in reviewing a performance of Bloch's Concerto Grosso for
strings and piano, wrote of Bloch's capacity for developing his ideas in
a modern format: "the humanistic Bloch is present . . . Bloch's power and
sincerity impose in this piece too. His capacity for developing and sus-
taining his ideas is second to no living composer's. Dignity and weight
enter what he touches. The new piece seems to show the vehement
modern observing others diddling with eighteenth-century forms."[111]

*   *   *

GEORGIA O'KEEFFE AND ELLEN KOENIGER

Perhaps the most significant figure to enter 291's door in the years between 1910 and 1920 was Georgia O'Keeffe. Although she had come to see the Rodin drawings at 291 in 1908, it was not until 1916 that Stieglitz saw O'Keeffe's drawings, secretly brought to him by her friend, Anita Pollitzer.

Discouraged by the continuing war, in which he felt unable to take sides, Stieglitz needed a new light in his life. Many of his friends had departed or there were rifts in old relationships. And his marriage was becoming increasingly difficult. In general, it was a dark period. In his words: "Much of the enthusiasm that had existed at 291 gradually disappeared because of the war. Close friends seemed to fall by the wayside. I could not turn 291 into a political institution, nor could I see Germany as all wrong and the allies as all right. The work going on at the gallery, I felt, was universal. Colleagues tried to prove to me that Beethoven was no German, that all the cruelty in the world came from Germany and that every Frenchman and Englishman was a saint. I was truly sick at heart."[112]

Stieglitz had hoped to devote an issue of *Camera Work* to the role of the subconscious in art, with a major article by A. A. Brill, a disciple and translator of Sigmund Freud's work, and color illustrations by psychiatric patients to be interspersed with children's work shown at 291. But because the war made the appropriate color printing processes inaccessible, Stieglitz could not realize this and several other projects involving color printing, which discouraged him.[113]

Stieglitz wrote to Paul Burty Haviland on 5 July 1916, despairing that no platinum paper was being manufactured because of the war, and noting that 291 was very quiet, and that he was putting together a complete portfolio of issues of 291 for Haviland and the Metropolitan Museum in that quiet time:

> Dear Haviland,
> I spent the whole of yesterday – the 4th – at 291 undisturbed. And after nine hours of doing but one thing I finally got three portfolios of 291 finished – one for you, one for your brother George, and one for the Metropolitan Museum (not an order!) . . . The one for you is the most complete yet put together . . . Besides the portfolios, I have sent you Deluxe copies, Nos. 1–8, 9, 10–11, 12 to complete the set you have. Is there anything missing? Let me know. A complete portfolio certainly makes a magnificent impression . . . I'll be glad though, when I'm

through with the portfolio business as it was fight-fight-fight for any inch of ground . . . I have finally, too, gotten another complete number of *Camera Work* together. It will be more of a record than anything else, but an interesting one. Weather has been rain-rain-rain, so that I've had no chance to print in weeks – months. And, to boot, all man-ufacture of platinum paper has been stopped. At 291 all is very quiet. Marie goes off on a 7 week vacation next week. I manage to keep busy. The Picabias sailed ten days ago – I was at the pier. He seemed a little stronger. I like both of them as much as ever.

I wonder how you are – I suppose on the job. And fully acclimated to your surroundings.

Warm wishes to be remembered. The fellows often speak of you and of course all miss you.

With heartfelt greetings,
Your Old,
Stieglitz.[114]

A new flame was kindled within Stieglitz as he looked at O'Keeffe's drawings: "Examining the first drawing, I realized that I had never seen

246   Alfred Stieglitz, *Georgia O'Keeffe: A Portrait*, 4 June 1917

247   Alfred Stieglitz, *Georgia O'Keeffe: A Portrait*, 4 June 1917

anything like it. All my tiredness vanished."[115] He responded with his famous words: "Finally, a woman on paper. A woman gives of herself. The miracle has happened."[116] Stieglitz seems to have found there part of the ideal of "Woman" that he had been seeking since reading Goethe's *Faust* as a young boy. There was, to him, a spirit and sexuality inherent in those free-flowing charcoal drawings by the twenty-nine-year-old O'Keeffe that captivated the fifty-two-year-old Stieglitz.

Without O'Keeffe's knowledge, Stieglitz hung her work in the spring of 1916, although he had written to her in January saying that he might like to show her work. The young O'Keeffe was initially upset at Stieglitz's arrogance in hanging her work without her permission. Upon confronting him, though, she was quickly convinced he had done the right thing. She was to write to him that July, "Nothing you do with my drawings is 'nervy.' I seem to feel that they are as much yours as mine."[117]

Stieglitz's viewing and showing of O'Keeffe's drawings seems to have been a catalyst for a breakthrough in his own photographic work in the summer of 1916. At Lake George he photographed a series of images of Ellen Koeniger, the niece of the photographer Frank Eugene. In that series of approximately a dozen photographs, printed in crisp gelatin silver rather than platinum or palladium, Stieglitz created a Modernist portrait. Ellen's strong athletic body is emphasized by her bare skin and the transparent fabric of her bathing suit. The series was made within a few minutes in the bright sunlight, as Ellen went in and out of the water. The sequence is very cinematic, recording Ellen's changing gestures – her arms raised, her body twisted, close-up shots, or longer shots. There is a joy in her face that seems to relish her freedom of movement and connection with the water. Ellen's body is well formed, muscular, free to move as she wishes. She is a twentieth-century woman, not constricted by nineteenth-century conventions of propriety. She is almost Olympian in her stature. Stieglitz captures well the significance of her freedom of movement.

One of the most striking images in the series is a close-up of Ellen's back, where her clinging bathing suit emphasizes the curves and lines of her body and light and shadow interact on her behind. Weston Naef has noted that this latter picture is "arguably the strongest picture in the group because it deals with pure form in an experimental way informed by Modernism and because it epitomizes in one picture the several aspects of the bathing-suit scenes. This sequence was previously unseen because it had not been published or exhibited. It informs us of Stieglitz's method of making a series of exposures of a particular subject."[118] This

248–52 Alfred
Stieglitz, *Ellen
Koeniger, Lake
George*, 1916

series, although it lacks the passion and sexuality of some of the Georgia O'Keeffe composite portraits, may be seen as a precursor to the concentrated studies Stieglitz made of O'Keeffe, beginning in 1917.

THE LAST DAYS OF 291

Stieglitz turned fifty-three on New Year's Day 1917. It was to be a year of beginnings and endings: the year he began to photograph O'Keeffe; the final year for 291. He showed the work of Marsden Hartley, John Marin, Stanton McDonald Wright, Gino Severini, and Georgia O'Keeffe.

Severini was the only European shown that season and his exhibition marked the first time Futurist paintings had been shown in New York, since they had not been included in the Armory Show. It is perhaps not surprising that several of the works shown had dance motifs, such as *Danseuse=Hélice=Mer* (*Dancer=Helix=Sea*, 1915, Metropolitan Museum of Art, New York), given Stieglitz's interest in music and dance. The exhibition also illustrated the beginning of a change in Severini's *oeuvre* from movement-filled Futurist pieces to quieter, more classical Cubist pieces, such as *Femme et Enfant* (*Woman and Child*, 1916, Fisk University, Nashville, Tennessee). The fragmented nature of modern life became translated into both a dynamic synthesis and synthetic dynamism in Severini's dance pieces. Stieglitz's selection of Severini's diamond-shaped *Danseuse=Hélice=Mer* also points to a shared interest in conceptual ideas and wit. In the painting Severini equated the idea of a spiral with images of a dancer and with the sea. The title contains a pun, since in French and Italian "helix" and "propeller" are translated by the same word. So that dance become analogous. Severini, like a number of artists and writers, was captivated by the idea of flight and the aerial feats of men such as the Wright brothers, Henri Farman, and Louis Blériot. Stieglitz just a few years before had celebrated flight in his 1910 images *A Dirigible* and *The Aeroplane*. A number of Severini's pieces were also seen to encompass elements of the "fourth dimension" that inspired Stieglitz and some of his contemporaries.

Stieglitz's support for the avant-garde and for the conceptual is also evident from his display at 291 of Marcel Duchamp's *Fountain*, his "ready made" porcelain urinal from J. L. Mutt Ironworks, signed "R. Mutt." The piece had been intended for the large first exhibition of the newly formed American Society of Independent Artists, comprising approximately 200 works, which opened at the Grand Central Palace in New York on 9 April 1917. The urinal, however, was seen as an indecent joke by all of the directors of exhibition except the visual-arts patron Walter Arensberg. At 291, Stieglitz photographed the controversial piece, of which Arensberg said, "A lovely form has been revealed, freed from its functional purpose, therefore a man clearly has made an aesthetic contribution."[119] A cropped version of the photograph appeared in 1917 in *The Blind Man*, a small magazine published by Duchamp and Arensberg.

When the readymade arrived at 291, work by O'Keeffe was hanging. Stieglitz chose to place the porcelain piece in front of a 1913 Marsden Hartley painting of German soldiers going to battle, with similar curved forms to the urinal. Just five days before the opening of the American Society of Independent Artists exhibition, the United States had declared war on Germany. A piece such as Hartley's could not be hung in the wake of strong anti-German sentiment and thus was on the floor. Stieglitz's photograph of Duchamp's piece was also mounted onto part of a page of the periodical *291* in 1917, in support of the spirit of the Dada movement.

Stanton Macdonald-Wright's exhibition from 20–31 March 1917, with its strong Synchronist imagery, was striking and was the artist's first one-man show in New York. Macdonald-Wright thought in terms of musical chords based on triads of colors, and was interested in the emotional values that colors might have. By equating color chords of the chromatic circle with equivalent notes of the musical scale, Macdonald-Wright and fellow Synchronists such as Morgan Russell sought a harmonious and balanced spectrum. Macdonald-Wright was particularly influenced by the Orphist–Cubist artist Robert Delaunay and by Kandinsky. His multicolored, swirling hues, often integrating parts of the human form, quickly engage the viewer, who becomes caught up in a color mist.

The last exhibition at 291, from 13 April to 14 May was Georgia O'Keeffe's one-person show of watercolors, drawings, and oils, as well as a small phallic sculpture she had made in 1916. Much of the critical response to O'Keeffe's early work had its roots in Symbolist language. William Murrell Fisher wrote of the 1917 show at 291: "Of all things earthly, it is in music that one finds any analogy to the emotional content of these drawings, to the gigantic swirling rhythms and the exquisite tendernesses so powerful and sensitively rendered. And music is the condition toward which, according to Pater, all art constantly aspires. Well, plastic art in the hands of O'Keeffe seems now to have approximated that."[120]

The O'Keeffe show was both an end and a beginning: an end to 291, and a beginning to O'Keeffe's life with Stieglitz on a professional and personal level, as well as a beginning of her role in the development of American modern art.

Stieglitz took a series of approximately eight images of the exhibition and sent them to O'Keeffe in Texas. One of the installation shots shows the small sculpture "bowing" toward one of O'Keeffe's charcoal drawings, *No. 12 Special* (1916), from which swirling lines reach toward the sculpture. In Stieglitz's photograph "male" and "female" seem to incline toward each other in dance-like gestures.

Stieglitz also chose to photograph another drawing of O'Keeffe's, *No. 9 Special* (1915), which had appeared in the 291 group show in 1916. The wave- and flame-like forms of O'Keeffe's piece may be seen as visual metaphors for the art of dance. The metaphor of dance as a flame was prevalent among writers of the time, and the dancer Loïe Fuller, whom Stieglitz had seen perform, was noted for her fire dance.

The writer and poet Paul Valéry also turned to the metaphor of the flame in his symposium *L'Ame et la danse* (*The Soul and the Dance*), published in 1921, in which Socrates speaks eloquently about dance: "Does she not look though she was living quite at her ease in an element comparable to fire, in a highly subtle essence of music and motion, while she inhales inexhaustible energy . . . O flame! Living and divine! What is a flame but not the movement itself?"[121] Valéry saw dance as a kind of state of intoxication and the dancer as capable of carrying others to that state. The dancer was a wave, "celebrating the mysteries of absence and presence."[122] Stieglitz's selection of O'Keeffe's flame- and wave-like forms, as well as other dance imagery by artists such as Severini and Rodin, is perhaps significant in light of Valéry's poetic imagery. It is unclear if Stieglitz had any direct exposure to Valéry while in France or through Picabia, but he was reported to have heard a reading by Valéry at one of Paul Rosenfeld's weekly soirées in November 1924.[123]

Stieglitz's organization of a variety of exhibitions that had strong connections to music and dance in the 291 years may perhaps be viewed as one path to the "Gesamtkunstwerk" that Wagner espoused. Stieglitz's attendance at so many operas, concerts, ballets, and other cultural events as a young student clearly made a strong impression on him, and developed his interest in music. It seems understandable that he would be attracted to artists whose work was rooted in music and dance. In supporting work where a variety of the senses could participate, Stieglitz appeared to be striving for a "total art" where synaesthesia played an important role and where the dynamism of modern life could be expressed in new spatio-temporal modes of expression. Indeed, he seemed to "sing the multicolored and polyphoric surf of revolutions"[124] that the Futurists espoused.

But Stieglitz could not sustain his efforts at 291. The war and increasing financial problems caused him to close his beloved gallery. On 31 May 1917, he wrote to O'Keeffe: ". . . I have decided to rip 291 to pieces after all. I can't bear to think that its walls which held your drawings and the children's should be in charge of anyone else but myself . . . No the walls must come down – and very soon – in a few days. So that I am sure they're down. Others should move in and build anew."[125] And he wrote to O'Keeffe again on 24 June: "I didn't tell you this afternoon I set Zoler ripping down more shelving in the old little room – and ripping down the remaining burlap – I made a photograph of him – he enjoyed the job – and I enjoyed the destruction – and his enjoyment. – The place looks as if it had been raped by the terrible Germans!"[126]

In June 1917 the last issue of *Camera Work* appeared. It was devoted to Paul Strand and was, in many ways, a funeral for Pictorialism. Strand's clean Modernist lines and abstracted forms were printed on thick, hard paper to emphasize the directness of his expression. Gone was the soft, delicate Japanese tissue paper of previous issues. Stieglitz had also shown Strand's photographs from 13 March to 3 April 1916 as a foil to the Forum Exhibition of Modern American Painters held at the same time at the Anderson Gallery. For Stieglitz, no significant photographic work apart from Strand's had been made in the last ten years in the United States or in Europe. Describing the illustrations, stieqlitz wrote, "The work is brutally direct. Devoid of trickery and of any 'ism,' devoid of any attempt to mystify an ignorant public . . . These photographs are the direct expression of today . . . In their presentation we have intentionally emphasized the spirit of their brutal directness."[127]

Camera Work had come to an end. The short life of the proto-Dada periodical *291*, on which Stieglitz had collaborated, had come to end. The workspace for the two publications had in part been in the back room of the gallery. Now that was closed. Stieglitz sadly described his selling of the last issues of *291*:

> Once *291* came to an end, and the gallery 291 closed in 1917, I didn't
> know what to do with the nearly eight thousand copies of the publi-

cation that remained. I called in a rag picker. It was wartime. The cost of paper was high. Perhaps my gesture was a satirical one. The rag picker offered five dollars and eighty cents for the lot, including the wonderful Imperial Japan 'Steerage' prints. I handed the money to my part-time secretary, and said, "Here, Marie. This may buy you a pair of gloves – or two."

I kept the greater part of the deluxe edition, but, in time, I destroyed most of that. I had no feeling whatsoever about the transaction except that it was another lesson. I asked myself why an official of a Berlin museum had been so willing to pay a hundred dollars for a print of *The Steerage* while my American friends did not want one at the cost of two dollars.[128]

Stieglitz's photograph *The Last Days of 291* captures his state of despair. It shows the backs of pictures; issues of *Camera Work* on the floor; on the rear shelf, an old broom; dried, dying foliage, perhaps bittersweet; and a sculptural bust with a bandage on his head. Two other sculptures are shrouded in gauze. The central figure, with its peeling paint, holds a makeshift sword in chains at his waist. Burlap from the walls is heaped on the floor. It is a funereal scene.

After 291 closed, Stieglitz paid $10 a month rent for the next year in order to have a place to get away from his house and failing marriage, and to have a professional mailing address. There was nothing on exhibition but people seemed still to seek out Stieglitz. That winter was extremely cold, the worst in decades. Stieglitz recalled, "I sat in the desolate, empty, filthy, rat-holed, ill-smelling little space that originally was part of 291. Or I walked up and down in my overcoat, my cape over the coat, hat on, and I still would be freezing . . . I had nowhere else to go – no working place, no club, no money. I felt somewhat as Napoleon must have on his retreat from Moscow. The world seemed sad and gray. There was not only the war, but also labor unrest. The heydays of 291 were over. Yet I stuck to my post."[129] Fortunately, the interior decorator, S. B. Lawrence, based nextdoor to 291, offered to let Stieglitz and his friends, who still came to 291, warm themselves by his coal stove.

In his sadness, Stieglitz also reached out to Gertrude Stein across the Atlantic:

Times are terrifically hard over here . . . Then too, one must remember that there is no real feeling for art, or love for art in the United States as yet. It is still considered a great luxury, something which is

253   Alfred Stieglitz, *The Last Days of 291*, 1917

really not necessary. And all this in spite of the so-called interest in old masters and the millions spent for them by people like Altman and Morgan. Was not Altman the landlord of our little 291? Did he not double the rent virtually on the day on which he bought the property and incidentally bought a new Rembrandt? Did he ever know that 291 was fighting tooth and nail, single-handed in this vast country of ours, for the very thing he thought he loved?[130]

In actuality, Stieglitz had made more inroads than he thought in his fight for photography as a fine art, for modern art, and in general for a living spirit that was dynamic, creative, and humanistic. He had fostered photography and the other arts as editor, gallery director, and constant advocate for his cause. In his own work, too, he continually pushed the boundaries of the photographic medium, moving from Pictorialism to "straight photography." In those later years of the 291 era, he was, as Weston Naef has noted, "an apostle of clarity. He simplified his subjects to their bare essence, eliminating the extraneous. Unity, logic, and the beauty of line are hallmarks of his style and result in the clarity that became his signature. Stieglitz invites us to see the duality that is often overlooked in everyday existence, he strives to express in his photographs elements of structure and content that are unseen on the surface of his subjects."[131]

His photographs also ask the viewer to contemplate both the seen and the unseen, and in many instances they serve as a bridge from the visible to the invisible. In the end, he found his own truth, one that encompassed as indefatigable spirit that, like an Olympic flame, was to travel many directions in its influence. As Stieglitz himself wrote, "When an artist finds his own truth, he will discover that it fits with traditional truths, with those that endured over a long period of time. Originally, whether or not the artist reveals a truth that happens to be traditional is never a question that concerns him. If he says what he must, from the depths of his own experience, it will automatically lie in the great tradition of truth. It is this that I mean in spirit when I say that all true things are equal to one another."[132]

With the closing of 291 and the final issue of *Camera Work*, many of the artists that had surrounded Stieglitz in those small rooms on lower Fifth Avenue, scattered; such a community would not really be formed again. Some such as Steichen traveled a divergent path, as he moved into a more commercial world. Artists such as John Marin enjoyed a productive career and remained close to Stieglitz. Marsden Hartley and Arthur Dove had uneven careers, and Dove, in particular, came to be seen as a forerunner to the Abstract Expressionists. O'Keeffe, with her independent spirit, developed her own voice. In some instances, Stieglitz became very protective of her work, and refused to sell it if he did not think the buyer was appropriate. O'Keeffe and Stieglitz, at various points, may be seen to have had reciprocal influences on each other.[1] Their words in 1915 and 1916 were perhaps prophetic: she, in 1915, "I believe I would rather have Stieglitz like something – anything I had done – than anyone else I know of . . . If I ever make anything that satisfies even so little – I am going to show it to him to find out if it's any good."[2] And he, in 1916, "Those drawings – how I understand them. They are as if I saw them as part of myself."[3] The critic Henry Tyrell's 1917 interpretation of O'Keeffe's watercolor, *Blue Lines X* (1916) may well be read as a description of O'Keeffe and Stieglitz in their early years together:

> Two lives, a man's and a woman's, distinct yet invisibly all joined together by mutual attraction, grow out of the earth like two graceful saplings, side by side, straight and slender, though their fluid lines undulate in unconscious rhythmic sympathy, as they react and react upon one another, "there is another self I long to meet without which life, my life is incomplete." But as the man's line broadens or thickens, with worldly growth, the woman's becomes finer as it aspires spiritually upward, until it faints and falls off sharply – not to break, however, but to recover firmness and resume its growth, straight heaven ward as before, farther apart from the other self and though never wholly sundered, yet never actually joined.[4]

Their relationship was to change over time as each grew older, and O'Keeffe became increasing independent. The passion of their early years evolved into a relationship that was often volatile and long distance, as O'Keeffe spent more and more time in New Mexico, while Stieglitz remained in New York, either in Manhattan or at Lake George.

In 1924, O'Keeffe and Stieglitz had their first and only joint exhibition, organized by Stieglitz. O'Keeffe showed images of trees and leaves while Stieglitz showed his images of clouds, which seem very painterly next to O'Keefe's paintings. The curator Elizabeth Hutton Turner has noted, "Whether inspired by the earth or the sky, Stieglitz and O'Keeffe shared the same intuition. Their images struck a common chord, which they attributed to nature and experience and characterized as 'music.'"[5] He described her work as "songs of consciousness" and "she maintained she found music in Stieglitz's photographs whether viewed 'right side up or upside down or sideways.'"[6]

It is doubtful whether Stieglitz could have produced his series of cloud photographs, his *Equivalents*, without the foundation work of his youth. As has been seen, he photographed various aspects of clouds and the sky from his youth onward. Nor could he have produced the remarkable composite portrait of O'Keeffe without the groundwork laid in his photographs of other women in his early years – his own daughter, Katharine Rhoades, Ellen Koeniger.

Stieglitz wrote, "I can do nothing because another does it, nothing that is not for me to do because of some deep inner need. I clarify for myself alone. I am interested in putting down an image only of what I have seen, not what it means to me. It is only after I have put down an equivalent of what has moved me that I can even begin to think about its meaning . . . I feel that all experiences in life are one, if truly seen. So that what one puts down in any particular form must be an equivalent of any other truly felt experience."[7] The clouds, the landscape, the trees, the street scenes, the buildings, the people Stieglitz knew and met, were all part of the fabric of his experience and existence before they were incorporated into photographic images and, in his final photographs, became equivalents for his life experience and feelings.

Besides being equivalents in some instances, his photographs over the years also helped define a sense of place for Stieglitz and others – New York City, Lake George, Katwyk, Gutach, Chioggia, Venice. These places became unique and special through the lens of Stieglitz's camera. But these photographs of particular places also often went beyond geography, to include elements of autobiography and metaphor that could carry

254   Alfred Stieglitz, *Equivalent, Portrait of Georgia, No. 3, Songs of the Sky, No. 2,*
1923

the image to the realm of the universal. As the photographer Robert Adams later noted: Geography is, if taken alone, sometimes boring, auto-biography is frequently trivial, and metaphor can be dubious, but taken together, as in the best work of people like Alfred Stieglitz and Edward Weston, the three kinds of information strengthen each other and rein-force what we all work to keep intact – an affection for life."[8] Adams went on to compare Stieglitz with the poet Theodore Roethke, finding that the two were allies, each "a poet, a describer of things, a recorder of Form independent of stories, [Roethke] an ally of the photographer Alfred Stieglitz, who observed that 'Beauty is the universal seen.'[9]

Stieglitz's development as a photographer from the day he bought his first camera as a young student in Berlin to his last days of photographing in 1937, was marked by intensity and continual striving for perfection. From Pictorialism to straight photography, Stieglitz pushed for honest, pure visual imagery. He was a child of European naturalism and of Romanticism, which evolved into Symbolism. But he also knew the clean, ordered lines of classicism. And finally, there was Modernism, which Stieglitz helped foster and develop into the twentieth century. In his later years, after 291 closed, Stieglitz pushed for the development of an American art and culture, but he did not forget his European roots, nor the Europeans whose work he brought to the United States – Rodin, Picasso, Matisse, Severini, Kandinsky.

Stieglitz's exposure to multiple art forms as a young man and student was a significant foundation for his development as a photographer, writer, editor, and gallery director, providing him with a wider field of reference and exposure to diverse modes of expression. Museum visits, attendance at concerts, operas, and the books he read were all signifi-cant elements that contributed to his creative expression. His early mentors and supporters, such as his father Edward, Professor Hermann Vogel, the artist Wilhelm Hasemann, or his friend and fellow photogra-pher Edward Steichen, were all part of the tapestry of experiences and influences that informed his work. That tapestry also contained the artists who frequented his galleries, the contributors to *Camera Notes* and *Camera Work*, and the women who influenced his life or became his photographic subjects – Emmy, Kitty, Marie Rapp, Ellen Koeniger, and Georgia O'Keeffe.

Through the work there runs an ever-present thread of musicality. Music was frequently a part of Stieglitz's life, and found its way into the very soul of his work. In his photographs, he provided a special music for the viewer. He offered proportion, rhythm, harmonies of earth and sky, and colors of the gray scale as part of that musicality. As Estelle Justim has noted, "Like music, his abstract forms are a notation of the vibrations of the universe. Music is the arithmetic of the cosmos and Stieglitz's 'music' is photography's music to the eye."[10] The musicality inherent in much of Stieglitz's imagery and in the work of other artists whom he supported may be seen as an ongoing musical score that began when he was a young student and continued to his last photographs.

Indeed, Stieglitz himself might be seen as a modern-day Orpheus. Like Orpheus, the son of the sun god Apollo and the muse Calliope, a musician and poet, Stieglitz frequently enchanted those around him. As a number of artists at the turn of the century portrayed Orpheus as a poet, prototypical artist, martyr, and priest, so too did Stieglitz's admirers elevate him to the role of a god-like figure. Stieglitz's song was intense, and his work fulfilled the criteria that John Marin set forth in 1922 – that the test of a work of art was whether a work could "sing." The brush or camera was to become a musical instrument that must be made to sing of life.[11]

This notion of song and its connection to spiritual expression seemed to find its roots in rhythms of the American soul and landscape, particularly in the 1920s and 1930s. Writers such as Sherwood Anderson in *Mid-American Chants* (1918), or Walt Whitman in "Song of Myself" (1855) or "Song of the Open Road" (1856) also emphasized the notion of song. Anderson "felt that Americans hungered for the expression of the soul – or song. To catch this song and sing it would do much – make much clear."[12]

Stieglitz as Orpheus, as priest; Stieglitz as Svengali, as Wagner's Hans Sachs, as impresario; Stieglitz as writer, as editor, as autocrat, or as searcher for the eternal Woman – who was the real Stieglitz? His life and work defy an answer. Those who admired him frequently saw him as god-like; they became disciples in a quasi-religious community, committed to the world of art and freedom of individual expression. A mythology has grown up surrounding Stieglitz, generated by his followers and his own writings, particularly those compiled and edited by Dorothy Norman, the young woman who came into Stieglitz's life at age twenty-one in 1926, when she visited his intimate gallery. Stieglitz's detractors saw him as controlling, as a dictator, opinionated, and garrulous to the extreme.

In Stieglitz's world, there always seemed to be a battle that needed to be waged, sometimes small, sometimes large. The word "fight" appeared frequently in his writings. In a letter to J. Dudley Johnston at the British

Royal Photographic Society in 1923, Stieglitz recalled his fight up to that point in his life:

> I have all but killed myself for Photography. My passion for it is greater than ever. It's forty years that I have fought its fight – and I'll fight to the finish – single-handed and without money if need be. It is not photographs – it is not photographers – I am fighting for. And my own photographs I never sign. I am not fighting to make a "name" for myself. Maybe you have some feeling for what the fight is for. It's a world's fight. This sounds mad. But so is *Camera Work* mad. All that's born of spirit seems mad in these [days] of materialism run riot."[13]

There seems to be little middle ground in responding to or understanding Stieglitz. But the middle ground, if any objectivity is to be found at all, perhaps lies in the paradoxical nature of Stieglitz's personality and core. He was a man who was gregarious, a conversationalist and raconteur, yet he was a man of intense private reflection. There were sometimes "hours of quiet," posted in his galleries. He often craved attention, but was also a loner in his ideas and ideals. He was democratic in believing that art should be available to everyone: "Art is not in reality the property of anyone . . . Art is for everyone."[14] But Stieglitz was also an elitist in his thinking, wanting to rise above the mainstream and materialism. He was eclectic in many of his tastes, interested in many things, from billiards to horse racing to photography and the other arts. But he was also single-minded, often focusing relentlessly on his 'cause' or argument. He loved New York City, with its energy and transition into a modern world. But he sought refuge in his beloved Lake George – its peaceful shoreline and still waters. Even as a young student he divided his time between city and country – Berlin and Gutach, or Venice and Chioggia.

For many he could hardly be described as a family man, leaving his first wife and spending little time with his daughter Kitty. But he went every summer to his large sprawling family home at Lake George, filled with visiting relatives, particularly when his parents were living. His mother's death in 1922 upset him; he appeared to bury his grief in his work. He loved "Woman" and women but also needed the camaraderie of his male colleagues.

He was American, believed in an American spirit, but had many of his roots in Europe, roots he never denied. He was both a Romantic and a Classicist, exhibiting tendencies toward both in the form and content of his photographs. He shared in the Symbolist aesthetic, but was also comfortable in the world of rationality and logic. He was both visually and verbally articulate.

Perhaps, above all, he was both artist and scientist, competent in chemistry, laboratory methods, and the evolving technology related to cameras, lenses, developing, and printing processes. He saw his galleries as laboratories, but he married the role of the scientist with the creative spirit of the artist, striving to push deep within the human psyche to have a better understanding of an inner human spirit that was invisible.

Stieglitz believed in life, as an affirming and evolving force. "I am . . . we die . . . Life is . . . let us get on with it . . . let life develop from within, spontaneously, in sacred spirit . . . with dignity. Fearlessly . . . nourish the life-force in man."[15] Stieglitz was a perfectionist in pursuing an affirmation of this life spirit. But he also associated perfection with death. Once when asked what a perfect photograph was, he replied:

> I will be sitting with the plate of a picture I have just taken in my hands. It will be the picture I have always known that some day I would be able to take. It will be the perfect photograph, embodying all that I ever have wished to say. I will just have developed it; just have looked at it; just have seen that it was exactly what I wanted. The room will be empty, quiet. The walls will be bare – clean. I will sit looking at the picture. It will slip from my hands, and break as it falls to the ground. I will be dead. They will come. No one will ever have seen the picture nor know what it was."[16]

Stieglitz's paradoxical nature will perhaps always be enigmatic for many. And perhaps there is no one Stieglitz but a multifaceted Stieglitz, who grew, changed, evolved through his career. For those he touched, he often helped form, inform, and transform their lives, both positively and negatively. To go beyond personality, it is his work – his photographs, his editorship of *Camera Notes* and *Camera Work*, and his fostering of artists at his galleries, that will be his enduring spirit.

At age eighty-two, on 13 July 1946, Stieglitz died after suffering a massive heart attack two days earlier. He had been at his gallery, An American Place, looking through some boxes of plates he had made during his student days in Europe. That early work still meant something to him.

About twenty people attended a small, brief service held at Frank Campbell's funeral home in New York, including Paul Strand, Edward Steichen, and Georgia O'Keeffe. There were no lengthy tributes, no

255   Lake George, close to where Stieglitz's ashes were scattered, 2002

music, few flowers. He was laid in a simple pine coffin, lined with a white
sheet. Although Steichen and Stieglitz had traveled divergent paths,
Steichen came and placed a pine bough on the black shrouded coffin,
which he said was from "Alfred's tree" on Steichen's Connecticut farm.[17]
Stieglitz's body was cremated and his ashes scattered at the base of an
old tree not far from Oaklawn, on the quiet shoreline of Lake George,
a lifelong source of renewal and inspiration. Stieglitz's own epitaph for
himself, as recorded by Dorothy Norman, read, "At last it can be said
of me, by way of an epitaph, that I cared."[18]

The basis for an ultimate judgment of Stieglitz's contribution and place
in twentieth century art is also to found in his own words. In a letter to
Thomas Hart Benton that he wrote the day after his seventy-first
birthday, 2 January 1935, he proclaimed, "When finally I am to be
judged I think I'll have to be judged by my own photographic work, by
Camera Work, by the way I've lived, and by the way I have conducted
a series of interindependent demonstrations in the shape of exhibitions
covering over forty years."[19] The "light" of Stieglitz's work, begun in his
youth, was not to be extinguished. He left a living legacy that would
shine brightly and distinctly for generations to come. It is for that legacy
of freedom, and the creative expression of an intense, inner spirit, that
we in the twenty-first century should be grateful.

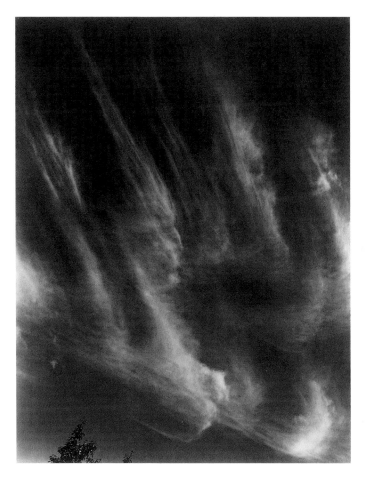

256   Alfred Stieglitz, *Equivalent*, 1930

Appendices

I PHOTOGRAPHIC PROCESSES: A BRIEF EXPLANATION

Albumen print: Originally introduced in 1850, this was a common method of photographic printing in the nineteenth century. Albumen was used as a binding agent for silver salts on the paper, and gave a shiny surface. Increased contrast was possible with this method.

Aristotype or gelatino-chloride or collodio-chloride print: These were the first emulsions on paper to be made commercially at the end of the nineteenth century. With contact with the negative, the paper provided very fine-grained images of a brownish color.

Autochrome: This process involved direct color photography. A glass plate was covered first with varnish, then with tiny grains of potato starch, dyed with the three primary colors in equal proportion. Another layer of varnish and a panchromatic gelatin-bromide emulsion was applied on top of the starch layer. The autochrome plate required a long exposure time and then was developed by a reversal process, resulting in a color glass transparency. The positive colored impression was then fixed, washed, and varnished. The coated plates were manufactured in large quantities by the Lumière brothers' company in France between 1907 and 1940.

Carbon print: This process was patented in 1864, the year Stieglitz was born. A thin piece of paper or tissue was coated with a gelatine emulsion, then set in potassium bichromate to make the paper light-sensitive. When exposed, in contact with the negative, the bichromated gelatin would harden, depending on the amount of light received. The tissue was then attached to a support paper and the unhardened areas were washed away, leaving a positive, reversed print.

Gum-bichromate print: These prints were made by brushing paper, usually textured drawing paper, with gum arabic, dichromated salt, and pigment, which became light-sensitive when dry. When exposed to light through a negative, the gum would harden in proportion to the light received. Water was used to remove the unhardened material, leaving a positive image. During development the photographer could manipulate the process with a brush or sponge. Painterly effects could thus be achieved. Different colors could be achieved by multiple printings of the same negative on the initial sheet of paper.

Gelatin silver print: This process has been used widely in the twentieth century and was used extensively by Stieglitz from the 1920s. Light-sensitive silver salts were mixed with gelatin and white pigment and brushed onto paper. The paper was exposed to light through a negative and the salts would darken in response to the amount of light received. It was easy to achieve a sharply detailed image since the silver would remain suspended in the gelatin and rest on coated paper.

Platinum and palladium prints: The platinum process was particularly popular with the Pictorial photographers from the 1880s to World War I. Here paper was coated with a solution of iron and platinum salts (palladium salts for the palladium process, usually producing warmer, sepia-toned prints). When dry, the paper was exposed to light through a negative and then developed. The process allowed for a wide range of tonal values with subtle gradations. Normally, platinum prints were silvery-gray.

Photogravure (also known as a heliogravure in Europe): This was a photo-mechanical reproduction process, an intaglio aquatint method on a prepared metal plate (usually copper). It was used to reproduce photographs in large editions, such as *Camera Work* editions. Printing was usually carried out on a hand press, although larger editions were made on a flatbed press. The process allowed for excellent definition on the final print.

Half-tone process: This photomechanical process involved the use of a meshed screen, which allowed for the transfer of half-tones. The number of dots per inch of the screen determined the quality of the final printed image. The images produced did not usually contain the fine definition of a photogravure.

Number 1, January 1903

PHOTOGRAPHS: six by Gertrude Käsebier; one by Alfred Stieglitz, *Hand of Man*; one by A. Radclyffe Dugmore.

PAINTINGS (B&W): one by D. W. Tryon; one by Pierre Puvis de Chavannes.

TEXTS: by Alfred Stieglitz, Charles Caffin, Dallett Fuguet, John Barrett Kerfoot, Sidney Allan (Sadakichi Hartmann), Edward Steichen, Joseph Keiley, and others.

Number 2, April 1903

PHOTOGRAPHS: twelve by Edward Steichen (and one advertisement for Kodak).

TEXTS: articles on Edward Steichen by Charles Caffin and Sadakichi Hartmann; miscellaneous by R. Child Bayley, Dallett Fuguet, John Barrett Kerfoot, and Eva Watson-Schütze.

Number 3, July 1903

PHOTOGRAPHS: five by Clarence White; three by Ward Muir; one by J. C. Strauss; one by Joseph Keiley; one by Alfred Stieglitz, *The Street: Design for a Poster*; one by Alvin Langdon Coburn.

PAINTINGS: one by Mary Cassatt; one by Eugène Boudin; one by Rembrandt.

TEXTS: Charles Caffin on Clarence White; miscellaneous by John Barrett Kerfoot, Dallett Fuguet, Ward Muir, and others; quotations from James McNeill Whistler, Peter Henry Emerson.

INSERTS: Facsimile of handwritten piece too late for previous issue by Maurice Maeterlinck, "Je Crois"; principles and membership list of Photo-Secession: "Fellows" including "Founders and Council"; Associates.

Number 4, October 1903

PHOTOGRAPHS: six by Frederick Henry Evans; one by Alfred Stieglitz, *The Flatiron Building*; one by Arthur E. Becher.

TEXTS: George Bernard Shaw on F. H. Evans; miscellaneous by Sadakichi Hartmann, Dallett Fuguet, John Barrett Kerfoot, Charles Caffin, Joseph Keiley, and Edward Steichen.

Number 5, January 1904

PHOTOGRAPHS: six by Robert Demachy; one by Prescott Adamson; one by Frank Eugene (Smith).

TEXTS: Joseph Keiley on Robert Demachy; Sadakichi Hartmann on criticism; miscellaneous by F. H. Evans, Dallett Fuguet, and others; quotations from James McNeill Whistler.

Number 6, April 1904
PHOTOGRAPHS: six by Alvin Langdon Coburn; two by Will A. Cadby; one by W. B. Post.
TEXTS: Charles Caffin on Alvin Langdon Coburn; Sadakichi Hartmann on Carnegie exhibit; miscellaneous by Will A. Cadby, Dallett Fuguet, and others.

Number 7, July 1904
PHOTOGRAPHS: six by Theodor and Oscar Hofmeister; two by Robert Demachy; one by Edward Steichen; one by Mary Devens.
TEXTS: Ernst Juhl on the Hofmeisters; Robert Demachy on gum prints; miscellaneous by A. K. Boursault, F. H. Evans, and others; appeal to subscribers.

Number 8, October 1904
PHOTOGRAPHS: six by J. Craig Annan; one by Alvin Langdon Coburn; one by F. H. Evans; six silhouette portraits by John Barrett Kerfoot.
TEXTS: Joseph Keiley on J. Craig Annan; John Barrett Kerfoot on silhouettes and satire; Alfred Stieglitz on foreign exhibits; miscellaneous others.

Number 9, January 1905
PHOTOGRAPHS: five by Clarence White; one by Edward Steichen; four by Eva Watson-Schütze.
TEXTS: Joseph Keiley on Eva Watson-Schütze; John W. Beatty on Clarence White; F. H. Evans on the 1904 London photographic salon; John Barrett Kerfoot on satire; new series of reprints of New York critics, here on "First American Salon in New York"; miscellaneous others; quotations from Sebastian Melmoth.

Number 10, April 1905
PHOTOGRAPHS: seven by Gertrude Käsebier; two by C. Yarnall Abbott; one by E. M. Bane.
OTHER ART: one Outamaro print; paintings by Thomas W. Dewing and Sandro Botticelli, *Primavera* (b&w).
TEXTS: Roland Rood on plagiarism; Charles Fitzgerald (a generally antagonistic critic on the *New York Sun*, often reprinted later in *Camera Work*), "Edward Steichen: Painter and Photographer"; miscellaneous others.

Number 11, July 1905
PHOTOGRAPHS: six by David Octavius Hill; two by Edward Steichen; one by Robert Demachy; two by A. Horsley Hinton.
TEXTS: J. Craig Annan on David Octavius Hill; Dallett Fuguet on art and originality; John Barrett Kerfoot (satire); various technical pieces; Alfred Stieglitz announces *Camera Work*'s plans for 1906.

Number 12, October 1905
PHOTOGRAPHS: ten by Alfred Stieglitz: *Horses* (1904), *Winter, Fifth Avenue* (misdated 1892, taken February 1893), *Going to the Post* (1904), *Spring* (1901), *Nearing Land* (1904), *Katherine* (1905), *Miss S. R.* (1904), *Ploughing* (1904), *Gossip, Katwyck* (1894), *September* (1899); three by F. Benedict Herzog.
OTHER ART: reprinted hieroglyphics and cave sketches (half page); two by Giotto; one by Sandro Botticelli (detail from *Primavera*); one by Diego Velázquez.
TEXTS: Charles Caffin on "Verities and Illusions"; Roland Rood on the evolution of art; announcement of the opening of the Little Galleries of the Photo-

Secession Gallery around 1 November; miscellaneous others; quotations from Sebastian Melmoth.

Number 13, January 1906

PHOTOGRAPHS: three by Hugo Henneberg; four by Heinrich Kühn; five by Hans Watzek.

OTHER ART: Edward Steichen poster of Photo-Secession.

TEXTS: F. Mathies-Masuren on Hugo Henneberg, Heinrich Kühn, and Hans Watzek; Charles Caffin "Verities & Illusions 11"; F. H. Evans on the 1905 London Salon (with a list of American photos shown); miscellaneous others.

Number 14, April 1906

PHOTOGRAPHS: nine by Edward Steichen; four by Alfred Stieglitz of exhibitions at 291, Edward Steichen in March, Clarence White and Gertrude Käsebier in February, and opening exhibition November–January (two images). One Edward Steichen cover design (woman with globe).

TEXTS: George Bernard Shaw, "The Unmechanicalness of Photography" and review of a London exhibition; John Barrett Kerfoot (satire); reprints of critics on Photo-Secession Gallery shows; calendar of shows.

Special Steichen supplement, April 1906

PHOTOGRAPHS: sixteen by Edward Steichen, including portraits of Eleanora Duse, Maurice Maeterlinck, J. P. Morgan, and August Rodin, and several half-tones (hand-colored).

TEXTS: Maurice Maeterlinck, "I Believe."

Number 15, July 1906

PHOTOGRAPHS: five by Alvin Langdon Coburn; one by George Bernard Shaw, portrait of Alvin Langdon Coburn; one by Edward Steichen, experiment in three-color photography, unretouched half-tone plate printed directly by engraver from three diapositives; one by George Henry Seeley.

TEXTS: articles by Charles Caffin and Roland Rood; George Bernard Shaw on Alvin Langdon Coburn; John Barrett Kerfoot, "The ABC of Photography, A–G"; miscellaneous others, including report on First Pennsylvania Academy photo show arranged by Joseph Keiley, Edward Steichen, and Alfred Stieglitz; sales of around $2,800 for prints averaging $45+ from gallery shows during 1905–6.

Number 16, October 1906

PHOTOGRAPHS: seven by Robert Demachy; three by C. (Emile Joachim Constant) Puyo; two by René LeBègue.

TEXTS: Robert Demachy on Rawlins oil process; Charles Caffin on recent shows; John Barrett Kerfoot, "The ABC of Photography, H–N"; miscellaneous others.

Number 17, January 1907

PHOTOGRAPHS: six by Joseph Keiley; two by F. Benedict Herzog; one by Harry Cogswell Rubincam; one by A. Radclyffe Dugmore.

OTHER ARTS: two by James Montgomery Flagg, two-color satiric watercolor "portraits."

TEXTS: Charles Caffin on F. Benedict Herzog: John Barrett Kerfoot, "The ABC of Photography, O–T' ", F. H. Evans on the London Salon 1906; miscellaneous others.

Number 18, April 1907
PHOTOGRAPHS: six by George Davison; two by Sarah C. Sears; two by William B. Dyer.
TEXTS: Charles Caffin, "Symbolism and Allegory"; R. Child Bayley on Pictorial photography; John Barrett Kerfoot, "The ABC of Photography, U–Z"; Robert Demachy on "modified" prints, answered by George Bernard Shaw; F. H. Evans; Frank Meadow Sutclyffe; miscellaneous others.

Number 19, July 1907
PHOTOGRAPHS: five by J. Craig Annan; one by Edward Steichen.
TEXTS: Robert Demachy on the "Straight Print"; miscellaneous by Dallett Fuguet, Charles Caffin, John Barrett Kerfoot, and others.

Number 20, October 1907
PHOTOGRAPHS: six by George Henry Seeley; three Alfred Stieglitz "snapshots", *From My Window, New York* (post-1898), *From My Window, Berlin* (1888–90), *In the New York Central Yards* (1903); one by W. Renwick.
TEXTS: Alfred Stieglitz, "The New Color Photography" (first report on Lumière autochromes; his first experiments with the process were in June 1907); Joseph Keiley on Gertrude Käsebier; C. A. Brasseur on color photography; miscellaneous others.

Number 21, January 1908
PHOTOGRAPHS: twelve by Alvin Langdon Coburn.
TEXTS: (unsigned) "Is Photography a New Art?"; Charles Caffin and others. Delay of a color issue explained.

Number 22, April 1908 (color number)
PHOTOGRAPHS: three by Edward Steichen, *BS, On the Houseboat, Lady H.* (reproduced in four-color half-tones by A. Bruckmann & Co., Munich).
TEXTS: Edward Steichen, "Color Photography"; Charles Caffin and J. C. Strauss on the expulsion of Alfred Stieglitz from the New York Camera Club; list of over forty members of the Camera Workers, a new group of photographers who had resigned from the Camera Club, with headquarters at 122 East 25th Street; miscellaneous others, including reviews of Auguste Rodin drawings at 291 in January.

Number 23, July 1908
PHOTOGRAPHS: sixteen by Clarence White.
TEXTS: Charles Caffin on a Clarence White and George Henry Seeley exhibition; reprints of critics on Henri Matisse exhibition; Alfred Stieglitz, "Frilling and Autochromes"; miscellaneous others.

Number 24, October 1908
PHOTOGRAPHS: seven by Adolph de Meyer; one by William E. Wilmerding; two by Guido Rey.
TEXTS: George Besson interviews artists including Auguste Rodin and Henri Matisse about Pictorial photography; Charles Caffin, "The Camera Point of View in Painting and Photography"; miscellaneous others.

Number 25, January 1909
PHOTOGRAPHS: five by Annie W. Brigman; one by Emma Spencer; one by C. Yarnall Abbott; two by Frank Eugene, including a portrait of Alfred Stieglitz.

TEXTS: Charles Caffin, "Henri Matisse and Isadora Duncan"; John Barrett Kerfoot on Henri Matisse; J. Nilsen Laurvik on Annie W. Brigman; miscellaneous others: Photo-Secession members' list.

Number 26, April 1909
PHOTOGRAPHS: six by Alice Boughton; one by J. Craig Annan; one by George Davison.
TEXTS: Benjamin de Casseres, "Caricature and New York"; Sir (Caspar) Purdon Clarke on "Art" and Oscar Wilde on "The Artist"; J. Nilsen Laurvik on the show *International Photography* at the National Arts Club: miscellaneous others.

Number 27, July 1909
PHOTOGRAPHS: five by Herbert G. French; four by Clarence White and Alfred Stieglitz (collaboration).
TEXTS: H. G. Wells, "On Beauty"; Benjamin de Casseres on Pamela Colman Smith; Charles Caffin on Adolph de Meyer and Alvin Langdon Coburn shows; New York critics on Alfred Maurer and John Marin at 291; quotations from Oscar Wilde; miscellaneous others.

Number 28, October 1909
PHOTOGRAPHS: six by David Octavius Hill; one by George Davison; one by Paul Burty Haviland; one by Marshall R. Kernochan; one by Alvin Langdon Coburn.
TEXTS: unsigned piece on Impressionism; Charles Caffin on Edward Steichen's pictures of Rodin's *Balzac* and on the Dresden international photo show; quotations from Friedrich Nietzsche, "To the Artist Who is Eager for Fame"; miscellaneous others.

Number 29, January 1910
PHOTOGRAPHS: ten by George Henry Seeley.
CARICATURES: four by Marius de Zayas.
TEXTS: Sadakichi Hartmann; Julius Meier-Graefe on Henri de Toulouse-Lautrec lithographs: other critics on Photo-Secession Galleries exhibition; miscellaneous others.

Number 30, April 1910
PHOTOGRAPHS: ten by Frank Eugene.
CARICATURES: one by Marius de Zayas, of Alfred Stieglitz.
TEXTS: William D. MacColl on art criticism; Sadakichi Hartmann on composition; Charles Caffin on Edward Steichen; New York critics on Edward Steichen, John Marin, and Henri Matisse; miscellaneous others, including announcement of Albright Gallery show in Rochester (November).

Number 31, July 1910
PHOTOGRAPHS: fourteen by Frank Eugene.
TEXTS: Max Weber, "The Fourth Dimension from a Plastic Point of View" and "Chinese Dolls and Modern Colonists"; Paul Burty Haviland in defense of including other arts at 291 gallery and in *Camera Work*; Sadakichi Hartmann on Marius de Zayas; New York critics on *Younger American Painters* show; miscellaneous others.

Number 32, October 1910

PHOTOGRAPHS: five by J. Craig Annan; one by Clarence White; advertisement by Alvin Langdon Coburn.

DRAWINGS: two by Matisse (nudes); one by Gordon Craig (stage design).

TEXTS: Sadakichi Hartmann on Puritanism; J. Craig Annan on photography as "artistic expression"; Benjamin de Casseres on "Decadence and Mediocrity"; Elie Nadelman, "My Drawings"; miscellaneous others.

Number 33, January 1911

PHOTOGRAPHS: fifteen by Heinrich Kühn (some mezzotint, some duplex half-tone).

TEXTS: Charles Caffin, Joseph Keiley, Alvin Langdon Coburn, and others on Albright Gallery show; Sadakichi Hartmann, "What Remains?"; Max Weber, poem to primitive Mexican art; miscellaneous others.

Numbers 34–35, April–July 1911

PHOTOGRAPHS: four by Edward Steichen, Auguste Rodin and *Balzac*.

DRAWINGS: Auguste Rodin, two gravures, seven colored collotypes.

TEXTS: Benjamin de Casseres; Agnes Ernst Meyer; Sadakichi Hartmann on Auguste Rodin; George Bernard Shaw, "A Page from Shaw"; Marius de Zayas on the Paris Salon d'Automne; Charles Caffin on Paul Cézanne; Marius de Zayas on Pablo Picasso; L. F. Hurd, Jr.; miscellaneous others.

Number 36, October 1911

PHOTOGRAPHS: sixteen by Alfred Stieglitz: *The City of Ambition* (1910), *The City Across the River* (1910), *The Ferry Boat* (1910), *The Mauretania* (1910), *Lower Manhattan* (1910), *Old and New New York* (1910), *The Aeroplane* (1910), *A Dirigible* (1910), *The Steerage* (1907), *Excavating, New York* (1911), *The Swimming Lesson* (1906), *The Pool – Deal* (1910), *The Hand of Man* (1902), *In the New York Central Yards* (1903), *The Terminal* (1892), *Spring Showers, New York* (1903).

DRAWINGS: one by Pablo Picasso.

TEXTS: Benjamin de Casseres, "The Unconscious in Art"; quotations from Henri Bergson and Plato; Alvin Langdon Coburn, "The Relation of Time to Art"; miscellaneous others.

Number 37, January 1912

PHOTOGRAPHS: nine by David Octavius Hill (and Robert Adamson).

TEXTS: Benjamin de Casseres on modernity and decadence; Sadakichi Hartmann on originality; Henri Bergson on the object of art; Archibald Henderson on George Bernard Shaw and photography; Maurice Maeterlinck on photography; Charles Caffin on Adolph de Meyer; Gelett Burgess, "Essays in Subjective Symbolism"; miscellaneous others.

Number 38, April 1912

PHOTOGRAPHS: five by Annie W. Brigman; eight by Karl F. Struss.

TEXTS: Benjamin de Casseres, "The Ironical in Art"; Sadakichi Hartmann, "The Esthetic Significance of the Motion Picture"; reprints of New York critics; miscellaneous others.

Number 39, July 1912
PHOTOGRAPHS: six by Paul Burty Haviland; one by H. Mortimer Lamb.
PAINTINGS: two John Marin watercolors (three-color half-tone).
DRAWINGS: two by Manuel Manolo.
CARICATURES: one by Marius de Zayas, of Alfred Stieglitz.
TEXTS: Marius de Zayas, "The Sun Has Set"; Sadakichi Hartmann on Henri Matisse; quotations from Wassily Kandinsky's "On the Spiritual in Art" (pre-English translation); J. Nilsen Laurvik on John Marin; Sadakichi Hartmann on children's drawings; miscellaneous others.

Special Number, August 1912
PAINTINGS: five by Henri Matisse; three by Pablo Picasso.
DRAWINGS: two by Pablo Picasso.
SCULPTURES: two by Henri Matisse; two by Pablo Picasso (all half-tone photo reproduction).
TEXTS: Editorial on contents; Gertrude Stein, "Henri Matisse" and "Pablo Picasso" (first publication of her work in the United States).

Number 40, October 1912
PHOTOGRAPHS: fourteen by Adolph de Meyer.
TEXTS: John Galsworthy, "Vague Thoughts on Art"; Hutchins Hapgood, "A New Form of Literature"; quotations from the letters of Vincent van Gogh; miscellaneous others.

Number 41, January 1913
PHOTOGRAPHS: five by Julia Margaret Cameron; four by Alfred Stieglitz, two entitled *A Snapshot, Paris* (1911), *The Asphalt Paver, New York* (1892), *Portrait, S. R.* (1904).
TEXTS: Marius de Zayas, "Photography" and "The Evolution of Form-Introduction"; reprints from New York critics; miscellaneous others.

Special Number, June 1913
PAINTINGS: three by Paul Cézanne; one by Vincent Van Gogh; two by Pablo Picasso; one by Francis Picabia.
DRAWINGS: one by Pablo Picasso (half-tone photo reproduction).
TEXTS: Gertrude Stein, "Portrait of Mabel Dodge at the Villa Curonia"; Mabel Dodge, "Speculations"; Gabrielle Buffet, "Modern Art and the Public"; Francis Picabia, "Vers L'Amorphisme"; Benjamin de Casseres, "The Renaissance of the Irrational"; miscellaneous others; "Are You Interested in the Deeper Meaning of Photography?"

Numbers 42–43, April–July 1913 (published November)
PHOTOGRAPHS: fourteen by Edward Steichen (including duogravures).
PAINTINGS: three by Edward Steichen (reproduced in three-color half-tones).
TEXTS: Marius de Zayas, "Photography and Artistic Photography"; Mary Steichen, poem; New York critics on 291; John Marin, "Statement on his Show"; Francis Picabia, "Preface to His Show"; Marius de Zayas, "Preface to His Show"; John Weichsel, "Cosmism or Amorphism?"

Number 44, October 1913 (published March 1914)
PHOTOGRAPHS: one by Edward Steichen; one by Alfred Stieglitz, *Two Towers, New York*; one by Annie W. Brigman.

DRAWINGS: seven by Abraham Walkowitz (collotype reproductions).

TEXTS: Tributes to Joseph Keiley (died January) by Dallett Fuguet, John Barrett Kerfoot, R. Child Bayley, William Murrell (Fisher), the editors; Oscar Bluemner on Abraham Walkowitz; reprints of New York critics; miscellaneous others.

Number 45, January 1914 (published June)

PHOTOGRAPHS: eight by J. Craig Annan.

TEXTS: Mina Loy, "Aphorisms on Futurism"; Marsden Hartley, foreword for exhibition; Mabel Dodge on Marsden Hartley; Gertrude Stein, "From a Play by Gertrude Stein on Marsden Hartley"; reprints of New York critics; notice of photo shows planned for 291; miscellaneous others.

Number 46, April 1914 (published October)

PHOTOGRAPHS: two by Paul Burty Haviland; one by Frederick H. Pratt.

CARICATURES: ten by Marius de Zayas.

TEXTS: John Weichsel, "Artists and Others"; poems by Katharine Rhoades and Mina Loy; Marius de Zayas on caricature; Paul Burty Haviland on Marius de Zayas; poem by "S.S.S." (Alfred Stieglitz's sister Selma); shows planned.

Number 47, July 1914 (published January 1915)

No illustrations.

TEXTS: Alfred Stieglitz, "What is 291?" Replies: Mabel Dodge, Hutchins Hapgood, Charles E. S. Rasay, Adolf Wolff, Hodge Kirnan, Annie W. Brigman, Clara Steichen, Ward Muir, Abby Hedge Coryell, Frank Pease, Stephen Hawes, Rex Stovel, Alfred Kreymborg, Francis Bruguière, Ethel Montgomery Andrews, Frances Simpson Stevens, Djuna Barnes, Paul Burty Haviland, Charles Demuth, Konrad Cramer, Charles Daniel, Anna C. Pellew, Helen R. Gibbs, H. Mortimer Lamb, Marsden Hartley, Arthur B. Davies, Arthur G. Dove, John W. Breyfogle, William Zorach, Velida, Max Merz, Eugene Meyer, Jr., Arthur B. Carles, Emil Zoler, J. Nilsen Laurvik, S.S.S., Christian Brinton, N. E. Montross, Hugh H. Breckenridge, Helen W. Henderson, Ernest Haskell, Frank Fleming, Lee Simonson, Arthur Hoeber, William F. Gable, A. Walkowitz, F. W. Hunter, Oscar Bluemner, C. Duncan, Katharine Rhoades, Agnes Ernst Meyer, Marion H. Beckett, Clifford Williams, Samuel Halpert, Man Ray, Marie J. Rapp, Charles Caffin, Dallett Fuguet, Belle Greene, Edward Steichen, Hippolyte Havel, Henry McBridge, Torres Palomar, John Weichsel, John Barrett Kerfoot, Francis Picabia, Marius de Zayas, John Marin.

Number 48, October 1916

PHOTOGRAPHS: one by Frank Eugene; six by Paul Strand; one by Arthur Allen Lewis; one by Francis Bruguière; six by Alfred Stieglitz, exhibitions at 291: *Negro Art* (November 1914), *German and Viennese Photographers* (March 1906), *Detail, Picasso, Braque* (January 1915), *Nadelman, room 1* (December 1915), *Nadelman, room 2* (December 1915).

TEXTS: 291 exhibitions 1914–16; Marius de Zayas, "Modern Art in Connection with Negro Art"; A. E. Meyer on Marion H. Beckett and Katharine Rhoades; Elie Nadelman on his show; Abraham Walkowitz on his show; Marsden Hartley on his show; C. Duncan and Evelyn Sayer on "Georgia O'Keeffe, C. Duncan and René Lafferty"; New York critics reprints; announcing "291, a new publication"; reprint from 291, July–August 1915 of Marius de Zayas piece; unsigned, "291 and the Modern Gallery"; Marsden Hartley, "Epitaph for A. S."

Numbers 49–50, June 1917 (final issue)
PHOTOGRAPHS: eleven by Paul Strand, including *The White Fence, Abstraction Porch Shadows*, and *Abstraction Bowls*.
TEXTS: Paul Strand, "Photography"; W. Murrell Fisher on O'Keeffe drawings and paintings; Charles Caffin on 1916–17 season shows at 291; Stanton MacDonald Wright, Foreword to his show; extract from letter from Frank Eugene; miscellaneous others.

3   EXHIBITION SCHEDULE OF THE LITTLE GALLERIES OF THE PHOTO-SECESSION (LATER CALLED 291)[2]

1905

24 November–4 January 1906   Exhibition of members' work.

1906

10 January–24 January   Exhibition of French photographers: Robert Demachy, E. J. Puyo, Constant Le Bègue.

26 January–4 February   Photographs by Herbert French

5 February–19 February   Photographs by Gertrude Käsebier and Clarence White.

21 February–7 March   British exhibition: J. Craig Annan, Frederick H. Evans, David Octavius Hill.

9 March–24 March   Photographs by Edward Steichen.

7 April–28 April   German and Austrian photographers: Heinrich Kühn, Hugo Henneberg, Theodor and Oscar Hofmeister, Hans Watzek.

10 November–30 December   Exhibition of members' work.

1907

5 January–24 January   Drawings by Pamela Colman Smith.

25 January–12 February   Photographs by Adolph de Meyer and George Henry Seeley.

19 February–5 March   Photographs by Alice Boughton, William B. Dyer, C. Yarnall Abbot

11 March–10 April   Photographs by Alvin Langdon Coburn.

18 November–30 December   Exhibition of members' work.

1908

2 January–21 January   Drawings by Auguste Rodin

7 February–25 February   Photographs by George Henry Seeley.

26 February–11 March   Etchings by Willi Geiger and Donald Shaw McLaughlan; drawings by Pamela Colman Smith.

12 March–25 April   Drawings, lithographs, watercolors, and etchings by Henri Matisse

8 December–30 December   Exhibition of members' work.

1909

4 January–16 January	Caricatures by Marius de Zayas; autochromes by J. Nilsen Laurvik.
18 January–1 February	Photographs by Alvin Langdon Coburn.
26 February–22 February	Photographs in color and monochrome by Adolph de Meyer.
26 February–10 March	Etchings, drypoints, and bookplates by Allen Lewis.
17 March–27 March	Drawings by Pamela Colman Smith.
30 March–17 April	Sketches in oil by Alfred Maurer; water colors by John Marin.
21 April–7 May	Photographs of Auguste Rodin's *Balzac* by Edward Steichen.
18 May–2 June	Exhibition of Japanese prints from the F. W. Hunter Collection, New York.
24 November–17 December	Monotypes and drawings by Eugene Higgins.
20 December–14 January 1910	Lithographs by Henri de Toulouse-Lautrec.

1910

21 January–5 February	Color photographs by Edward Steichen.
7 February–19 February	Watercolors, pastels, and etchings by John Marin.
23 February–6 March	Drawings and reproductions of paintings by Henri Matisse.
9 March–21 March	Younger American Painters: D. Putnam Brinley, Arthur Carles, Arthur Dove, Laurence Fellowes, Marsden Hartley, John Marin, Alfred Maurer, Edward Steichen Max Weber.
21 March–18 April	Drawings and watercolors by Auguste Rodin.
26 April–indefinitely	Caricatures by Marius de Zayas.
18 November–8 December	Lithographs by Edward Manet, Paul Cézanne, Pierre August Renoir, and Henri de Toulouse-Lautrec; drawings by August Rodin; paintings and drawings by Henri Rousseau.
10 December–8 January 1911	Drawings and etchings by Gordon Craig.

1911

11 January–31 January	Drawings and paintings by Max Weber.
2 February–22 February	Watercolors by John Marin.
1 March–25 March	Watercolors by Paul Cézanne.
28 March–25 April	Drawings and watercolors by Pablo Picasso: *Complete Evolution Through Cubism*.
Exact date unknown	Watercolors by Gelett Burgess.
18 December–15 January 1912	Photographs by Adolph de Meyer.

1912

18 January–3 February	Paintings by Arthur Carles.
7 February–26 February	Paintings and drawings by Marsden Hartley.
27 February–12 March	Pastels by Arthur Dove.
14 March–6 April	Sculpture and drawings by Henri Matisse.
11 April–10 May	Watercolors and pastels by children aged two to eleven.
Exact date unknown	Sculptures by Manuel Manolo.
20 November–12 December	Caricatures by Alfred J. Frueh.
15 December–14 January 1913	Drawings and paintings by Abraham Walkowitz.

1913

20 January–15 February	Watercolors by John Marin.
24 February–15 March	Photographs by Alfred Stieglitz.
17 March–5 April	Exhibition of New York studies by Francis Picabia.
8 April–20 May	Exhibition by Marius de Zayas.
19 November–3 January 1914	Drawings, pastels, and watercolors by Abraham Walkowitz.

1914

12 January–14 February	Paintings by Marsden Hartley.
18 February–11 March	Second exhibition of children's work (drawings by boys aged eight to fourteen).
12 March–4 April	Sculpture by Constantine Brancusi
6 April–6 May	Paintings and drawings by Frank Burty Haviland
9 November–8 December	African sculpture
9 December–11 January	Drawings and paintings by Pablo Picasso and Georges Braque; archaic Mexican pottery and carvings; kalograms by Torres Palomar.

1915

12 January–26 January	Paintings by Francis Picabia.
27 January–22 February	Paintings by Marion H. Beckett and Katharine Rhoades.
23 February–26 March	Oils and watercolors by John Marin.
27 March–17 April	Third exhibition of children's work.
10 November–7 December	Drawings and paintings by Oscar Bluemner.
8 December–17 January 1916	Sculpture and drawings by Elie Nadelman.

1916

18 January–12 February	John Marin watercolors.
14 February–12 March	Drawings and watercolors by Abraham Walkowitz.
13 March–3 April	Photographs by Paul Strand.
4 April–22 May	Paintings by Marsden Hartley

23 May–5 July	Drawings by Georgia O'Keeffe; watercolors by C. Duncan; oils by René Lafferty.
22 November–20 December	Watercolors and drawings by Georgia S. Engelhard, a ten-year-old child.
27 December–17 January	Watercolors by Abraham Walkowitz.

1917

22 January–7 February	Marsden Hartley, recent work.
14 February–3 March	Watercolors by John Marin.
6 March–17 March	Paintings, drawings, and pastels by Gino Severini.
20 March–31 March	Paintings and sculpture by Stanton Macdonald-Wright.
3 April–14 May	Watercolors, drawings, and oils by Georgia O'Keeffe

The Photo-Secession.[3]

So many are the enquiries as to the nature and aims of the Photo-Secession and requirements of eligibility to membership therein, that we deem it expedient to give a brief résumé of the character of this body of photographers.

The object of the Photo-Secession is: to advance photography as applied to pictorial expression; to draw together those Americans practicing or otherwise interested in the art, and to hold from time to time, at varying places, exhibitions not necessarily limited to the productions of the Photo-Secession or to American work.

It consists of a *Council* (all of whom are Fellows); *Fellows* chosen by the Council for meritorious photographic work or labors in behalf of pictorial photography, and *Associates* eligible by reason of interest in, and sympathy with, the aims of the Secession.

In order to give Fellowship the value of an honor, the photographic work of a possible candidate must be individual and distinctive, and it goes without saying that the applicant must be in thorough sympathy with our aims and principles.

To Associateship are attached no requirements except sincere sympathy with the aims and motives of the Secession. Yet, it must not be supposed that these qualifications will be assumed as a matter of course, as it has been found necessary to deny the application of many whose lukewarm interest in the cause with which we are so thoroughly identified gave no promise of aiding the Secession. It may be of general interest to know that quite a few, perhaps entitled by their photographic work to Fellowship, have applied in vain. Their rejection being based solely upon their avowed or notoriously active opposition or equally harmful apathy. Many whose sincerity could not be questioned were refused Fellowship because the work submitted was not equal to the required standard. Those desiring further information must address the Director of the Photo-Secession, Mr. Alfred Stieglitz, 1111 Madison Avenue, New York.

List of Members.
Fellows.

JOHN G. BULLOCK	Philadelphia	
WM. B. DYER	Chicago	
FRANK EUGENE	New York	
DALLETT FUGUET	New York	Founders
GERTRUDE KÄSEBIER	New York	and
JOSEPH T. KEILEY	New York	Council.
ROBERT S. REDFIELD	Philadelphia	
EVA WATSON SCHÜTZE	Chicago	
EDUARD J. STEICHEN	New York	

Fellows—Continued.

ALFRED STIEGLITZ . . . . New York ⎤
EDMUND STIRLING . . . . Philadelphia ⎟ Founders
JOHN FRANCIS STRAUSS . . . . New York ⎬ and
CLARENCE H. WHITE . . . . Ohio ⎦ Council.
ALVIN LANGDON COBURN . . . . Boston
MARY DEVENS . . . . Boston
WM. B. POST . . . . Maine
S. L. WILLARD . . . . Chicago

Associates.

PRESCOTT ADAMSON . . . . Philadelphia
WM. P. AGNEW . . . . New York
A. C. BATES . . . . Cleveland, O.
EDWARD LaVELLE BOURKE . . . . Chicago
ANNIE W. BRIGMAN . . . . Oakland, Cal.
NORMAN W. CARKHUFF . . . . Washington, D.C.
WM. E. CARLIN . . . . New York
J. MITCHELL ELLIOT . . . . Philadelphia
DR. MILTON FRANKLIN . . . . New York
HERBERT G. FRENCH . . . . Cincinnati
GEO. A. HEISEY . . . . Newark, O.
SAM. S. HOLZMAN . . . . New York
MARSHALL P. KERNOCHAN . . . . New York
SARAH H. LADD . . . . Portland, Ore.
CHESTER ABBOTT LAWRENCE . . . . New York
FRED. K. LAWRENCE . . . . Chicago
OSCAR MAURER . . . . San Francisco
WILLIAM J. MULLINS . . . . Franklin, Pa.
OLIVE M. POTTS . . . . Philadelphia
HARRY B. REID . . . . New York
HARRY C. RUBINCAM . . . . Denver
T. O'CONOR SLOANE . . . . Orange, N. J.
WALTER P. STOKES . . . . Philadelphia
MRS. GEORGE A. STANBERY . . . . Zanesville, O.
KATHARINE STANBERY . . . . Zanesville, O.
GEO. B. VAUX . . . . Philadelphia
MARY VAUX . . . . Philadelphia
LILY E. WHITE . . . . Portland, Ore.
MYRA WIGGINS . . . . Salem, Ore.
ARTHUR W. WILDE . . . . Philadelphia

NOTES

OPENING QUOTATIONS

1 Herman Melville, "Art," cited in Ellmann, 1976, p. 305.
2 Alfred Stieglitz, Letter to Guido Bruno, 28 December 1946, ASA/YCAL.
3 Ansel Adams, quoted in Norman, 1947, p. 15.
4 Frank Lloyd Wright, Norman, 1947, p. 14.
5 Henri Cartier-Bresson, Norman, 1947, p. 18.
6 Amanda K. Coomaraswamy, quoted in Norman, 1938, p. 175.
7 Alfred Stieglitz, quoted in Norman, 1938, pp. 78–79.

PROLOGUE

1 Alfred Stieglitz, quoted in Caffin, 1971, p. 36.
2 Ashton, 1971, p. 152.
3 Stieglitz, 1923a.
4 Alfred Stieglitz, letter to Sherwood Anderson, 1 November 1923, ASA/YCAL.
5 Alfred Stieglitz, letter to Hart Crane, 10 December 1923, ASA/YCAL.
6 Alfred Stieglitz, letter to J. Dudley Johnston, 3 April 1925, RPSA.
7 Herbert Seligmann, quoted in Norman, 1947, p. 14.
8 Norman, 1947, p. 7.
9 Alfred Stieglitz, quoted in Dorothy Norman, "Introduction to an American Seer," *Aperture*, 8, 1, 1960, p. 36.

I   THE NINETEENTH CENTURY

1 Walt Whitman, "Out of the Cradle Endlessly Rocking," quoted by William Carlos Williams, introduction, to Whitman, 1971.
2 Walt Whitman, "Song of the Open Road," in Whitman, 1971, p. 105.
3 Alfred Stieglitz, quoted in Norman, 1973, p. 15.
4 Alfred Stieglitz, quoted in Norman, 1973, p. 16.
5 Whelan, 1997, pp. 15–16.
6 Alfred Stieglitz, quoted in Norman, 1973, p. 20.
7 Alfred Stieglitz, quoted in Norman, 1940–1, pp. 158–60.
8 Thomas Jefferson, quoted in Sinnott, 1993, p. 9.

9 Bryant, 1872–4, vol. 2, p. 256.

10 Stoddard 1874, pp. 30–1.

11 Alfred Stieglitz, quoted in Norman, 1973, p. 19.

12 Alfred Stieglitz, quoted in Norman, 1973, p. 18.

13 Whelan, 1997, p. 53.

14 "Autographs," vol. 1, ASA/YCAL.

15 Alfred Stieglitz, letter to Edward Stieglitz, 8 December 1877, ESP/YCAL.

16 Rosenfeld, 1934, p. 39.

17 Alfred Stieglitz, quoted in Norman, 1973, p. 20.

18 Hatfield, 1963, p. 211.

19 Goethe, 1969 (trans.), p. 346.

20 Nancy Newhall, unpublished manuscript, National Gallery of Art, Washington, D.C., p. 7.

21 Johann Wolfgang von Goethe, quoted in Hatfield, 1963, p. 166.

22 Johann Wolfgang von Goethe, quoted in Ballerini, 1984, p. 106.

23 Berman, 1982, pp. 85–6.

24 Alfred Stieglitz, quoted in "Thoroughly Unprepared," *Twice a Year*, ed. Dorothy Norman, 10–11 (1943): pp. 245, 248.

25 Lowe, 1983, p. 61.

26 Edward Stieglitz, letter to Wilhelm Hasemann, 25 May 1882, private collection. "Sie haben meiner Familie ein lebenstreues Bild meines lieben Sohne zuertheilt – & wird Ihr Name ein Hauswort sein & verbleiben bei mir & meinen Kindern! Eine fast ebenso große Freude gewährte mir neben der . . . des Bildes der Umstand, wie sehr ich einen erheblichen Fortschritt in Ihren Schöpfungen wahrnehme, hauptsächlich da wo es sich um das Colorit handelt – & bin nicht wenig erstaunt, daß Sie in Aquarell – auf dessen Boden Sie noch so selten geschafft – so Vorzügliches zu leisten vermögen. So werden Sie weiterschreiten, mein lieber bescheidener Freund & Lehrer & eingereiht werden in die Reihe deutscher Künstler, welchen es ernst um ihre Kunst ist & schließlich das schaffen, was Geschlechter um Geschlecter sich noch nach Jahren & Jahren erfreuen können-. So sage ich Ihnen denn gute Nacht mit ebenso freudigen als dankbarem Herzen. Ihr getreuer Ed. Stieglitz".

27 Alfred Stieglitz, letter to Adolph Werner, 18 April 1882 ASA/YCAL.

28 Alfred Stieglitz, letter to Wilhelm Hasemann, 31 October 1882, private collection: "Mein lieber Herr Hasemann wie erstaunt ich war wie ich gestern morgen zu Tische kam und die schöne Postkarte von Ihnen fand. Es ist eine herrliche Zeichnung und gefiel jedem sehr gut, Erdmann Encke, inclusiv – Der letzere und Frau lassen herzlich grüssen – Wie es mir geht, etc. haben Sie höchst wahrscheinlich alles von Papa gehört [der sich in Gutach aufhielt] und ich kann nur wieder sagen, dass ich tief im Studium stecke. mit herzlichstem Grüss und bestem Dank – ihr Alfred Stieglitz."

29 Bowles, 1893, p. 240.

30 Bowles, 1893, p. 241.

31 Rosenfeld, 1934, p. 41.

32 Emile Zola, letter to *Alfred Stieglitz*, 22 May 1884, ASA/YCAL.

33 Schorske, 1981, pp. 60–70.

34 Flint, 1947, pp. 37–8.

35   Alfred Stieglitz, quoted in Norman, 1973, p. 32.

36   Isidore de Seville, quoted in Tillyard, 1983, p. 497.

37   René Descartes, quoted in Thomas, 1985, p. 28.

38   Charles Baudelaire, "La Musique," translated in Lockspeiser, 1973, pp. 79, 83.

39   Pater, 1873, p. 9.

40   Nietzsche, 1956, p. 10.

41   Nietzsche, 1968, p. 11.

42   Alfred Stieglitz, quoted in Norman, 1973, pp. 31–2.

43   "Willst du dich selber kennen. So siehen wie die andern es treiben. Willst du die Andern verstehen, blick in dem eigenes Herz." ASA/YCAL.

44   Lowe, 1983, pp. 79–80.

45   Alfred Stieglitz, quoted in Craven, 1944, p. 14.

46   Vogel, 1882, introduction.

47   Vogel, 1882, p. 157.

48   He noted this, in particular, in an article in the *Photographic Times* (13 August 1883), pp. 403–4.

49   Alfred Stieglitz, quoted in "Photography and Painting." *Twice a Year* 5–6 (1940–1): 145–7. Norman, ed., no. 5/6, 1940–41, pp. 145–7.

50   Alfred Stieglitz, quoted in Norman, 1973, p. 32.

51   The album is in the collection of the National Gallery of Art, Washington.

52   *The Truant* appeared in the *Photographic Times* 23, 1 December 1893, p. 645, the *Photographic Times* 26, May 1895, p. 297, and the *American Amateur Photographer*, 7 May 1895, p. 204. A version of *The Harvest* with a fuller background and sky included was published in *Der Amateur Photograph* 1, 1887 (unpaginated), titled *Die Ernte*.

53   Morris Loeb, quoted in Greenough, 2002, I, pp. 4–7.

54   See later discussion of their work together in Katwyk in 1894.

55   Whelan, 1997, p. 84.

56   Bry, 1965, p. 11.

57   See Greenough, 2002, for complete histories of publication of specific images.

58   Alfred Stieglitz, quoted in "Alfred Stieglitz and His Latest Work," 1896, p. 161.

59   Stieglitz, 1889a, p. 7.

60   Stieglitz, 1889a.

61   *Camera Work*, April 1903, p. 37.

62   Stieglitz, 1889a, p. 8.

63   Stieglitz, 1889a, p. 9.

64   Bry, 1965, p. 11.

65   Emerson, 1886.

66   Stieglitz, 1892a.

67   Stieglitz, 1899d, p. 528.

68   Peter Henry Emerson, quoted in Newhall, 1975, p. 137.

69   Stieglitz, 1889d, p. 202.

70   *Sie Photographische Rundschau* 5 (1888): 7.

71   Stieglitz, 1892c, p. 60.

72   Stieglitz, 1892c, p. 61.

73   Stieglitz, 1892c, p. 61.

74   Peter Henry Emerson, quoted in Newhall, 1975, p. 114.

75   Charles Hastings, letter to Alfred Stieglitz, 7 August 1890, ASA/YCAL.

76   *Cloud Study in Biarritz* is known through an auction catalogue for Christie's, New York, 26 May 1982, lot 68.

77   The image appeared as an illustration in Adams, 1897, p. 78.

78   Whelan, 1997, pp. 101–2.

79   Seligmann, 1966, p. 102.

80   Seligmann, 1966, p. iv.

81   Stieglitz, 1892d.

82   Stieglitz, 1905b, p. 164.

83   "The Linked Ring Information Sheet," in Harker, 1979, n.p.

84   Alfred Stieglitz, quoted in Greenough, 2002, p. 51.

85   Greenough, 2002.

86   Stieglitz, 1897, p. 27.

87   Alfred Stieglitz, quoted in Norman, 1938, pp. 96–7.

88   Alfred Stieglitz, quoted in Norman, 1963.

89   Corbin, 1903, p. 259.

90   Corbin, 1903, p. 272.

91   Corbin, 1903, pp. 263–4.

92   Bunnell, 1978, p. 3. In this article, Bunnell also gives the locations and dates for the Herbert Small Collection photographs.

93   Alfred Stieglitz, quoted in Greenough, 2002, p. 69. On the same page are listed the numerous publications in which this image was reproduced.

94   Georges Lecomte, quoted in Clark, 1999, p. 30.

95   Georges Lecomte, quoted in Clark, 1999, p. 30.

96   Whelan, 1997, p. 130.

97   Alfred Stieglitz, letter to Wilhelm Hasemann, 18 June 1894. Private collection.

98   Stieglitz and Schubart, 1895, pp. 9–10.

99   Jackson, 1978, p. 228.

100   Alfred Stieglitz, letter to Wilhelm Hasemann, 9 January 1895, private collection. (See p. 165 for a copy of the complete letter.) "Meine Frau und ich denken oft an Gutach, und beide möchten zu gerne sehr bald wieder hinkommen. Es ist viel schöner dort wie hier in dieser schmützigen Stadt wo alles nach dem dollar jagt . . . seit einem Monat haben wir unser eigen Heim, wo es recht germütlich ist . . . ich hatte gerne von du letzen Sommer ein Bildchen abgekauft aber das Geld wollte nicht aussreichen . . . aber habe ich heute Dir ungefahr die Photographien gesandt, die Du auch verteilen wirst, d.h. behalte wie Dir gefallt und die andern verschenke an Reiss. Liebich, etc. Es kommen noch mehr . . . lass mich wissen ob Herr Reiss oder Liebich gewisse Bilder haben wollen . . . Willst Du Keine Schneelandschaftmal malen? Wir sprachen doch davon.

Meine Frau lässt vielmals grüssen.

Dein Freund,

Alfred Stieglitz".

101   Alfred Stieglitz, letter to Wihelm Hasemann, 29 May 1896, private collection. "Ich habe viel vor, meine '94er Reise hat sich sehr gelohnt vom photographischen Standpunkt aus . . . Gutach muss noch ein mal herhalten . . . Wir denken oft an die nette Zeit die wir zusammen verweilt."

102   Lizzie Stieglitz, letter to Wihelm Hasemann, 17 May 1899, private collection. "Empfehlen Sie mich bitte ihrer lieben Frau – durch Alfreds und Emmy's begeisterte Erzählungen kenne ich Sie alle – und seien Sie selbst freundlichst gegrüsst von Lizzie Stieglitz."

103   Alfred Stieglitz, letter to Wilhelm Hasemann, 23 August 1894, private collection. (See p. 165 for a copy of the complete letter.) "Hier wimmelte es von Motiven aller Arten. Es ist wo möglich noch reich haltiger wie Gutach, da man Alles hat was man sich denken kann, nur kein Gebirg, sonst aber Alles. Ich habe trotz Regen und Sturm darauf los photographiert – und werde dir von New York manches schicken."

104   Stieglitz and Schubart, 1895, pp. 11–12.

105   "Chronique des Arts," *Sun and Shade* 4/1 (September 1891), p. 1. Author unknown.

106   Stieglitz, 1899c.

107   Pater, 1873, p. 133.

108   Keiley, 1899b, n.p.

109   Alfred Stieglitz, letter to Wilhelm Hasemann, 23 August 1894, private collection. (See p. 165 for a copy of the complete letter.) "Von Antwerpen reisten wir nach dem Haag, waren die Rembrandts sehr imponierten . . . Die Rembrandts sind fabelhaft, man kennt ihn nicht ehe man seine Bilder in Holland gesehen – Von New York auf bekam ich Nachricht dass die Karten von Herr Reiss und und Liebich grosse Freude bereiteten."

110   Hartmann, 1900a, p. 59.

111   Dreiser, 1899b, p. 324.

112   Dreiser, 1899b, pp. 329–31.

113   Publication committee announcement, *Camera Notes* 1/1 (July 1897), p. 3.

114   Peterson, 1993, p. 19. See this book for a complete listing of the photographic images by Alfred Stieglitz and others that appeared in *Camera Notes*.

115   Young, 1898.

116   The lengthy reviews occurred in *Camera Notes*, issues 2/3, pp. 113–20, 123–32; 3/3, pp. 135–38, 141–48, 151–70; 4/3, pp. 189–204, 207–27; 5/4, pp. 279–84, 287–99.

117   Keiley, 1899a, pp. 120–23.

118   See fig. 158 for a copy of parts of the catalogue.

119   Fuguet, 1902.

120   Arthur Dow, quoted in Moffatt, 1977, p. 110.

121   Alfred Stieglitz et al. *Camera Notes*. July 1902, Vol. 6, No. 1. p. 3.

122   Peterson, 1993, p. 60.

123   Stieglitz, 1898b, p. 205.

124   Caffin, 1972, p. 49.

125   Dimock, 2001, pp. 10–12.

126　See Trachtenberg 1989 for an in depth discussion and comparison of Lewis Hine's and Alfred Stieglitz's photographs. See also Jussim, 1978.

127　Alfred Stieglitz, quoted in the wall text for his photograph *Georgia O'Keeffe* (1921), at the exhibition *Twentieth-Century Photographs*, at the Metropolitan Museum of Art, New York, 2002.

128　Whelan, 1997, p. 156.

129　Emmeline Obermeyer Stieglitz, letters to Alfred Stieglitz, ASA/YCAL.

130　Alfred Stieglitz, letter to Emmeline Obermeyer Stieglitz, 7 February 1919, ASA/YCAL.

131　Kitty Stieglitz, letters to Alfred Stieglitz, 1904–22, ASA/YCAL.

132　Alfred Stieglitz, letter to Kitty Stieglitz, 7 April 1919, ASA/YCAL.

133　Stieglitz 1940–1.

134　Kitty Stieglitz, letters to Alfred Stieglitz, 1904–22, ASA/YCAL.

2　THE TWENTIETH CENTURY

1　Walt Whitman, "Song of Myself" in Whitman, 1971, pp. 48–50.

2　Alfred Stieglitz quoted in, Newhall, 1989, pp. 118–19.

3　Alfred Stieglitz, quoted in Norman, 1938, p. 110.

4　Stieglitz, 1898a.

5　Steichen, 1963, n.p., facing plate 3.

6　Stieglitz, Editorial, *Camera Notes*, 1 July 1901.

7　Stieglitz, 1943.

8　Stieglitz, 1903b, p. 3.

9　Stieqlitz, 1903b, p. 3.

10　Alfred Stieglitz, quoted in Clifford and Zigrosser, 1944, p. 5.

11　Stieglitz, 1903c.

12　Edward Steichen, quoted in Homer and Johnson, 2002, p. 16. Homer and Johnson's comprehensive discussion of the 1902 Arts Club exhibit marked its 100th anniversary.

13　Alfred Stieglitz, letter to Richard Gilder, 15 March 1902, CC/NYPL.

14　Homer and Johnson, 2002, p. 29.

15　Laurvik, 1911, p. xxv.

16　Naef, 1996, p. 1.

17　Corbin, 1903, pp. 260–2.

18　Stieglitz, 1946–7.

19　Roth, 2001, p. 7.

20　Stieglitz, 1903a.

21　Roberts, 1997a, p. 31.

22　For further discussion of Mallarmé's aesthetic theories, and his "Divagations," see Lehmann, 1950.

23　Mallarmé, 1953, pp. 43–6.

24　Ernst Mach, quoted in Yves Kobry, 1995, p. 46.

25　Robert Goldwater discusses Symbolism and Synthetism in Goldwater, 1979. See particularly pp. 72–5.

26   Green, 1973, p. 12.

27   Green, 1973, p. 13.

28   Hartmann, 1911b.

29   Bluemner, 1913a.

30   Caffin, 1909.

31   For a brief listing of what appeared in particular issues of *Camera Work*, see Appendix II.

32   Alfred Stieglitz, letter to J. McIntosh, 31 August 1910. RPSA.

33   Alfred Stieglitz, quoted in Naef, 1995, p. 18.

34   The gallery was described in *Camera Work*, 14 April 1906, p. 48.

35   Kerfoot, 1911.

36   Charles Fitzgerald, quoted in *Camera Work* 14, April 1906, p. 33.

37   [Ernst], 1908, n.p.

38   Stieglitz, 1907a.

39   Pamela Colman Smith, quoted in "Pictured Music," 1908, p. 174.

40   Arthur Wesley Dow, quoted in Moffatt, 1977, p. 63.

41   Parsons, 1975, n.p.

42   De Casseres, 1909.

43   See Appendix III for a full listing of exhibitions at 291.

44   Alfred Stieglitz, quoted in McCausland, 1946.

45   *Camera Work* 30, April 1910, p. 48.

46   Kiefer, 1991, p. 298.

47   Ernst Mach, quoted in Kiefer, 1991, p. 274.

48   Stieglitz, 1915a, pp. 36–8, 40–2, 70–3.

49   Craven, 1935, p. 312.

50   Hamilton, 1970, p. 378. See this article for a more detailed discussion of the specific titles and works collected by Stieglitz.

51   Stieglitz, 1942.

52   Sekula, 1975, pp. 41–2.

53   Sekula, 1975, p. 42.

54   Alfred Stieglitz, quoted in Whelan, 2000, p. 197.

55   Stieglitz, 1938, p. 81.

56   Stieglitz, 1907b, pp. 24, 25.

57   Socrates, "Plato's Dialogues," quoted in *Camera Work* 36, October 1911.

58   De Casseres, 1911.

59   Alfred Stieglitz, letter to F. J. Mortimer, 10 October 1910. RPSA.

60   Foreword, Buffalo, 1910.

61   Alfred Stieglitz, telegram to Emmeline Obermeyer Stieglitz, November 1910, ASA/YCAL.

62   Keiley, 1911.

63   Hartmann, 1911a.

64   Hartmann, 1910.

65   De Zayas, 1916, p. 41.

66   See Whelan, 1997, p. 296.

67   Alfred Stieglitz, letter to Paul Haviland, 6 August 1911, FH/MO.

68   Alfred Stieglitz, letter to the editor, *New York Evening Sun*, 18 December 1911.

69   "The Future Futurists," 1912. Article found in Stieglitz's scrapbook, ASA/YCAL. Author unknown.

70   Review of children's art at 291, *New York Evening Sun*, 27 August 1912. Article found in Stieglitz's scrapbook, ASA/YCAL. Author unknown.

71   "Some Remarkable Work By Very Young Artists," n.d. Article found in Stieglitz's scrapbook, ASA/YCAL. Author unknown.

72   Brown, 1955, p. 47.

73   Arthur Davies, quoted in Baur, 1951, p. 6.

74   Kenyon Cox, quoted in Brown, 1955, p. 53.

75   Frank Jewett Mather, Jr., quoted in Brown, 1955, p. 53.

76   Shapiro, 1971, p. 206.

77   Arnason, 1965, p. 410.

78   Royal Cortissoz, quoted in *Camera Work* 42–3, April–July 1913.

79   Francis Picabia, quoted in Eddy, 1914, p. 220.

80   Francis Picabia, quoted in Hapgood, 1913.

81   *Camera Work* 41, January 1913, p. 24.

82   Arthur Hoeber, quoted in *Camera Work* 41, January 1913, p. 26.

83   Oscar Bluemner, Diary, 4 July 1925, AAA/SI (340:1516–19).

84   Oscar Bluemner, Diary, 4 July 1925, AAA/SI (340:1745).

85   Yousuf Karsh, quoted in Jussim, 1989, p. 93.

86   Cramer, 1947, p. 721.

87   Hodge Kirnon, quoted in *Camera Work* 47, July 1914, p. 16.

88   Alfred Stieglitz, letter to R. Child Bayley, 1 November 1916, quoted in Greenough and Hamilton, 1983, p. 201.

89   Miller, 1942.

90   Rugg, 1934, p. 98.

91   Marin, 1934, p. 118.

92   Hartley, 1934, p. 121.

93   Demuth, 1914, p. 122.

94   Dove, 1934, p. 122.

95   Arthur Dove and Alfred Stieglitz, quoted in Morgan, 1985, pp. 41–51.

96   Robert M. Crunden. *Body and Soul: The Making of American Modernism* (New York: Basic Books, 2000) p. 5.

97   Dijkstra, 1969, p. 145.

98   William Carlos Williams, "Spring Strains," quoted in Dijkstra, 1969, p. 64.

99   Theodore Dreiser, *The Genius*, quoted in Rabb, 1995, pp. 191–2.

100   Kandinsky, 1977, p. 51.

101   Rosenfeld, 1924, pp. 238–9, 251.

102   Sadakichi Hartmann, quoted in Schiffmann, 1951, p. 251.

103   Charles Caffin, quoted in *Camera Work* 13, January 1906, pp. 43–4.

104   Rosenfeld, 1924, pp. 281–5.

105   Frank, 1919, p. 180.

106   Alfred Stieglitz, quoted in Whelan, 1997, p. 419.

107   Johnson, 1976, p. 7.

108   Alfred Stieglitz, letter to Ernest Bloch, 1 July 1922, quoted in Schenkenberg, 1980, p. 6.

109   Ernest Bloch, letter to Paul Strand, 1922, quoted in Schenkenberg, 1980, p. 8.

110   Alfred Stieglitz, letter to W. Orison Underwood, 30 April 1914, quoted in Greenough and Hamilton, 1983, p. 197. Sarah Greenough's introductory essay, "Alfred Stieglitz and the Idea Photography," discusses the notion of idea photography more fully.

111   Rosenfeld, 1967, p. 57.

112   Alfred Stieglitz, quoted in Norman, 1973, p. 124.

113   Norman, 1973, p. 130.

114   Alfred Stieglitz, letter to Paul Haviland, 5 July 1916, FH/MO.

115   Alfred Stieglitz, quoted in Norman, 1973, p. 130.

116   Alfred Stieglitz, quoted in McCausland, 1946.

117   Georgia O'Keeffe, letter to Alfred Stieglitz, 27 July 1916, quoted in Pollitzer, 1988, pp. 140–1.

118   Naef, 1995, n.p.

119   Walter Arensberg, quoted in Wood, 1985, p. 29.

120   Fisher, 1917, p. 5.

121   Paul Valéry, quoted in Sorrell, 1981, p. 341.

122   Paul Valéry, quoted in Sorrell, 1981, p. 341.

123   Whelan, 1997, pp. 474–5.

124   Filippo Tommaso Marinetti, *The Foundation and Manifesto of Futurism*, 1909, quoted in Chipp, 1968, pp. 284–5.

125   Alfred Stieglitz, letter to Georgia O'Keeffe, 31 May 1917, ASA/YCAL.

126   Alfred Stieglitz, letter to Georgia O'Keeffe, 24 June 1917, ASA/YCAL.

127   Stieglitz, 1917.

128   Alfred Stieglitz, quoted in Norman, 1973, p. 127.

129   Alfred Stieglitz, quoted in Norman, 1973, pp. 134–5.

130   Alfred Stieglitz, quoted in Gallup, 1953, pp. 87–8.

131   Naef, 1996, n.p.

132   Alfred Stieglitz, quoted in Norman, 1973, p. 175.

EPILOGUE

1   See Arrowsmith and West, 1992, for an in-depth look at their reciprocal influences.

2   Georgia O'Keeffe, quoted in Arrowsmith and West, 1992, n.p.

3   Alfred Stieglitz, quoted in Arrowsmith and West, 1992, n.p.

4   Henry Tyrell, quoted in Arrowsmith and West, 1992, n.p.

5   Turner, 1992, p. 79.

6   Turner, 1992, pp. 81, 85.

7   Alfred Stieglitz, quoted in Norman, 1960, p. 36.

8   Adams, 1996, p. 14.

9   Adams, 1996, p. 36.

10   Jussim and Lindquist-Cook, 1985, p. 85.

11   John Marin, quoted in *Manuscripts* 4, December 1922, p. 11.

12   Anderson, 1918, p. 16.

13   Alfred Stieglitz, letter to L. Dudley Johnston, 15 October 1923, quoted in Greenough and Hamilton, 1983, p. 217; original letter at the Royal Photographic Society Archives, Bath, England.

14   Stieglitz, 1938, p. 85.

15   Alfred Stieglitz, quoted in Norman, 1973, p. 229.

16   Stieglitz, 1938, p. 109.

17   Whelan, 1997, p. 573.

18   Alfred Stieglitz, quoted in Norman, 1973, p. 229.

19   Alfred Stieglitz, letter to Thomas Hart Benton, 2 January 1935, quoted in Greenough and Hamilton, 1983, p. 219.

APPENDICES

1   Listings of *Camera Work* contents from Lowe, 1983, pp. 423–7, with additions from the author. Listings are found also in other sources on *Camera Work*.

2   Listings of exhibitions at the Little Galleries of the Photo-Secession and 291 from Taylor, 1973, pp. 221–4, and Norman, 1973, pp. 232–5.

3   Supplement of *Camera Work*, no. 3, July 1903, Milne Special Collections, Dimond Library, University of New Hampshire, Durham, N.H.

SELECTED BIBLIOGRAPHY

Archive sources

Alfred Stieglitz Archive, Yale University Collection of American Literature, Beinecke Rare Book and Manuscript Library, Yale University, New Haven, Connecticut: ASA/YCAL.

Archives of American Art, Smithsonian Institute, Washington, D.C.: AAA/SI.

Century Collection, Manuscripts and Archives, New York Public Library: CC/NYPL.

Edward Stieglitz Papers, Yale University Collection of American Literature, Beinecke Rare Book and Manuscript Library, Yale University, New Haven, Connecticut: ESP/YCAL.

Fonds Haviland, Musée D'Orsay, Paris: FH/MO.

Kunstbibliothek, Berlin.

Museum of Modern Art, New York.

Philadelphia Museum and Library, Philadelphia.

The Royal Photographic Society Archives, Bath, UK: RPSA.

University of Arizona, Center for Creative Photography, Tuscson, Arizona.

Printed Sources

Abrahams, Edward. "Alfred Stieglitz and/or Thomas Hart Benton." *Arts* 55 (June 1981): 108–13.

Adams, Robert. *Beauty in Photography*. New York: Aperture, 1996.

Adams, W. I. Lincoln. *Sunlight and Shadow: A Book for Photographers Amateur and Professional*. New York: Baker and Taylor Company, 1897.

Agee, William C. *Synchronism and Color Principles in American Painting, 1910–1930*. New York: M. Knoedler & Co., 1965.

Allan, Sidney [Sadakichi Hartmann]. "A New Departure in Photography." *The Lamp* 29 (February 1904): 21–5.

"Alfred Stieglitz and His Latest Work." *The Photographic Times* 4 (April 1896): 161–9.

"Alfred Stieglitz, Artist, and His Search for the Human Soul," *New York Herald* (8 March 1908): 5.

Alter, Judith. *Dancing and Mixed Media: Early Twentieth-Century Modern Dance Theory in Text and Photography*. New York: Peter Lang, 1994.

Anderson, Sherwood. *Mid-American Chants*. New York: John Lane Co., 1918.

Arnason, H. H. *History of Modern Art*. Englewood Cliffs, New Jersey: Prentice Hall, 1965.

Arrowsmith, Alexandra, and Thomas West, eds. *Two Lives, Georgia O'Keeffe and Alfred Stieglitz: A Conversation in Paintings and Photographs*. New York: Harper Collins, 1992.

Ashton, Dore. *A Reading of Modern Art*. Rev. ed. New York: Harper and Row, 1971.

Association of American Painters and Sculptors. *The Armory Show: International Exhibition of Modern Art, 1913*. New York: Arno Press, 1973.

Bailey, Craig R. "The Art of Marius de Zayas." *Arts Magazine* 53 (September 1978): 136–44.

Ballerini, Julia. "The Incomplete Camera Man." *Art in America* (January 1984): 106.

Barth, Ansgar, ed. *Wilhelm Hasemann, Schwarzwaldmaler, 1850–1913*. Druckerei-Engelberg-Hempelmann, 2000.

Barth, Ansgar, and Werner Liebich. *Gutach*. Konstanz: Verlag Stadler, 2000.

Baur, John. *Revolution and Tradition in Modern American Art*. Cambridge, Mass.: Harvard Univesity Press, 1951.

Baudelaire, Charles. "Philosophic Art." In *The Painter of Modern Life and Other Essays*. Translated by Jonathon Mayne. London: Phaidon Press, 1964.

Benson, E. M. "Alfred Stieglitz: The Man and the Book." *The American Magazine of Art* (January 1936): 36–42.

Bergson, Henri. "An Extract from Bergson." *Camera Work* 36 (October 1911): 20–1.

———. *Creative Evolution*. Translated by Arthur Mitchell. New York: The Modern Library, 1944.

Berman, Marshall. *All That is Solid Melts into Air: The Experience of Modernity*. New York: Penguin Books, 1982.

Bieber, Dietrich. *German Grobe*. Katwyk: Katwyk Museum, 1999.

Blake, Rodney [Selma Stieglitz Schubart, pseud.]. *Random Rhythms*. New York: Publishers Press Publishing Company, 1924.

Bloch, Suzanne. *Ernest Bloch, Creative Spirit*. New York: Jewish Music Council of the National Jewish Welfare Board, 1976.

Bluemner, Oscar. "Audiater et Altera Para: Some Plain Sense on the Modern Art Movement." *Camera Work, special issue* (June 1913): 32. 1913a.

———. "Walkowitz." *Camera Work*, 44 (October 1913): 25–38. 1913b.

Bourne, Randolph. "The War and the Intellectuals." *The Seven Arts* (June 1917): 133–46.

Bowles, Mary. "Wilhelm Hasemann's Home in the Black Forest." *The Magazine of Art* (May 1893): 239–43.

Brassai. "A Letter from Alfred Stieglitz." *Camera* 48 (January 1969): 37.

Brennan, Marcia. *Painting Gender, Constructing Theory: The Alfred Stieglitz Circle and American Formalist Aesthetics.* Cambridge, Mass. and London: MIT Press, 1999.

Brooks, Van Wyck. *America's Coming-of-Age.* New York: B.W. Huebsch, 1915.

Brown, Milton. *American Painting from the Armory Show to the Depression.* Princeton: Princeton University Press, 1955.

———. *The Story of the Armory Show.* New York: Joseph H. Hirshhorn Foundation, 1963.

Bruno, Guido. "The Passing of 291." *Pearson's Weekly* 13 (March 1918): 402–3.

Bry, Doris. *Alfred Stieglitz.* Washington, D.C.: National Gallery of Art, 1958.

———. *Alfred Stieglitz: Photographer.* Boston: Museum of Fine Arts, 1965.

Bryant, William Cullen. *Picturesque America.* New York: D. Appleton and Co., 1872–4.

Buerger, Janet. *The Last Decade: The Emergence of Art Photography in the 1890s.* Rochester, New York: International Museum of Photography at George Eastman House, 1984.

Buffalo Fine Arts Academy and Albright Art Gallery. *Catalogue for the International Exhibition of Pictorial Photography.* Buffalo, New York: Buffalo Fine Arts Academy and Albright Art Gallery, 1910.

Bunnell, Peter. "Alfred Stieglitz and *Camera Work.* *Camera* (December 1969): 8–27.

———. "Some Observations on a Collection of Stieglitz Early New York Photographs." *Center for Creative Photography* 6 (April 1978): 1–19.

———, ed. *A Photographic Vision: Pictorial Photography, 1889–1923.* Salt Lake City: Peregrine Smith, Inc., 1980.

Caccini, P. Angelo. *Basilica of Saints John and Paul.* Padua: Editions G. Deganello, 1988.

Caffin, Charles H. "Photography as a Fine Art: Alfred Stieglitz and His Work." *Everybody's Magazine* 4 (April 1901): 359–71.

———. "Symbolism and Allegory." *Camera Work* 18 (April 1907): 17–22.

———. "Henri Matisse and Isadora Duncan." *Camera Work* 25 (January 1909): 19–20.

———. *Art for Life's Sake: An Application of the Principles of Art to the Ideals and Conduct of Individual and Collective Life.* New York: Prang, 1913.

———. *Photography as a Fine Art.* New York: Doubleday, Page & Co., 1901. Reprint, Hastings-on-Hudson: Morgan and Morgan, 1972.

Caffin, Charles H, and Caroline Caffin. *Dancing and Dancers of Today: The*

Modern Revival of Dancing and Art. New York: Dodd, Mead & Co., 1912.

Camfield, William A. *Francis Picabia: His Art, Life and Times*. Princeton: Princeton University Press, 1979.

Chipp, Herschel B., ed. *Theories of Modern Art*. Berkeley: University of California Press, 1968.

Clair, Jean. *Symbolist Europe – Lost Paradise*. Montreal: Musée des Beaux Arts, 1995.

Clark, T. J. *Farewell to an Idea*. New Haven and London: Yale University Press, 1999.

Clifford, Henry, and Carl Zigrosser. *History of an American: Alfred Stieglitz, 291, and After*. Philadelphia: Philadelphia Museum of Art, 1944.

Cohen-Solal, Annie. *Painting American*. New York: Alfred Knopf, 2001.

Copeland, Roger, and Marshall Cohen, eds. *What is Dance? Readings in Theory and Criticism*. New York: Oxford University Press, 1983.

Corbin, John. "The Twentieth-Century City." *Scribner's Magazine* 33 (March 1903): 259–72.

Corn, Wanda M. *The Color of Mood*. San Francisco: H.H. De Young Memorial Museum, 1972.

———. "Apostles of the New American Art: Waldo Frank and Paul Rosenfeld." *Arts Magazine* 54 (February 1980): 159–63.

Cramer, Konrad. "Stupendous Stieglitz." Photographic Society of American Journal (November 1947).

Craven, Thomas. *Modern Art: The Men, the Movements, the Meaning*. New York: Simon and Schuster, 1935.

———. "Stieglitz: Old Master of the Camera." *Saturday Evening Post* (8 January 1944): 14.

Crunden, Robert M. *American Salons: Encounters with European Modernism, 1885–1917*. New York: Oxford University Press, 1993.

———. *Body and Soul: The Making of American Modernism*. New York: Basic Books, 2000.

Davidson, Abraham A. *Early American Modernist Painting, 1910–1935*. New York: Harper & Row, 1951.

Davison, George. "To American Photographers." *The American Amateur Photographer*, 6 (January 1894): 3–7.

De Casseres, Benjamin. "Pamela Colman Smith." *Camera Work* 27 (July 1909): 19.

———. "The Unconscious in Art." *Camera Work* 36 (October 1911).

Demuth, Charles, "Lighthouses and Fog." *Camera Work* 47 (July 1914).

De Zayas, Marius. [Untitled] *291* 5–6 (July–August 1915): n.p.

———. [Untitled] *291* 7–8 (September–October 1915): n.p.

———. *African Negro Art: Its Influence on Modern Art*. New York: Modern Gallery, 1916.

————. "How, When, and Why Modern Art Came to New York." *Arts Magazine* 54 (April 1980): 96–126.

De Zayas, Marius, and Paul Haviland. *A Study of the Modern Evolution of Plastic Expression*. New York: 291, 1913.

Dijkstra, Bram. *The Hieroglyphics of a New Speech: Cubism, Stieglitz and the Early Poetry of William Carlos Williams*. Princeton: Princeton University Press, 1969.

Dimock, George. *Priceless Children: American Photographs, 1890–1925*. Greensboro, North Carolina: Weatherspoon Art Museum, 2001.

Doty, Robert. *Photo-Secession: Photography as a Fine Art*. Rochester, New York: George Eastman House, 1960.

Dougherty, James. *Walt Whitman and the Citizen's Eye*. Baton Rouge: Louisiana State University Press, 1993.

Dove, Arthur. "A Different One." In *America and Alfred Stieglitz: A Collective Portrait*, edited by Frank, Waldo et al. New York: Doubleday, Doran & Co., 16, 1934.

Dow, Arthur Wesley. *Composition*. Boston: J.M. Bowles, 1899.

————. *Theory and Practice of Teaching Art*. 2nd ed. New York: Teachers College, Columbia University Press, 1912.

————. "Modernism in Art." *Magazine of Art* 8 (January 1917): 113–16.

Dreiser, Theodore. "A Master of Photography." *Success Magazine* 2 (10 June 1899): 471. 1899a.

————. "The Camera Club of New York." *Ainslee's Magazine* 4 (October 1899): 324–35. 1899b.

————. "A Remarkable Art." *The Great Round World* (3 May 1902): 430–4.

Eddy, Arthur Jerome. *Cubists and Post-Impressionism*. Chicago: A.C. McClurg and Company, 1914.

Eisler, Benita. *O'Keeffe and Stieglitz: An American Romance*. New York: Doubleday, 1991.

Eldredge, Charles C. "The Arrival of European Modernism." *Art in America* 61 (July–August 1973): 35–41.

————. *American Imagination and Symbolist Painting*. New York: Grey Art Gallery and Study Center, New York University, 1979.

Ellmann, Richard, ed. *The New Oxford Book of American Verse*. New York: Oxford University Press, 1976.

Emerson, Peter Henry. "Photography: A Pictorial Art." Amateur Photographer (19 March 1886): 138–9.

————. *Naturalistic Photography for Students of the Art*. 2nd ed. London: Sampson Low, 1889. Reprint, New York: Arno Press, 1973.

Émile-Zola, Francois, and Massin Émile-Zola. *Zola, Photographer*. New York: Henry Holt, 1988.

Engelhard, Georgia. "The Face of Alfred Stieglitz." *Popular Photography* 19 (September 1946): 52–5, 120–6.

———. "Alfred Stieglitz – Father of Modern Photography." *The Camera* 69 (June 1947): 48–53, 102–3.

Ernst, Agnes. "The New School of the Camera." *New York Morning Sun*, (26 April 1908).

Falk, Peter. *Frank S. Hermann: A Separate Reality*. White Plains, New York: Sound View Press, 1988.

Fanning, Patricia, ed. *New Perspectives on F. Holland Day*. North Easton, Mass.: Stonehill College and the Norwood Historical Society, 1998.

Farber, Richard. *Historic Photographic Processes*. New York: Allworth Press, 1998.

Fisher, William Murrell. "Georgia O'Keeffe: Drawings and Paintings at 291." *Camera Work* 49–50 (June 1917).

Flint, Ralph. "Prize Song." In *Stieglitz Memorial Portfolio*. Edited by Dorothy Norman. New York: Twice a Year Press, 1947.

Frank, Waldo. *Our America*. New York: Boni and Liveright, 1919.

———. "The Poetry of Hart Crane." *New Republic* 50 (16 March 1927): 116–17.

———. *The Re-Discovery of America: An Introduction to a Philosophy of American Life*. New York: Charles Scribner's Sons, 1929.

Frank, Waldo, Lewis Mumford, Paul Rosenfeld, Dorothy Norman, and Harold Rugg, eds. *America and Alfred Stieglitz: A Collective Portrait*. New York: The Literary Guild, 1934.

Franko, Mark. *Dancing Modernism/Performing Politics*. Bloomington and Indianapolis: Indiana University Press, 1995.

Frizot, Michel, ed. *A New History of Photography*. Cologne: Könemann Verlag, 1998.

Fry, Roger. "A Postscript on Post-Impressionism." *The Nation* 8 (24 December 1910): 536–7.

———. "Preface to the Second Exhibition of Post-Impressionist Art, Grafton Galleries." In *Vision and Design*. Middlesex, England: Penguin Books, 1920, 1940.

Fuguet, Dallett. "Maxims for Artistic Beginners." *Camera Notes* 53 (January 1902): 188.

Fuller, John. "Seneca Stoddard and Alfred Stieglitz." *History of Photography* 19/2 (Summer 1995): 150–8.

"The Future Futurists." *New York Tribune*, (31 March 1912): part 5: 4.

Gallup, Donald, ed. *The Flowers of Friendship: Letters Written to Gertrude Stein*. New York: Alfred Kropf, 1953.

Gee, Helen. *Stieglitz and the Photo-Secession*. Trenton: New Jersey State Museum, 1975.

"Gems from the Forthcoming International Photographic Salon." *New York Herald*, (4 November 1906): 4.

Goethe, Johann Wolflgang von. *Faust: Parts I and II*. Translated by George Madison Priest. New York: Alfred Knopf, 1969.

Goldwater, Robert. *Symbolism*. New York: Harper and Row, 1979.

Green, Jonathan, ed. *Camera Work: A Critical Anthology*. Millerton, New York: Aperture, Inc., 1973.

Greenough, Sarah. "*The Flatiron* by Alfred Stieglitz." *Bulletin, University of New Mexico Art Museum* 10 (1976–77): 15–18. Also published in *Exposure* 15 (September 1977): 28–9.

———. "From the American Earth: Alfred Stieglitz's Photographs of Apples." *Art Journal* 41 (Spring 1981): 46–54.

———. "Alfred Stieglitz's Photographs of Clouds." Ph.D. diss., University of New Mexico, 1984.

———. *Modern Art and America: Alfred Stieglitz and His New York Galleries*. Washington, D.C.: National Gallery of Art, 2000.

———. *Alfred Stieglitz: The Key Set, Volume One, 1886–1922*. New York and Washington, D.C.: Harry Abrams and the National Gallery of Art, 2002.

Greenough, Sarah, and Juan Hamilton. *Alfred Stieglitz: Photographs and Writings*. New York: Calloway Editions, and Washington, D.C.: National Gallery of Art, 1983.

Griffith, Bronwyn. *Ambassadors of Progress, American Women Photographers in Paris, 1900–1907*. Washington D.C.: Library of Congress, 1990.

Haines, Robert E. "Image and Idea: The Literary Relationships of Alfred Stieglitz." Ph.D. diss., Stanford University, 1967.

———. *The Inner Eye of Alfred Stieglitz*. Washington D.C.: University Press of America, 1982.

Hamilton, George Heard. "The Alfred Stieglitz Collection." *Metropolitan Museum Journal* 3 (1970): 371–92.

Hapgood, Hutchins. "A Paris Painter." *New York Globe and Commercial Advertiser* (20 February 1913): 12.

———. *A Victorian in the Modern World*. New York: Harcourt Brace, 1939.

Harker, Margaret F. *The Linked Ring*. London: Heinemann, 1979.

Hartley, Marsden. *Adventures in the Arts, Informal Chapters on Painters, Vaudeville and Poets*. New York: Boni and Liveright, 1921.

Hartley, Marsden. "291 and the Brass Bowl." In *America and Alfred Stieglitz: A Collective Portrait*, edited by front Waldo et al. New York: Doubleday, Doran & Co., 1934.

Hartmann, Sadakichi. "An Art Critic's Estimate of Alfred Stieglitz." *Photographic Times* 30 (June 1898): 257–62.

———. "The New York Camera Club." *Photographic Times* (February 1900): 59. 1900a.

———. "Alfred Stieglitz." *Photographische Rundschau* 14 (1900): 237–40. 1900b.

———. "Ein Ruckblick auf die Saison in Amerika, 1900 bis 1901." *Photographische Rundschau* 14 (1900): 237–41. 1900c.

———. "On the Lack of Culture." *Camera Work* 6 (April 1904): 19–22. 1904a.

———. "The Photo-Secession Exhibition at the Carnegie Art Galleries, Pittsburgh, PA." *Camera Work* 6 (April 1904): 47–51. 1904b.

———. "The Photo-Secession: A New Pictorial Movement." *The Craftsman* (April 1904): 30–7. 1904c.

———. "De Zayas." *Camera Work* 21 (July 1910): 31.

———. "What Remains." *Camera Work* 33 (January 1911): 32. 1911a.

———. "Rodin's Balzac." *Camera Work* 34–5 (April–July 1911): 21. 1911b.

Haskell, Barbara. *Arthur Dove*. Boston: New York Graphic Society, 1975.

———. *Marsden Hartley*. New York: New York University Press, 1980.

Hatfield, Henry. *Goethe: A Critical Introduction*. New York: New Directions Books, 1963.

Haviland, Paul. [Untitled] *291* 1 (March 1915): n.p.

———. [Untitled] *291* 7–8 (September–October 1915): n.p.

Hayes, Jeffrey. "Oscar Bluemner's Late Landscapes: The Musical Color of Fateful Experience." *Art Journal* (Winter 1984): 352–60.

Haz, Nicholas. "Alfred Stieglitz, Photographer." *The American Annual of Photography* (1936): 7–17.

Henderson, Linda Dalrymple. *The Fourth Dimension and Non-Euclidean Geometry in Modern Art*. Princeton: Princeton University Press, 1983.

———. "Mabel Dodge, Gertrude Stein, and Max Weber: A Four-Dimensional Trio." *Arts Magazine* 57 (September 1982): 106–11.

"Hermann Vogel." *The Philadelphia Photographer* 10 (1873): 28–31.

Hinton, A. Horsley. *Practical Pictorial Photography*. London: Hazell, Watson, and Viney, 1900.

Hoffman, Katherine Ann. *An Enduring Spirit: The Art of Georgia O'Keeffe*. Metuchen, New Jersey and London: Scarecrow Press, 1984.

———. *Georgia O'Keeffe: A Celebration of Music and Dance*. New York: George Braziller, 1997. 1997a.

———. "The Multicolored and Polyphonic Surf of Revolution." In *Mediterranean Perspectives: Philosophy, Literature, History and Art*, edited by James Caraway. New York: Dowling College Press, 1997, 1997b.

Hoffman, Michael, ed. "Spirit of an American Place." *Bulletin of the Philadelphia Museum of Art* 76 (Winter 1980): 331.

Holme, Charles, ed. *Art in Photography*. New York and London: The Studio, 1905.

———. *Colour Photography and Other Recent Developments of the Art of the Camera*. London: The Studio, 1908.

Homer, William. "Alfred Stieglitz and the American Aesthete." *Arts Magazine* 49 (September 1974): 25–8.

———. *Avant-Garde: Painting and Sculpture in America, 1910–25*. Willington, Delaware: Delaware Art Museum, 1975.

———. "Stieglitz, 291, and Paul Strand's Early Photography." *Image* (19 June 1976): 10–19.

———. *Alfred Stieglitz and the American Avant-Garde*. Boston: New York Graphic Society, 1977.

———. *Frank S. Hermann*. New York: Marbella Gallery, 1982.

———. *Alfred Stieglitz and the Photo-Secession*. Boston: New York Graphic Society, 1983.

Homer, William, and Catherine Johnson. *Stieglitz and the Photo-Secession, 1902*. New York: Viking Books, 2002.

Humphrey, Marmaduke. "Triumphs in Amateur Photography – Alfred Stieglitz." *Godey's* 136 (December 1897): 581–92.

Hyland, Douglas. *Marius de Zayas: Conjurer of Souls*. Lawrence, Kansas: Spencer Museum of Art, 1981.

Jackson, John Binkerhoff. "Reading the Landscape." In *The Interpretation of Ordinary Landscapes*, edited by D. W. Meing. Oxford: Oxford University Press, 1978.

Johnson, Eric. "Ernest Bloch, A Composer's Vision." *Camera* (February 1976): 6–37.

Jussim, Estelle. "Icons or Ideology: Stieglitz and Hine." In *Photography: Current Perspectives*, edited by Jerome Liebling. Rochester, New York: Light Impressions, 1978.

———. "Technology or Aesthetics: Alfred Stieglitz and Photogravure." *History of Photography* 3 (January 1979): 81–92.

———. *Slave to Beauty: The Eccentric Life and Controversial Career of F. Holland Day*. Boston: David R. Godine, 1981.

———. "The Psychological Portrait." In James Borcomen, Estelle Jussim, and Philip Pocock, *Karsh: The Art of the Portrait*. Ottawa: National Gallery of Art, 1989.

Jussim, Estelle, and Elizabeth Lindquist-Cook. *Landscape as Photograph*. New Haven and London: Yale University Press, 1985.

Kandinsky, Wassily. *Concerning the Spiritual in Art*. Translated by M. T. H. Sadler. London: Constable & Co., 1914. Reprint, New York: Dover Publications, 1977.

Kandinsky, Wassily, and Franz Marc. *Documents of Twentieth-Century Art: The Blaue Reiter Almanac*. New York: The Viking Press, 1974.

Keiley, Joseph T. "The Philadelphia Salon: Its Origin and Influence." *Camera Notes* 2 (January 1899): 113–32. 1899a.

———. *Exhibition of Photographs by Alfred Stieglitz*. New York: Camera Club, 1899, 1899b.

———. "American Pictorial Photographers – Alfred Stieglitz." *Photography*, (February 1904): 147–51.

———. "The Buffalo Exhibition." *Camera Work* 33 (January 1911): 27.

Kent, Richard John. "Alfred Stieglitz and the Maturation of American Culture." Ph.D. diss., Johns Hopkins University, 1974.

Kerfoot, John. "The Game of the Galleries." *Camera Work* 33 (January 1911): 45.

Kettlewell, James. "Artists of Lake George, 1776–1976." Glens Falls: The Hyde Collection, 1976.

Kiefer, Geraldine Wojno. *Alfred Stieglitz: Scientist, Photographer, and Avatar of Modernism, 1880–1913*. New York and London: Garland Publishing, Inc., 1991.

Kobry, Yves. "The Depths of an Eqo." In Jean Clair, Pierre Theboqe et al. *Lost Paradise: Symbolist Europe*. Montreal: Musée des Beaux-Arts, 1995.

Krauss, Rosalind. "Alfred Stieglitz's 'Equivalents.'" *Arts* 54 (February 1980): 134–7.

Kreymborg, Alfred. "Stieglitz and 291." *New York Morning Telegraph* (14 June 1914).

Laurvik, J. Nilsen. "The New Color Photography." *Century Magazine* 75 (January 1908): 322–30.

———. "Alfred Stieglitz, Pictorial Photographer." *International Studio* 44 (August 1911): xx–xxvii.

———. *Is It Art? Post-Impressionism, Futurism, Cubism*. New York: The International Press, 1913.

Lehmann, A. G. *The Symbolist Aesthetic in France, 1885–1895*. Oxford: Basil Blackwell, 1950.

Leonard, Neil. "Alfred Stieglitz and Realism." *Art Quarterly* 29/3–4. (1966): 277–86.

Le Rider, Jacques. "Böcklin entre antique et moderne." *La Revue du Musée d'Orsay* (Autumn 2001).

Levin, Gail. "Wassily Kandinsky and the American Avant-Garde, 1912–1950." Ph.D. diss., Rutgers University, 1976.

———. "Konrad Cramer: Link from the German to the American Avant-Garde." *Arts Magazine* 56 (February 1982): 145–9.

———. *Synchronism and American Color Abstraction, 1916–1929*. Chicago: University of Chicago Press, 1989.

Levinson, Jerrold. *Music, Art and Metaphysics: Essays in Philosophical Aesthetics*. Ithaca and London: Cornell University Press, 1990.

Lipsey, Roger. "Double Portrait – Alfred Stieglitz and Ananda Coomaraswamy" *Aperture* 16/3, 1972.

Lockspeiser, Edward. *Music and Painting: A Study in Corporative Ideal from Turner to Schoenberg*. New York: Horper and Row, 1973.

Longwell, Dennis. *Steichen: The Master Prints 1895–1914: The Symbolist Years*. New York: The Museum of Modern Art, 1978.

Lowe, Sue Davidson. *Stieglitz – A Memoir/Biography*. New York: Farrar, Straus, and Giroux, 1983.

Lukach, Joan J. "Severini's 1917 Exhibition at Stieglitz's 291." *Burlington Magazine* 113 (April 1971): 196–209.

Lynes, Barbara Buhler. *O'Keeffe, Stieglitz and the Critics, 1916–1929.* Chicago: University of Chicago Press, 1989.

Lyons, Nathan. *Photographers on Photography.* Englewood Cliffs, New Jersey: Prentice Hall, 1966.

MacDonald, M. Irwin. "The Fairy Faith and Pictures of Music." *The Craftsman* 23 (October 1912): 23.

Makela, Maria. *The Munich Secession.* Princeton: Princeton University Press, 1990.

Mallarmé, Stéphone. *Mallarmé: Selected Prose Poems, Essays, and Letters.* Translated by Bradford Cook. Baltimare: John Hopkins University Press, 1953.

Margolis, Marianne Fulton. "Philadelphia Photographic Salons, 1898–1901." *Image* 22 (September 1978): 2–10.

———. *Camera Work: A Pictorial Guide.* New York: Dover Publications, 1978.

Marin, John. "The Man and the Place." In *America and Alfred Stieglitz: A Collective Portrait,* edited by Frank, Waldo, et al. New York: Doubleday, Doran & Co., 1934.

———. *The Selected Writings of John Marin.* Edited by Dorothy Norman. New York: Pellegrini and Cudahy, 1949.

May, Henry F. *The End of American Innocence: A Study of the First Years of Our Own Time.* New York: Knopf, 1959.

McCausland, Elizabeth. "Georgia O'Keeffe in a Retrospective Exhibition." *Spring Field Republic* (26 May 1946): 6.

Mellquist, Jerome, and Lucie Wiese, eds. *Paul Rosenfeld: Voyager in the Arts.* New York: Creative Age Press, 1948.

Mendelsohn, Joyce. *Touring the Flatiron.* New York: New York Landmarks Conservancy, 1999.

Miller, Henry. "Stieglitz and Marin." *Twice a Year* 8–9 (1942): 152–3.

Moffatt, Frederick C. *Arthur Wesley Dow.* Washington, D.C.: Smithsonian Institute Press and National Collection of Fine Arts, 1977.

Morgan, Ann Lee, ed. *Dear Stieglitz, Dear Dove.* Newark: University of Delaware Press, 1985.

"Mr. Stieglitz's Special Lantern Slide Exhibition." *Journal of the Society of Amateur Photographers of New York* 3 (February 1896): 13–14.

Muir, Ward. "Alfred Stieglitz: An Impression." *Amateur Photographer* 57 (24 March 1913): 285–6.

Mulligan, Therese, ed. *The Photography of Alfred Stieglitz.* Rochester, New York: George Eastman House, 2000.

Munson, Gorham. *Destinations: A Canvas of American Literature since 1900.* New York: J.H. Sears, 1928.

Naef, Weston. *The Painterly Photograph, 1890–1914.* New York: The Metropolitan Museum of Art, 1973.

———. *The Collection of Alfred Stieglitz: Fifty Pioneers of Modern Photography*. New York: Viking Press, 1978.

———. *In Focus: Alfred Stieglitz*. Los Angeles: The J. Paul Getty Museum, 1995.

———. *Alfred Stieglitz: Seen and Unseen*. Los Angeles: The J. Paul Getty Museum, 1996.

———. *Peter Henry Emerson: The Fight for Photography as a Fine Art*. Millerton, New York: Aperture, 1975.

———. *From Adams to Stieglitz: Pioneers of Modern Photography*. New York: Aperture Foundation, 1989.

———. Unpublished manuscript and notes on Stieglitz. National Gallery of Art, Washington, D.C.

Newhall, Beaumont. *Photography: Essays and Images*. New York: Museum of Modern Art, 1980.

Nietzsche, Friedrich Wilhelm. *The Birth of Tragedy and the Genealogy of Morals*. New York: Doubleday, 1956.

———. *The Portable Nietzsche*. Edited and translated by Walter Kaufmann. New York: Viking Press, 1968.

Niven, Penelope. *Steichen: A Biography*. New York: Clarkson Potter, 1997.

Norman Dorothy. "Writings and Conversations of Alfred Stieglitz." *Twice a Year* 1 (fall – Winter 1938).

———. "An Introduction to an American Seer." *Aperture* 8/1 (1960).

———. "Stieglitz's Experiments in Life." *New York Times Megazine* (29 December 1963): 9.

———. *Alfred Stieglitz: An American Seer*. Millerton, New York: Aperture, 1973.

———. Alfred Stieglitz. The Aperture History of Photography Series. Millerton, New York: Aperture, 1976.

———. *Alfred Stieglitz*. New York: Aperture Foundation, 1989.

———, ed. "Ten Stories." *Twice a Year* 5–6 (1940–1): 158–60.

———, ed. *Stieglitz: A Memorial Portfolio, 1864–1946*. New York: Twice a Year Press, 1947.

Norton, Minerva Brace. *In and Around Berlin*. Chicago: A.C. McClurg and Co., 1890.

O'Brien, Kathryn. *The Great and the Gracious on Millionaire's Row: Lake George in its Glory*. Utica, New York: North Country Books, Inc., 1978.

O'Keeffe, Georgia. Georgia O'Keeffe: A Portrait by Alfred Stieglitz. New York: Metropohtan Museum of Art: 1978.

Oppenheim, William G. "Distinguished Photographers of Today: Alfred Stieglitz." *The Photographic Times* 23 (1 December 1893): 689–93.

Pagé, Suzanne, ed. *Francis Picabia*. Paris: Musée d'Art Moderne de la ville de Paris, 2002.

Parker, William, ed. *Art and Photography: Forerunners and Influences*. Utah: Peregrine Smith, Inc. 1985.

Parsons, Melinda Boyd. *To All Believers: The Art of Pamela Colman Smith*. Delaware: Delaware Art Museum, 1975.

Pater, Walter. *The Renaissance: Studies in Art and Poetry*. New York, 1873.

Peeler, David. *The Illuminating Mind in American Photography: Stieglitz, Strand, Weston, Adams*. Rochester, New York: University of Rochester Press, 1998.

Peterson, Christian. *Alfred Stieglitz's "Camera Notes"*. New York: W.W. Norton and Minneapolis: Minneapolis Institute of Art, 1993.

"Pictorial Photography from America." *The Amateur Photographer* (12 October 1900): 282–4.

"Pictured Music." *Current Literature* 45 (August 1908).

Pollitzer, Anita. *A Woman on Paper: Georgia O'Keeffe*. New York: Simon and Schuster, 1988.

Poore, Henry R. *The New Tendency in Art: Post-Impressionism Cubism, Futurism*. Garden City, New York: Doubleday, Page and Company, 1913.

Poivert, Michel, and Hélène Pinet. *Le Salon de Photographie: Les Ecoles Pictorialistes en Europe et aux Etats-Unis vers 1900*. Paris: Musée Rodin, 1993.

Pringle, Andrew. "The Naissance of Art in Photography." *The Studio* 1 (June 1893): 87–95.

Pultz, John, and Catherine B. Scallen. *Cubism and American Photography 1910–1930*. Williamstown, Massachusetts: Sterling and Francine Clark Art Institute, 1981.

Rabb, Jane, ed. *Literature and Photography, Interactions 1840–1990*. Albuquerque: University of New Mexico Press, 1995.

Risatti, Howard. "American Critical Reaction to European Modernism, 1908–1917." Ph.D. diss., University of Illinois at Urbana-Champaign, 1978.

———. "Music and the Development of Abstraction in America: The Decade Surrounding the Armory Show." *Art Journal* 59 (July 1979): 8–13.

Roberts, Pam. "Alfred Stieglitz, 291 Gallery and *Camera Work*." In *Camera Work: The Complete Illustrations, 1903–1917*, edited by Pam Roberts. Cologne: Benedikt Taschen Verlag, 1997. 1997a.

———, ed. *Camera Work: The Complete Illustrations, 1903–1917*. Cologne: Benedikt Taschen Verlag, 1997. 1997b.

Rodgers, Timothy Robert. "Making the American Artist: John Marin, Alfred Stieglitz and Their Critics, 1909–1936." Ph.D. diss., Brown University, 1994.

Rolland, Romain. "America and the Arts." *The Seven Arts* 1 (November 1916): 52–6.

Rood, Roland. "The 'Little Galleries' of the Photo-Secession." *American Amateur Photographer* 17 (December 1905): 506–9.

Rookmaaker, H. R. *Gauguin and 19th-Century Art Theory*. Amsterdam: Swets and Zeitlinger, 1972.

Rosen, Charles. *The Frontiers of Meaning: Three Informal Lectures on Music*. New York: Hill and Wang, 1994.

Rosenblum, Naomi, *A World History of Photography*. 3rd ed. New York: Abbeville Press, 1997.

Rosenfeld, Paul. "Stieglitz." *The Dial* 70 (April 1921): 397–409.

———. *Port of New York: Essays on Fourteen Moderns*. New York: Harcourt, Brace, and Company, 1924.

———. *Musical Portrait*. New York: Harcourt, Brace, and Company, 1925.

———. "The Boy in the Dark Room". In *America and Alfred Stieglitz: A Collective Partrait*, edited by Waldo Frank. New York: Doubleday, Doran and Co., 1934.

———. "Alfred Stieglitz." *Twice a Year* 14–15 (1946–7): 203–10.

———. *By Way of Art*. New York: Coward-McCann, Inc., 1928. Reprint, Freeport, New York: Books for Libraries Press Inc., 1967.

Roth, Andrew. *The Book of 101 Books: Seminal Photographic Books of the Twentieth Century*. New York: PPP Editions, 2001.

Rugg, Harold. "The Artist and the Great Transition." In *America and Alfred Stieglitz: A Collective Portrait*, edited by Frank Waldo et al. New York: Doubleday, Doran and Co., 1934.

Sadler, Michael T. H. "After Gauguin." *Rhythm, Art, Music, and Literature* 1 (Spring 1912): 23–9.

Savery, James C. "Photo-Secession." *The Burr McIntosh Monthly*. 12/49 (April 1907): n.p.

Schenkenberg, Bonnie Ford. *Ernest Bloch, Photographer and Composer*. Tucson: Centre for Creative Photography, 1980.

Schiffmann, Joseph. "The Alienation of the Artist: Alfred Stieglitz." *American Quarterly*, 3 (1951).

Schloss, Carol. *In Visible Light*. New York and Oxford: Oxford University Press, 1987.

Schorske, Carl. *Fin-de-Siècle Vienna: Politics and Culture*. New York: Vintage Books, 1981.

Scott, Temple. "Fifth Avenue and the Boulevard Saint-Michel." *Forum* 28 (December 1910): 665–85.

Sekula, Allan. "On the Invention of Photographic Meaning." *Artforum* 13 (January 1975): 37–45.

Seligmann, Herbert J. "Music and Words." *New York Tribune* (18 November 1923).

———. *Alfred Stieglitz Talking*. New Haven: Yale University Library, 1966.

Shapiro, Meyer. "Rebellian in Art." In *America in Crisis*, edited by David Aaron. Hamden, Connecticut: Archon Books, 1971.

Sheehy, Helen. *Eleanora Duse*. New York: Alfred Knopf. 2003.

Sillevis, John, ed. *Katwijk in de Schildekunst*. Katwijks Museum, 1995.

Sinnòtt, Trip. *Tea Island, A Perfect Gem*. New York: Attic Studio Press, 1993.

Sorell, Walter. *Dance in Its Time*. New York: Doubleday, 1981.

Steichen, Edward. *A Life in Photography*. Garden City, New York: Doubleday and Company, 1963.

Stewart, Doug. "Stieglitz in Focus." *Smithsonian Magazine* (June 2002): 70–80.

Stieglitz, Alfred. "A Word or Two About Amateur Photography in Germany." *Amateur Photographer* 5 (25 February 1887): 96–7.

———. "A Day in Chioggia." *Amateur Photographer* prize tour issue (June 1889): 7–9. 1889a.

———. "A Plea for Art in America." *Photographic Mosaics* 28 (June 1889): 7–9. 1889b.

———. "Eine kurze unparteiische Übersicht der Amateur – Leistungen in der Kunst – Abteilung der Berlin Jubiläums–Ausstellung." *Photographische Rundschau* 3 (October 1889): 332–4. 1889c.

———. "The Berline Exhibition." *American Amateur Photographer* (November 1889): 202–4. 1889d.

———. "The Platinotype Process and the New York Amateur." *American Amateur Photographer* 4 (April 1892): 153–5. 1892a.

———. "The Berlin Exhibition." *American Amateur Photographer* 1 (1892): 135–7. 1892b.

———. "Cortina and Sterzing." *Amateur Photographer* (1892): 60–1. 1892c.

———. "A Plea for Art in Photography." Photographic Mosaics 28 (1892): 136–7. 1892d.

———. "The Joint Exhibition at Philadelphia." *American Amateur Photographer* 5 (June 1893): 249–54.

———. "A Plea for a Photographic Art Exhibition." In *American Annual of Photography and Photographic Times Almanac for 1895*. New York: 1895. 1895a.

———. "Pictorial Photography in the United States, 1895." In *Photograms of the Year 1895*. New York: Tennant and Ward, 1895. 1895b.

———. "The American Photographic Salon." In *American Annual of Photography and Photographic Times Almanac for 1896*. New York: 1896.

———. "The Hand Camera – Its Present Importance." In *American Annual of Photography and Photographic Times Almanac for 1897*. New York: 1897.

———. "Exhibition of F. H. Day's Work." *Camera Notes* (April 1898): 119. 1898a.

———. "Night Photography with the Introduction of Life." In *American Annual of Photography and Photographic Times Almanac for 1898*. New York: 1898. 1898b.

———. "Reviews and Exchanges." *Camera Notes* 3 (October 1899): 11–12. 1899a.

————. "The Progress of Pictorial Photography in the United States." In *American Annual of Photography and Photographic Times Almanac for 1899*. New York: 1899. 1899b.

————. "My Favorite Picture." *Photographic Life* 1 (1899): 88. 1899c.

————. "Pictorial Photography." *Scribner's* 26 (1899): 528–37. 1899d.

————. "Why American Pictorial Work Is Absent from the Paris Exhibition." *Amateur Photographer* 32 (20 July 1900): 44.

————. "The Phiadephia Salon." *Camera Notes* 5 (October 1901): 121–2.

————. "Painters on Photographic Juries." *Camera Notes* 6 (July 1902): 27–30. 1902a.

————. "The Photo-Secession at the National Arts Club, New York." In *Photograms of the Year 1902*. New York: Tennant and Ward, 1902. 1902b.

————. "Introduction." *Camera Work* (January 1903): 15–16. 1903a.

————. "The Photo-Secession." In *Bausch and Lomb Lens Souvenir*. Rochester, New York: Bausch and Lomb Optical Company, 1903. 1903b.

————. "The Photo-Secession." Typescript. 7 June 1903. ASA/YCAL. 1903c.

————. "The Photo-Secession and the St. Louis Exposition," *Amateur Photographer* 39 (14 April 1904): 287–8.

————. "Platinum Printing," In *Picture Taking and Picture Making*. Rochester, New York: Eastman Kodak Company, 1898. Later published in *The Modern Way of Picture Making*. Rochester, New York: Eastman Kodak Company, 1905. 1905a.

————. "Simplicity in Composition." In *The Modern Way of Picture Making*. Rochester, New York: Eastman Kodak Company, 1905. 1905b.

————. "The Editor's Page." *Camera Work* 17 (January 1907): 37. 1907a.

————. "The New Color Photography: A Bit of History." *Camera Work* 20 (October 1907): 20–5. 1907b.

————. *The Photo-Secession and Its Opponents: Five Letters*. New York: Privately Published by Stieglitz, 1910. 1910a.

————. *The Photo-Secession and Its Opponents: Another Letter – the Sixth*. New York: Privately Published by Stieglitz, 1910. 1910b.

————. "The Exhibition of Pictorial Photography at the Albright Art Gallery." *Academy Notes* 6 (1911): 11–13.

————. "Address by Alfred Stieglitz." *Photo Era* 28 (March 1912): 134.

————. "What is 291?" *Camera Work* (January 1915). 1915a.

————. "One Hour's Sleep – Three Dreams." *291* 1 (March 1915): n.p. 1915b.

————. "Photographs by Paul Strand." *Camera Work* 48 (October 1916): 11–12. 1916a.

————. "Foreword." In *The Forum Exhibition of Modern American Painters*. New York: The Anderson Galleries, 1916. 1916b.

———. "Our Illustrations." *Camera Work* 49–50. (June 1917): 36.

———. "How I Came to Photograph Clouds." *Amateur Photographer and Photography* 56 (1923): 255. 1923a.

———. "Some of the Reasons." In *The Complete Photographer*, edited by R. Child Bayley. Revised edition. New York: McClure Phillips and Company, 1923. 1923b.

———. "From Notes Made by Stieglitz, 1938." *Twice a Year* 1 (1938).

———. "Who Am I?" *Twice a Year* 5–6 (1940–1).

———. "How *The Steerage* Happened." *Twice a Year* 8–9 (1942): 175–8.

———. "Stories." *Twice a Year* 10–11 (1943): 264.

———. "Six Happening I: Photographing the Flat-Iron Building, 1902–3." *Twice a Year* 14–15 (1946–7): 188–90.

Stieglitz, Alfred, and Louis H. Schubart. "Two Artists' Haunts." *Photographic Times* 26 (1895): 9–12.

"Stieglitz." *The Amateur Photographer* home portraiture issue (7 October 1887): 13.

"Stieglitz." *The Amateur Photographer* photographic holiday work (11 July 1888): 18.

Stoddard, Seneca Ray. *Lake George (Illustrated), A Book of Today*. Albany: Weed, Persons and Co., 1874.

Strand, Paul. "Alfred Stieglitz and a Machine." *MSS* 2 (March 1922): 6–7.

———. "The Art Motive in Photography." *British Journal of Photography* 70 (5 October 1923): 612–15.

———. "Stieglitz: An Appraisal." *Popular Photography* (July 1947): 88–98.

———. *A Retrospective Monograph*. Millerton, New York: Aperture, 1971.

Suffolk, Randall, ed. *Arthur Davies, Dweller on the Threshold*. Glens Falls, New York: The Hyde Collection, 2001.

Symons, Arthur. *Studies in the Seven Arts*. London: A. Constable and Company, 1906.

Szarkowski, John. *Photography until Now*. New York: Museum of Modern Art, 1989.

———. *Alfred Stieglitz at Lake George*. New York: Museum of Modern Art, 1995.

Taft, Robert. *Photography and the American Scene*. New York: Macmillan, 1938. Reprint, New York: Dover Publications, 1964.

Tarshis, Jerome. "Alfred Stieglitz, Editor." *Portfolio* (August–September 1979): 50–5.

Tashjian, Dickran. *William Carlos Williams and the American Scene, 1920–1940*. Berkeley: University of California Press, 1978.

Taylor, Larry Hugh. "Alfred Stieglitz and the Search for American Equivalents." Ph.D. diss., University of Illinois at Champaign-Urbana, 1973.

Thomas, Downing. *Music and the Origins of Language: Theories of the French Enlightenment*. Cambridge: Cambridge University Press, 1985.

Thomas, F. Richard. *Literary Admirers of Alfred Stieglitz*. Carbondale, Illinois: Southern Illinois University Press, 1983.

Thornton, Gene. *Masters of the Camera: Stieglitz, Steichen and their Successors*. New York: Holt, Rinehart, and Winston, 1976.

Tillyard, E. M. W. "The Cosmic Dance." In *What is Dance: Reading in Theory and Criticism*, edited by Roger Copeland and Morshall Cohen. New York: Oxford University Press, 1983.

Trachtenberg, Alan. *Classic Essays on Photography*. New Haven: Leete's Island Books, 1980.

———. "Camera Work/Social Work." In *Reading American Photographs: Images as History, Matthew Brady to Walker Evans*, edited by Alan Trachtenberg. New York: Hill and Wang, 1989.

Travis, David. *Photography Rediscovered: American Photography 1900–1930*. New York: Whitney Museum, 1979.

Troncale, Tony. *The Camera Club of New York, 1888–1988*, Camera Club of New York, 1988.

Tudor, Hart P. "The Analogy of Sound and Color." *Cambridge Magazine* (2 March 1918): 480–3.

Turner, Elizabeth Hutton. "I can't Sing so I Paint." In *Two Lives, Georgia O'Keeffe and Alfred Stieglitz: A Conversation in Paintings and Photographs*. New York: Harper Collins, 1992.

Valéry, Paul. *Aesthetics*. Translated by Ralph Manheim. New York: Pantheon Books, 1964.

Vogel, Hermann W. *Handbook of the Practice and Art of Photography*. Philadelphia: Benerman and Wilson, 1871.

———. *The Chemistry of Light and Photography in their Applications to Art, Science, and Industry*. New York: D. Appleton, 1882.

Weber, Brom, ed. *The Letters of Hart Crane, 1916–1932*. Berkeley: University of California Press, 1965.

Weber, Max. "Chinese Dolls and Modern Colorists." *Camera Work* 31 (July 1910): 51.

———. *Cubist Poems*. London: Elin Mathews, 1914.

Welling, William. *Photography: The Formative Years*. New York: Thomas Crowell Co. 1978.

Werner, Alfred. *Max Weber*. New York: Harry N. Abrams, Inc., 1974.

Wertheim, Arthur F. *The New York Little Renaissance: Iconoclasm, Modernism, and Nationalism in American Culture*. New York: New York University Press, 1976.

Whelan, Richard. *Alfred Stieglitz: A Biography*. New York: Da Capo Press, 1997.

———. *Stieglitz on Photography: His Selected Essays and Notes*. New York: Aperture, 2000.

Whitman, Walt. *The Illustrated Leaves of Grass*. Edited by Howard Chapnick. New York: Madison Square Press, 1971.

Wickstrom, Richard. *Selections from "Camera Work": Transformations in Pictorial Photography*. Iowa: University of Iowa Museum of Art, 1980.

Williams, William Carlos. *In the American Grain*. New York: Random House, 1925. Reprint, New York: New Directions, 1956.

Willis, Paul. "A Talk with the Photo-Secession." *The Photographer* (2 July 1904): 151.

Wood, Beafrice. *I Shock Myself*. Ojai, California: Billingham Press, 1985.

Wood, John. *The Art of the Autochrome*. Iowa City: University of Iowa Press, 1993.

Wright, Williard Huntington. *Modern Painting: Its Tendency and Meaning*. New York: John Lane Co., 1915.

———. "The Aesthetic Struggle in America." *Forum* 55 (February 1916): 201, 220.

———. *The Creative Will, Studies in the Philosophy and the Syntax of Aesthetics*. New York: John Lane Co., 1916.

Young, Daniel. "The Other Side – A Communication." *Camera Notes* 2/2 (October 1898): 46–9.

Zilczer, Judith Katy. "The Aesthetic Struggle in America, 1913–1918: Abstract Art and Theory in the Stieglitz Circle." Ph.D. diss., University of Delaware, 1975.

———. "Synaesthesia and Popular Culture: Arthur Dove, George Gershwin, and the 'Rhapsody in Blue.'" *Art Journal* (Winter 1984): 361–6.

Zoller, Andreas. *Künstler Kolonien im deutschen Südwesten*. Schwarzwald-Baar-Heuberg: Edition Kunststiftung Hohenkarpfen. 1994.

ILLUSTRATIONS

All photographs by the author (K. Hoffman) are © Katherine Hoffman.

References to "NGA Key Set" are to the catalogue by Sarah Greenough of the "Key Set" of Stieglitz's photographs in the National Gallery of Art, Washington, D.C.

14   Wilhelm Hasemann, *Gutach*, 19 August 1883, drawing of Alfred Stieglitz and possibly his sister, postcard addressed to Edward Stieglitz, Yale Collection of American Literature, Beinecke Rare Book and Manuscript Library

15   Wilhelm Hasemann, drawing of a Gutach scene, postcard written by Alfred Stieglitz to his sister Flora, 10 April 1882, Yale Collection of American Literature, Beinecke Rare Book and Manuscript Library

16   K. Hoffman, the Technische Hochschule, Berlin, 2002

17   The University of Berlin, *c*.1880–1900, postcard, private collection

18   Alfred Stieglitz, *Snowscape (Berlin)*, 1888–90, lantern slide, © The Art Institute of Chicago, 1986.3320

19   Alfred Stieglitz, *Winter (Berlin)*, 1887, lantern slide, Yale Collection of American Literature, Beinecke Rare Book and Manuscript Library

20   Unter den Linden and Ecke Friedrichstrasse with the Café Bauer, Berlin, 1885, postcard, private collection

21   Unknown photographer, *Eleanora Duse*, n.d., Yale Collection of American Literature, Beinecke Rare Book and Manuscript Library

22   Playbill from Stieglitz's Scrapbook eight, Yale Collection of American Literature, Beinecke Rare Book and Manuscript Library

23   Alfred Stieglitz, pages from Scrapbook eight, *c*.1896–97, Yale Collection of American Literature, Beinecke Rare Book and Manuscript Library

24   K. Hoffman, Klosterstrasse, Berlin, 2002

25   Alfred Stieglitz, *Professor Vogel*, platinum print, 1885, private collection

26   Alfred Stieglitz, *Untitled* (possibly Tiergarten, Berlin) *c*.1888, private collection

27   K. Hoffman, Tiergarten, Berlin, 2002

28   Wilhelm Hasemann, *Tiergarten, Berlin*, 1871, oil sketch, private collection

29   Wilhelm Hasemann, *Clouds, Berlin*, 1871, oil sketch, private collection

30   K. Hoffman, memorial to Queen Luise, 2003 (cf. photograph by Stieglitz in NGA Key Set, fig. 30)

31   K. Hoffman, memorial to Queen Luise (base), 2003

32   K. Hoffman, statue of Goethe, Tiergarten, Berlin, 2003 (cf. photograph by Stieglitz of 1886 in NGA Key Set, fig. 31)

33   Alfred Stieglitz, photograph of a collage of photographic portraits of Stieglitz taken by Erdmann Encke, 1883, Philadelphia Museum of Art: From the collection of Dorothy Norman, 1997

34   Alfred Stieglitz, "*My Room*" (Behren Strasse, Berlin), 1885–6, Yale Collection of American Literature, Beinecke Rare Book and Manuscript Library

35   Alfred Stieglitz, *Mittenwald*, 1886, lantern slide, The Museum of Modern Art, New York

36   Alfred Stieglitz, *Self-Portrait* – (?)*Bavaria*, 1886, Yale Collection of American Literature, Beinecke Rare Book and Manuscript Library

37   Alfred Stieglitz, *Bavaria (Figure Asleep in a Cemetery)*, 1886, Yale Collection of American Literature, Beinecke Rare Book and Manuscript Library

38   Alfred Stieglitz, *Lake and Mountain (On Lake Thun, Switzerland)*, 1886, lantern slide (1894), George Eastman House, International Museum of Photography and Film, Rochester

39   Alfred Stieglitz, *Frank Simon "Sime" Hermann*, 1894, platinum print, The J. Paul Getty Museum, Los Angeles © Estate of Georgia O'Keeffe

40   Alfred Stieglitz, *Self-portrait, Freienwalde, an-der-Oder*, 1886, platinum print, Yale Collection of American Literature, Beinecke Rare Book and Manuscript Library

41   Unknown photographer, *Stieglitz and His Friends*, 1887, Yale Collection of American Literature, Beinecke Rare Book and Manuscript Library

42   K. Hoffman, the approach to Bellagio, 2001

43   Alfred Stieglitz, *Maria, Bellagio*, 1887, lantern slide, George Eastman House, International Museum of Film and Photography, Rochester, New York

44   Alfred Stieglitz, *Leone, Bellagio*, 1887, lantern slide, private collection

45   Alfred Stieglitz, *Bellagio*, 1887 (print 1894), Philadelphia Museum of Art: Gift of Sue Davidson Lowe

46   K. Hoffman, steps at Bellagio, 2001

47   Alfred Stieglitz, *The Last Joke – Bellagio*, or *A Good Joke*, 1887, platinum print, The Museum of Modern Art, New York

48   Alfred Stieglitz, *At Lake Como*, 1887, photogravure, The Photographic Times 23, December 1893; 684, New York Public Library

49   Alfred Stieglitz, *Untitled (Woman Washing)*, 1887, private collection

50   Alfred Stieglitz, *Woman Washing, Europe*, (?)1884–6, Philadelphia Museum of Art: From the Collection of Dorothy Norman, 1967

51   Alfred Stieglitz, *Lake Garda*, c.1887, lantern slide, The Museum of Modern Art, New York City

52   K. Hoffman, Lake Garda, 2001

53   Alfred Stieglitz, *Kettle Cleaner, Lake Como*, 1887, platinum print, private collection

54   K. Hoffman, Chioggia, 2001

55   K. Hoffman, Chioggia, 2001

56   Alfred Stieglitz, *On the Bridge, Chioggia*, 1887, platinum print, private collection

57   Alfred Stieglitz, *Stones of Venice (Chioggia)*, 1887 (print 1894), chloride print, © The Art Institute of Chicago, Alfred Stieglitz Collection, 1949.700

58   K. Hoffman, Ponte Vigo, Chioggia, 2001

59   Alfred Stieglitz, *Boats*, c.1887, platinum print, private collection

60   Alfred Stieglitz, *Untitled, (?)Italian fisherman*, c.1887, platinum print, private collection

61   Alfred Stieglitz, *Marina*, 1887, lantern slide, private collection

62   Alfred Stieglitz, *A Venetian Gamin*, 1887, gelatin silver print, Philadelphia Museum of Art: The Alfred Stieglitz Collection 1949

63   Alfred Stieglitz, *Landscape (November Days) (near Munich)*, 1887, chloride print, © The Art Institute of Chicago, The Alfred Stieglitz Collection, 1949.692

64   K. Hoffman, The Quarters at Four Seasons Hotel, formerly Oaklawn, Lake George, 2002

65   Alfred Stieglitz, *Oaklawn*, photograph on a postcard, December 1903 , from Edward Stieglitz to Wilhelm Hasemann, private collection

66   Alfred Stieglitz, *Oaklawn, Lake George*, 27 August 1897, Yale Collection of American Literature, Beinecke Rare Book and Manuscript Library

67   Alfred Stieglitz, *Stieglitz Family at Oaklawn, Lake George*, 1888 lantern slide, Yale Collection of American Literature, Beinecke Rare Book and Manuscript Library

68   Alfred Stieglitz, *The Parlor at Oaklawn, Lake George*, 1907, chloride print, © The Art Institute of Chicago, Alfred Stieglitz Collection, 1949.715

69   Alfred Stieglitz, *Listening to the Crickets*, 1891, lantern slide, Yale Collection of American Literature, Beinecke Rare Book and Manuscript Library

70   Alfred Stieglitz, *Maggie Foord*, c.1888, lantern slide, Yale Collection of American Literature, Beinecke Rare Book and Manuscript Library

71   Alfred Stieglitz, *Untitled (The Dock at Lake George)*, 1890s, private collection

72   Alfred Stieglitz, *Meeting of Day and Night, Lake George*, 1896, lantern slide, © The Art Institute of Chicago, 1986.3323, photograph by Greg Williams,

73   Alfred Stieglitz, *Evening, Lake George*, 1890s, private collection

74   Alfred Stieglitz, *Clouds*, c.1888, platinum print, private collection

75   Alfred Stieglitz, *Lake George*, c.1895, platinum print, Yale Collection of American Literature, Beinecke Rare Book and Manuscript Library

76   Alfred Stieglitz, *Untitled (Lake George)*, c.1890, Yale Collection of American Literature, Beinecke Rare Book and Manuscript Library

77   Alfred Stieglitz, *Equivalent (Clouds)*, 1924 or 1926, Leica print, Yale Collection of American Literature, Beinecke Rare Book and Manuscript Library

78   Cover and page from the Jubilee Exhibition catalogue, *Catalog der Photographischen Jubiläums-Ausstellung*, Berlin, 1889, private collection

79   Alfred Stieglitz, *Jubilee Exhibition, Berlin: Main Hall*, 1889, George Eastman House, International Museum of Photography and Film, Rochester, New York

80   Alfred Stieglitz, *Sun Rays, Paula*, 1889, lantern slide, Yale Collection of American Literature, Beinecke Rare Book and Manuscript Library

81   Alfred Stieglitz, *Paula*, 1889, platinum print, private collection

82   Alfred Stieglitz, *Weary*, 1890, gelatin silver print, 1920s/30s, J. Paul Getty Museum © Estate of Georgia O'Keeffe

83   Alfred Stieglitz, *Peasant*, c.1890, platinum print, private collection

84   Alfred Stieglitz, *Lago di Misurina*, 1890s, private collection

85   Alfred Stieglitz, *Self-Portrait, Cortina*, c.1890, platinum print, 1895/96, Adirondack Museum, Blue Mountain Lake, New York

86   Alfred Stieglitz, *The Last Load*, 1890, lantern slide, The Museum of Modern Art, New York

87   Alfred Stieglitz, *A Street in Sterzing*, inscribed 1887, probably 1890, platinum print, © The Art Institute of Chicago, The Alfred Stieglitz Collection, 1949.699

88   Alfred Stieglitz, *Untitled (?Biarritz)*, c.1890, private collection

89   K. Hoffman, Arcachon, 2002

90   K. Hoffman, Ile de Ré, 2002

91   Alfred Stieglitz, *Mid-Ocean* from *Sunlight and Shadow* by W. I. Lincoln Adams, New York: Baker & Taylor Co., 1897, p. 78

slide, Yale Collection of American Literature, Beinecke Rare Book and Manuscript Library

115   Alfred Stieglitz, *A Wet Day on the Boulevard*, 1894, photogravure, © The Art Institute of Chicago, Alfred Stieglitz Collection, 1949.887

116   K. Hoffman, The Old England Store, Paris, 2002

117   Alfred Stieglitz, *The Eiffel Tower*, 1894, lantern slide, The Museum of Modern Art, New York

118   Alfred Stieglitz, *On the Seine-Near Paris*, 1894, photogravure, George Eastman House, International Museum of Photography and Film, Rochester, New York

119   Alfred Stieglitz, *Landscape (Mid Ice and Snow)*, 1894, chloride print, © The Art Institute of Chicago, Alfred Stieglitz Collection, 1949.691, photograph by Greg Williams

120   Alfred Stieglitz, *The Jungfrau from Murren*, 1894, lantern slide, George Eastman House, International Museum of Photography and Film, Rochester, New York

121   Alfred Stieglitz, *Mountain Bridges*, 1894, lantern slide, George Eastman House, International Museum of Photography and Film, Rochester, New York

122   Alfred Stieglitz, *Grindelwald Glacier*, 1894, lantern slide, George Eastman House, International Museum of Photography and Film, Rochester, New York

123   Alfred Stieglitz, *The Two Fashions, Venice*, 1894, lantern slide, George Eastman House, International Museum of Photography and Film, Rochester, New York

124   Alfred Stieglitz, *Venetian Scenes (A)*, 1894, Philadelphia Museum of Art: From the Collection of Dorothy Norman 1997

125   Alfred Stieglitz, *Church Entrance, Santi Giovanni e Paolo*, 1894, lantern slide, Philadelphia Museum

126   K. Hoffman, Santi Giovanni e Paolo, Venice, 2002

127   Alfred Stieglitz, *Portrait – "An Arrangement,"* from *Burr McIntosh Monthly*, April 1907, private collection

128   Alfred Stieglitz, *A Venetian Well*, 1894, lantern slide, George Eastman House, International Museum of Photography and Film, Rochester, New York

129   Alfred Stieglitz, *Venice*, 1894, lantern slide, George Eastman House, International Museum of Photography and Film, Rochester, New York

130   Alfred Stieglitz, *A Venetian Canal*, 1894, 1920s/30s's gelatin silver print, The J. Paul Getty Museum © Estate of Georgia O'Keeffe

131   Alfred Stieglitz, *A Venetian Canal*, 1894, photogravure (1897), © The Art Institute of Chicago, Alfred Stieglitz Collection, 1949.701

132   Alfred Stieglitz, *Venice*, 1894, Art Institute of Chicago Alfred Stieglitz Collection

133   Postcard from Alfred Stieglitz to Wilhelm Hasemann, 18 June 1894, private collection

134   Alfred Stieglitz, *Pride of the Black Forest*, 1894, lantern slide, The Museum of Modern Art, New York

135   K. Hoffman, Gutach, 2002

161   Alfred Stieglitz, *Reflections: Night, New York*, 1897, photogravure, Philadelphia Museum of Art: From the Collection of Dorothy Norman, 1968

162   Alfred Stieglitz, *Icy Night, New York*, 1898, carbon print, © The Art Institute of Chicago, Alfred Stieglitz Collection, 1949.689

163   Alfred Stieglitz, prints from Photographic Journal of a Baby, 1900, Yale Collection of American Literature, Beinecke Rare Book and Manuscript Library

164   Alfred Stieglitz, prints from Photographic Journal of a Baby, 1900, Yale Collection of American Literature, Beinecke Rare Book and Manuscript Library

165   Alfred Stieglitz, *Baby Being Fed by Emmy*, 1899, lantern slide, Yale Collection of American Literature, Beinecke Rare Book and Manuscript Library

166   Alfred Stieglitz, *Katherine, Lake George*, 1899, lantern slide, Yale Collection of American Literature, Beinecke Rare Book and Manuscript Library

167   Alfred Stieglitz, *Kitty with Mother*, 1902, Yale Collection of American Literature, Beinecke Rare Book and Manuscript Library

168   Alfred Stieglitz, *Kitty Stieglitz Holding a Book*, 1904, Yale Collection of American Literature, Beinecke Rare Book and Manuscript Library

169   Alfred Stieglitz, *Family at the Beach*, 1900, Yale Collection of American Literature, Beinecke Rare Book and Manuscript Library

170   Alfred Stieglitz, *Steichen and Kitty*, n.d., Yale Collection of American Literature, Beinecke Rare Book and Manuscript Library

171   Alfred Stieglitz, *Spring (Kitty)*, 1901, photogravure, Lee Gallery, Winchester, Massachusetts

172   Alfred Stieglitz, *Kitty and Emmeline*, c.1905–6, Yale Collection of American Literature, Beinecke Rare Book and Manuscript Library

173   Alfred Stieglitz, *The Swimming Lesson (Kitty)*, 1906, photogravure, Lee Gallery, Winchester, Massacusetts

174   Alfred Stieglitz, *Kitty Holding a Plant*, n.d., Yale Collection of American Literature, Beinecke Rare Book and Manuscript Library

175   Alfred Stieglitz, *Kitty*, 1908, lantern slide, © The Art Institute of Chicago, 1986.3340, photograph by Greg Williams

176   Alfred Stieglitz, *Katherine Stieglitz*, 1910, autochrome, Yale Collection of American Literature, Beinecke Rare Book and Manuscript Library

177   Alfred Stieglitz, *Katherine Stieglitz*, 1910, autochrome, Yale Collection of American Literature, Beinecke Rare Book and Manuscript Library

178   Alfred Stieglitz, *Kitty in Profile*, 1912, print, Yale Collection of American Literature, Beinecke Rare Book and Manuscript Library

179   Alfred Stieglitz, *Kitty Stieglitz*, 1907, autochrome, The J. Paul Getty Museum © Estate of Georgia O'Keeffe

180   Alfred Stieglitz, *Katherine*, 1905, photogravure, Yale Collection of American Literature, Beinecke Rare Book and Manuscript Library

181   Alfred Stieglitz, *Lou Schramm and Daughter*, ?1890–94 The J. Paul Getty Museum © Estate of Georgia O'Keeffe

182   Alfred Stieglitz, *Untitled (Georgia E. with Teddy Bear)*, ?1916, lantern slide, © The Art Institute of Chicago, 1986.3346, photograph by Greg Williams

183   Kitty Stieglitz, *Still Life*, n.d., tempera, Yale Collection of American Literature, Beinecke Rare Book and Manuscript Library

184 Alfred Stieglitz, *Spring Showers, New York*, 1900–1, photogravure, Lee Gallery, Winchester, Massachusetts

185 Alfred Stieglitz, *The Street – Design for a Poster*, 1900–01, photogravure, Lee Gallery, Winchester, Massachusetts

186 K. Hoffman, winter in New York City, 2002

187 Alfred Stieglitz, *Rockefeller Center from the Shelton Hotel, New York City*, 1935, gelatin silver print, Collection Centre Canadian d'Architecture/Canadian Centre for Architecture, Montreal

188 Alfred Stieglitz, *Tree in Snow, New York City*, 1900–2, lantern slide, © The Art Institute of Chicago, 1986.3325

189 Alfred Stieglitz, *Snapshot, From My Window, New York*, 1902, photogravure, Lee Gallery, Winchester, Massachusetts

190 Alfred Stieglitz, *Snapshot, From My Window, Berlin*, probably 1904, photogravure, Lee Gallery, Winchester, Massachusetts

191 The first page of an article on the Photo-Secession by James Savery, published in *Burr McIntosh Monthly*, April 1907 (clipped by Stieglitz in a scrapbook), private collection

192 Alfred Stieglitz, *The Hand of Man*, 1902, photogravure, Lee Gallery, Winchester, Massachusetts

193 Alfred Stieglitz, *In the New York Central Yards*, 1903, photogravure, Lee Gallery, Winchester, Massachusetts

194 Alfred Stieglitz, *The Flat-iron*, 1903, photogravure, Lee Gallery, Winchester, Massachusetts

195 The Flatiron Building as seen in a postcard of 1905, private collection

196 K. Hoffman, the Flatiron Building, 2002

197 Alfred Stieglitz, *Going to the Start*, 1904, photogravure, Lee Gallery, Winchester, Massachusetts

198 Alfred Stieglitz, *Nearing Land*, 1904, photogravure, Lee Gallery, Winchester, Massachusetts

199 Graflex advertisement in *Camera Work*, April 1907, Dimond Library, Milne Special Collection, University of New Hampshire, Durham, New Hampshire

200 "The ABC of Photography," from *Camera Work*, October 1906, Dimond Library, Milne Special Collection, University of New Hampshire, Durham, New Hampshire

201 Alfred Stieglitz, *Landscape, the Tyrol*, 1904, The J. Paul Getty Museum © Estate of Georgia O'Keeffe

202 Alfred Stieglitz, *Ploughing*, 1904, photogravure, Lee Gallery, Winchester, Massachusetts

203 Alfred Stieglitz, *Horses*, 1904, photogravure, Lee Gallery, Winchester, Massachusetts

204 Alfred Stieglitz, *Miss S. R.*, 1904, photogravure, George Eastman House, International Museum of Photography and Film, Rochester, New York

205 Alfred Stieglitz or Paul Strand, photograph of the building at 291 Fifth Avenue, 1917, Yale Collection of American Literature, Beinecke Rare Book and Manuscript Library

206a   Alfred Stieglitz, photograph of the Little Galleries of the Photo-Secession with the Kühn, Henneberg, and Watzek exhibition, March 1906, Yale Collection of American Literature, Beinecke Rare Book and Manuscript Library

206b   Alfred Stieglitz, installation view of the Picasso/Braque exhibition at 291, January 1915, Yale Collection of American Literature, Beinecke Rare Book and Manuscript Library

207a   Alfred Stieglitz, Negro art exhibition, November 1914, photogravure, Library of Congress, Washington, D.C.

207b   Alfred Stieglitz, Brancusi sculpture exhibition, March 1914, photogravure, Library of Congress, Washington, D.C.

208   Alfred Stieglitz, installation views of the Nadelman exhibition, December 1915, photogravures, Library of Congress, Washington, D.C.

209   Pamela Colman Smith, *Beethoven Sonata No. 11*, 1907, watercolor on paper board, Yale Collection of American Literature, Beinecke Rare Book and Manuscript Library

210   Alfred Stieglitz, *The Steerage*, 1907, photogravure, Lee Gallery, Winchester, Massachusetts

211   Alfred Stieglitz, *Oaklawn*, 1910, autochrome, Yale Collection of American Literature, Beinecke Rare Book and Manuscript Library

212   Alfred Stieglitz, *Frank Eugene*, 1907, autochrome, Yale Collection of American Literature, Beinecke Rare Book and Manuscript Library

213   Alfred Stieglitz, *Dorothy Schubart*, 1915, autochrome, Yale Collection of American Literature, Beinecke Rare Book and Manuscript Library

214   Alfred Stieglitz, *Alfred and Emmeline Stieglitz*, 1910, autochrome, Yale Collection of American Literature, Beinecke Rare Book and Manuscript Library

215   Statement to the Press by Alfred Stieglitz, 26 September 1907, Century Collection, New York Public Library, New York City

216   Alfred Stieglitz, *Paul Haviland*, 1914, Leica print no.50-c, platinum, Yale Collection of American Literature, Beinecke Rare Book and Manuscript Library

217   Alfred Stieglitz, *Old and New New York*, 1910, photogravure, Collection Centre Canadian d'Architecture/Canadian Centre for Architecture, Montreal

218   Alfred Stieglitz, *The City of Ambition*, 1910, photogravure, Lee Gallery, Winchester, Massachusetts

219   Alfred Stieglitz, *Two Towers – New York*, 1911, photogravure, Lee Gallery, Winchester, Massachusetts

220   Alfred Stieglitz, *Excavating, New York*, 1911, photogravure, Lee Gallery, Winchester, Massachusetts

221   Alfred Stieglitz, *Lower Manhattan*, 1910, photogravure, Lee Gallery, Winchester, Massachusetts

222   Alfred Stieglitz, *City Across the River*, 1910, photogravure, Lee Gallery, Winchester, Massachusetts

223   Alfred Stieglitz, *Mauretania*, 1910, photogravure, Lee Gallery, Winchester, Massachusetts

224   Alfred Stieglitz, *Self-Portrait*, 1907 (NGA Key Set: 1911), The J. Paul Getty Museum © Estate of Georgia O'Keeffe

Adirondack Museum (NGA Key Set: *Music – A Sequence of Ten Cloud Photographs, No. II*), Blue Mountain Lake, New York

246   Alfred Stieglitz, *Georgia O'Keeffe: A Portrait*, 4 June 1917, platinum print, The J. Paul Getty Museum © Estate of Georgia O'Keeffe

247   Alfred Stieglitz, *Georgia O'Keeffe: A Portrait*, 4 June 1917, platinum print, The J. Paul Getty Museum © Estate of Georgia O'Keeffe

248   Alfred Stieglitz, *Ellen Koeniger, Lake George*, 1916, The J. Paul Getty Museum © Estate of Georgia O'Keeffe

249   Alfred Stieglitz, *Ellen Koeniger, Lake George*, 1916, The J. Paul Getty Museum © Estate of Georgia O'Keeffe

250   Alfred Stieglitz, *Ellen Koeniger, Lake George*, 1916, The J. Paul Getty Museum © Estate of Georgia O'Keeffe

251   Alfred Stieglitz, *Ellen Koeniger, Lake George*, 1916, The J. Paul Getty Museum © Estate of Georgia O'Keeffe

252   Alfred Stieglitz, *Ellen Koeniger, Lake George*, 1916, The J. Paul Getty Museum © Estate of Georgia O'Keeffe

253   Alfred Stieglitz, *The Last Days of 291*, 1917, gelatin silver print, Philadelphia Museum of Art: From the Collection of Dorothy Norman 1967

254   Alfred Stieglitz, *Equivalent, Portrait of Georgia, No. 3, Songs of the Sky, No. 2*, 1923, The J. Paul Getty Museum © Estate of Georgia O'Keeffe

255   K. Hoffman, Lake George, close to where Stieglitz's ashes were scattered, 2002

256   Alfred Stieglitz, *Equivalent*, 1930, gelatin silver print, The J. Paul Getty Museum © Estate of Georgia O'Keeffe

INDEX